A Networked Self

A Networked Self examines self presentation and social connection in the digital age. This collection brings together new theory and research on online social networks by leading scholars from a variety of disciplines. Topics addressed include self presentation, behavioral norms, patterns and routines, social impact, privacy, class/gender/race divides, taste cultures online, uses of social networking sites within organizations, activism, civic engagement and political impact.

Zizi Papacharissi is Professor and Head of the Communication Department at the University of Illinois-Chicago. She is author of *A Private Sphere: Democracy in the Digital Age* and editor of *Journalism and Citizenship: New Agendas*, also published by Routledge.

A Networked Self

Identity, Community, and Culture on Social Network Sites

Edited by Zizi Papacharissi

Routledge
Taylor & Francis Group

NEW YORK AND LONDON

First published 2011
by Routledge
711 Third Avenue, New York, NY 10017

Simultaneously published in the UK
by Routledge
2 Park Square, Milton Park, Abingdon, Oxon OX14 4RN

Routledge is an imprint of the Taylor & Francis Group, an informa business

© 2011 Taylor & Francis

Typeset in Perpetua by Wearset Ltd, Boldon, Tyne and Wear

Library of Congress Cataloging in Publication Data

A networked self : identity, community and culture on social
network sites / Zizi A. Papacharissi, editor.
p. cm.
Includes bibliographical references and index.

1. Online social networks–Psychological aspects. 2. Identity
(Psychology) 3. Information technology–Social aspects. I.
Papacharissi, Zizi.
HM742.N49 2010
302.30285–dc22
2010002502

ISBN13: 978-0-415-80180-5 (hbk)
ISBN13: 978-0-415-80181-2 (pbk)
ISBN13: 978-0-203-87652-7 (ebk)

Contents

Acknowledgments

This edited volume is the result of encouragement, trust, and inspiration from a variety of colleagues, several of whom are also contributors to the volume. The editor would like to thank Steve Jones for his suggestions and support. I also appreciate the encouragement provided by my editor, Matthew Byrnie, to move forward with a proposal on a volume on social network sites. The day-long conference that brought contributors to *A Networked Self* together, and was hosted by the Department of Communication at the University of Illinois-Chicago, would not have been possible without the generous endorsement of the College of Liberal Arts and Sciences, and our Dean Dr. Dwight McBride, and I thank him warmly for his faith in my vision. My research assistant Kelly Quinn helped preserve sanity at the various planning stages of the volume and conference, with her knack for planning, insight and thoughtful interventions. Doctoral candidates at the University of Illinois-Chicago Maggie Griffith and Gordon Carlson deserve thanks for their help with organizing and chairing sessions for the Networked Self conference. My colleagues and students at the University of Illinois-Chicago and Temple University make my everyday network of interaction fun, and thus provide me with a never-ending source of energy. Finally, this volume enabled me to collaborate with people whose work I admire, and to this end, I thank all the volume contributors for being who they are.

has roughly the same number of friends, and it's very difficult to find individuals that are significantly richer or significantly poorer in the terms of their social ties than the average person. So, despite the randomness by which the links are placed, the randomness gets averaged out, and in the end we all become very similar to each other.

Now, we need to question whether this is correct. Do we honestly believe that real networks—society, the Internet, or other systems—are truly random, decided by chance? No one would question that there is a large degree of randomness in the way we make friends and in the way certain things are connected. But is that all, or is there more to it? To answer this question, about a decade ago we started to collect large data sets, large maps of networks, with the idea that we needed to examine real networks to understand how they actually worked. Our first choice was the World Wide Web, a large network where nodes and documents were linked using URLs. It wasn't a philosophical decision, it was simply available data that we could actually map out. We started in 1999 from the main page of University of Notre Dame and followed the links. Then we followed the links on the pages we reached. It was a terribly boring process, so we built a software to do this—these days, it is called a search engine. But unlike Google, who runs similar search engines, we didn't care about the content of the pages. We only cared about the links and what they were actually connected to. So at the end of the day, this robot returned a map in which each node corresponds to a Web page and the links tell you the connection to another page that can be made with a single click.

What was our expectation? Well, Web pages are created by individuals who significantly differ from one another. Some people care about social systems. Others care about the Red Sox or the White Sox, and still others care about Picasso. And what people put on Web pages reflect these personal interests. Given the huge differences between us, it's reasonable to expect that a very large network would have a certain degree of randomness. And we expected that when we counted how many links each Web page had, the network would follow Poisson distribution, as predicted by the random network model. Surprisingly, however, our results showed something different. We found a large number of very small nodes with only a few links each, and a few very highly connected nodes. We found what we call a "power law distribution." That is, $P(k) \sim k^{-\gamma}$ where $P(k)$ is the probability that a node has k links and is called the "degree exponent."

What is a power law distribution? A power law distribution appears on a regular plot as a continuously and gradually decreasing curve. Whereas a Poisson distribution has an exponentially decaying tail, one that drops off very sharply, a power law distribution has a much slower decay rate resulting in a long tail. This means that not only are there numerous small nodes, but that these numerous small nodes coexist with a few very highly connected nodes, or hubs.

To illustrate, a random network would look similar to the highway system of the United States, where the cities are the nodes and the links are the highways connecting them. Obviously, it doesn't make sense to build a hundred highways going into a city, and each major city in the mainland U.S. is connected by a highway. So if you were to draw a histogram of the number of major highways that meet in major cities, you would find the average to be around two or three. You wouldn't find any city that would have a very large number of highways going in or out. In comparison, a map of airline routes shows many tiny airports and a few major hubs that have many flights going in and out; these hubs hold the whole network together. The difference between these two types of networks is the existence of these hubs. The hubs fundamentally change the way the network looks and behaves. These differences become more evident when we think about travel from the east coast to west coast. If you go on the highway system, you need to travel through many major cities. When you fly, you fly to Chicago and from Chicago you can reach just about any other major airport in the U.S. The way you navigate an airline network is fundamentally different from the way you navigate the highway system, and it's because of the hubs.

So we saw that the Web happens to be like the airline system. The hubs are obvious—Google, Yahoo, and other websites everybody knows—and the small nodes are our own personal Web pages. So the Web happens to be this funny animal dominated by hubs, what we call a "scale-free network." When I say "scale-free network," all I mean is that the network has a power law distribution; for all practical purposes you can visualize a network as dominated by a few hubs. So we asked, is the structure of the Web unique, or are there other networks that have similar properties?

Take for example the map of the Internet. Despite the fact that in many people's minds the Internet and Web are used interchangeably, the Internet is very different from the Web because it is a physical network. On the Web, it doesn't cost any more money to connect with somebody who is next door than it does to connect to China. But with the Internet, placing a cable between here and China is quite an expensive proposition.

On the Internet the nodes correspond to routers and the links correspond to physical cables. Yet, if one inspects any map of the Internet, we see a couple of major hubs that hold together many, many small nodes. These hubs are huge routers. Actually, the biggest hub in the United States is in the Midwest, in a well-guarded underground facility. We'll see why in a moment. Thus, like the Web, the Internet is also a hub-dominated structure. I want to emphasize that the Web and the Internet are very different animals. Yet, when you look at their underlying structures, and particularly if you mathematically analyze them, you will find that they are both scale-free networks.

Let's take another example. I'm sure everybody here is familiar with the Kevin Bacon game, where the goal is to connect an actor to Kevin Bacon. Actors are connected if they appeared in a movie together. So Tom Cruise has a Kevin Bacon number one because they appeared together in *A Few Good Men*. Mike Myers never appeared with Kevin Bacon—but he appeared with Robert Wagner in *The Spy Who Shagged Me*, and Robert Wagner appeared with Kevin Bacon in *Wild Things*. So he's two links away. Even historical figures like Charlie Chaplin or Marilyn Monroe are connected by two to three links to Bacon. There is a network behind Hollywood, and you can analyze the historical data from all the movies ever made from 1890 to today to study its structure. Once again, if you do that, you will find exactly the same power law distribution as we saw earlier. Most actors have only a few links to other actors but there are a few major hubs that hold the whole network together. You may not know the names of the actors with few links because you walked out of the movie theater before their name came up on the screen. On the other hand there are the hubs, the actors you go to the movie theater to see. Their names are on the ads and feature prominently on the posters.

Let's move to the subject of this conference, online communities. Here, the nodes are the members. And though we don't know who they are, their friends do, and these relationships with friends are the links. There are many ways to look at these relationships. One early study from 2002 examined email traffic in a university environment, and sure enough, a scale-free network emerged there as well. Another studied a pre-cursor to Facebook, a social networking site in Sweden, and exactly the same kind of distribution arose there. No matter what measure they looked at, whether people just poked each other, traded email, or had a relationship, the same picture emerged: most people had only few links and a few had a large number.

But all the examples I have given you so far came from human-made systems, which may suggest that the scale-free property is rooted in something we do. We built the Internet, the Web, we do social networking, we do email. So perhaps these hubs emerge as something intrinsic in human behavior. Is it so?

Let's talk about what's inside us. One of the many components in humans is genes, and the role of the genes is to generate proteins. Much of the dirty work in our cells is done not by the genes, but by the proteins. And proteins almost never work alone. They always interact with one another in what is known as protein–protein interaction. For example, if you look in your blood stream, oxygen is carried by hemoglobin. Hemoglobin essentially is a molecule made of four proteins that attach together and carry oxygen. The proteins are nodes in a protein–protein interaction network, which is crucial to how the cell actually works. When it's down, it brings on disease. There's also a metabolic network inside us, which takes the food that you eat and breaks it down into the components that the cells can consume. It's a network of chemical reactions. So the point is that there are many networks in our cells. On the left-hand side of this figure is the metabolic network of the simple yeast organism. On the right-hand side is the protein–protein interaction network. In both cases, if you analyze them mathematically you will observe a scale-free network; visually you can see the hubs very clearly.

Figure 1.2 Protein interaction network of yeast, an organism often studied in biological labs. Each node corresponds to a protein and two proteins are linked together if there is experimental evidence that they interact with each other in the cell. The color of the nodes denote their essentiality: dark grey proteins are those without which the organism cannot survive, while light grey are those that the organism can live without. Note the uneven link distribution: most proteins link to one or a few nodes only, while a few proteins act as hubs, having links to dozens of other proteins.

When you think about it, this is truly fascinating because these networks have emerged through a four-billion-year evolution process. Yet they converge to exactly the same structure that we observe for our social networks, which raises a very fundamental question. How is it possible that cells and social networks can converge with the same architecture?

One of the goals of this talk is to discuss the laws and phenomena that are recurrent in different types of networks, summarizing them as organizing principles. The first such organizing principle is the scale-free property which emerges in a very large number of networks. For our purposes, it just simply means that many small nodes are held together by a few major hubs. Yet, there is a second organizing property that many of you may be aware of, often called either the "six degrees" or the "small world" phenomenon. The idea behind it is very straightforward: you pick two individuals and try to connect them. For example, Sarah knows Ralph, Ralph knows Jason, Jason knows Peter, so you have a three-handshake distance between Sarah and Peter. This phenomenon was very accurately described in 1929 by the Hungarian writer Frigyes Karinthy, in a short story that was published in English about two years ago and translated by a professor at UIC, Professor Adam Makkai. The idea entered the scientific literature in 1967 thanks to the work of Stanley Milgram, who popularized the "six degrees of separation" phrase after following the path of letters sent out from a particular town.

No matter what network you look at, the typical distances are short. And by short we mean that the average separation between the nodes is not a function of how many nodes the network has, but rather the logarithm of the number of nodes, which is a relatively small number. This is not a property of social networks only. We see it in the Web. We see it in the cell. We see it in all different types of networks. The small world phenomenon is important because it completely destroys the notion of space. Indeed, two people can be very far away if you measure their physical distance. And yet, when you look at the social distance between them, it is typically relatively short.

Now let's come back to the central question that I raised earlier. I have given several examples of networks that were documented to be scale-free. How is it possible that such different systems—the Web, the Internet, the cell, and social networks—develop a common architecture? What's missing from the random network model that doesn't allow us to capture the features of these networks? Why are hubs in all these networks?

To answer these questions, we must return to the random model, to Erdős and Rényi's hypothesis, which contains several assumptions that you might not have noticed. Their model depicts a society of individuals by placing six billion dots on a screen and connecting them randomly. But their fundamental assumption is that the number of nodes remains unchanged while you are making the connections. And I would argue that this is not necessarily correct. The networks we see have always gone through, and continue to go through, an expansion process. That is, they are always adding new nodes, and this growth is essential to the network.

Let's inspect the Web. In 1991 there was only one Web page out there, Tim Berners-Lee's famous first page. And now we have more than a trillion. So how do you go from one to more than a trillion nodes? The answer is one node at a time, one Web page at a time, one document at a time, whether a network expands slowly or fast, or does so node-by-node. So if we are to model the Web, we can't just simply put up a trillion nodes and connect them. We need to reproduce the process by which the network emerged in the first place. How would we do that? Well you assume that there is growth in the system, by starting with a small network and adding new nodes, and somehow connecting the new nodes to existing nodes.

The next question that comes up right away: how do we choose where to connect the node? Erdős and Rényi actually gave us the recipe. They said, choose it randomly. But this is an assumption that is not borne out by our data. It turns out that new nodes prefer to link to highly connected nodes. The Web is the best example. There are a trillion pages out there. How many do you know personally? A few hundred, maybe a thousand? We all know Google and Yahoo, but we're much less aware of the rest of the trillion which are not so highly connected. So our knowledge is biased toward pages with more connections. And when we connect, we tend to follow our knowledge. This is what we call "preferential attachment" and simply means that we can connect to any node, but we're more likely to connect to a node with a higher degree

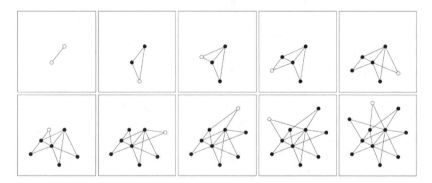

Figure I.3 Birth of a scale-free network. The scale-free topology is a natural consequence of the ever-expanding nature of real networks. Starting from two connected nodes (top left), in each panel a new node, which is shown as an open dot, is added to the network. When deciding where to link, new nodes prefer to attach to the more connected nodes. Thanks to growth and preferential attachment, a few highly connected hubs emerge.

than to one with a smaller degree. It's probabilistic: the likelihood of me connecting to a certain Web page is proportional to how many links that page already has. This is often called the "Matthew Effect" from Merton's famous paper, and is also sometimes called "cumulative advantage." The bottom line is that there is a bias toward more connected nodes. If one node has many more links than another, new nodes are much more likely to connect to it. So, big nodes will grow faster than less connected nodes.

One of the most beautiful discoveries of random network theory is that if we keep adding links randomly, at a certain moment a large network will suddenly emerge. But the model discussed above suggests a completely different phenomenon: the network exists from the beginning, and we just expand it. There is no magic moment of the emergence of the network. In evolving network theory, we look at the evolution of the system rather than the sudden emergence of the system. So if we take this model and grow many nodes, you will find that the emerging network will be scale-free and the hubs will naturally emerge. This is the third organizing principle: hubs emerge via growth and preferential attachment.

Now let's be realistic. There are lots of other things going on in a complex networked system in addition to those I have just described. One thing we learned mathematically is that as long as the network is growing, and as long as there is some process that generates preferential attachment, a network is scale-free. Thus, one of the reasons there are so many different networks that are scale-free is because the criteria for their emergence is so minimal.

The next question that naturally comes up concerns one of this model's predictions: the earliest nodes in the network become the biggest hubs. And the later the arrival, the less chance a node has to become big. There is way of mathematically expressing this occurrence: each node increases its degree as the square root of time. This means that the longer you are in the system, the more connected you are. So, can any of us become hubs if we are late-comers? Well, there are obvious examples of this happening. Google was a relative latecomer to the WWW and yet it's the biggest hub today. So, how can you be a late-comer and become very highly connected? Is there a mechanism for this?

One way to describe the Google phenomenon is with the concept of fitness. What is fitness? Fitness is the node's ability to attract links. It's not the likelihood of finding a Web page, but rather once you've found a Web page, it's the probability that you will connect to it. It's not the chance of running into a person. But once you've met the person, will you want to see him or her again? Thus, fitness is the ability to attract links after these random encounters. To model the impact of fitness, we assign a parameter for each node which represents its ability to compete for links. You can build it into preferential attachment, because now the likelihood that you will connect to a certain node is the product of the fitness and the number of links. The number of links is there because it tells us how easy it is to find the node. If a node is very highly connected, it is easy to bump into it. But the fitness tells me the likelihood that I will actually link to it, once I find it.

If you solve this fitness-driven model analytically, you will find that each node will increase its links following a power law, but the exponent by which the node grows is unique to the node. What does this mean? It means that there's a possibility for a node to come in late with a higher fitness and grow faster than the earlier-arriving nodes. Now, if the fitness of the new node is only marginally higher than the other nodes, it will take a long time to catch up. But if it's significantly higher, then the node will actually grow larger than any of the others. One of the reasons it's so hard to beat Google today—that is, to grow as large as Google is as a late-comer—is that there has to be a significantly higher fitness to overcome the time lag.

Fitness also makes a somewhat disturbing prediction, allowing for the possibility of a "winner takes all" situation. In the language of physics, this is what we call a "Bose–Einstein condensation," and simply means that a node with significantly higher fitness will grab all the links. As the network grows, this node will completely dominate the system, much more so than a hub in a scale-free network. Let me explain the difference between a scale-free network and a "winner takes all" network. In a scale-free network, as the network expands, the market share of the biggest hub will decrease in time. That is, even though the biggest hub will get larger and larger, the fraction of the total links in the full network that connect to it will slowly decay. In a case where you have a "winner takes all" situation, the market share of the biggest hub will remain constant. An example is the Windows operating system, which has an 85% market share in operating systems. That's a winner takes all situation because its share has stayed relatively constant over that of Apple and Linux. So, to summarize, competition in networks is driven by fitness; the fittest nodes are the ones who will turn slowly into hubs. So it's very important to think about where fitness comes from. And, obviously, if you want to compete, you need to think about how to increase your fitness.

The next questions that come up are, "So what—should we even care?" and "Do these hubs have any consequences that are important?" It turns out that there are many consequences. One is illustrated by the concept of robustness, which means that complex systems maintain their basic functions even under errors and failures. For example, in my cells there are many errors. Yet I can carry on speaking, despite the fact that something in my cells has gone wrong. Another example is the Internet, where at any time hundreds of routers are not working, yet the Internet still functions. So how do we think about the data survey for approximately 10 million individuals. We know exactly when each user called, who they called, and so on. You can see, in fact, that there are almost invisible links that connect different groups together; these are weak links and they are highlighted in light grey. There are some communities that are highly interconnected, and these links are highlighted in dark grey. Recalling the concept of the strength of weak ties from Mark Granovetter, this figure shows that the strong ties are indeed within the communities, and the weak ties are used mainly to connect communities together.

What we don't see, however, is that the weak ties matter for information transfer. In this figure, though we have a fundamental perception of communication, we really don't know the strength of the ties. But in the full network we do: we can simply look at how often each individual speaks with another and assign a weight between them based on the frequency and the time spent together on the phone. If we do this, we can create a weighted network. As a comparison, we can generate a second network, a reference network, where the average weighted link is exactly the same as the empirical network, but where every connection between the nodes has the same weight. Now, if we model a piece of information spreading through each of these two networks, we find that information spreads much more slowly in the empirical network than in the reference network. This is in complete agreement with Granovetter's theory: information gets stuck in the communities and takes time to spread because ties between communities are weak.

But from an individual's perspective, where does new information come from? Does it typically spread through weak ties from one community to another, or will it come from a strong tie within the community? If all the links are equal, new information arrives to the individual from the ties that are normally weak. It very rarely comes from the strong ties. When we add the real weights to the links, however, we find that information doesn't come from either the weak ties or the strong ties; it arrives through intermediate ties. The reason is simple. People rarely use their weak ties because they very rarely communicate through them. It takes forever for you to get in touch with the person you are weakly connected to. Information doesn't come from the strong ties either, though, because strong ties are part of groups where all individuals have the same information. We find that information comes from somewhere in between. We call this the "weakness of weak and strong ties in social systems."

So to wrap this up, today I've outlined some of the distinctive properties that recur in networks. But what really is network science? From my perspective, it's an attempt to understand the networks emerging in nature, technology, and society using a unified set of tools and principles. It is a new field and a new discipline, and what really excites me is that despite recurring

Part I

Context

Communication Theory and Social Network Sites

Chapter 1

Interaction of Interpersonal, Peer, and Media Influence Sources Online

A Research Agenda for Technology Convergence

Joseph B. Walther, Caleb T. Carr,
Scott Seung W. Choi, David C. DeAndrea,
Jinsuk Kim, Stephanie Tom Tong, and
Brandon Van Der Heide

Developments in communication technologies are raising new questions and resurrecting old questions about the interplay of interpersonal, mass, and peer communication. Questions about the interplay of mass media and interpersonal processes are not altogether new. Yet new communication technologies demand a revised view of mass and interpersonal processes. New technologies blur the boundaries between interpersonal and mass communication events and/or the roles that communicators take on using new systems. Arguments have been made that the "convergence" of old and new media demands new and unified perspectives on traditionally segregated processes.

Some of the questions about the convergence of communication sources deserve reconsideration in light of recent technological developments, many of which were unforeseen when previous pronouncements were articulated, that change relationships of mass and interpersonal sources. More specifically, some new communication technologies are changing the manner of reception by which individuals acquire information from institutional, interpersonal, and peer information sources. Technology changes the temporal and contiguous presentations of these sources, and may in fact change the information processing and social influence dynamics among these sources; that is, the sequence with which sources are sampled or the simultaneousness with which they appear may have potent effects on the information processing filters and biases.

"Media convergence" is a term that has been used to connote several phenomena that are brought about by advancements in telecommunication technology that may change some aspect of the communication process. Sometimes the term refers to the blending of previously individuated mass media: One can watch movies on one's computer, for example. We wish to discuss another kind of convergence: The potential for simultaneous communication via computers of both conceptually mass and interpersonal channels. For example, one can examine the NYTimes.com while chatting about its content with a friend via Instant Messenger; one can draw political news from a blogger, and post an individual reaction on that blog as a comment. Moreover, in addition to mass and interpersonal sources, new communication technology has made incredibly salient another information source, virtual communities and other forms of peer-generated information, which is accessible at a previously impossible level. This addition may further affect the balance of sources of social influence in several settings.

How these information streams influence individuals, of course, is not a magic bullet. We believe that in many cases a deeper understanding of the use and influence of these sources may be derived through a renewed focus on the interpersonal goals that may drive users' information-seeking and processing. How these new juxtapositions of institutional, peer, and interpersonal sources may change information-processing patterns, and effects of information consumption will have much to do with the interplay of motives that drive particular interactions.

Technology has also generated new forms of communication, in social networking sites and other systems, which bridge the structural and functional characteristics of mass/interpersonal/peer communication. Such technologies invite research that will advance understanding of how individuals conceptualize communication, instantiate communication strategies, and interpret new mediated message forms and content.

The purposes of the present work are several. First, we revisit approaches to the division and interaction of mass and interpersonal communication processes, to see what questions and assertions have been raised that may continue to guide understanding of these processes as they unfold via new technologies. Second, we will attempt to articulate an expanded perspective on the interplay of institutional, peer, and interpersonal sources through contemporary communication technologies, and to articulate research agendas that can help in understanding of the information-processing patterns that such convergent forms make likely. Third, we identify new forms and functions of mediated communication that challenge previous classifications, in order to invoke principles that may focus research to help explain these new phenomena.

Perspectives on Mass/Interpersonal Divisions and Mergers

Traditionally, mass communication processes have been conceptualized as one-way message transmissions from one source to a large, relatively undifferentiated and anonymous audience. Interpersonal communication involves smaller numbers of participants who exchange messages designed for, and directed toward, particular others. Interpersonal communication has been considered a two-way message exchange between two or more individuals in which communication strategies are shaped by the instrumental and relational goals of the individuals involved, and knowledge about one another's idiosyncratic preferences (see for review Berger & Chaffee, 1989; Cappella, 1989).

Several landmark works involve both mass communication and interpersonal processes to render a comprehensive understanding of particular phenomena. The manner in which most people form and change opinions of politics, style, and other cultural issues is well-known to involve mass media messages and interpersonal discussions (e.g., Katz, 1957; Katz & Lazarsfeld, 1955; Lazarsfeld, Berelson, & Gaudet, 1944). Similarly, the integration of mass and interpersonal processes is necessary in order to understand the diffusion of innovations, a communication process that incorporates both mass and interpersonal communication in its very conceptualization (Reardon & Rogers, 1988).

Despite their organic relationship in some contexts, a review of their conceptual and disciplinary differences shows that the exploration of mass and interpersonal processes often takes place in isolation of one another. This separation helps to make clear how they operate together when they do, as well as to set the stage for consideration of their interactions, mergers, and/or convergences. Several commentators have illuminated the causes and consequences of a disciplinary divide between mass and interpersonal communication research. Wiemann, Hawkins, and Pingree (1988) attributed the division to historical and academic/bureaucratic differences. Reardon and Rogers (1988) argued that the division developed as a result of scholars' efforts to define their distinctive contributions to social science. Interpersonal scholars followed the tradition of psychology and social psychology from the 1920s–1930s. Key sources such as Heider's (1958) *Psychology of Interpersonal Relations* and the approaches employed by psychologists, sociologists, and anthropologists such as Argyle, Goffman, and Bateson, respectively, helped to solidify the relevance of social scientific research on face-to-face interaction and relationships (Reardon & Rogers, 1988), leading to the sub-area of interpersonal communication. Mass media research evolved primarily from sociology and political science (Reardon & Rogers, 1988). Mass media research examined how mediated messages affect large audiences. These alternative sub-areas allowed scholars to focus, define, and justify their academic endeavors.

Despite its historical utility, this division has been lamented for a variety of reasons. The most prevalent concern is a lack of synthesis between mass and interpersonal communication in terms of the theories and research methods that have developed under alternative foci, to the extent that scholars with functionally similar interests may not be aware of the scientific work being performed outside of their area of specialization (Berger & Chaffee, 1988; Pingree, Wiemann, & Hawkins, 1988; Reardon & Rogers, 1988). Cross-disciplinary integration can expand understanding and contribute to more comprehensive approaches to measurement, critics argue, as well as surface for greater scrutiny underlying assumptions inherent in individual specializations (Pingree et al., 1988). Berger and Chaffee (1988) argued that theorizing with a common purpose is the way to unify the field as a whole. Subfields pursuing similar issues without the knowledge of one another can lead to greater division and weakened theoretical results, whereas shared purposes, language, and research areas can provide frameworks for the creation of new theories that examine processes of communication as a whole.

In addition to these general arguments for a merger of mass and interpersonal research approaches, advocates have argued that new communication technologies have the potential to merge the very processes conventionally considered as pertaining to mass communication or interpersonal communication, and that the merger of processes demands the merger of approaches in order to understand such phenomena. For example, Reardon and Rogers (1988) suggested that new interactive media did not neatly fit into preexisting areas of study. They claimed that a new epistemological approach to communication research may be needed. Several observers suggested that new technologies defy easy categorization as either interpersonal or mass media channels because of their interactive nature (Cathcart & Gumpert, 1986; Newhagen & Rafaeli, 1996; O'Sullivan, 1999, 2005; Pingree et al., 1988; Reardon & Rogers, 1988). Thus, commentators hold out hope that "this technological change may facilitate a long-needed paradigm shift in communication science" (Reardon & Rogers, 1988, p. 297) since analytic approaches from mass or interpersonal communication traditions may be insufficient to grasp the effects of new technologies in communication dynamics.

Cathcart and Gumpert's (1986) initial exploration into the mass/personal merger led them to speculate about a "new typology" they termed "mediated interpersonal communication" which they defined as "any person-to-person interaction where a medium has been interposed to transcend the limitations of time and space" (p. 30). They argued that new analytics are needed for such forms since the interposition of media changes the quality and quantity of information exchanged, influences personal behaviors and attitudes, and shapes an individual's self image. Some 20 years later, without a new typology per se, the study of computer-mediated communication (CMC) has done much to flesh out a number of issues that Cathcart and Gumpert identified (see, for review, Walther, 2006).

Likewise, O'Sullivan (1999, p. 580) argued that "The functional convergence of mass and interpersonal channels, perhaps best represented by the Internet, is both a challenge and an opportunity for scholars to pursue convergence of the two areas of study." More recently, O'Sullivan (2005) suggested that there are and have been unique blends of "masspersonal" communication, not only in Internet forms but through unconventional appropriations of conventional media, when individuals use traditional mass communication channels for interpersonal communication, traditional interpersonal communication channels for mass communication, and new communication channels to generate mass communication and interpersonal communication simultaneously. One recalls the example of proposing marriage by sending the request over the Jumbotron at a major sporting event, in front of screaming throngs of onlookers.

Despite the call for synthesis, the publication of synthetic interpersonal/mass approaches to communication and new technology has not accelerated. O'Sullivan's (1999) analysis of articles in *Human Communication Research* since its creation in 1974 to 1999 showed that less than 3% of articles offered "synthesis scholarship," and the frequency of such synthesis did not increase after the Winter 1988 issue calling for rapprochement of mass and interpersonal communication research. Results of similar analyses for other major communication journals such as *Communication Monographs*, the *Journal of Communication*, and *Communication Research* over the same time period showed that a small and sporadic amount of synthesis research has continued after several endorsements (O'Sullivan, 1999). Much has changed since 1999 with respect to the prevalence of the very technologies that may require synthetic approaches, and the number of articles in our journals (and journals themselves) devoted to those technologies has changed as well.

Integrating mass and interpersonal dynamics may be easier said than done. Adherents of each tradition who focus on new technology sometimes fail to realize their sub-disciplinary biases. For instance, *interactivity*, which is frequently mentioned in association with new technology, may connote different things for different analysts: New media are relatively *more* interactive than traditional sources, to mass communication researchers; new media are *less* interactive than traditional sources, to interpersonal communication researchers (Walther, Gay, & Hancock, 2005). Others caution that analysis of emergent forms of Internet communication defy a simplistic merger of traditional mass and interpersonal perspectives altogether. Caplan (2001), for instance, argues that CMC involves mixtures of traditional features of mass and interpersonal communication in unique and recombinant ways: In CMC, senders can be sources of mass communication (e.g., personal Web pages, participating in a large online forum) and an interpersonal communication partner (e.g.,

Instant Messaging, online chatting) at the same time. Receivers in CMC can be anonymous audience members (lurkers), and can also be the targets of instant personalized messages. Additionally, in CMC, message processes are not constrained by time or physical space. Caplan argued that these fundamental differences between CMC and traditional mass or interpersonal communication systems cannot be understood by simply "merging" or "bridging" mass and interpersonal perspectives; they are fundamentally new processes that require a new paradigmatic approach.

Although most predate the study of contemporary electronic communication technologies, some efforts to bring specific mass and interpersonal processes together have appeared throughout the years. These integrations provide stimulating launching points for reconsideration of communication processes in light of recent changes in the media and interpersonal landscapes. The following discussion reviews some exemplars, and suggests extensions of their potential application with respect to new media.

Functional Perspective on Information-Seeking

In his essay, "Mass Media and Interpersonal Channels: Competitive, Convergent, or Complementary?," Chaffee (1986) discussed the convergent (overlapping) and complementary (differentiated) roles that traditional mass and interpersonal channels play in the acquisition and dissemination of communication messages. Chaffee's essay reminds readers that information sources are less likely to be selected on the basis of whether they are mass or interpersonal channels; other criteria are more important selection determinants. For instance, an interpersonal source may have more or less *credibility* on a particular topic than a mass media source. Alternatively, mass media sources may not provide the same degree of *access* to information on a particular topic as might be available by asking an interpersonal acquaintance. No single information source is the end of the process: An individual may seek information on a topic from one target, and seek elaboration or a second opinion from another target. Chaffee concluded that "The traditional concept of a directional 'two step' or 'multi step' flow fails to capture the cyclical and reciprocal nature of this process" (1986, p. 76).

Chaffee's (1986) conceptualization of access and credibility issues, as stronger determinants of information-seeking than media versus interpersonal forms, have important implications in the contemporary technological landscape.

The *access* criterion that Chaffee (1986) identified has been transformed radically, in several ways, with dramatic implications. Chaffee asserted that we seek information from media or interpersonal channels largely based on topic, timing, and immediate accessibility. In Chaffee's time, access considerations may have led an individual to choose an interpersonal or media source depending on which source was more able to deliver information on a specific topic most readily. If it was unlikely that TV news or a newspaper would soon carry information on a topic of interest, one might seek a knowledgeable friend. In the age of the Internet, however, a wide array of information is accessible on demand. Because of the availability of the Internet, traditional mass media or interpersonal sources may be less likely to be easy-access starting points for information-seeking. The search engine puts a virtual encyclopedia on every desk.

Furthermore, this radical degree of access seems to have obviated traditional credibility concerns in terms of preferences and acceptability of sources. Chaffee (1986) argued that credibility—the expertise and trustworthiness of a source—rather than the channel, plays the greatest role in our acceptance of information. This may no longer be the case, at least in some contexts. Search engine users generally exhibit the tendency to "satisfice" when seeking information online, relying on Google's hierarchical display of search results by relevance, regardless of the source of the pages referenced, in guiding their information acquisition (Pan et al., 2007). In a study of health and medical information-seeking, Eysenbach and Köhler (2002) asked focus groups of Internet users how they selected credible sources of health information online. Respondents offered reasonable criteria, such as the institutional source of the information, author credentials, and recency of updating. When the same respondents were led to a computer lab and asked to find answers to specific health-related questions, however, they relied almost exclusively on the top-to-bottom rankings of search engine results, with no particular evaluation of source credibility using the criteria they themselves had articulated moments before (see also Metzger, Flanagin, & Zwarun, 2003; Walther, Wang, & Loh, 2004).

As we suggested above, another dramatic shift brought on by electronic technology's changes in information access pertains not only to the convergence of media (television, newspapers, movies, and the Internet), but also the more fundamental convergence of mass, interpersonal, and peer channels (mass media sources on the one hand, and synchronous or asynchronous discussion with peers, family, and/or friends on the other). In the contemporary media landscape, individuals may consume traditional mass media information from electronic mass media. For example, individuals may watch a Presidential candidate debate on the computer via CNN.com or even on YouTube while they simultaneously or subsequently chat about that debate (and re-run the good parts) online with peers or provocateurs. How does the presence of peers affect perception and interpretation of the political messages? In the above scenario, do the chatroom messages complement the information being provided by the political candidate or vice versa? Does the simultaneous convergence of information from two sources have the same degree of influence as the traditional type of flow, in which information from one source precedes information from the other source in a distinct temporal order? The Internet and CMC subvert previous patterns with regard to the sequence of communication flows among sources.

Research has provided some insights into the possible effects of online discussions about both political races and public service announcements (PSAs). Price and Cappella (2002) found that online political discussion promoted civic engagement; 60 groups of citizens engaged monthly in real-time CMC discussions about issues facing the country and the ongoing 2000 presidential campaign. Price and Cappella found that discussion participants recalled more pro and con arguments over issues than they had held before the discussions. This change correlated with increases in participants' political knowledge. As a result of participants' online discussions, attitudes and behaviors were altered: Those who had engaged in online political discussion were more likely to vote and perform civic duties than individuals who did not participate in the discussions. Whether these effects are due in any way to CMC rather than discussion per se was not addressed.

Chatroom discussions also facilitate ironic effects on the persuasive potential of PSAs. David, Cappella, and Fishbein (2006) explored how adolescents' online discussions that followed the viewing of weak or strong anti-marijuana PSAs affected their attitudes. Results showed that online group interaction after weak PSA exposure led to more pro-marijuana attitudes and beliefs than those in the no-chat conditions. A sample of seventh- and twelfth-grade students were assigned to four treatments crossing strong versus weak PSAs with chat versus no-chat conditions, in groups of 10–20 at a time, with participants using pseudonymous nicknames when they discussed the PSAs. David et al. proposed that high sensation seekers were likely to process the PSA messages in a biased manner. These individuals dominated the online discussions, eclipsing others who might have favored the PSAs' messages but who remained relatively silent. As a result, the outspoken participants influenced others negatively with respect to the PSAs' intended effect on marijuana attitudes. Both of these studies demonstrate potent effects of online chat, but did not examine whether online discussions offer dynamics which differ from those potentially garnered from face-to-face discussions.

Other research on social discussion of PSAs has reached alternative conclusions, but these studies employed face-to-face discussion rather than online chat. Kelly and Edwards (1992) assigned female college students to several groups, some who observed anti-drug PSAs without discussion and others who observed the PSAs and engaged in discussion afterwards. Results were mixed overall, but the discussion of PSAs had a significant positive effect on some attitudinal outcomes. Warren et al. (2006) also compared the utility of class-room videos on adolescents' substance-use rates, alone or accompanying face-to-face discussions. Only with discussion were videos effective in reducing drug use in that sample. Comparing these results to those of David et al. (2006), there appear to be differences in the effects of online versus offline discussion of anti-drug PSAs.

Although David et al. (2006) did not consider online chats to provide any-thing other than a methodological convenience for the capture of adolescents' discussions, there is reason to believe that CMC exerted some effect. The research on social influence in online settings under the aegis of the social iden-tification and deindividuation (SIDE) model of CMC (Reicher, Spears, & Postmes, 1995) sheds some light on the issue. Several studies offer compelling evidence that short-term anonymous online chats bestow extraordinary pres-sure on participants to conform to normative positions in group discussions (Sassenberg & Boos, 2003; see, for review, Postmes, Spears, & Lea, 1999), and that these dynamics are diluted in face-to-face settings. Thus, effects of CMC in the discussion of PSAs or other media messages should be expected to differ from offline discussions. David et al. (2006) did note that the older and more influential teens were generally considered to have higher social status than younger ones and more likely to have had prior experience with mari-juana. It is just such social identification dynamics that should lead to more pronounced effects in CMC than face-to-face interaction. Social identification and peer group influence in CMC should be a useful element in explaining a variety of influence effects in the new technological landscape, as we will illus-trate further below.

Multiple Information Sources and Peer Influence: Web 2.0

Do asynchronous comments about videos affect perceptions of videos the same way that chatroom discussions undermined the potential influence of anti-drug PSAs? Do comments appearing adjacent to YouTube videos affect perception of the videos? There is a need for further research on how social influence transpires under various conditions where online peer discussion co-appear with institutionally authored messages or other messages that bear the conven-tional characteristics of mass media. These situations are made radically acces-sible by the convergence of mass, peer, and interpersonal communication channels. Online chatrooms, asynchronous discussion boards, and various types of commenting and referral systems provide salient group dynamics.

Indeed, we wish to suggest that one of the most fruitful approaches to understanding new technology may be through consideration of the multiple and simultaneous social influence agents embodied in the channels that these technologies make salient.

Much attention has been given to Web 2.0 (O'Reilly, 2005), which encapsulates websites built to facilitate interactivity and co-creation of content by website visitors in addition to original authors. In the original Web, personal and institutional Web pages were changeable but not dynamic (Papacharissi, 2002). Feedback to a website's content was made through other channels—primarily email—if at all. The traditional Web was a one-to-many medium, and in that respect was similar to other mass communication channels (Trenholm, 1999). More recent technologies allow for interactivity on websites. For example, Facebook, a social networking site, allows users to place comments on their friends' "walls," thereby co-creating their friends' homepages (Levy, 2007).

Web 2.0 provides new forms of communication among individuals and groups. In addition to social network sites on which one's associates can contribute content to one's Web-based profile, it includes picture-sharing systems that allow users to append "tags" to content that facilitate later searching, linking, and the discovery of conceptually or visually similar content on others' sites; video-sharing systems like YouTube, where users upload and share videos, and may publically comment on those videos either verbally or with additional videos; wikis, which are collaboratively edited documents; reputation systems such as those on product vendor sites, on which customers can post their evaluations of products and vendors, or on auction sites such as eBay where sellers and buyers are numerically and verbally rated for others to see, as well as sites that specifically solicit ratings of instructors such as RateMyProfessor.com. All of these forms allow ostensible peers—other users—to interact, without having to disclose much about one's offline identity or qualifications. The sites are populated by relatively anonymous peers. As such, they are prone to the kinds of influence that social identification facilitates. Moreover, we may say that the peers are not simply peers, but peers exhibiting "optimal heterophily" (Rogers & Shoemaker, 1971): They are like us in terms of interests and in their shared perspective (e.g., also customers rather than vendors, students rather than teachers) except for one important difference: They have experience with the specific target (vendor, professor, etc.) while we do not. Thus their trustworthiness and relative expertise should be quite strong. Indeed, Sundar and Nass (2001) found that people more highly value information presented on computers when they believe that the information was selected by other (unidentified) computer users. In an experiment that presented identical news stories on computers to subjects, ostensibly peer-selected stories were preferred, as opposed to stories that appeared to have been chosen by news editors, computer algorithms, or even by the subject him- or herself. When other users were perceived to be the source of online news, the stories were liked more and perceived to be higher in quality, and were perceived to be more representative of news.

Casting Web 2.0 as an interface that presents multiple sources of influence demands that we explore whether and how peers' (users') additions to Web pages affect other users' perceptions of the original author's mass media message. Several studies have begun in this direction.

These effects are clear in online recommender systems, or reputation systems: Tools explicitly designed to display peers' evaluations of various targets. Their foci range from product reviews and vendor reviews to professor reviews. The impact of peers' online comments also arise when viewing users' reactions to online news stories, and even to comments about individuals as they appear in people's Facebook profiles. In terms of vender reviews, Resnick, Zeckhauser, Friedman, and Kuwabara (2000) established that the quality of one's ratings as a seller on eBay—ostensibly generated by a prospective buyer's peers—renders a demonstrable monetary influence on the prices one is able to garner for the goods one sells. Edwards, Edwards, Quing, and Wahl (2007) experimentally examined the impact of online peer reviews of college faculty in RateMyProfessor.com on students' perceptions of faculty. Edwards et al. proposed that online reviews are believed to be authored by individuals similar to the receiver. After reviewing contrived positive peer reviews for a professor on RateMyProfessor.com, and watching a video showing a sample of the professor's lecture, students rated the instructor more attractive and credible. On the other hand, when students read negative peer evaluations, they rated the instructor as less attractive and less credible, despite watching the identical lecture video. This research found similar results with respect to attitudes toward course material and learning. Edwards et al. concluded that the interactive Web has the ability to manipulate offline beliefs and actions, by affecting students' perceptions of credibility and attractiveness, their affective learning, and state motivation in the educational process.

Reliance on online user-generated recommendation systems has become a normal strategy by which prospective shoppers, healthcare users, and hobbyists evaluate the credibility of online sellers or service providers, according to research by Metzger, Flanagin, and Medders (in press). A series of focus group discussions uniformly indicated that Internet users frequently rely on

> tools such as feedback systems, testimonials, and reputation systems as ways to help them make credibility evaluations. Many participants indicated that they looked at the number of testimonials or reviews available

online, paid attention to the proportion of negative to positive reviews, or relied more heavily on negative versus positive reviews.

The influence of Web-based social comments on perceptions of individuals extends beyond the inspection of recommender systems, and even beyond the *deliberate* consideration of others' comments. Peers' online comments can also influence readers' attitudes and perceptions about the news. In Lee, Jang, and Kim's (2009) experiment, undergraduates viewed online news stories addressing teacher compensation packages. Alongside the stories, peers' comments appeared either to agree or disagree with the actions that the news story presented. Those who read comments opposing the issues rated the story more negatively. In addition to affecting their own attitudes regarding the news, the online comments also affected readers' perceptions of public sentiment about the teacher compensation issue: Participants who read other ostensible readers' comments perceived that public sentiment about teacher compensation packages was more congruent with the direction of attitudes appearing in the posted comments. Taken together, these results indicate that third-party online commentary not only influences individuals' attitudes regarding the specific target of others' comments, but it also influences individuals' perceptions on the attitudes of the general online community.

The effect of third-party comments, and other attributes of third-party agents, also extends to perceptions of individuals who created online profiles in social network systems. Walther, Van Der Heide, Kim, Westerman, and Tong (2008) found that the content of friends' postings on profile owners' "walls" in the Facebook social network site affects perceptions of profile owners' credibility and attractiveness. The physical appearance of one's friends, as shown in those wall postings, affects the perceived physical appearance of the profile owner, as well. Additional research shows that when there is a discrepancy between a Facebook profile owner's self-disclosed extraversion and perceived attractiveness, and the imputation of those characteristics implied by wall postings, others' comments override the profile owners' claims (Walther, Van Der Heide, Hamel, & Shulman, 2009).

While new communication technology can make peers and their potential influence exceptionally salient, the basis of online influence dynamics need not rest in group identification and social identities, as the SIDE model claims. In some circumstances new communication technologies make individuals salient, raising the potential influence of interpersonal sources as well. Several social network systems within Web 2.0 applications make salient what one's friends are doing, not just what a diffuse group of anonymous peers have to say. For instance, although it is clear that the definition of "friend" is stretched rather thin in Facebook, where the 250–275 average number of friends an individual specifies and links with (Vanden Boogart, 2006; Walther et al., 2008) exceeds by far the 10–20 close relationships people tend to sustain in traditional relationships (Parks, 2007), among this huge amalgamation may be one's closest affiliates. Facebook prompts users to describe, and the system displays, what films and TV shows these friends are watching, what political views they hold, and what events they are attending. Even the Web-based DVD-by-mail system, Netflix, offers users the opportunity to share information automatically about what movies chosen friends have rented and how they rated them.

To summarize, one important avenue of research for the convergence of sources that new technology promotes will be to understand the various avenues and interactions of social influence agents who co-appear (or are closely within clicking reach) in Web 2.0 interfaces. Another potentially important line of research goes beyond the impact of the overwhelming presence of what friends and peers think and do in terms of social influence on receivers. The dynamics we have considered so far have focused on how individuals passively use the social information made manifest by participative social technologies, in terms of how such information shapes receivers' own perceptions and decisions.

If individuals come to guide their own media information-seeking and information-processing in order to attempt to satisfy other social goals through subsequent or simultaneous interactions with social partners, convergent social technologies make possible a separate set of dynamics. For example, do friends and family members watch broadcasted political debates for the express purpose of gathering talking points with which to deride certain parties' candidates in interpersonal conversations with relational partners? If so, do these motivations affect attention to and processing of candidates' messages? Other research on traditional communication sets the stage for a contemporary re-examination of just such possibilities.

"Communicatory Utility" in Media Information-Seeking

The predominant view of the two-step flow of individuals' use of mass media and interpersonal encounters suggests that individuals garner information from the media that they then elaborate in interpersonal encounters, to understand the issues that the media discuss. In distinction to the primacy of the issue suggested in such an approach, Atkin (1972) demonstrated how interpersonal motivations drive mass media information-seeking in order to fulfill interpersonal goals. Atkin (1973) defined *behavioral adaptation* as one of the primary motivations to seek information: Because of an individual's "need [of] information that is useful for directing anticipated behavior" (p. 217), people garner information from mass media when they anticipated future communication with others about some topic. As such, while information garnered from mass media sources may provide its consumers with matter related to the topic, it also provides *communicatory utility*—awareness about a topic about which the individual expects to interact—with respect to further conversations.

In establishing these constructs, Atkin (1972) analyzed survey data that revealed an association between the number of conversations people had with others about the news and the number of news sources to which one was exposed. Atkin also found a significant association between the degree to which individuals discussed an ongoing presidential campaign with their family and friends and the degree to which they sought information about that campaign, even after controlling for individuals' level of interest in the campaign (as well as education level and socioeconomic status of participants). In other words, even when people were not interested in the presidential campaign, they sought information about the campaign because they knew they would be called upon to have interpersonal discussions about it. To further establish the effect, Atkin (1972) conducted an original experiment in which he led subjects to different levels of expected future interaction on various news topics of a local or national relevance. Expected future communication about a topic significantly predicted the extent to which participants reported information-seeking on that particular topic. Similar findings are reported by Wenner (1976), who found that some people who watched television did so because it provided a vehicle for conversation, and Lull (1980), who found that media were often used relationally to facilitate interpersonal communication. Similar effects have been found in more recent studies as well (e.g., Southwell & Torres, 2006). In short, one drive to employ mass media information is because of prospective discussion about it among interpersonal acquaintances.

Atkin's (1972) notion of communicatory utility is intriguing on several counts. Clearly it offers another insight into the merger of mass and interpersonal events, but it connects the utilization of mass communication to a superordinate interpersonal functionality. It is intriguing in terms of the questions it raises with respect to the availability of mass and interpersonal sources in the current technological landscape: Do individuals peruse electronic mass media, as well as websites or recommendation systems online, in order to fuel discussions with friends? Do these discussions precede or co-occur with the perusal of information sources, rather than follow them the next day at lunch? That is, does a question (or an anticipated question) in an online chat with a friend or friends prompt an information search *in situ*? All of these variations are germane to the notion of communicatory utility online, and they raise information-processing questions that pertain to the timing and specifiability of information sought when interpersonal discussion and media searching can take place contemporaneously.

Communicatory utility is a concept that helps to explain an example offered above: Individuals might watch a political debate not in order to gather information with which to make a voting decision, but rather, to have ammunition with which to derogate some candidates. Yet Atkin's original formulation of the utility construct offered little in the way of information about what kinds of interpersonal goals might be served by sampling media, other than to be able to hold one's own conversationally. By expanding the range of interpersonal goals one may consider, the potential of communicatory utility can go beyond helping us to understand media consumption, to help illuminate issues of media information processing.

We posit that the specific interpersonal goal(s) that prompt an individual's media consumption shape attention to variations in the content and features of the topical information one consumes, affecting its interpretation and recall. For instance, collectively derogating political candidates or office-holders may be an activity that relational partners use to reinforce the similarity of their attitudes. This, of course, is not restricted to online news and online chats, but may be a general purpose, cross-media communication function. As such, one may not watch a debate or speech with an open mind in an effort to make political decisions. Rather, one may watch for the illogical assertions and dumb mistakes a disliked speaker utters.

These notions raise the question of whether purposive sampling of mass media information is biased by specific interpersonal goals. If so, how? How does biased sampling affect attention, repetition, inference, and retention? Goals may vary in any number of dimensions with respect to instrumental, identity, or relational issues (Clark & Delia, 1979; Graham, Argyle, & Furnham, 1980) in the service of needs for inclusion, affection, and/or control (Schutz, 1966). The goals of an online chat may include the desire to impress a conversational partner. This could take the form of a desire to maintain status, as may have been the case in the adolescent chats observed by David et al. (2006), consistent with Heider's (1958) balance theory. Do adolescent students who crave inclusion with outspoken sensation-seekers look for anti-drug YouTube videos accompanied by derisive user comments, to which they add their own derision? Alternatively, interpersonal goals may reflect a desire to express attitudinal agreement and convey interpersonal similarity in order to impress a prospective relationship partner. If the expression of one's attitude becomes a strategy subordinated to a goal of expressing solidarity with another person, one's sampling of media messages is likely to be exercised in a manner which allows one to express the socially utilitarian attitude. Thus when individuals pursue relational goals, they may focus their media sampling and the potentially counter-attitudinal advocacy they generate. In this way relational goals affect the attention, selection, interpretation, and retention of media information.

The currency of this proposition is that information-seeking and processing may be different in traditional environments, where media exposure and interpersonal discussion are separated by some interval of time, compared to the new media environment in which mass and interpersonal channels may be sampled (and re-sampled) simultaneously. Even in offline group discussions, communicators share or withhold information in a biased manner due to the social motives they bring to discussions, such as maintaining good relations, obviating conflict, or gaining status; validation from others further biases information sharing (Wittenbaum, Hollingshead, & Botero, 2004). Computer-mediated communication may exacerbate this tendency. CMC has particularly dynamic properties that facilitate selective self-presentation in the pursuit of relational goals, facilitated by unique characteristics of the channel and the context in which it is deployed (Walther, 1996). Studies show that CMC allows users fluidly to adapt their self-presentation to their expectations or observations of a conversational partner in order to facilitate impressions and positive interactions, in both asynchronous statements (e.g., Thompson, Murachver, & Green, 2001; Walther, 2007) and adaptive synchronous interactions (e.g., Herring & Martinson, 2004). Web users are well aware of the impressions they construct in the pursuit of relationships, and consider carefully the balance between honest disclosure versus socially desirable distortion in selecting communication strategies to attract others online (Gibbs, Ellison, & Heino, 2006). For these reasons, it is important to improve understanding of how these Internet-magnified motivations affect message processing.

New Message Forms

Finally, an approach to new communication technology from the perspective of mass, peer, and interpersonal communication and communicators' goals may offer approaches to new communication forms, the understanding of which begs real analysis. Although there may be many aspects of CMC that are analytically novel in structure and purpose (see Caplan, 2001), we focus here on a potential hybrid of mass and interpersonal messaging: Public interpersonal messages posted on social network sites. Although these sites have been the focus on intense research activity of late, very little research has formally considered the goals guiding users as they compose messages. Ultimately, we believe, a goals-based approach will help us to understand how the users of such systems conceive of these publicly shared messages, which, given that communication technologies are often best understood in terms of their actual appropriations (see DeSanctis & Poole, 1994), will allow us to learn much about their utility as communication tools and the messages they convey.

An example becoming very well-known is the Facebook feature, wall postings. Person A, who Person B has specified in the system as a "friend" (a person with privileges to see and contribute to portions of Person B's profile) can post an interpersonal verbal message (accompanied by Person A's photo, by default) to Person B's profile wall. These postings often appear to express interpersonal affection, comment on some mutual event in the past or future, or proclaim relational status (among best friends forever!). However, it is also known to all involved—posters and profile-owners—that such messages can also be read by all the other people connected to Person B's social network of friends. It is, by definition, a public message, bordering on being broadcasted (or at least, narrowcasted within the social network) for others to see. Facebook users have noted that one of the main uses for social networking technology is relational maintenance (Lampe, Ellison, & Steinfield, 2006). Are such wall posts "mass" messages or "interpersonal" messages?

The exchange of messages that are inherently interpersonal and at the same time public is rare, and comparable to few other communication forms. The notion of posting on a "wall" may conjure the image of graffiti, which share communication characteristics with Facebook. Rodriguez and Clair (1999) note that graffiti are participatory exchanges: An individual writes a message which others independently observe and to which they potentially reply. Graffiti also share characteristics of mass media messages: Messages are transmitted by a sender to many receivers, mediated by the wall on which they are written. Graffiti rely on asynchronous interactivity (Robshaw, 1996), like Facebook, although the lack of photos and other individual authors' signifiers obviously limits graffiti's social networking and relational maintenance utility.

In one sense wall postings may constitute "tie signs" (Morris, 1977). In their material manifestations offline, where they are less content-rich than Facebook messages, tie signs function as public symbols of interpersonal connections, or "signals that a couple is to be treated as a bonded pair" (Burgoon, Buller, & Woodall, 1989, p. 318), and can include touch behaviors or articles of clothing, jewelry, decorations, or other adornments that belong to, or signal mutual belonging to, another person. A woman wearing a particular man's sweater, or a half-heart pendant, can constitute such public signifiers of relational belonging. They do not always explicate who the relational partner is, the way a Facebook posting makes obvious and visual. Yet Facebook postings do contain content, and the construction of that public/private content may be intriguing.

Facebook posts certainly qualify as that which O'Sullivan (2005) called "masspersonal communications," yet this characterization only helps to raise rather than answer questions about their function and strategic aspects. How does their knowledge about the public visibility of their otherwise private conversation affect friends' construction of Facebook wall posts? Is there conscious or unconscious collusion in the collaborative construction of personal identity online—are there "rules" of Facebook postings (e.g., if I do not post pictures of myself drinking, my friends don't discuss it) that define friendship online, or that distinguish between close versus weak friendship constructions? Do private codes appear on wall postings, and if so, to communicate meaning to the friend or to signal exclusivity to others? Do supportive wall postings buffer offline public embarrassments, even if there is no ostensible content-based connection between the events? What communicatory utility does a Facebook posting provide for other conversations—or, what communicatory utility does "real life" offer for self-promotion and relational signification on Facebook? Unless one commands a flock of paparazzi, rarely before these participative social network technologies could people make such varied public displays of affection, among such different levels of relationships, in such an enduring and broadcast manner. What users think as they construct these masspersonal messages is a new domain of inquiry that reference to interpersonal goals and audience considerations will help to address. Web 2.0 sites are by nature interactive environments, not just site-to-user, but user-to-user and user-to-public as well. Consequently, the way people learn to interact may also be evolving.

In conclusion, we reiterate a new perspective on the merger of various communication processes in the common interface that some new communication technologies provide. The first analytic keystone is to recognize that new interfaces bring into proximity or simultaneity information from several types of sources. Analysis proceeds by identifying the presence and salience of type of sources such as institutional, interpersonal, and/or peer, and to assess the sources of credibility relevant to each source in situ with respect to communicators' goals. A second analytic keystone is the recognition not only that interpersonal contacts motivate media information-seeking, but that an expanded range of particular interpersonal goals may be found to affect information processing in potentially different ways; different relational motivations such as status seeking, maintenance, or relationship initiation may bias information sampling from various media and affect the ultimate interpretations derived from them. These dynamics may be especially potent when conversations guide media consumption simultaneously, as the Internet not only allows but promotes.

References

Atkin, C. K. (1972). Anticipated communication and mass media information-seeking. *Public Opinion Quarterly, 36*, 188–199.

Atkin, C. K. (1973). Instrumental utilities and information-seeking. In P. Clarke (Ed.), *New models for communication research* (pp. 205–242). Beverly Hills, CA: Sage.

Berger, C. R., & Chaffee, S. H. (1988). On bridging the communication gap. *Human Communication Research, 15*, 311–318.

Berger, C. R., & Chaffee, S. H. (1989). Levels of analysis: An introduction. In C. R. Berger & S. H. Chaffee (Eds.), *Handbook of communication science* (pp. 143–145). Newbury Park, CA: Sage.

Burgoon, J. K., Buller, D. B., & Woodall, W. G. (1989). *Nonverbal communication: The unspoken dialogue*. New York, NY: Harper & Row.

Caplan, S. E. (2001). Challenging the mass-interpersonal communication dichotomy: Are we witnessing the emergence of an entirely new communication system? *Electronic Journal of Communication, 11*(1). Online, available at: www.udel.edu/communication/web/onlinepubs/Caplan-ejc-v11no1.html (accessed October 26, 2007).

Cappella, J. N. (1989). Interpersonal communication: Definitions and fundamental questions. In C. R. Berger & S. H. Chaffee (Eds.), *Handbook of communication science* (pp. 184–239). Newbury Park, CA: Sage.

Cathcart, R., & Gumpert, G. (1986). Mediated interpersonal communication: Toward a new typology. In G. Gumpert & R. Cathcart (Eds.), *Inter/media: Interpersonal communication in a media world* (3rd ed., pp. 26–40). New York, NY: Oxford University Press.

Chaffee, S. H. (1986). Mass media and interpersonal channels: Competitive, convergent, or complimentary? In G. Gumpert & R. Cathcart (Eds.), *Inter/media: Interpersonal communication in a media world* (3rd ed., pp. 62–80). New York, NY: Oxford University Press.

Clark, R. A., & Delia, J. C. (1979). *Topoi* and rhetorical competence. *Quarterly Journal of Speech, 65*, 187–206.

David, C., Cappella, J. N., & Fishbein, M. (2006). The social diffusion of influence among adolescents: Group interaction in a chat room environment about antidrug advertisements. *Communication Theory, 16*, 118–140.

DeSanctis, G., & Poole, M. S. (1994). Capturing the complexity in advanced technology use: Adaptive structuration theory. *Organization Science, 5*, 121–147.

Edwards, C., Edwards, A., Qing, Q., & Wahl, S. T. (2007). The influence of computer-mediated word-of-mouth communication on student perceptions of instructors and attitudes toward learning course content. *Communication Education, 53*, 255–277.

Eysenbach, G., & Köhler, C. (2002). How do consumers search for and appraise health information on the world wide web? Qualitative study using focus groups, usability tests, and in-depth interviews. *British Medical Journal, 324*, 573–577.

Gibbs, J. L., Ellison, N. B., & Heino, R. D. (2006). Self-presentation in online personals: The role of anticipated future interaction, self-disclosure, and perceived success in Internet dating. *Communication Research, 33*, 152–177.

Graham, J., Argyle, M., & Furnham, A. (1980). The goal structure of situations. *European Journal of Social Psychology, 10*, 345–366.

Heider, F. (1958). *The psychology of interpersonal relations*. New York, NY: Wiley.

Herring, S. C., & Martinson, A. (2004). Assessing gender authenticity in computer-mediated language use: Evidence from an identity game. *Journal of Language and Social Psychology, 23*, 424–446.

Katz, E. (1957). The two-step flow of communication: An up-to-date report on an hypothesis. *Public Opinion Quarterly, 21*, 61–78.

Katz, E., & Lazarsfeld, P. (1955). *Personal influence*. New York, NY: Free Press.

Kelly, K., & Edwards, R. (1992). Observations: Does discussion of advertising transform its effects? Yes sometimes—A case among college students and their response to anti-drug advertising. *Journal of Advertising Research, 32*(4), 79–83.

Lampe, C., Ellison, N., & Steinfield, C. (2006). A face(book) in the crowd. Proceedings of the twentieth anniversary Conference on Computer Supported Cooperative Work, Alberta, Canada, pp. 167–170.

Lazarsfeld, P., Berelson, B. R., & Gaudet, H. (1944). *The people's choice*. New York, NY/London: Columbia University Press.

Lee, E.-J., Jang, J.-W., & Kim, M.-J. (2009). *Interpersonal interactivity in online journalism: What do readers' comments on Internet news sites tell us?* Paper presented at the annual meeting of the National Communication Association, Chicago, November.

Levy, S. (2007). Facebook grows up. *Newsweek*, August 27, pp. 40–46.

Lull, J. (1980). The social uses of television. *Human Communication Research, 6*, 197–209.

Metzger, M. J., Flanagin, A. J., & Medders, R. B. (in press). Social and heuristic approaches to credibility evaluation online. *Journal of Communication*.

Metzger, M. J., Flanagin, A. J., & Zwarun, L. (2003). College student Web use, perceptions of information credibility, and verification behavior. *Computers in Education, 41*, 271–290.

Morris, D. (1977). *Manwatching: A field guide to human behavior*. New York, NY: Abrams.

Newhagen, J. E., & Rafaeli, S. (1996). Why communication researchers should study the Internet: A dialogue. *Journal of Communication, 46*, 4–13.

O'Reilly, T. (2005). *What is Web 2.0? Design patterns and business models for the next generation of software*, September 30. Online, available at: www.oreillynet.com/pub/a/oreilly/tim/news/2005/09/30/what-is-web-20.html (accessed September 25, 2007).

O'Sullivan, P. B. (1999). Bridging mass and interpersonal communication: Synthesis scholarship in HCR. *Human Communication Research, 25*, 569–588.

O'Sullivan, P. B. (2005). *Masspersonal communication: Rethinking the mass interpersonal divide*. Paper presented at the annual meeting of the International Communication Association, New York, May.

Pan, B., Hembrooke, H., Joachims, T., Lorigo, L., Gay, G., & Granka, L. (2007). In Google we trust: Users' decisions on rank, position, and relevance. *Journal of Computer-Mediated Communication, 12*(3). Online, available at: http://jcmc.indiana.edu/vol.12/issue3/pan.html (accessed October 22, 2007).

Papacharissi, Z. (2002). The self online: The utility of personal home pages. *Journal of Broadcasting & Electronic Media, 46*, 346–368.

Parks, M. R. (2007). *Personal networks and personal relationships*. Mahwah, NJ: Lawrence Erlbaum Associates.

Pingree, S., Wiemann, J. M., & Hawkins, R. P. (1988). Editor's introduction: Toward conceptual synthesis. In R. P. Hawkins, J. M. Wiemann, & S. Pingree (Eds.), *Advancing communication science: Merging mass and interpersonal processes* (pp. 7–17). Newbury Park, CA: Sage.

Postmes, T., Spears, R., & Lea, M. (1999). Social identity, normative content, and "deindividuation" in computer-mediated groups. In N. Ellemers, R. Spears & B. Doosje (Eds.), *Social identity: Context, commitment, content* (pp. 164–183). Oxford, UK: Blackwell.

Price, V., & Cappella, J. N. (2002). Online deliberation and its influence: The electronic dialogue project in campaign 2000. *IT & Society, 1*, 303–329.

Reardon, K. K., & Rogers, E. M. (1988). Interpersonal versus mass media communication: A false dichotomy. *Human Communication Research, 15*, 284–303.

Reicher, S., Spears, R., & Postmes, T. (1995). A social identity model of deindividuation phenomena. *European Review of Social Psychology, 6*, 161–198.

Resnick, P., Zeckhauser, R., Friedman, E., & Kuwabara, K. (2000). Reputation systems. *Communications of the ACM, 43*(12), 45–48.

Robshaw, B. (1996). Toilet seats of learning. *New Statesman, 125*(13), p. 53.

Rodriguez, A., & Clair, R. P. (1999). Graffiti as communication: Exploring the discursive tensions of anonymous texts. *Southern Communication Journal, 65*, 1–15.

Rogers, E. M., & Shoemaker, F. F. (1971). *Communication of innovations*. New York, NY: Free Press.

Sassenberg, K., & Boos, M. (2003). Attitude change in computer-mediated communication: Effects of anonymity and category norms. *Group Processes & Intergroup Relations, 6*, 405–422.

Schutz, W. C. (1966). *The interpersonal underworld*. Palo Alto, CA: Science and Behavior Books.

Southwell, B. G., & Torres, A. (2006). Connecting interpersonal and mass communication: Science news exposure, perceived ability to understand science, and conversation. *Communication Monographs, 73*, 334–350.

Sundar, S. S., & Nass, C. (2001). Conceptualizing sources in online news. *Journal of Communication, 51*, 52–72.

Thompson, R., Murachver, T., & Green, J. (2001). Where is the gender in gendered language? *Psychological Science, 12*, 171–175.

Trenholm, S. (1999). *Thinking through communication: An introduction to the study of human communication*. Needham Heights, MA: Allyn & Bacon.

Vanden Boogart, M. R. (2006). *Uncovering the social impact of Facebook on a college campus*. Unpublished master's thesis, Kansas State University, Manhattan, Kansas. Online, available at: http://krex.k-state.edu/dspace/bitstream/2097/181/1/MatthewVandenBoogart2006.pdf (accessed July 5, 2007).

Walther, J. B. (1996). Computer-mediated communication: Impersonal, interpersonal, and hyperpersonal interaction. *Communication Research, 23*, 3–43.

Walther, J. B. (2006). Nonverbal dynamics in computer-mediated communication, or :(and the net :('s with you, :) and you :) alone. In V. Manusov & M. L. Patterson (Eds.), *Handbook of nonverbal communication* (pp. 461–479). Thousand Oaks, CA: Sage.

Walther, J. B. (2007). Selective self-presentation in computer-mediated communication: Hyperpersonal dimensions of technology, language, and cognition. *Computers in Human Behavior, 23*, 2538–2557.

Walther, J. B., Gay, G., & Hancock, J. T. (2005). How do communication and technology researchers study the Internet? *Journal of Communication, 55*, 632–657.

Walther, J. B., Van Der Heide, B., Hamel, L., & Shulman, H. (2009). Self-generated versus other-generated statements and impressions in computer-mediated communication: A test of warranting theory using Facebook. *Communication Research, 36*, 229–253.

Walther, J. B., Van Der Heide, B., Kim, S., Westerman, D., & Tong, S. T. (2008). The role of friends' behavior on evaluations of individuals' Facebook profiles: Are we known by the company we keep? *Human Communication Research, 34*, 28–49.

Walther, J. B., Wang, Z., & Loh, T. (2004). The effect of top-level domains and advertisements on health web-site credibility. *Journal of Medical Internet Research, 6* (3). Retrieved October 29, 2007 from www.jmir.org/2004/3/e24/.

Warren, J. R., Hecht, M. L., Wagstaff, D. A., Elek, E., Ndiaye, K., Dustman, P., et al. (2006). Communicating prevention: The effects of the keepin' it REAL classroom videotapes and televised PSAs on middle-school students' substance use. *Journal of Applied Communication Research, 34*, 209–227.

Wenner, L. A. (1976). Functional analysis of TV viewing for older adults. *Journal of Broadcasting, 20*, 77–88.

Wiemann, J. M., Hawkins, R. P., & Pingree, S. (1988). Fragmentation in the field—and the movement toward integration in communication science. *Human Communication Research, 15*, 304–310.

Wittenbaum, G. M., Hollingshead, A. B., & Botero, I. C. (2004). From cooperative to motivated information sharing in groups: Moving beyond the hidden profile paradigm. *Communication Monographs, 71*, 286–310.

Chapter 2

Social Network Sites as Networked Publics

Affordances, Dynamics, and Implications

danah boyd

Social network sites have gained tremendous traction recently as popular online hangout spaces for both youth and adults. People flock to them to socialize with their friends and acquaintances, to share information with interested others, and to see and be seen. While networking socially or for professional purposes is not the predominant practice, there are those who use these sites to flirt with friends-of-friends, make business acquaintances, and occasionally even rally others for a political cause. I have been examining different aspects of social network sites, primarily from an ethnographic perspective, for over six years. In making sense of the practices that unfold on and through these sites, I have come to understand social network sites as a genre of "networked publics."

Networked publics are publics that are restructured by networked technologies. As such, they are simultaneously (1) the space constructed through networked technologies and (2) the imagined collective that emerges as a result of the intersection of people, technology, and practice. Networked publics serve many of the same functions as other types of publics—they allow people to gather for social, cultural, and civic purposes, and they help people connect with a world beyond their close friends and family. While networked publics share much in common with other types of publics, the ways in which technology structures them introduces distinct affordances that shape how people engage with these environments. The properties of bits—as distinct from atoms—introduce new possibilities for interaction. As a result, new dynamics emerge that shape participation.

Analytically, the value of constructing social network sites as networked publics is to see the practices that unfold there as being informed by the affordances of networked publics and the resultant common dynamics. Networked publics' affordances do not dictate participants' behavior, but they do configure the environment in a way that shapes participants' engagement. In essence, the architecture of a particular environment matters and the architecture of networked publics is shaped by their affordances. The common dynamics fall out from these affordances and showcase salient issues that participants must regularly contend with when engaging in these environments. Understanding the properties, affordances, and dynamics common to networked publics provides a valuable framework for working out the logic of social practices.

The purpose of this chapter is to map out the architecture of networked publics, beginning with the bits-based nature of digital environments and then moving on to show how the affordances of networked publics are informed by the properties of bits and highlighting common dynamics that emerge from those affordances. Before examining these various properties, affordances, and dynamics, I will begin with a discussion of what constitutes publics in order to account for the conceptualization of networked publics. In introducing the notion of architecture, I will also map out some of the critical features of social network sites as a type of networked public.

Publics and Networked Publics

Networked publics must be understood in terms of "publics," a contested and messy term with multiple meanings that is used across different disciplines to signal different concepts. One approach is to construct "public" as a collection of people who share "a common understanding of the world, a shared identity, a claim to inclusiveness, a consensus regarding the collective interest" (Livingstone, 2005, p. 9). In this sense, a public may refer to a local collection of people (e.g., one's peers) or a much broader collection of people (e.g., members of a nation-state). Those invested in the civic functioning of publics often concern themselves with the potential accessibility of spaces and information to wide audiences—"the public"—and the creation of a shared "public sphere" (Habermas, 1991). Yet, as Benedict Anderson (2006) argues, the notion of a public is in many ways an "imagined community." Some scholars contend that there is no single public, but many publics to which some people are included and others excluded (Warner, 2002).

Cultural and media studies offer a different perspective on the notion of what constitutes a public. In locating the term "public" as synonymous with "audience," Sonia Livingstone (2005) uses the term to refer to a group bounded by a shared text, whether a worldview or a performance. The audience produced by media is often by its very nature a public, but not necessarily a passive one. For example, Michel de Certeau (2002) argues that consumption and production of cultural objects are intimately connected, and Henry Jenkins (2006) applies these ideas to the creation and dissemination of media. Mizuko Ito extends this line of thinking to argue that "publics can be reactors, (re)makers and (re)distributors, engaging in shared culture and knowledge through discourse and social exchange as well as through acts of media reception" (Ito, 2008, p. 3).

It is precisely this use of public that upsets political theorists like Jurgen Habermas, who challenge the legitimacy of any depoliticized public preoccupied "with consumption of culture" (Habermas, 1991, p. 177). Of course, not all political scholars agree with Habermas' objection to the cultural significance of publics. Feminist scholar Nancy Fraser argues that publics are not only a site of discourse and opinion but "arenas for the formation and enactment of social identities" (Fraser, 1992), while Craig Calhoun argues that one of Habermas' weaknesses is his naive view that "identities and interests [are] settled within the private world and then brought fully formed into the public sphere" (Calhoun, 1992, p. 35).

Networked publics exist against this backdrop. Mizuko Ito introduces the notion of networked publics to "reference a linked set of social, cultural, and technological developments that have accompanied the growing engagement with digitally networked media" (Ito, 2008, p. 2). Ito emphasizes the networked media, but I believe we must also focus on the ways in which this shapes publics—both in terms of space and collectives. In short, I contend that networked publics are publics that are restructured by networked technologies; they are simultaneously a space and a collection of people.

In bringing forth the notion of networked publics, I am not seeking to resolve the different discursive threads around the notion of publics. My approach accepts the messiness and, instead, focuses on the ways in which networked technologies extend and complicate publics in all of their forms. What distinguishes networked publics from other types of publics is their underlying structure. Networked technologies reorganize how information flows and how people interact with information and each other. In essence, the architecture of networked publics differentiates them from more traditional notions of publics.

How the Properties of Bits and Atoms Shape Architecture

While Frank Lloyd Wright defined architecture as "life" (Wright & Gutheim, 1941, p. 257), there is no broadly accepted definition (Shepheard, 1994). Yet, in the everyday sense, architecture typically evokes the image of the design of physical structures—buildings, roads, gardens, and even interstitial spaces. The product of architecture can be seen as part engineering, part art, and part socially configuring, as structures are often designed to be variably functional, aesthetically pleasing, and influential in shaping how people interact with one another. The word "architecture" is also used in technical circles to refer to the organization of code that produces digital environments. Drawing on all of these uses, architecture can also serve as an important conceptual lens through which to understand structural differences in technologies in relation to practice (Papacharissi, 2009).

Physical structures are a collection of atoms, while digital structures are built out of bits. The underlying properties of bits and atoms fundamentally distinguish these two types of environments, define what types of interactions are possible, and shape how people engage in these spaces. Both William Mitchell (1995, p. 111) and Lawrence Lessig (2006, pp. 1–8) have argued that "code is law" because code regulates the structures that emerge. James Grimmelmann argues that Lessig's use of this phrase is "shorthand for the subtler idea that code does the work of law, but does it in an architectural way" (Grimmelmann, 2004, p. 1721). In looking at how code configures digital environments, both Mitchell and Lessig highlight the ways in which digital architectures are structural forces.

The difference between bits and atoms as architectural building blocks is central to the ways in which networked publics are constructed differently than other publics. More than a decade ago, Nicholas Negroponte (1995) mapped out some core differences between bits and atoms to argue that digitization would fundamentally alter the landscape of information and media. He pointed out that bits could be easily duplicated, compressed, and transmitted through wires; media that is built out of bits could be more easily and more quickly disseminated than that which comprises atoms. During that same period, Mitchell (1995) argued that bits do not simply change the flow of information, but they alter the very architecture of everyday life. Through networked technology, people are no longer shaped just by their dwellings but by their networks (Mitchell, 1995, p. 49). The city of bits that Mitchell lays out is not configured just by the properties of bits but by the connections between them.

The affordances of networked publics are fundamentally shaped by the properties of bits, the connections between bits, and the way that bits and networks link people in new ways. Networked publics are not just publics networked together, but they are publics that have been transformed by networked media, its properties, and its potential. The properties of bits regulate the structure of networked publics, which, in turn, introduces new possible practices and shapes the interactions that take place. These can be seen in the architecture of all networked publics, including social network sites.

Features of Social Network Sites

Social network sites are similar to many other genres of social media and online communities that support computer-mediated communication, but what defines this particular category of website is the combination of features that allow individuals to (1) construct a public or semi-public profile within a bounded system, (2) articulate a list of other users with whom they share a connection, and (3) view and traverse their list of connections and those made by others within the system (boyd & Ellison, 2007). Features and functionality vary across different social network sites, providing a variety of different public and private communication channels, but I want to focus on four types of features that play a salient role in constructing social network sites as networked publics—profiles, Friends lists, public commenting tools, and stream-based updates. These different features showcase how bits are integrated into the architecture of networked publics.

Profiles

Profiles are not unique to social network sites, but they are central to them. Profiles both represent the individual and serve as the locus of interaction. Because of the inherent social—and often public or semi-public—nature of profiles, participants actively and consciously craft their profiles to be seen by others. Profile generation is an explicit act of writing oneself into being in a digital environment (boyd, 2006), and participants must determine how they want to present themselves to those who may view their self-representation or those who they wish might. Because of this, issues of fashion and style play a central role in participants' approach to their profiles.

In addition to being a site of self-representation, profiles are a place where people gather to converse and share. Conversations happen *on* profiles and a person's profile reflects their engagement with the site. As a result, participants do not have complete control over their self-representation. Although features may allow participants to restrict others' contributions to their profile, most participants welcome the contribution of images and comments.

Profiles are also a site of control, allowing participants to determine who can see what and how. While social network site profiles can be accessible to anyone—"truly public"—it is common for participants to limit the visibility of their profiles, making them "semi-public." Semi-public profiles are still typically available to a broad audience, comprised of friends, acquaintances, peers, and interesting peripheral ties. In this way, profiles are where the potential audience is fixed, creating a narrower public shaped by explicit connection or affiliation.

Friends Lists

On social network sites, participants articulate who they wish to connect with, and confirm ties to those who wish to connect with them. Most social network sites require connections to be mutually confirmed before being displayed. Each individual's Friends list is visible to anyone who has permission to view that person's profile.

The public articulation of Friends on a social network site is not simply an act of social accounting. These Friends are rarely only one's closest and dearest friends. The listing of Friends is both political and social. In choosing who to include as Friends, participants more frequently consider the implications of excluding or explicitly rejecting a person as opposed to the benefits of including them. While there are participants who will strictly curtail their list of Friends and participants who gregariously seek to add anyone, the majority of participants simply include all who they consider a part of their social world. This might include current and past friends and acquaintances as well as peripheral ties, or people that the participant barely knows but feels compelled to include. The most controversial actors are those who hold power over the participant, such as parents, bosses, and teachers. For many participants, it is more socially costly to include these individuals than it is to include less intimate ties.

One way of interpreting the public articulation of connections on social networks is to see it as the articulation of a public. These Friends are the people with whom the participants see themselves connecting en masse. For some participants, it is important to make certain that these individuals are all part of the same social context; for others, mixing different social contexts is acceptable and desirable. How a participant approaches the issue of social contexts shapes who they may or may not include as Friends.

In theory, truly public profiles can be accessed by anyone. In reality, an individual's audience is typically much smaller than all people across all space and all time. Even when participants choose to make their profiles widely accessible or seek broad audiences, very few people are likely to look. In determining who to account for as viewers when interacting in networked publics, few participants consider every possible person to be their audience. Instead, they imagine an audience that is usually more constrained by who they wish to reach and how they wish to present themselves (Marwick & boyd, in press). On social network sites, people's imagined—or at least intended—audience is the list of Friends that they have chosen to connect with on the site. This is who participants expect to be accessing their content and interacting with them. And these are the people to whom a participant is directing their expressions. By serving as the imagined audience, the list of Friends serves as the intended public. Of course, just because this collection of people is the intended public does not mean that it is the actual public. Yet, the value of imagining the audience or public is to adjust one's behavior and self-presentation to fit the intended norms of that collective.

Tools for Public Communication

Most social network sites provide various tools to support public or semi-public interactions between participants. Group features allow participants to gather around shared interests. A more commonly used tool for public encounters is the commenting feature that displays conversations on a person's profile (aka "The Wall" on Facebook and "Comments" on MySpace). Comments are visible to anyone who has access to that person's profile, and participants use this space to interact with individuals and cohorts. Looking at the content, one might argue that there is little value to the conversations that take place, especially since teen conversations can often be boiled down to, "Yo! Wazzup?" "Not much . . . how you?" "Good . . . whatcha doing?" "Nothing . . . you?" "Nothing. I'm bored." "Me too." While this typed conversation may appear to have little communicative efficacy, the ritual of checking in is a form of social grooming. Through mundane comments, participants are acknowledging one another in a public setting, similar to the way in which they may greet each other if they were to bump into one another on the street. Comments are not simply a dialogue between two interlocutors, but a performance of social connection before a broader audience.

In conjunction with the comments section, both Facebook and MySpace have implemented features that allow participants to broadcast content to Friends on the sites. MySpace initially did this with a feature called "bulletins," which allowed for blog-esque messages to be distributed. After Facebook implemented "status updates" to encourage the sharing of pithy messages, MySpace introduced a similar feature. All of these features allow individuals to contribute content, which is then broadcast to Friends primarily via a stream of updates from all of their Friends. In some cases, these updates are then re-displayed on a person's profile and available for comments. While individual updates are arguably mundane, the running stream of content gives participants a general sense of those around them. In doing so, participants get the sense of the public constructed by those with whom they connect.

Together, profiles, Friends lists, and various public communication channels set the stage for the ways in which social network sites can be understood as publics. In short, social network sites are publics both because of the ways in which they connect people en masse and because of the space they provide for interactions and information. They are networked publics because of the ways in which networked technologies shape and configure them.

Structural Affordances of Networked Publics

Networked technologies introduce new affordances for amplifying, recording, and spreading information and social acts. These affordances can shape publics and how people negotiate them. While such affordances do not determine social practice, they can destabilize core assumptions people make when engaging in social life. As such, they can reshape publics both directly and through the practices that people develop to account for the affordances. When left unchecked, networked technologies can play a powerful role in controlling information and configuring interactions. This is one fault line that prompts resistance to and demonization of new technologies. Much of the concern stems from how the technology's affordances inflect understood practices.

The content of networked publics is made out of bits. Both self-expressions and interactions between people produce bit-based content in networked publics. Because of properties of bits, bits are easier to store, distribute, and search than atoms. Four affordances that emerge out of the properties of bits play a significant role in configuring networked publics:

Persistence: Online expressions are automatically recorded and archived.

Replicability: Content made out of bits can be duplicated.

Scalability: The potential visibility of content in networked publics is great.

Searchability: Content in networked publics can be accessed through search.

To account for the structure of networked publics, I want to map out these different elements, situate them in a broader discussion of media, and suggest how they shape networked publics and people's participation. Although these affordances are intertwined and co-dependent, I want to begin by looking at each one differently and considering what it contributes to the structure of networked publics.

Persistence: What One Says Sticks Around

While spoken conversations are ephemeral, countless technologies and techniques have been developed to capture moments and make them persistent. The introduction of writing allowed people to create records of events, and photography provided a tool for capturing a fleeting moment. Yet, as Walter Ong (2002) has argued, the introduction of literacy did more than provide a record; it transformed how people thought and communicated. Furthermore, as Walter Benjamin (1969) has argued, what is captured by photography has a different essence than the experienced moment. Both writing and photography provide persistence, but they also transform the acts they are capturing.

Internet technologies follow a long line of other innovations in this area. What is captured and recorded are the bytes that are created and exchanged across the network. Many systems make bits persistent by default and, thus, the text that one produces becomes persistent. Yet, do people interpret the content in the same way as they did when it was first produced? This is quite unlikely. The text and the multimedia may be persistent, but what sticks around may lose its essence when consumed outside of the context in which it was created. The persistence of conversations in networked publics is ideal for asynchronous conversations, but it also raises new concerns when it can be consumed outside of its original context.

While recording devices allow people to record specific acts in publics, the default is typically that unmediated acts are ephemeral. Networked technology inverted these defaults, making recording a common practice. This is partially due to the architecture of the Internet, where dissemination requires copies and records for transmission and processing. Of course, while original records and duplicated records can in theory be deleted (or, technically, overwritten) at any point in the process, the "persistent-by-default, ephemeral-when-necessary" dynamic is relatively pervasive, rendering tracking down and deleting content once it is contributed to networked publics futile.

Replicability: What's the Original and What's the Duplicate?

The printing press transformed writing because it allowed for easy reproduction of news and information, increasing the potential circulation of such content (Eisenstein, 1980). Technology has introduced a series of tools to help people duplicate text, images, video, and other media. Because bits can be replicated more easily than atoms, and because bits are replicated as they are shared across the network, the content produced in networked publics is easily replicable. Copies are inherent to these systems.

In a world of bits, there is no way to differentiate the original bit from its duplicate. And, because bits can be easily modified, content can be transformed in ways that make it hard to tell which is the source and which is the alteration. The replicable nature of content in networked publics means that what is replicated may be altered in ways that people do not easily realize.

Scalability: What Spreads May Not Be Ideal

Technology enables broader distribution, either by enhancing who can access the real-time event or widening access to reproductions of the moment. Broadcast media like TV and radio made it possible for events to be simultaneously experienced across great distances, radically scaling the potential visibility of a given act and reshaping the public sphere (Starr, 2005). While such outlets allow content to scale, distribution outlets are frequently regulated (although this did not stop "pirates" from creating their own broadcast publics (Walker, 2004)). The Internet introduced new possibilities for distribution; blogging alone allowed for the rise of grassroots journalism (Gillmor, 2004) and a channel for anyone to espouse opinions (Rettberg, 2008).

The Internet may enable many to broadcast content and create publics, but it does not guarantee an audience. What scales in networked publics may not be what everyone wishes to scale. Furthermore, while a niche group may achieve visibility that resembles "micro-celebrity" (Senft, 2008), only a small fraction receives mass attention, while many more receive very small, localized attention. Scalability in networked publics is about the *possibility* of tremendous visibility, not the guarantee of it.

Habermas' frustration with broadcast media was rooted in the ways that broadcast media was, in his mind, scaling the wrong kinds of content (Habermas, 1991). The same argument can be made concerning networked media, as what scales in networked publics is often the funny, the crude, the embarrassing, the mean, and the bizarre, "ranging from the quirky and offbeat, to potty humor, to the bizarrely funny, to parodies, through to the acerbically ironic" (Knobel & Lankshear, 2007). Those seeking broad attention, like politicians and wannabe celebrities, may have the ability to share their thoughts in networked publics, but they may not achieve the scale they wish. The property of scalability does not necessarily scale what individuals want to have scaled or what they think should be scaled, but what the collective chooses to amplify.

Searchability: Seek and You Shall Find

Librarians and other information specialists have long developed techniques to make accessing information easier and more effective. Metadata schemes and other strategies for organizing content have been central to these efforts. Yet, the introduction of search engines has radically reworked the ways in which information can be accessed. Search has become a commonplace activity among Internet users.

As people use technologies that leave traces, search takes on a new role. While being able to stand in a park and vocalize "find" to locate a person or object may seem like an element of a science fiction story, such actions are increasingly viable in networked publics. Search makes finding people in networked publics possible and, as GPS-enabled mobile devices are deployed, we will see such practices be part of other aspects of everyday life.

Central Dynamics in Networked Publics

The affordances of networked publics introduce new dynamics with which participants must contend. Many of these dynamics are not new, but they were never so generally experienced. Analyzing how broadcast media transformed culture, Joshua Meyrowitz (1985) articulated that the properties of media change social environments and, thus, influence people and their behavior. He examined how broadcast media's ability to rework scale reconfigured publics, altered the roles that people play in society, complicated the boundaries between public and private, collapsed distinct social contexts, and ruptured the salience of physical place in circumscribing publics. Just as many of the affordances of networked media parallel those of broadcast media, many of the dynamics that play out in networked publics are an amplification of those Meyrowitz astutely recognized resulting from broadcast media. Three dynamics play a central role in shaping networked publics:

Invisible audiences: Not all audiences are visible when a person is contributing online, nor are they necessarily co-present.

Collapsed contexts: The lack of spatial, social, and temporal boundaries makes it difficult to maintain distinct social contexts.

The blurring of public and private: Without control over context, public and private become meaningless binaries, are scaled in new ways, and are difficult to maintain as distinct.

As people engage with networked publics, they are frequently forced to contend with the ways in which these dynamics shape the social environment. While such dynamics have long been part of some people's lives, they take on a new salience in networked publics because of their broad reach and their pervasiveness in everyday life. Let's briefly consider each dynamic.

Invisible Audiences: To Whom Should One Speak?

In unmediated spaces, it is common to have a sense for who is present and can witness a particular performance. The affordances of networked publics change this. In theory, people can access content that is persistent, replicable, scalable, and searchable across broad swaths of space and time. Lurkers who share the same space but are not visible are one potential audience. But so are those who go back to read archives or who are searching for content on a particular topic.

People in certain professions have long had to contend with invisible audiences. In producing content for the camera, microphone, or printing press, journalists and actors sometimes prepare for invisible audiences by imagining the audience and presenting themselves to that imagined audience. When TV began, studio audiences were tremendously common because it helped people gauge their performances. This audience was not the complete audience, but the feedback was still valuable for the performers. Likewise, some journalists perform for those who provide explicit feedback, intentionally avoiding thinking about those who are there but invisible. Performing for imagined or partial audiences can help people handle the invisible nature of their audience. These practices became a part of life in networked publics, as those who contributed tried to find a way to locate their acts.

Knowing one's audience matters when trying to determine what is socially appropriate to say or what will be understood by those listening. In other words, audience is critical to context. Without information about audience, it is often difficult to determine how to behave, let alone to make adjustments based on assessing reactions. To accommodate this, participants in networked publics often turn to an imagined audience to assess whether or not they believe their behavior is socially appropriate, interesting, or relevant.

Collapsed Contexts: Navigating Tricky Social Situations

Even when one knows one's audience, it can be challenging to contend with groups of people who reflect different social contexts and have different expectations as to what's appropriate. For some, the collapsing of contexts in broadcast media made expressing oneself challenging. Consider the case of Stokely Carmichael, which Meyrowitz (1985, p. 43) details in his book. Carmichael was a civil rights leader in the 1960s. He regularly gave speeches to different audiences using different rhetorical styles depending on the race of the audience. When Carmichael began addressing broad publics via television and radio, he had to make a choice. There was no neutral speaking style and Carmichael's decision to use black speaking style alienated white society. While Carmichael was able to maintain distinct styles as long as he was able to segment social groups, he ran into trouble when broadcast media collapsed those social groups and, with them, the distinct contexts in which they were embedded.

Networked publics force everyday people to contend with environments in which contexts are regularly colliding. Even when the immediate audience might be understood, the potential audience can be far greater and from different contexts. Maintaining distinct contexts online is particularly tricky because of the persistent, replicable, searchable, and scalable nature of networked acts. People do try to segment contexts by discouraging unwanted audiences from participating, or by trying to limit information to make searching more difficult, or by using technologies that create partial walls through privacy settings. Yet a motivated individual can often circumvent any of these approaches.

Some argue that distinct contexts are unnecessary and only encourage people to be deceptive. This is the crux of the belief that only those with something to hide need privacy. What is lost in this approach is the ways in which context helps people properly contextualize their performances. Bilingual speakers choose different languages depending on context, and speakers explain concepts or describe events differently when talking to different audiences based on their assessment of the audience's knowledge. An alternative way to mark context is as that which provides the audience with a better understanding of the performer's biases and assumptions. Few people detail their life histories before telling a story, but that history is often helpful in assessing the significance of the story. While starting every statement with "as a person with X identity and Y beliefs and Z history" can provide context, most people do not speak this way, let alone account for all of the relevant background for any stranger to understand any utterance.

Networked publics both complicate traditional mechanisms for assessing and asserting context as well as collapse contexts that are traditionally segmented. This is particularly problematic because, with the audience invisible and the material persistent, it is often difficult to get a sense of what the context is or should be. Collapsing of contexts did take place before the rise of broadcast media, but often in more controlled settings. For example, events like weddings, in which context collisions are common, are frequently scripted to make everyone comfortable. Unexpected collisions, like running into one's boss while out with friends, can create awkwardness, but since both parties are typically aware of the collision, it can often be easy to make quick adjustments to one's behavior to address the awkward situation. In networked publics, contexts often collide such that the performer is unaware of audiences from different contexts, magnifying the awkwardness and making adjustments impossible.

Blurring of Public and Private: Where are the Boundaries?

Additionally, as networked publics enable social interactions at all levels, the effects of these dynamics are felt at much broader levels than those felt by broadcast media and the introduction of other forms of media to publics.

These dynamics alter interactions among very large and broad collections of people, but they also complicate the dynamics among friend groups and collections of peers. They alter practices that are meant for broad visibility and they complicate—and often make public—interactions that were never intended to be truly public. This stems from the ways in which networked media, like broadcast media (Meyrowitz, 1985), blurs public and private in complicated ways. For those in the spotlight, broadcast media often appeared to destroy privacy. This is most visible through the way tabloid media complicated the private lives of celebrities, feeding on people's desire to get backstage access (Turner, 2004). As networked publics brought the dynamics of broadcast media to everyday people, participants have turned their social curiosity toward those who are more socially local (Solove, 2007).

Some argue that privacy is now dead (Garfinkel, 2001) and that we should learn to cope and embrace a more transparent society (Brin, 1999). That is a naive stance, both because privacy has been reshaped during other transformative moments in history (Jagodzinski, 1999) and because people have historically developed strategies for maintaining aspects of privacy even when institutions and governments seek to eliminate it (McDougall & Hansson, 2002; Toch, 1992). For these reasons, I argue that privacy is simply in a state of transition as people try to make sense of how to negotiate the structural transformations resulting from networked media.

People value privacy for diverse reasons, including the ability to have control over information about themselves and their own visibility (Rossler, 2004, pp. 6–8). Social network sites disrupt the social dynamics of privacy (Grimmelmann, 2009). Most importantly, they challenge people's sense of control. Yet, just because people are adopting tools that radically reshape their relationship to privacy does not mean they are interested in giving up their privacy.

Defining and controlling boundaries around public and private can be quite difficult in a networked society, particularly when someone is motivated to publicize something that is seemingly private or when technology complicates people's ability to control access and visibility. What remains an open question is how people can regain a sense of control in a networked society. Helen Nissenbaum (2004) argues that we need to approach privacy through the lens of contextual integrity, at least in terms of legal protections. I believe that we need to examine people's strategies for negotiating control in the face of structural conditions that complicate privacy and rethink our binary conceptions of public and private. While public and private are certainly in flux, it is unlikely that privacy will simply be disregarded.

Transformation of Publics

While I have accounted for the ways in which the affordances of networked publics and the dynamics that unfold mirror those which take place due to other technologies or for distinct populations, what is significant about this stems from how such factors are more broadly transforming everyday life for broad swaths of the public at large. The affordances of networked publics rework publics more generally and the dynamics that emerge leak from being factors in specific settings to being core to everyday realities.

The changes brought on by networked technologies are more pervasive than those by earlier media. Because content and expressions contributed to networked publics is persistent and replicable by default, the possibility of acts being scaled, searchable, and thus viewed is heightened. Physical spaces are limited by space and time, but, online, people can connect to one another across great distances and engage with asynchronously produced content over extended periods. This allows people to work around physical barriers to interaction and reduces the cost of interacting with people in far-off places.

Yet, at the same time, many people are unmotivated to interact with distant strangers; their attention is focused on those around them. Andy Warhol argued that mass media would guarantee that, "in the future everyone will be world-famous for fifteen minutes" (Hirsch, Kett, & Trefil, 2002). As new media emerged, artists and writers countered this claim by noting, "in the future everyone will be famous for fifteen people" (Momus, 1992; Weinberger, 2002, p. 104). In networked publics, attention becomes a commodity. There are those who try to manipulate the potential scalability of these environments to reach wide audiences, including politicians and pundits. There are also those who become the object of widespread curiosity and are propelled into the spotlight by the interwoven network. There are also the countless who are not seeking or gaining widespread attention. Yet, in an environment where following the content of one's friends involves the same technologies as observing the follies of a celebrity, individuals find themselves embedded in the attention economy, as consumers and producers. While new media can be reproduced and scaled far and wide, it does not address the ways in which attention is a limited resource.

Persistence and replicability also complicate notions of "authenticity," as acts and information are not located in a particular space or time and, because of the nature of bits, it is easy to alter content, making it more challenging to assess its origins and legitimacy. This issue has long been a part of discussions about reproductions and recordings, with Walter Benjamin (1969, p. 220) suggesting that art detached from its time and space loses its "aura," and Philip Auslander (1999, p. 85) arguing that aura is in the relationship between performances and their recordings. Authenticity is at stake in networked publics because altering content in networked publics is both easy and common. Code, text, images, and videos are frequently modified or remixed. While remix is politically contentious, it reflects an active and creative engagement with cultural artifacts (Lessig, 2005), amplifying ongoing efforts by people to make mass culture personally relevant by obliterating the distinctions between consumers and producers. How people alter content in networked publics varies. Alterations can be functional (e.g., altering code to make it work in a new environment), aesthetic (e.g., altering images to remove red eye), political (e.g., modifying famous photos to make political statements (Jenkins, 2006)), or deceptive (e.g., altering text to make it appear as though something was said that was not). This magnifies questions of what is original, what is a copy, and when does it matter?

While there are limits to how many people can be in one physical space at a time, networked publics support the gathering of much larger groups, synchronously and asynchronously. Networked publics make one-to-many and many-to-many interactions far easier. In essence, networked media allows anyone to be a media outlet (Gillmor, 2004), and with this comes the potential of scalability. Yet an increase in people's ability to contribute to publics does not necessarily result in an increase in their ability to achieve an audience. The potentials of scalability raise questions about the possible democratizing role that networked media can play when anyone can participate and contribute to the public good (e.g., Benkler, 2006). Unfortunately, networked publics appear to reproduce many of the biases that exist in other publics—social inequalities, including social stratification around race, gender, sexuality, and age, are reproduced online (Chen & Wellman, 2005; Hargittai, 2008). Political divisions are also reproduced (Adamic & Glance, 2005) such that even when content scales in visibility, it may not cross sociopolitical divisions. Those using networked media to contribute to the dissemination of news selectively amplify stories introduced by traditional media outlets, replicating offline cultural foci (Zuckerman, 2008). Although networked publics support mass dissemination, the dynamics of "media contagion" (Marlow, 2005) show that what spreads depends on the social structure underlying the networked publics. In other words, scalability is dependent on more than just the properties of bits.

Implications for Analysis

The affordances of networked publics and the resultant dynamics that emerge are transforming publics. While marking networked publics as a distinct genre of publics is discursively relevant at this moment, it is also important to acknowledge that the affordances of networked publics will increasingly shape publics more broadly. As social network sites and other genres of social media become increasingly widespread, the distinctions between networked publics and publics will become increasingly blurry. Thus, the dynamics mapped out here will not simply be constrained to the domain of the digital world, but will be part of everyday life.

The rise of social network sites has introduced ever-increasing populations to the trials and tribulations of navigating networked publics. Many of the struggles that take place on social network sites are shaped by the properties of bits, the affordances of networked publics, and the resultant dynamics. While some of the specific factors are not unique to networked publics, the prevalence of social network sites has introduced these affordances and dynamics to a much broader subset of the population.

This is not to say that what emerges in social network sites is simply determined by the technical affordances, or that the dynamics described here predict practices. Rather, participants are implicitly and explicitly contending with these affordances and dynamics as a central part of their participation. In essence, people are learning to work within the constraints and possibilities of mediated architecture, just as people have always learned to navigate structures as part of their daily lives.

In my earlier analysis on American teenagers' participation in social network sites (boyd, 2008), I highlighted that teens can and do develop strategies for managing the social complexities of these environments. In some ways, teens are more prepared to embrace networked publics because many are coming of age in a time when networked affordances are a given. Adults, on the other hand, often find the shifts brought on by networked publics to be confusing and discomforting because they are more acutely aware of the ways in which their experiences with public life are changing. Yet, even they are adjusting to these changes and developing their own approaches to reconfiguring the technology to meet their needs.

As social network sites and other emergent genres of social media become pervasive, the affordances and dynamics of networked publics can shed light on why people engage the way they do. Thus, taking the structural elements of networked publics into account when analyzing what unfolds can provide a valuable interpretive framework. Architecture shapes and is shaped by practice in mediated environments just as in physical spaces.

References

Adamic, L. A. & Glance, N. (2005). The political blogosphere and the 2004 U.S. election: Divided they blog. *Proceedings of Knowledge Discovery in Data, Chicago, IL* (pp. 36–43). ACM.

Anderson, B. (2006). *Imagined communities: Reflections on the origin and spread of nation-alism* (new ed.). New York, NY: Verso.

Auslander, P. (1999). *Liveness: Performance in a mediatized culture.* London: Routledge.

Benjamin, W. (1969). The work of art in the age of mechanical reproduction. In W. Benjamin (Ed.), *Illuminations* (H. Zohn, Trans.) (pp. 217–252). New York, NY: Schocken Books.

Benkler, Y. (2006). *The wealth of networks: How social production transforms markets and freedom.* New Haven, CT: Yale University Press.

boyd, d. (2006). Friends, friendsters, and MySpace Top 8: Writing community into being on social network sites. *First Monday, 11* (12).

boyd, d. (2008). *Taken out of context: American teen sociality in networked publics.* PhD Dissertation, School of Information, University of California-Berkeley, Berkeley, CA.

boyd, d. m. & Ellison, N. (2007). Social network sites: Definition, history, and scholarship. *Journal of Computer-Mediated Communication, 13* (1), 11.

Brin, D. (1999). *The transparent society: Will technology force us to choose between privacy and freedom?* New York, NY: Basic Books.

Calhoun, C. (1992). Introduction. In C. Calhoun (Ed.), *Habermas and the public sphere* (pp. 1–50). Cambridge, MA: MIT Press.

Chen, W. & Wellman, B. (2005). Minding the cyber-gap: The Internet and social inequality. In M. Romero & E. Margolis (Eds.), *The Blackwell companion to social inequalities* (pp. 523–545). Malden, MA: Blackwell.

de Certeau, M. (2002). *The practice of everyday life.* Berkeley and Los Angeles, CA: University of California Press.

Eisenstein, E. L. (1980). *The printing press as an agent of change.* Cambridge: Cambridge University Press.

Fraser, N. (1992). Rethinking the public sphere: A contribution to the critique of actually existing democracy. In C. Calhoun (Ed.), *Habermas and the public sphere* (pp. 109–142). Cambridge, MA: MIT Press.

Garfinkel, S. (2001). *Database nation: The death of privacy in the 21st century.* Sebastopol, CA: O'Reilly Media.

Gillmor, D. (2004). *We the media: Grassroots journalism by the people, for the people.* Sebastopol, CA: O'Reilly Media.

Grimmelmann, J. (2004). Regulation by software. *Yale Law Journal, 114,* 1719–1758.

Grimmelmann, J. (2009). Facebook and the social dynamics of privacy. *Iowa Law Review, 94,* 1137–1206.

Habermas, J. (1991). *The structural transformation of the public sphere: An inquiry into a category of bourgeois society.* Cambridge, MA: MIT Press.

Hargittai, E. (2008). The digital reproduction of inequality. In D. Grusky (Ed.), *Social Stratification* (pp. 936–944). Boulder, CO: Westview Press.

Hirsch, E. D., Kett, J. F., & Trefil, J. S. (2002). *The new dictionary of cultural literacy.* Boston, MA: Houghton Mifflin.

Ito, M. (2008). Introduction. In K. Vernelis (Ed.), *Networked publics* (pp. 1–14). Cambridge, MA: MIT Press.

Jagodzinski, C. M. (1999). *Privacy and print: Reading and writing in seventeenth-century England.* Charlottesville, VA: University of Virginia Press.

Jenkins, H. (2006). *Convergence culture: Where old and new media collide.* New York, NY: New York University Press.

Knobel, M. & Lankshear, C. (2007). Online memes, affinities, and cultural production. In M. Knobel & C. Lankshear (Eds.), *A new literacies sampler* (pp. 199–228). New York, NY: Peter Lang.

Lessig, L. (2005). *Free culture: The nature and future of creativity.* New York, NY: Penguin.

Lessig, L. (2006). *Code: Version 2.0.* New York, NY: Basic Books.

Livingstone, S. (2005). *Audiences and publics: When cultural engagement matters for the public sphere.* Portland, OR: Intellect.

McDougall, B. S. & Hansson, A. (Eds.) (2002). *Chinese concepts of privacy.* Leiden: Brill.

Marlow, C. A. (2005). *The structural determinants of media contagion.* PhD Thesis, Media Arts and Sciences, Massachusetts Institute of Technology, Cambridge, MA.

Marwick, A. & boyd, d. (in press). I tweet honestly, I tweet passionately: Twitter users, context collapse, and the imagined audience. *New Media & Society.*

Meyrowitz, J. (1985). *No sense of place: The impact of electronic media on social behavior.* New York, NY: Oxford University Press.

Mitchell, W. J. (1995). *City of bits: Space, place, and the infobahn.* Cambridge, MA: MIT Press.

Momus. (1992). Pop stars? Nein Danke! *Grimsby Fishmarket.* Online, available at: http://imomus.com/index499.html (accessed December 3, 2008).

Negroponte, N. (1995). *Being digital.* New York, NY: Vintage Books.

Nissenbaum, H. (2004). Privacy as contextual integrity. *Washington Law Review, 79* (1), 101–139.

Ong, W. J. (2002). *Orality and literacy.* London: Routledge.

Papacharissi, Z. (2009). The virtual geographies of social networks: A comparative analysis of Facebook, LinkedIn and ASmallWorld. *New Media & Society, 11*, 199–220.

Rettberg, J. W. (2008). *Blogging.* Cambridge: Polity Press.

Rossler, B. (2004). *The value of privacy.* Cambridge: Polity.

Senft, T. M. (2008). *Camgirls: Celebrity and community in the age of social networks.* New York, NY: Peter Lang.

Shepheard, P. (1994). *What is architecture? An essay on landscapes, buildings, and machines.* Cambridge, MA: MIT Press.

Solove, D. (2007). "I've got nothing to hide" and other misunderstandings of privacy. *San Diego Law Review, 44*, 745.

Starr, P. (2005). *The creation of the media: Political origins of modern communication.* New York, NY: Basic Books.

Toch, H. (1992). *Living in prison: The ecology of survival.* Washington, DC: American Psychological Association.

Turner, G. (2004). *Understanding celebrity.* London: Sage.

Walker, J. (2004). *Rebels on the air: An alternative history of radio in America.* New York, NY: New York University Press.

Warner, M. (2002). *Publics and counterpublics.* Cambridge, MA: MIT Press.

Weinberger, D. (2002). *Small pieces loosely joined: A unified theory of the Web.* Cambridge, MA: Perseus.

Wright, F. L. & Gutheim, F. E. (1941). *On architecture: Selected writings (1894–1940).* New York, NY: Grosset and Dunlap.

Zuckerman, E. (2008). What bloggers amplify from the BBC. *My Heart's in Accra.* Online, available at: www.ethanzuckerman.com/blog/2005/01/28/what-bloggers-amplify-from-the-bbc/. (accessed December 3, 2008).

Chapter 3

Social Networking

Addictive, Compulsive, Problematic, or Just Another Media Habit?[1]

Robert LaRose, Junghyun Kim, and Wei Peng

Social networking services have become a highly popular online activity in recent years with 75% of young adults online, aged 18 to 24, reporting that they have a profile (Lenhart, 2009). Social network sites have become such an obsession with some that they raise concerns about the potential harmful effects of their repeated use, known in the popular press as "Facebook addiction" (Cohen, 2009). For many Internet users, social networking has perhaps indeed become a media habit, defined (after LaRose, 2010; Verplanken & Wood, 2006) as a form of automaticity in media consumption that develops as people repeat media consumption behavior in stable circumstances. How might repeated social networking evolve from a "good" habit that merely indulges a personal media preference into a "bad" habit with potentially harmful life consequences that might rightfully be termed compulsive, problematic, pathological, or addictive? And, is social networking any more or less problematic than other popular Internet activities?

Although the extent of Internet pathology by any name, and indeed its very existence, are open to question (Shaffer, Hall, & Vander Bilt, 2000; Widyanto & Griffiths, 2007), the attention of scholars continues to be drawn to the harmful effects of excessive Internet consumption. In a national survey, 6% of U.S. adults said a relationship had suffered as a result of their Internet use (Aboujaoude, Koran, Gamel, Large, & Serpe, 2006). Correlational studies have linked Internet use and psycho-social maladjustment (e.g., Caplan, 2007; LaRose, Lin, & Eastin, 2003; McKenna & Bargh, 2000; Morahan-Martin & Schumacher, 2000; Young & Rogers, 1998). Internet usage disorder has been proposed as a new category of mental illness (Block, 2008), including a subcategory of email/text messaging that might subsume social networking.

Whether social networking habits are especially problematic or not, they are a distinctive media consumption phenomenon that harkens back to previous studies of television addictions (Kubey & Csikszentmihalyi, 2002). An understanding of Internet habits can extend models of media behavior to incorporate habitual, automatic consumption patterns as well as those that result from active selection processes (LaRose & Eastin, 2004). The current premise is that problematic media behaviors are habits that have gotten out of control (cf. Marlatt, Baer, Donovan, & Kivlahan, 1988) and that they begin as media favorites, defined here as the preferred media activity within a particular medium. Media favorites are themselves habits, as evident when items now recognized as indicators of habit strength (e.g., watching "because it is there" and because "it is part of a daily ritual") entered into a factor analysis of the uses and gratifications of favorite TV program types (Bantz, 1982). Verplanken and Orbell (2003) found that media consumption was highly correlated to habit strength while Wood, Quinn, and Kashy (2002) reported that over half of all media behaviors recorded in an experience sampling study were habit-driven. Yet clearly not all media habits spin out of control to become problematic, so how might we explain why some do and others do not? And is social networking one of the habits that is especially likely to do so?

Two competing explanations of problematic media habits have emerged in the communication literature: a social skill account that explains Problematic Internet Use (PIU) as compensation for social incompetence in the offline world (Caplan, 2005) and a socio-cognitive model of unregulated media use (LaRose et al., 2003). The present research comparatively evaluates and then integrates these two perspectives. To arrive at an understanding of social networking habits and their potential for abuse, we will first integrate the two perspectives.

The Social Skill Model of PIU

Caplan (2005, p. 721) defined PIU as a "multidimensional syndrome consisting of cognitive and behavioral symptoms that result in negative social, academic or professional consequences." Building on Davis' (2001) description of pathological Internet use in relation to symptoms of impulse control disorders, and on other researchers who drew upon symptoms of pathological gambling and substance abuse, Caplan (2002) developed a multidimensional measure of PIU dimensions. They were mood alteration, social benefits, negative outcomes, compulsivity, excessive time, preoccupation, and interpersonal control.

Predicated on repeated observations that negative life consequences are especially associated with social uses of the Internet, the social skill model posits that compulsive Internet use is the direct result of preference for online social interaction ("social benefits" in the earlier factor analysis), which in turn is inversely related to self-presentational skills (previously dubbed "interpersonal control"). Compulsive use was the causal antecedent of negative outcomes of Internet use, such as missing social engagements. Thus, the social skill account explained PIU as a form of compensation for defective real-world social skills. This model was a moderately good fit, accounting for 10% of the variance in negative outcomes (Caplan, 2005).

The resulting social skill model omitted three dimensions of PIU (Caplan, 2003): mood alteration, excessive time, and withdrawal. These additional variables can be interpreted within the competing socio-cognitive model.

The Socio-Cognitive Model of Unregulated Internet Use

In the socio-cognitive model of unregulated Internet use (LaRose et al., 2003), expected outcomes are key determinants of media behavior. So, for example, the expectation that social networking will relieve loneliness should predict social networking use. This corresponds to the "mood alteration" dimension of PIU. Internet usage is also determined by self-efficacy, or belief in one's capability to organize and execute a particular course of action, such as the person's perceived ability to use social networking to make new friends.

The socio-cognitive self-regulatory mechanism describes how humans exercise—but also how they may lose—control over media behavior. Deficient self-regulation is defined as a state in which self-regulatory processes become impaired and self-control over media use is diminished (LaRose et al., 2003). In the model of unregulated Internet use, overall Internet usage was a function of self-reactive outcome expectations and self-efficacy. Usage was further predicted by two dimensions of deficient self-regulation, one of which was associated with lack of awareness and attention[2] and a second that was associated with lack of controllability and intentionality.[3] The latter was causally related to the former and was itself predicted in turn by self-reactive outcome expectations and self-efficacy. Self-efficacy was also causally related to self-reactive outcome expectations and to the controllability/intentionality variable.

New Perspectives of Habitual Behavior

Deficient self-regulation aligns with conceptions of habit found in current research in social psychology (e.g., Verplanken & Orbell, 2003; Wood & Neal, 2007) that define habits as a form of automaticity, which in turn is thought to have four facets: lack of awareness, lack of attention, lack of controllability, and lack of intentionality. The dimensions underlying the construct are unclear, however. Verplanken and Orbell (2003) arrived at a unidimensional solution that incorporated three of the four facets of automaticity.[4] LaRose et al. (2003) empirically derived two dimensions that incorporated all four, as described above. Caplan's (2002) compulsive use dimension reflected a lack of controllability ("Unsuccessful attempts to control use") while his withdrawal dimension had items that Verplanken and Orbell (2003) identified with inattention ("Miss being online if I can't go on it") and the excessive time dimension betrayed a lack of intentionality ("Go online for longer time than I intended").

Recent developments in the neurology and social psychology of automaticity call for a conceptual re-assessment. On a neurological level, repeated behaviors gradually shift from conscious cortical control to automated responses governed by the basal ganglia, a group of nuclei in the cerebrum (Yin & Knowlton, 2006). Thus, consciously framed reasons for Internet use, such as Caplan's mood alteration dimension, are distinguishable from habit. The four facets of automaticity are independent in that they can be manipulated separately (Saling & Phillips, 2007) so the differing number of dimensions may reflect varying combinations among the four dimensions of automaticity that are found across behaviors (Saling & Phillips, 2007).

Caplan's (2002) dimensions of compulsive use, excessive time, and withdrawal included items that correspond to lack of controllability, intentionality, and attention, respectively, but a dimension indicating lack of awareness was not found.

The socio-cognitive concept of self-regulation incorporates all four facets of automaticity, and these can be re-framed in terms of sub-processes of the self-regulatory mechanism (Bandura, 1986). Here, deficient self-regulation is abandoned in favor of habit as an umbrella concept describing the overall weakness of self-regulation that encompasses two sub-processes associated with habits. Habit formation is in part a deficiency in self-observation. As behavior is repeated, individuals become less attentive to the immediate consequences of its performance and rely on cognitive shortcuts to prompt behavior, such as environmental cues or internal mood states, rather than consciously considering the behavior on each successive occurrence. This conserves scarce attentional resources, freeing the individual to process new information while placing repeated choices "on automatic," below the level of conscious awareness. Habits are maintained through a failure of self-reaction, the mechanism through which individuals apply their own incentives to modify their behavior and its outcomes, such as administering rewards for moderate behavior or indulging feelings of guilt for excessive media behavior. In the absence of such corrective measures, deficient self-reaction also diminishes attentiveness to behavior and therefore contributes to deficient self-observation.

An Integrated Model of Internet Habits

The socio-cognitive model of unregulated Internet use therefore incorporates dimensions of PIU not found in the social skill account of the syndrome. The mood alteration dimension of PIU (Caplan, 2002) corresponds to self-reactive outcome expectations, withdrawal is related to deficient self-observation, and excessive use is located in deficient self-reaction along with compulsivity. The socio-cognitive model of unregulated Internet use described above arrays these in a causal model suggested by a well-established theory of human behavior. Both models may now be understood to explain habitual Internet behavior, one focusing on the amount of consumption and the other on its consequences.

Comparing the two, the social skill account identifies negative life outcomes as a separate, dependent variable. Since such outcomes are a necessary condition for the diagnosis of impulse control disorders (Shaffer et al., 2000), this is an important addition. Three changes in terminology will help to further integrate the two models: Compulsive use is re-labeled deficient self-reaction to be consistent with the social cognitive model. Negative outcomes from Caplan's model are designated as negative life consequences to avoid confusion with outcome expectations in the SCT model. Finally, the antecedent variable of the social skill account is re-labeled deficient social skill to reflect the wording of its operational definition and clarify its conceptual relationship to preference for online social interaction.

Substituting negative life consequences for overall Internet usage as the dependent variable produces a socio-cognitive model of PIU shown in Figure 3.1. The rationale is the time inelasticity hypothesis (Nie, 2001) that holds that time spent on the Internet subtracts from the time available for other activities. Consistent with this view, an excessive time factor had a significant and positive zero-order correlation with negative outcomes[5] (Caplan, 2003) and the operational definition of the latter asks about harm to other activities that result from Internet use. The substitution of negative consequences for Internet usage, rather than its addition to the previous LaRose et al. (2003) model, is to achieve parsimony; otherwise, the Social Cognitive model of PIU would include links to negative consequences not only from usage but also from the other variables related to usage in the original model. Also for parsimony's sake, self-efficacy can be deleted on the assumption that sufficient levels of self-efficacy are achieved in the process of elevating an activity to a favorite so that the former becomes inoperative as a predictor of usage and hence of the negative life consequences that might follow.

HI: Negative life consequences of favorite Internet activities are explained by depression, self-reactive outcome expectations, deficient self-observation, and deficient self-reaction.

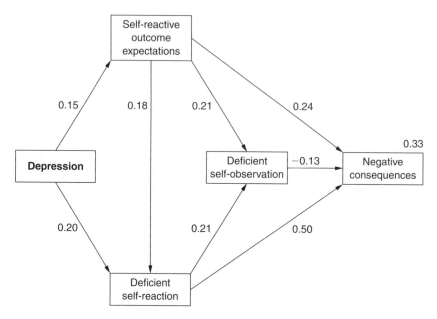

Figure 3.1 Socio-cognitive model of problematic Internet use.

This model provides an alternative explanation of negative life consequences from the social skills account. Depression causes a negative cognitive bias through which individuals slight their own successes at maintaining self-control and blame themselves for failure (Bandura, 1991), thus undermining effective self-reaction. Dysphoric moods also stimulate the seeking of self-reactive outcomes (or "mood alteration" in Caplan, 2002) to dispel those moods (see also Zillmann & Bryant, 1985). Repeated efforts to obtain self-reactive outcomes cause deficient self-observation as behavioral control shifts to non-conscious processes governed by the basal ganglia (Yin & Knowlton, 2006). Self-observation is also weakened by deficient self-reaction as individuals abandon attempts to regulate their Internet behavior, making it less subject to conscious internal scrutiny. The conscious pursuit of favorite activities to cheer oneself up or to relieve loneliness causes mounting use, the socio-cognitive version of the classic "active media selection" hypothesis of uses and gratifications research (LaRose & Eastin, 2004). Deficient self-reaction and deficient self-observation also lead to mounting use as self-regulation fails and habit strength increases. Finally, the time allocated to favorite activities interferes with important activities, producing negative life consequences.

The social skill model can be incorporated by adding deficient social skills and preference for online interaction as antecedent variables to deficient self-reaction. Depression causes deficient social skills by impairing interpersonal communication and inviting rejection (Segrin & Abramson, 1994). Also, a preference for online social interaction would likely result from successful efforts to relieve dysphoric moods through online interactions. Thus, self-reactive outcome expectations should cause a preference for online social interaction (Figure 3.2).

H2: Depression will be positively related to deficient social skill.

H3: Self-reactive outcome expectations will be positively related to preference for online social interaction.

Is Social Networking More Problematic Than Other Online Activities?

A wide variety of online activities have been identified as "addictive" (Block, 2008) and, although social networking is not currently among them, it is perhaps only a function of the relative newness of the activity. However, the appropriateness of the term "addictive" and related constructions, including

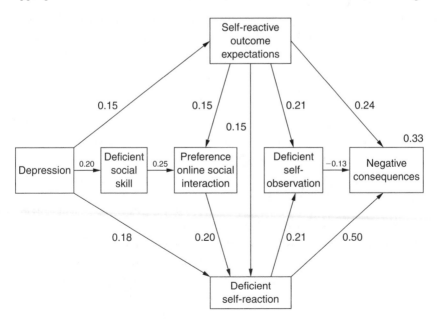

Figure 3.2 Integrated model of PIU.

compulsive, pathological, and problematic, are themselves problematic in that there appear to be so few truly addictive/compulsive/pathological/problematic users included in such research that they are more properly considered studies of online media habits in normal populations. That is because the criteria used to assess pathology, by whatever name, are based on self-reported responses to interval level scales with the average levels of endorsement typically at or below the midpoint of the scales among the general student populations that are typical of this stream of research. And, self-reports of symptoms (e.g., agreeing that family relationships have been damaged as a result of social networking based on one or two instances of being late for dinner) are lax compared to the assessments of trained clinicians. Also, the self-reported symptoms fail to rule out other psychiatric conditions (e.g., mania, impulse control disorders, pathological gambling, sexual compulsions) that may explain the behavior in question. Using rigorous criteria that would attribute pathology only to those who strongly agree that they have suffered significant life consequences as a result of Internet use, it can be estimated that potentially problematic or addictive cases constitute something in the order of 1% to 5% of college student populations (e.g., Caplan, 2005; Dowling & Quirk, 2009), a handful of possible cases among the hundreds included in such surveys. As yet, there appears to be no research that offers a comparative analysis of the "addictiveness" of social networking in relation to other popular online pursuits.

If those were not truly studies of Internet addiction, then perhaps they were studies of Internet habits. The criteria used were drawn from the same sources, namely, the DSM IV criteria for pathological gambling and impulse control disorders (American Psychiatric Association, 1994) as measures of deficient self-regulation, and most of the items used in the operational definitions also match items from a validated measure of habits (the SRHI, Verplanken & Orbell, 2003).

There has been previous research of social networking habits, although not conducted under that rubric. Facebook Intensity (Ellison, Steinfield, & Lampe, 2007) was operationally defined (no conceptual definition was provided) by the number of Facebook friends, the amount of time spent on Facebook in a typical day, and several Likert-type questions that arguably included items tapping deficient self-observation ("Facebook has become part of my daily routine" and "Facebook is part of my everyday activity") and of deficient self-reaction ("I feel out of touch when I haven't logged onto Facebook for a while"). The average scores on the indicators of deficient self-observation were near the midpoints of the scales, indicating a moderate degree of habit formation. Internet uses (Bessiere, Kiesler, Kraut, & Boneva, 2008) conform to an often-used (if flawed, see LaRose, 2010) measure of Internet habits in that they ask respondents to indicate the frequency of past behavior. The "communicating with family and friends" and "communicating to meet people" dimensions thus can be construed to represent habitual use of online social networking. These were relatively weak habits, averaging 1–2 days a week for family and friends and close to "never" for meeting new people, although it should be noted that these data were collected before social networking services were established. Still, it is interesting to note that communication with family and friends was indulged more frequently than information or entertainment habits. Also, the communication habits were moderately to highly correlated (0.60–0.54) with entertainment/escape uses, the latter being possible indicators of the pursuit of self-reactive outcomes in the present account. However, neither study offered unambiguous comparisons of the habit-forming potential of social networking compared to other online activities.

Consistent with the social skill account, a preference for online social interaction should logically play a more important role in activities that focus on social interaction, such as social networking and messaging, than those in which social interaction is more peripheral, such as downloading media files, online shopping, and online games. That is because the most natural way of making up for social deficiencies in the offline world and expressing a preference for online social interaction would seem to be participation in online socializing. Both the absolute level of the preference for online social interaction and the magnitude of its relationship to deficient self-reaction (called "compulsive use" in the original social skills account of Caplan, 2005) should thus be greatest for online social activities. And if compensation for offline social deficiencies is what makes the Internet especially "problematic," then negative consequences should be more strongly associated with that preference among social activities than for other activities.

H4: a. Preference for online social interaction and b. deficient social skills will be greater among those with social activities as favorite Internet activities than for other activities.

H5: Social activities will have more negative consequences than for other activities.

H6: a. Deficient social skill will be more related to preference for online social interaction and b. in turn it will be more related to deficient self-reaction for social activities than others.

The socio-cognitive model makes no a priori assumptions about which Internet activities are more problematic than others but does suggest a means to identify the ones most likely to lead to problems: activities that become a primary means of relieving dysphoric moods. So, Internet pastimes with high levels of self-reactive outcome expectations and with the strongest relationships between those expectations and the other variables in the model are arguably the most likely to lead to serious life consequences. Thus, the following question might be answered:

RQ1: Which Internet activities are most problematic?

The present research integrates social skill and socio-cognitive perspectives of PIU. By examining social networking in comparison to other online activities, it tests the key assumptions underlying the social skill model and furthers our understanding of potentially harmful Internet habits.

Method

Participants

Students from two Midwestern universities enrolled in introductory communication classes were invited to participate in an online survey for extra credit. To diversify the sample, 134 students were surveyed at random from the on-campus student population at one of the universities (completion rate of 27%). This yielded 635 usable cases; 58% were female and 42% were male, with a median age of 20 (range 18 to 50).

Measures

Each respondent's favorite leisure activity on the Internet was the frame of reference. Eleven options were pre-listed[6] and 7% listed "other" favorites. The latter included a number of responses that could be matched to the pre-listed categories (e.g., eBay was recoded in the online shopping category). Distinctive "other" responses included "reading," webcomics, online forums, fantasy sports, news, and browsing/surfing. Since all of the latter involved downloading information from the Internet and were said to be leisure activities, it was decided to group them with the "downloading entertainment" category (24.4% of respondents). Similarly, chat, instant messenger and email were combined into "messaging" (21.1%), online shopping and auctions into "shopping" (2.4%), and online gaming and gambling into "gaming" (10.4%). Social networking accounted for the remaining favorites (41.6%).

To clarify the overlapping operational definitions of habit-related constructs, an exploratory factor analysis was performed on items from LaRose et al.'s (2003) measures of deficient self-regulation, Caplan's (2002) PIU scale, and the Self-Report Habit Index (SHRI, Verplanken & Orbell, 2003). This yielded three dimensions interpreted to be deficient self-observation (mean $= 4.77$, $sd = 1.37$, $\alpha = 0.88$),[7] deficient self-reaction (mean $= 2.77$, $sd = 1.25$, $\alpha = 0.87$),[8] and negative life consequences (mean $= 2.02$, $sd = 1.25$, $\alpha = 0.87$).[9] Except where noted, seven-point Likert type rating scales were used throughout.

Self-reactive outcome expectations (mean $= 4.05$, $sd = 1.45$, $\alpha = 0.82$) were borrowed from LaRose et al. (2003).[10] Depression was measured by three items from Mirowsky and Ross' (1992) short version of the CES-D depression scale, scored 1 for rarely or none of the time (less than one day in the last week) to 4 for all of the time (5–7 days) (mean $= 1.76$, $sd = 0.63$, $\alpha = 0.73$).[11] Self-efficacy was measured with three items specific to the focal favorite activity (mean $= 4.99$, $sd = 1.08$, $\alpha = 0.71$).[12] Deficient social skill was represented by two items (mean $= 4.71$, $sd = 1.19$, $\alpha = 0.62$) from the Self Monitoring Scale (Lennox & Wolfe, 1984).[13] Preference for online social interaction (mean $= 3.38$, $sd = 1.48$, $\alpha = 0.87$), was measured by three items from Caplan (2005).[14] Internet usage was the minutes spent on Internet on a typical weekday and weekend day, transformed by $\log_{10}$ (value $+1$) and added (mean $= 3.97$, $sd = 0.95$, $\alpha = 0.72$).

Data Analysis

Missing data were replaced with mean values for each component item and the items in each scale were averaged. SPSS version 16.0 (SPSS, 2007) was used for item analysis and the analysis of means. To prepare for path analysis, the multi-item indices were trimmed to retain the three to five items with the highest item–total correlations. The AMOS 16.0 (Arbuckle, 2007) structural equation modeling (SEM) program was used to test hypothesized path models. First, the path models previously reported in LaRose et al. (2003) and Caplan (2005) were replicated. Then, the socio-cognitive model of negative life consequences resulting from Internet use, shown in Figure 3.1, was tested. Finally, an integrated model incorporating both the socio-cognitive and social skills components was examined, shown in Figure 3.2.

Multigroup analysis was used to compare path coefficients across favorite activities by imposing cross-group equality constraints. The chi-square of the model with each path coefficient constrained to equality was compared against that of the unconstrained model. If the model fit of the constrained model was significantly worse than that of the unconstrained model, it was concluded that the coefficient was significantly different across groups (Kline, 1998). Those listing online shopping as their favorite activity were too few to support a separate analysis.

Results

Considering that CFI and NFI indices over 0.90 indicate acceptable fit (Bentler, 1990; Bollen, 1990), while RMSEA values below 0.06 mean a good fit (MacCallum, Brown, & Sugawara, 1996), the socio-cognitive model of unregulated Internet usage (LaRose et al., 2003) was confirmed in these data (χ^2 (3) = 0.211, n.s., NFI = 0.999, CFI = 1.00, RMSEA = 0.00). This model differed from Figure 3.1 in that Internet usage rather than negative life consequences was the ultimate dependent variable and self-efficacy preceded each of the other variables, save for depression. As was expected when examining favorite activities, self-efficacy was a significant predictor of neither Internet usage (r = 0.03, n.s.) nor negative life consequences (r = –0.06, n.s.), supporting the decision to eliminate self-efficacy to achieve greater parsimony.

The social skill model of PIU (Caplan, 2005) did not fit the current data well (χ^2 (3) = 34.7, p < 0.001, NFI = 0.889, CFI = 0.897, RMSEA = 0.129). The modification indices suggested a correlated error term between deficient social skills and compulsive Internet use (deficient self-reaction in the current terminology). This yielded a good fitting model (χ^2 (2) = 3.637, n.s., NFI = 0.988, CFI = 0.995, RMSEA = 0.036), albeit not one explicable through the social skills account.

The socio-cognitive model of PIU (Figure 3.1) was a good fit (χ^2 (2) = 2.583, n.s., NFI = 0.993, CFI = 0.998, RMSEA = 0.021) and explained 33% of the variance in negative life consequences. All of the expected causal links among variables were confirmed with path coefficients significant at the 0.001 level. Depression predicted self-reactive outcome expectations (β = 0.15) and deficient self-reaction (β = 0.20). Self-reactive outcome expectations preceded deficient self-reaction (β = 0.18), deficient self-observation (β = 0.21), and negative life consequences (β = 0.24). Deficient self-reaction also preceded deficient self-observation (β = 0.21) and negative consequences (β = 0.50). Finally, deficient self-observation also predicted negative consequences (β = –0.13), but this was an inverse relationship rather than the positive relationship found in the earlier model of unregulated Internet use (LaRose et al., 2003). With this exception, Hypothesis 1 extending the model of unregulated Internet use to a model of PIU was confirmed.

Adding two variables suggested by the social skills account resulted in an acceptable fit (χ^2 (9) = 41.546, p < 0.001, NFI = 0.923, CFI = 0.937, RMSEA = 0.076), although a previous model was a significantly better fit (chi-square (7) = 39.966, p < 0.001) and the addition of the social skills variable increased the ratio of chi-square to degrees of freedom above the recommended level of 3. Depression was directly related to deficient social skill ($\beta = 0.20$), confirming Hypothesis 2, while self-reactive outcome expectations preceded preference for online social interaction ($\beta = 0.15$), supporting Hypothesis 3. The path from self-reactive outcome expectations changed slightly ($\beta = 0.15$), but the remaining path coefficients and the overall variance explained in negative consequences were unchanged. The modification indices suggested a correlated error term between deficient social skills and deficient self-reaction, but this modification was not necessary to produce an acceptable fit.

In Table 3.1, one-way ANOVA with pre-planned contrasts was used to distinguish social (messaging and social networking) activities from others (downloading, gaming, and shopping).

Preference for online social interaction differed by activity ($F(4,629) = 3.12$, $p < 0.05$); however, the planned contrast was not significant ($t(29.6) = 0.956$, n.s., equal variances not assumed) and so H4a was rejected. Deficient social skills did not differ among activities ($F(4,629) = 0.756$, n.s.) so H4b was not supported. Negative consequences varied across favorites ($F(4,629) = 19.06$, $p < 0.001$) and the planned contrast was significant ($t(80.7) = -3.29$). However, the pattern of means was not the one proposed in H5, with gamers experiencing

Table 3.1 Mean comparisons by favorite Internet activity

Variable		SNSs	DWN	GAM	MSG	SHOP	F
	n	264	155	66	134	15	
Negative consequences	Mn	1.85[a]	1.97[a]	3.20[b]	1.86[a]	1.58[a]	19.06**
	sd	1.09	1.23	1.53	1.14	0.84	
Deficient self-reaction	Mn	2.84[a,b]	2.72[a]	3.39[b]	2.53[a]	1.77[c]	8.35**
	sd	1.24	1.25	1.38	1.10	0.67	
Deficient self-observation	Mn	5.10[a]	4.26[b]	4.34[b]	5.09[a]	3.24[c]	19.52**
	sd	1.23	1.44	1.40	1.21	1.14	
Self-reactive expectations	Mn	3.87[a]	3.96[a]	4.87[b]	4.25[a,b]	2.73[c]	10.89**
	sd	1.41	1.46	1.23	1.43	1.14	
Depression	Mn	1.84[a]	1.76[a,b]	1.69[a,b]	1.69[a,b]	1.47[b]	2.56*
	sd	0.66	0.63	0.60	0.56	0.42	
Preference for online	Mn	3.26[a]	3.25[a]	3.70[a]	3.67[a]	2.91[a]	3.124*
	sd	1.51	1.39	1.57	1.41	1.78	
Deficient social skills	Mn	4.74[a]	4.59[a]	4.80[a]	4.69[a]	5.00[a]	0.756
	sd	1.13	1.22	1.35	1.12	1.54	

Note
Common superscripts (i.e. [a], [b], [c]) denote common means within rows, Tukey HSD
**$p < 0.001$; *$p < 0.05$.

the most negative outcomes ($M = 3.20$, $SD = 1.53$) and about equal levels found among downloaders ($M = 1.97$, $SD = 1.23$), social networkers ($M = 1.85$, $SD = 1.09$), messagers ($M = 1.86$, $SD = 1.14$), and shoppers ($M = 1.58$, $SD = 0.84$).

To test Hypothesis 6, the integrated model was applied to four favorite activities and differences among path coefficients were examined (Tables 3.1 and 3.2). Online shopping had too few cases to be included and the results for gaming should be interpreted with caution for the same reason. There were no significant differences among the paths linking deficient social skills to the preference for online social interaction to deficient self-reaction. Therefore, hypothesis 6 was disconfirmed.

In answer to RQ1, online gaming had the highest overall level of negative consequences (Table 3.1) and also the highest levels of deficient self-regulation and self-reactive outcome expectations. However, the paths from depression to self-reactive outcome expectations, from self-reactive outcome expectations

Table 3.2 Path coefficient comparisons among favorite Internet activities

Path	Standardized β			
	SNSs	DWN	GAM	MSG
1 Depression → Self-reactive outcome expectation	0.15*	0.25**	0.02	0.12
2 Depression → Deficient social skill	0.23**	0.32**	0.06	0.04
3 Self-reactive outcome → Preference online social	0.09	0.03	0.20	0.24**
4 Deficient social skill → Preference online social	0.33**	0.32**	0.29*	0.12
5 Depression → Deficient self-reaction	0.15*	0.18*	0.31**	0.11
6 Preference online social → Deficient self-reaction	0.28**	0.18*	0.12	0.18*
7 *Self-reactive outcome → Deficient self-reaction*	*0.03*	*0.31***	*0.21*	*0.06*
8 *Deficient self-reaction → Deficient self-observation*	*0.35***	*0.16**	*0.14*	*0.03*
9 *Self-reactive outcome → Deficient self-observation*	*0.24***	*0.37***	*0.17*	*0.08*
10 Self-reactive outcome → Negative consequences	0.22**	0.20**	0.14	0.18*
11 Deficient self-reaction → Negative consequences	0.50**	0.51**	0.42**	0.44**
12 Deficient self-observation → Negative consequences	−0.07	0.02	−0.06	−0.22**
Variance explained in negative consequences (R2)	0.28	0.38	0.22	0.28

Notes
Italics denote significantly different path coefficients among groups ($p < 0.05$). *Significant path coefficient, $p < 0.05$; **Significant path coefficient $p < 0.001$. SNSs = Social networking services, DWN = Downloading, GAM = Gaming, MSG = Messaging.

to deficient self-reaction, and from self-reactive outcomes to negative consequences were not significant, so there was no evidence of a pattern of Internet use in the service of mood management. A case could also be made for downloading as the most problematic in that the latter two paths ($\beta = 0.25$, $\beta = 0.31$, and $\beta = 0.20$ respectively, all $p < 0.001$) were significant even though the levels of negative consequences, deficient self-reaction, and self-reactive outcome expectations were moderate compared to other activities. The links between depression and self-reactive outcomes ($\beta = 0.15$, $p < 0.05$) and between self-reactive outcomes and negative consequences ($\beta = 0.22$, $p < 0.001$) were significant for social networking, indicating its possible use for mood adjustment and its potential for interfering with important life activities. Also, the level of deficient self-reaction was higher for social networking than for all other activities, save for online gaming, although still below the midpoint of the scales used. Moreover, the link between self-reactive outcomes and deficient self-reaction was not confirmed ($\beta = 0.03$, n.s.), suggesting a behavior that is still under effective self-regulation.

Discussion

Prior studies of Internet habits, whether described as problematic (Caplan, 2005), addictive (Young & Rogers, 1998), or unregulated (LaRose et al., 2003) media behaviors, did not distinguish among different types of online activities. The current study asked the participants to focus on their favorite online activity; in order of popularity, they were social networking, downloading entertainment media files, messaging, gaming, and online shopping.

The present research re-examined the structure of media habits within socio-cognitive theory to articulate two dimensions associated with habitual use, deficient self-observation, and deficient self-reaction. Incorporating these concepts, LaRose et al.'s (2003) model of unregulated Internet use explained negative life consequences. In this model, depression preceded self-reactive outcome expectations and deficient self-reaction. Deficient self-reaction and self-reactive outcome expectations both predicted deficient self-observation and negative life consequences, and self-reactive outcome expectations also preceded deficient self-reaction. Deficient self-reaction, an indication of the lack of intentionality and lack of controllability of media habits, emerged as the single most powerful predictor of negative life consequences.

A second dimension of media habits, deficient self-observation, also predicted negative life consequences, but the sign of the relationship was opposite to the one expected. This might be interpreted to mean that, with repetition, individuals become inattentive to their favorite online activity as control over it gradually shifts from the cortex to (non-conscious) processes governed by the basal ganglia (Yin & Knowlton, 2006). They are then perhaps less likely to perceive that they "have a problem" by failing to recognize that their involvement with their favorite online activity has impacted their school, work, or social activities. This could be an act of denial or the result of lack of conscious awareness of the extent of their involvement in their favorite pastime. But there is also the possibility that the causal relationship is in the opposite direction of that proposed in the model; that is, that negative life consequences cause individuals to become more attentive to their media consumption behavior, causing deficient self-observation to decrease. That would be an indication of a moderating process through which effective self-regulation might be restored. A third possibility is that both mechanisms are in play, with the former operative at relatively early stages of habit formation when individuals are merely indulging in enjoyable activities and the latter when excessive indulgence has severe consequences.

However, the latter mechanism is unlikely to have played a major role in the current study since there were few, if any, "problematic" Internet users in the sample, a statement that can also be made about previous research involving student samples, including Caplan (2005) and LaRose et al. (2003). In the present sample, only seven individuals (four of whom listed gaming as their favorite online activity) strongly agreed that they had suffered even one of the three negative consequences associated with their favorite activity and thus might be said to be experiencing "severe" life consequences required for a diagnosis of a mental disease (Shaffer et al., 2000). But the consequences (missing work or social activities or dropping a grade in a class) are perhaps in themselves not dire enough to constitute a diagnosis of mental illness. Flunking out of school, for example, might be such a consequence, but those persons would not appear in the present sample of college students, nor in the previously cited ones.

Thus, what emerges is a model of habitual Internet activities rather than problematic ones. However, we would argue along with LaRose and Eastin (2004) that a further understanding of the mechanisms that contribute to habitual media consumption make an important contribution. The process by which media selections turn into favorite activities, whether or not they lead to negative consequences, should be of interest both to media scholars and to practitioners.

The social skill account fared less well than previously (Caplan, 2005), and did not produce an acceptable fit to the current data. The compulsive use variable of the social skill model, called deficient self-reaction here, was a consistent predictor of negative consequences across all activities. However, adding two variables introduced in Caplan's (2005) social skill model of PIU, deficient social skill and preference for online social interaction, did not improve the overall model fit nor did they increase the variance explained in negative life consequences compared to the socio-cognitive variables alone. Thus, the effects of the unique social skill variables may be accounted for by the socio-cognitive model. Moreover, Social Cognitive Theory offers an explanation for a connection between deficient social skill and deficient self-reaction that would be necessary to fit the current data: Both could reflect an underlying inability to regulate one's behavior effectively, both in the real-world social realm and in the online world.

At the time of Caplan's (2005) work, social uses of the Internet did not include social networking websites (e.g., MySpace, Facebook). Since these are now the dominant online activity among college students, it might be expected that the social skill account would be more powerful than ever, but it did not hold in the current study. Also, the social networking and messaging activities that might be expected to be most amenable to the social skill explanation did not differ from downloading or gaming with respect to the impact of deficient (real-world) social skill and preference for online social interaction. However, it might be argued that all of the favorite online activities examined here involve extensive social interaction. For example, multiplayer online games like World of Warcraft typically require online interactions to plan group activities, such as raids on other groups of players (Ducheneaut & Moore, 2004). File sharers interact to share their interests in entertainment and to locate rare or good-quality files to download (LaRose & Kim, 2007).

Among favorite online activities, there was little evidence that social networking services were especially problematic compared to other favorite online pursuits. Social networking, along with messaging, was associated with a higher degree of deficient self-observation compared to other favorite online activities, but it appeared that social networking behavior was still guided by effective self-regulation.

Online gaming was perhaps the most problematic since it was associated with the highest levels of negative consequences, deficient self-reaction, and self-reactive outcome expectations. And, four of the seven most problematic cases in the present sample were gamers. This confirmed recent findings that online gaming is one of the most likely reasons for compulsive Internet use (Meerkerk, Van Den Eijnden, & Garretsen, 2006). However, there were three vital "missing links" in the path model for gaming, from depression to self-reactive outcome expectations and then to deficient self-reaction and negative consequences, that would indicate a pattern of "self-medication" with online games as the "drug." This pattern was not found among the gamers in the present study.

To understand how favorites may change into problematic habits, consider that Figure 3.1 represents but one iteration in what can become a recurring cycle. Negative consequences lead to increased dysphoria, diminished self-regulation, and renewed efforts to adjust dysphoric states through further media use, leading to yet more negative consequences, and so on. Media consumption could become a classically conditioned response (i.e., a habitual reaction triggered by external stimuli such as the sight of one's computer) to dysphoric moods, resulting in a complete loss of self-control (i.e., highly deficient self-reaction), deepening the spiral until the individual "bottoms out" by experiencing the loss of job, marriage, or home. Such cases would conform to the etiology of addictive behavior (Marlatt et al., 1988).

Individuals might also exit the cycle in various ways. The experience of negative life consequences could heighten awareness of the activity and restore effective self-observation of the (negative) outcomes of excessive Internet behavior. Conscious efforts to reduce excessive use, such as indulging feelings of guilt or self-administering rewards for moderate behavior, would restore effective self-reaction and also re-direct attention to the behavior, further bolstering self-observation. With continual repetition, favorite activities might also lose their ability to modify dysphoric moods.

The present results lend new credence to the "time inelasticity" argument (Nie, 2001) to explain the negative effects of the Internet. The amount of usage of favorite Internet activities was directly related to negative consequences ($r = 0.32$, $p < 0.001$), suggesting that time displacement may account, in part, for negative effects of the Internet. Efforts to explain away such effects (e.g., Bargh & McKenna, 2004) may suffer from the same criticism that inspired the present research, that all Internet use is not the same. The positive effects of some types of Internet use may offset the negative effects of others and lead to misleading conclusions about underlying causal mechanisms.

For example, messaging differed from other favorites in that it was the only online activity for which there were significant paths from expected self-reactive outcomes to preference for online social interaction and from deficient self-observation to negative consequences, although both paths were significant across all activities in the combined sample. Also, messaging was the only activity for which the path from deficient social skill to preference for online interaction, a key link in the social skills account, was not significant. Unlike social networkers, among the messagers the paths from depression were not significant, nor was the path from deficient social skill to preference for online social interaction. Thus, the social skill account has merit for social networking but does not appear to account for online social interaction involving email and other forms of messaging. Rather than responding to unsatisfying real-world interactions by seeking new relationships online, the messagers may have learned to expect instant messages will maintain satisfying existing relationships.

Limitations

The present results may not be generalized to other populations. The Internet usage patterns of college students might be unique, both with regard to the use of social networking applications and with respect to the prevalence of problematic forms of use (Byun, Celestino, Mills, Ajecia, et al., 2009). Second, some of the more problematic applications of the Internet, such as online gambling and pornography, were not sufficiently prevalent in the current study to permit separate analyses. The negative consequences reported by the sample were also at the low ends of their respective scales. At-risk populations should be targeted for future data collection. Finally, structural equation modeling with cross-sectional data can only test assumptions about the direction of causality, not establish them conclusively.

Implications for Further Research

The present model of media might be expanded to include the third submechanism of self-regulation, judgmental process. LaRose and Kim (2007) found that holding behavior up to lax standards (e.g., the downloading behavior of other college students) decreased perceptions that self-regulation was deficient and thus might impair efforts to restore effective self-control.

Time-series studies should explore feedback loops in the current model; for example, a connection from the experience of negative life consequences to depression has not been explored in extant time-series research (Bessiere et al., 2008). The further connection between depression and self-reactive outcome expectations would in turn complete the "missing links" in a downward spiral through which media use mounts to offset dysphoric moods, resulting in further negative consequences as the media compete with other life activities, ending in a behavioral addiction (Marlatt et al., 1988).

Reward sensitivity has been identified as a possible underlying cause of the various types of disorders that have been identified with PIU/Internet Addiction (Hollander, 2006). Reward sensitivity might be understood in sociocognitive terms as a causal linkage between self-reactive outcome expectations for a favorite media activity and negative life outcomes. This concept should be tested as a possible mediator of that relationship.

Summary

The present research redefined what had been called problematic, addictive, or unregulated Internet behavior as habitual media consumption. Two competing explanations of the negative consequences of Internet use were compared and integrated into a model grounded in Social Cognitive Theory.

The causal mechanisms underlying favorite activities were found to differ. As the Internet absorbs and creates more forms of entertainment and interpersonal communication, it will be increasingly important to draw distinctions among online activities. However, based on the current results, social networking services appear to be no more problematic, addictive, or even habitual than others despite their widespread popularity and popular press accounts of "Facebook addiction."

Notes

1. The authors would like to thank the following students for their assistance in the completion of this research: Michelle Bruneau, Jennifer Beal, Dave Beaudoin, Christy Lee, Su Yun Cho. Correspondence should be addressed to the first author.
2. Termed "habit strength" in the original.
3. Called "deficient self-regulation" in the original.
4. They omitted indicators of un-intentionality on the premise, one not shared by other social psychologists (e.g., Wood & Neal, 2007), that habits are goal-directed automatic behaviors that therefore possess intentionality.
5. The relationship turned negative in multiple regression analysis, suggesting the existence of a suppressor variable.
6. Social networking (e.g., Facebook, MySpace), Downloading or streaming music, Downloading or streaming videos, Instant Messenger, Online gaming (e.g., Everquest, World of Warcraft), Online gambling, Online shopping, Online pornography, Chatrooms, Auctions (e.g., eBay), Email.
7. I do it without thinking. I do it automatically. It makes me feel weird if I do not do it. I do it without having to consciously remember. It is part of my usual routine.
8. I have to keep doing it more and more to get my thrill. I have a hard time keeping my use under control. I sometimes try to conceal how much time I spend on it from my family or friends. I feel guilty about the amount of time I spend on it. I would go out of my way to satisfy my urge to do it.
9. As a result of indulging your favorite activity, how likely are you to ... Miss class or work? Lose a grade in a course? Miss a social event?
10. As a result of indulging your favorite activity, how likely are you to ... Feel less lonely? Feel relaxed? Forget your problems? Feel better when you are down?
11. Below is a list of some of the ways you might have felt or behaved. Please tell us how often you have felt this way during the PAST WEEK by clicking the appropriate number: I was bothered by things that usually don't bother me, I had trouble keeping my mind on what I was doing, I felt depressed, I could not "get going."
12. It is easy for me to do. I am confident I have mastered all of its fine points. I am confident I can overcome any barrier to my enjoyment of it.
13. I have trouble changing my behavior to suit different people and different situations. Even when it might be to my advantage, I have difficulty putting up a good front (both reflected).
14. I am treated better online than in face-to-face relationships. I feel safer relating to others online rather than face-to-face. I am more confident socializing online than offline.

References

Aboujaoude, E., Koran, L. M., Gamel, N., Large, M. D., & Serpe, R. T. (2006). Potential markers for problematic Internet use: A telephone survey of 2,513 adults. *CNS Spectrum, 11*, 750–755.

AMA. (2007). *Report 12 of the council on science and public health (a-07)*. Paper presented to the American Medical Association.

American Psychiatric Association. (1994). *Diagnostic and statistical manual of mental disorders*, 4th ed. Washington, DC: Author.

Arbuckle, J. L. (2007). Amos 16.0. Spring House, PA: Amos Development Corporation.

Bandura, A. (1986). *Social foundations of thought and action*. Englewood Cliffs, NJ: Prentice Hall.

Bandura, A. (1991). Social cognitive theory of self-regulation. *Organizational Behavior and Human Decision Processes, 50*, 248–287.

Bantz, C. R. (1982). Exploring uses and gratifications—a comparison of reported uses of television and reported uses of favorite program type. *Communication Research, 9*, 352–379.

Bargh, J., & McKenna, K. (2004). The Internet and social life. *Annual Review of Psychology, 55*, 573–590.

Bentler, P. M. (1990). Comparative fit indexes in structural models. *Psychological Bulletin, 107*, 238–246.

Bessiere, K., Kiesler, S., Kraut, R., & Boneva, B. S. (2008). Effects of Internet use and social resources on changes in depression. *Information, Communication and Society, 11*(1), 47–70.

Block, J. J. (2008). Issues for DSM-V: Internet addiction. *American Journal of Psychiatry, 165*(3), 306–307.

Bollen, K. A. (1990). Overall fit in covariance structure models: Two types of sample size effects. *Psychological Bulletin, 107*, 256–259.

Byun, S., Celestino, R., Mills, J. E., Ajecia, C. D., et al. (2009). Internet addiction: Metasynthesis of quantitative research 1996–2006. *CyberPsychology & Behavior, 12*(2), 203–207.

Caplan, S. E. (2002). Problematic Internet use and psychosocial well-being: Development of a theory-based cognitive–behavioral measurement instrument. *Computers in Human Behavior, 18*, 553–575.

Caplan, S. E. (2003). Preference for online social interaction. *Communication Research, 30*, 625–648.

Caplan, S. E. (2005). A social skill account of Problematic Internet Use. *Journal of Communication, 55*, 721–736.

Caplan, S. E. (2007). Relations among loneliness, social anxiety, and Problematic Internet Use. *CyberPsychology & Behavior, 10*, 234–242.

Cohen, E. (2009). Five clues that you are addicted to Facebook. CNNHealth.com. Online, available at: www.cnn.com/2009/HEALTH/04/23/ep.facebook.addict/.

Davis, R. A. (2001). A cognitive–behavioral model of pathological Internet use. *Computers in Human Behavior, 17*, 187–195.

Dowling, N. A., & Quirk, K. L. (2009). Screening for Internet Dependence: Do the proposed diagnostic criteria differentiate normal from dependent Internet use? *Cyberpsychology & Behavior, 12*(1), 21–27.

Ducheneaut, N., & Moore, R. J. (2004). The social side of gaming: A study of interaction patterns in a massively multiplayer online game. Paper presented at the ACM conference on Computer-Supported Cooperative Work (CSCW2004), New York.

Ellison, N. B., Steinfield, C., & Lampe, C. (2007). The benefits of Facebook "friends": Social capital and college students' use of online social network sites. *Journal of Computer-Mediated Communication, 12*(4), article 1. Online, available at: http://jcmc. indiana.edu/vol.12/issue4/ellison.html.

Hollander, E. (2006). Behavioral and substance addictions: A new proposed DSM-V category characterized by impulsive choice, reward sensitivity, and fronto-striatal circuit impairment. *CNS Spectrum, 11*, 814.

Kline, R. B. (1998). *Principles and practice of structural equation modeling.* New York, NY: Guilford.

Kubey, R., & Csikszentmihalyi, M. (2002). Television addiction. *Scientific American, 286*(2), 74–81.

LaRose, R. (2004). Cybercompulsions: Media habits, media addictions and the Internet. In P. Lee, L. Leung, & C. So (Eds.), *Impact and issues in new media: Toward intelligent societies.* Cresskill, NJ: Hampton Press.

LaRose, R. (2010). The problem of media habits. *Communication Theory, 20*, 194–222.

LaRose, R., & Eastin, M. S. (2004). A social cognitive theory of Internet uses and gratifications: Toward a new model of media attendance. *Journal of Broadcasting and Electronic Media, 48*, 358–377.

LaRose, R., & Kim, J. (2007). Share, steal or buy? A social cognitive perspective of music downloading. *Cyberpsychology and Human Behavior, 10*, 267–277.

LaRose, R., Lin, C. A., & Eastin, M. S. (2003). Unregulated Internet usage: Addiction, habit, or deficient self-regulation? *Media Psychology, 5*, 225–253.

Lenhart, A. (2009). Pew Internet Project Data Memo (January 14). Online, available at: www.pewinternet.org/~/media/Files/Reports/2009/PIP_Adult_social_networking_data_memo_FINAL.pdf.pdf.

Lennox, R. D., & Wolfe, R. N. (1984). Revision of the self-monitoring scale. *Journal of Personality and Social Psychology, 46*, 1349–1364.

MacCallum, R. C., Brown, M. W., & Sugawara, H. M. (1996). Power analysis and determination of sample size for covariance structure modeling. *Psychological Methods, 1*, 130–139.

McKenna, K. Y. A., & Bargh, J. A. (2000). Plan 9 from cyberspace: The implications of the Internet for personality and social psychology. *Journal of Personality and Social Psychology, 75*, 681–694.

Marlatt, G. A., Baer, J. S., Donovan, D. M., & Kivlahan, D. R. (1988). Addictive behaviors: Etiology and treatment. *Annual Review of Psychology, 39*, 223–252.

Meerkerk, G. J., Van Den Eijnden, R. J., & Garretsen, H. F. (2006). Predicting compulsive Internet use: It's all about sex! *Cyberpsychology & Behavior, 9*, 95–103.

Mirowsky, J., & Ross, C. E. (1992). Age and depression. *Journal of Health and Social Behavior, 33*, 187–205.

Morahan-Martin, J., & Schumacher, P. (2000). Incidence and correlates of pathological Internet use among college students. *Computers in Human Behavior, 16*, 13–29.

Nie, N. H. (2001). Sociability, interpersonal relations, and the Internet: Reconciling conflicting findings. *The American Behavioral Scientist, 45*, 420–436.

Saling, L. L., & Phillips, J. G. (2007). Automatic behaviour: Efficient not mindless. *Brain Research Bulletin, 73*, 1–20.

Segrin, C., & Abramson, L. Y. (1994). Negative reactions to depressive behaviors: A communication theories analysis. *Journal of Abnormal Psychology, 103*, 655–668.

Shaffer, H. J., Hall, M. N., & Vander Bilt, J. (2000). "Computer addiction": A critical consideration. *American Journal of Orthopsychiatry, 70*, 162–168.

SPSS. (2007). *Statistical Package for the Social Sciences Version 16.0*. Chicago, IL: SPSS, Inc.

Verplanken, B., & Orbell, S. (2003). Reflections on past behavior: A self-report index of habit strength. *Journal of Applied Social Psychology, 33*, 1313–1330.

Verplanken, B., & Wood, W. (2006). Interventions to break and create consumer habits. *Journal of Public Policy & Marketing, 25*, 90–103.

Widyanto, L., & Griffiths, M. (2007). Internet addiction: Does it really exist? (revisited). In J. Gackenbach (Ed.), *Psychology and the Internet (2nd Edition)* (pp. 141–163). Orlando, FL: Academic Press.

Wood, W., & Neal, D. T. (2007). A new look at habits and the habit–goal interface. *Psychological Review, 114*, 843–863.

Wood, W., Quinn, J. M., & Kashy, D. (2002). Habits in everyday life: Thought, emotion and action. *Journal of Personality and Social Psychology, 83*, 1281–1297.

Yin, H. H., & Knowlton, B. J. (2006). The role of the basal ganglia in habit formation. *Nature Reviews Neuroscience, 7*, 464–476.

Young, K. S., & Rogers, R. C. (1998). The relationship between depression and Internet addiction. *Cyberpsychology and Behavior, 1*, 25–36.

Zillmann, D., & Bryant, J. (1985). Affect, mood and emotion as determinants of selective media exposure. In D. Zillmann & J. Bryant (Eds.), *Selective exposure to communication* (pp. 157–190). Hillsdale, NJ: Lawrence Erlbaum.

Chapter 4

Social Network Exploitation

Mark Andrejevic

> Herein lies the perversity of social networks: however radical they may be, they will always be data-mined. They are designed to be exploited.
>
> (Ippolita, Lovink, & Rossiter, 2009)

The commercial models that are rapidly invading and colonizing social life online are spilling over into the realm of the workplace proper—and not just for the bored-at-work network. Consider, for example, a recent account of the use of social networking sites like Facebook by job recruiters in the wake of the global financial downturn. After several months of looking for a job, an unemployed engineer profiled by the *New York Times* received a "Jobvite" from a former co-worker who found him through an online recruiting application that trawls sites like Facebook and LinkedIn. Such applications mark a shift in employers' use of social networking sites from surreptitious screening resources to recruiting databases and utilities for viral marketing. To avail themselves of employee social networks, companies piggyback applications supplied by so-called "software-as-service" companies like Appirio onto the social networking sites of employees. Appirio's application, for example, searches the networks and notifies employees "when new jobs open and which of their friends might be a good fit" (Weed, 2009). Aside from generating practical benefits for job seekers and companies, such applications extend workplace monitoring into the online social lives of employees. In this regard, the workplace is catching up with the marketing industry, which has been drawing on the power of interactivity to insert itself into realms of social practice hitherto largely beyond the gaze of market researchers and to convert the information employees generate into what Vincent Mosco (1989) has described as "cybernetic commodities."

If one of the characteristic developments of the interactive era has been the de-differentiation of sites of labor, domesticity, social life, and consumption, for some categories of workers, it is perhaps not surprising that the monitoring capacity of the workplace is reaching out into the realm of our increasingly digitally mediated social lives. More concretely, if digital technology makes it possible to work outside the office, recent innovations enable the workplace to exploit the productivity of our social lives outside the workplace.

Much has been made of the ambivalent or hybrid status of user-generated content creation as a site of both intrinsic reward and potential exploitation (see, for example, Arvidsson, 2007; Terranova, 2000; Banks & Humphreys, 2008). Thus, for example, Arvidsson argues that, "the post-Fordist production process directly exploits the communitarian dimension of social life" (p. 241). By capturing and channeling user-generated activity for marketing purposes, emerging forms of online commerce subsume the potential diversity of social life to narrower commercial interests. One important dimension of exploitation, for Arvidsson, "consists in making the productive sociality of consumers evolve on the premises of brands; to make it unfold through branded consumer goods in such ways that makes it produce measurable (and hence valuable) forms of attention" (p. 251). By contrast, Banks and Humphreys (2008) argue that online forms of co-creation complicate standard critiques of exploitation. Users clearly enjoy and benefit from online activities even as they generate value for commercial websites. The result, they suggest, might be better understood in terms of mutual benefit than exploitation:

> Rather than being a zero sum game where if companies derive economic benefit it negates social benefit to the users (and hence is couched in terms of exploitation), is this instead an example of a new articulation of a cooperative and non-zero sum game whereby different motivations and value regimes co-exist?
>
> (pp. 412–413)

We are left with a familiar back-and-forth: if people willingly submit to forms of online monitoring, they must be getting something out of it. After all, they have a choice of whether or not to use social networking sites and submit to the forms of commercial monitoring such use entails.

This chapter argues that more work needs to be done to clarify the relationship between willing participation and commercial exploitation. What is needed is an explanation of how a theory of exploitation might apply to the conditions under which user-generated content creates value. Rather than capitulating to the notion that notions of exploitation do not readily apply to the changed conditions of production associated with the provision of "free" or "immaterial" labor, this chapter provides a preliminary attempt to develop a theory of exploitation for the era of commercial social networking.

It is perhaps worth highlighting the workings of the corporate imagination at play in the fields of social networking to make it clear just how these sites are viewed as standing reserves of data for marketing purposes. For example, a press release by Appirio outlines the triple value of employee social networking data as a resource for recruiting, sales, and marketing—all of this without having to pay employees for providing the data. Appirio's marketing application piggybacks on Facebook,

> to increase the size of a company's "virtual account team" by leveraging relationships that employees might already have to approach strategic accounts or build customer relationships.... The employee can see if a friend has become a lead, bought a product, attended an event . . . etc. If the employee chooses they can contact their friend through Facebook to make a connection and ultimately help contribute to their company's bottom line (and maybe even their own bonus!).
>
> (*Market Wire*, 2009—note that the only compensation for the employee's "voluntary" participation is a *potential* bonus!)

But there is more: the same data that can provide leads for potential hires and clients serve treble duty by providing data for targeted marketing appeals: "Based on a search of keywords in friend profiles, the application makes recommendations of friends who might be interested in the offer, which users can then choose to take action on" (*Market Wire*, 2009). The application links data from the social networks of individual employees with a proprietary consumer relationship marketing database in order "to track leads, make follow-up offers, and report on campaign success to see how their viral campaigns stack up to other marketing programs" (*Market Wire*, 2009).

It is not hard to imagine marketers slapping their foreheads as the proverbial light bulb snaps on: all the work that the Internet generation has been doing to assemble extended social networks of hundreds or even thousands of Facebook "friends" can be harnessed not just by Facebook, but also by employers. The scenario outlined by Appirio is a fascinating if disturbing one: potential employees with large online social networks might be viewed as preferable hires because of the resources for viral marketing they bring to their company. Indeed, an extended social network might come to function not just as a form of online social capital, but also as online economic capital: an information asset that the digital worker must cultivate to be viable in the twenty-first-century workforce. It is all too easy to envision the proliferation of self-help books that provide instruction in how to cultivate extended networks of "high-quality" online friends in order to maximize one's potential value in the workplace. Within the context of the commercial deployment of social networking, the very notion of what constitutes a "quality" friendship becomes colonized by the promise of economic return-on-investment. The dystopian scenario envisioned by the capitalization of social networks is one of rationalized instrumentalism: the permeation of social networks by the quantifying logic of exchange value. It is a prospect foreshadowed by, for example, the title of an investment note on social networking put out by Lehman Brothers: "How Much are Your Friends Worth?" (the *Independent*, 2007)—and by the Facebook application "Friends for Sale," which invites participants to "Buy people and make them your pets! Make money as a shrewd pet investor or as a hot commodity" (Facebook, 2009a).

The Logic of Separation

The plan outlined by Appirio (and other startups developing strategies for "monetizing" the tremendous amounts of data generated by commercial social networking sites and, most recently, Twitter feeds), the details of employees' social lives along with the observations and opinions they share with one another are treated as *free* resources, readily available to employers for the purposes of recruiting, marketing, and sales. The cursory qualification by Appirio that employees can supply access to their networks "if they so choose" comes across as an empty gesture: what choice will they really have? Their online social resources are treated as one more capacity of labor. Withholding such resources might come to seem as strange as withholding other aspects of one's labor: like signing up for a job and then refusing to devote one's full mental or physical effort to the assigned tasks. In the information era, members of the digital working class have something else to sell as part of their labor power: their social networks, at least insofar as these are recorded and stored on commercial platforms like Facebook or otherwise available online.

As in the case of labor power, however, the "freely agreed upon" transaction that governs the use of this information will be shaped by existing power relations and structures of ownership. Or, to put it in somewhat different terms, submission to forms of commercial surveillance becomes one of the conditions of employment, just as submission to monitoring becomes, over time, a built-in condition of the wage–labor contract and, indeed, one of the reasons for the development and structure of group workplaces. If one of the expectations of wage–labor is the willing submission to workplace surveillance, applications like Appirio's entail normalizing the expansion of management's monitoring gaze to encompass not just workplace activities, but also the structure and details of employees' social lives. We might think of this expansion of reach as the contemporary appropriation of newly exploitable productive resources: a contemporary process of virtual enclosure of the commons of social life.

It is tempting to describe this act of appropriation as an act of expropriation—a contemporary form of "primitive accumulation" of resources: what Hesmondhalgh (2008), following David Harvey, has described in a slightly different context as, "the commodification of culture as accumulation by dispossession" (p. 107). Such a formulation, however, does not quite do justice to the type of appropriation envisioned by Appirio and similar applications, for they do not deprive employees of the productive use, at least for certain purposes, of their social network resources. Social networks as information resources are, in the sense described by economists, "non-rival" in use: employers can put them to work without depriving employees of them.

A more precise and accurate formulation is outlined by Massimo De Angelis (2001), who describes the forms of ongoing "primitive" accumulation necessary to capitalism's reproduction in terms of *separation*. The exploitation of new markets, in other words, entails the separation of resources from those who rely upon them. This process of separation facilitates the establishment of property rights that structure or restructure the terms of access to productive resources. As De Angelis (2001) puts it, "the characteristic extra-economic process of separation between people and means of production is a continuous and inherent process of capitalist production" (p. 4). Such "extra-economic" forms of separation include the pre-market establishment of property rights exemplified by the forcible seizure of assets, for example, or the structuring of legal regimes that assign rights to new forms of economic resources. When drug companies claim patent rights over traditional medicines, they are engaging in an enclosure of the commons analogous to the seizure and privatization of agricultural land. In both instances, the privatization process helps to secure control over access to productive resources. In turn, the separation of producers from the means of production contributes to the reproduction of ongoing forms of separation. As Marx put it, "Once this *separation* is given, the production process can only produce it anew, reproduce it, and reproduce it on an expanded scale" (2009, p. 6). Thus, land enclosure, for example, undergirds the alienation of workers from control over their own labor, which must be sold in exchange for access to the means of production.

To describe the appropriation of information resources produced by the social networking activity of employees in terms of separation is to interrogate the conditions whereby this information is made accessible to and productive for employers. The rise of online social networking as a commercially supported phenomenon combines new conveniences and affordances (access to email and social networking utilities, for example) with new forms of separation. To the extent that networked forms of sociability rely on privately owned and operated infrastructures like Facebook, they represent the separation of users from the means for producing online sociability. Those who control the means of online sociability thus have the power to set the terms of access to these resources. These terms include the establishment of certain rights over the information provided by users—rights that tend to be outlined in cursory, often incomprehensible and qualified fashion. Separation (the private control over online resources for sociability) begets separation (the establishment of certain rights of use over information generated by users).

Thus, the various "terms of use" and end-user license agreements posted by social networking sites are, in large part, constructed around the goal of asserting rights over the use, sale, and transfer of information collected online. Facebook's terms of use are explicit in this regard, stipulating that users provide the company with the right "to use, copy, publicly perform, publicly display, reformat, translate, excerpt . . . and distribute such User Content for any purpose, commercial, advertising, or otherwise . . ." (Facebook, 2009c). The sweeping and often vague terms of these agreements, coupled with the stipulation that the terms of use may change at any point in time drives home the point that the companies regard this information as theirs to do with as they see fit. In its privacy policy, Facebook makes a distinction between two types of information provided by users: "personal information you knowingly choose to disclose that is collected by us and Web Site use information collected by us as you interact with our Web Site [and other sites, as stipulated later in the policy]," but it seems apparent that it views *both* categories as proprietary information when used for marketing purposes (Facebook, 2009d). The site, for example, asserts the right to "collect information about you from other sources, such as newspapers, blogs, instant messaging services, and other users of the Facebook service through the operation of the service . . ." (2009d). The other social networking giant, MySpace, offers more opt-out options and a more fully articulated privacy policy, but nevertheless establishes its rights over user-generated information for a broad range of marketing purposes. Thus, it stipulates that it has the right to collect "other Related Data and non-PII [Personally Identifiable Information] including IP address, aggregate user data, and browser type. This data is used to manage and improve the MySpace Services, track usage, and for security purposes" (MySpace, 2008).

The combination of apparently rigorous and detailed privacy controls with vague and open-ended loopholes recurs further down in MySpace's policy: "Profile Information you provide in structured profile fields or questions . . ., information you add to open-ended profile fields and questions . . . and other non-PII and Related Data about you may also be used to customize the online ads you encounter" (MySpace, 2008). As if these terms do not make it clear enough, the privacy policy stipulates that it counts this information among the economic assets it can sell at will:

if MySpace sells all or part of its business or makes a sale or transfer of all or a material part of its assets . . . MySpace may transfer your PII [and, it seems fair to assume, all "Related Data"] to the party or parties involved in the transaction.

(MySpace, 2008)

The information generated by consumers who are presumably compensated through access to the site comprises a major part of the assets of the site.

The fact that online sociability is facilitated by separating users from the means of socializing and thereby creating an external, storable, and sortable collection of data about their social lives, renders the product of their online activity further alienable. Not only can Facebook use it, for example, to design and implement customized marketing campaigns, but the data can be put to use by the growing range of applications that piggy-back on the Facebook platform. In this case, the term "separation" refers to the fact that a digital intermediary is interposed into relations of sociability. That is to say, forms of socializing that once relied upon other resources, as well as new forms of sociability, are increasingly dependent upon an infrastructure provided by a third party. When we are "separated" from the means of socialization, this does not mean we do not have access to them; rather, we come to rely upon technologies for socialization that separate us from the information upon which our social lives rely. Crucial resources for sociability are no longer in our own hands (at least to the extent that they once were), but are separated from us and stored in servers owned and controlled by, for example, Facebook. Imagine how much of the data upon which current social interactions rely (at least for some groups) would be lost if Facebook were to disappear: millions of photos, posts, messages, pokes, links, and so on would be wiped away: an entire archive upon which a wide range of social connections relied. Many people would lose one of their primary modes of communication with certain "friends." We do not have to go far to figure out *why* people are so willing to use such sites: they provide a ready, convenient, and entertaining way of enriching, extending, and preserving our connections with others. What requires a bit more explanation is how we might discern, in a voluntary and rewarding activity, the traces of exploitation.

The result of the form of separation facilitated by Facebook is not the dispossession of users, but rather the alienability of the product of their online social activity: the fact that the fruits of this activity can become a resource whose uses range far beyond their control. Companies like Appirio seek to exploit this productivity when they develop applications that put the social resources of employees to work in ways that exceed the knowledge and control of those who created them. We might then note the parallels between the productive capacity of the work of online social networking and that of workplace labor: both rely for their exercise upon privately owned and controlled infrastructures (in the case of social networking sites, we might call these the means for the production of sociability). In both cases, access to these resources entails surrendering control over the product of collective activity to those who own the resources. It is important also to stress the differences between the two forms of value production. In the case of online social networks, control over the productive activity itself (as opposed to some of the product of this activity) is not (yet?) surrendered to those who own the means of sociability. That is to say, neither Facebook nor employers who avail themselves of applications like Appirio claim the right to dictate what employees do in their online social networks. In the case of Appirio, however, it is not hard to imagine how the imperatives of employers might come to colonize or shape social networking activities, especially if compensation is tied to the value they generate.

Another crucial difference between the productivity of online social networking and that of workplace labor is that the appropriation of products functions differently: employees do not lose their social networks just because their employers put the data they generate to work. Finally, unlike workplace labor, social networking is not directly tied to one's livelihood. Significantly, however, the scenario envisioned by Appirio directly links the two: one's social network becomes analogous in important respects to one's laboring capacities. That is to say, it becomes a productive resource, like one's education, skill set, training, and so on, that employers gain control over in order to generate value.

Exploiting Free Labor

Because activities like online social networking have the capacity to generate value, they fit into the broader categories of what has been described as "affective" and "immaterial" labor: not the manufacture of material products, but rather the production of networks of sociability, taste, and communication. Lazzarato describes immaterial labor as the "activity that produces the 'cultural content' of the commodity," noting that it "involves a series of activities that are not normally recognized as 'work'—in other words, the kinds of activities involved in defining and fixing cultural and artistic standards, fashions, tastes, consumer norms, and, more strategically, public opinion" (1996, p. 137). Such labor corresponds to what Michael Hardt (also following Lazzarato) describes as an "affective" form of immaterial labor: "the production and manipulation of affects," which "requires (virtual or actual) human contact and proximity" (1999, p. 93).

In each case, the form of labor in question tends to be "free": both unpaid (outside of established labor markets) and freely given, endowed with a sense of autonomy. The free and spontaneous production of community, sociality, and shared contexts and understandings remains both autonomous in principle from capital and captured in practice by it. As Hardt (1999) puts it, "in those networks of culture and communication, collective subjectivities are produced and sociality is produced—even if those subjectivities and that sociality are directly exploitable by capital" (p. 93). In her discussion of the "free labor" provided by chat-room moderators in exchange for access to online services, Terranova (2000) suggests that such productive activities can, in some contexts, be described as both voluntary and subject to exploitation: "Free labor is the moment where this knowledgeable consumption of culture is translated into productive activities that are pleasurably embraced and at the same time often shamelessly exploited" (p. 37).

There is nothing particularly new about the fact that individual consumers add value to cultural and material products. Why then describe such forms of work (a term which can be used to designate any activity that requires expenditure of effort) as *labor* (work that generates value)? Precisely because of the ways in which commercial digital media *capture* the details of activity that once eluded systematic forms of value extraction in order to turn them into information commodities. Writing before the explosive growth of commercial social networking sites, Terranova (2000) draws on the work of the Italian autonomists to describe this process as the creation of a "social factory," wherein, "work processes have shifted from the factory to society, thereby setting in motion a truly complex machine" (p. 36). Certainly not all work practices have migrated out of the factory—but the term captures the way in which the productive capacity of the "factory" has extended out into society at large. The social factory puts our pleasures, our communications, our sociability to work, capturing them in order to extract value from them. Terranova describes such forms of online labor as "Simultaneously voluntarily given and unwaged, enjoyed and exploited" (p. 36).

If we concede that activity which generates value for others can be described as labor, it is yet another step to make the case regarding why, as such, it might also be considered a form of exploitation. After all, the standard critique of exploitation relies on an account of coercion—even if this coercion is embedded in the social relations that structure the "freely" agreed upon labor contract. If, with Hardt (1999) and Terranova (2000), we are going to assert that the potential exists for the *exploitation* of so-called immaterial or free labor, we face the necessity of coming up with an understanding of the term that is adequate to the work being performed and the value extracted from it. In the face of contemporary critiques of attempts to mobilize the notion of exploitation, perhaps the first task is to define what exploitation is *not*. The mere fact that someone benefits from the efforts of another does not, in itself, constitute exploitation. In an online context, for example, the fact that others may benefit by having access to an open-source program or to the product of the collective contributions of others cannot be construed as prima-facie evidence of exploitation. The shared benefits of collaboration and the non-market benefits that economists describe as externalities are not indicators of exploitation.

Exploitation is also not definable solely in terms of subjective sensibility: it is not reducible to whether or not individuals *feel* they are the victims of exploitation. Such feelings may indeed be accurate, and yet they do not define exploitation. That is to say, exploitation may exist in the absence of a subjective sense of victimization. Moreover, this assertion relies not upon the resuscitation of notions of false consciousness, but rather upon a conception of alienation which, according to Holmstrom (1997), lies at the heart of a critical account of exploitation. For Marx, Holmstrom observes, the appropriation of control over workers' labor represents more than a means for capturing surplus value: it simultaneously reproduces the alienation of workers from the product of their labor: "Being congealed labor, the product is in some sense part of the producers. When it is taken away from them, they are thereby diminished, impoverished, denuded" (1997, p. 85). It is a formulation that draws not from the description of exploitation in *Das Kapital*, but from the 1844 manuscripts, where Marx (2009) forcefully elaborates the wages of estranged labor:

> The worker places his life in the object; but now it no longer belongs to him, but to the object. [. . .] What the product of his labor is, he is not. Therefore, the greater this product, the less is he himself.
>
> (p. 27)

It is worth recalling this overtly humanist formulation if only to note how neatly it anticipates the promises of the interactive economy: to return control to producers of their creative activity (that is, to overcome their estrangement from the product of their efforts), to build community (to overcome estrangement from others), and to facilitate our own self-understanding (to overcome estrangement from themselves). If anyone is directly invoking the language of Marx in the current conjuncture, it is not the critical theorists, but the commercial promoters of the interactive revolution. In this regard, we might enlist Holmstrom's formulation to turn the promise of digital empowerment back on itself by exploring the ways in which it fails to overcome the very forms of alienation it promised to remedy.

The promise of interactive participation takes shape against the background of the very alienation that was the object of Marx's critique. One of the preconditions for the promotion of Web 2.0 is thus the invocation of the forms of estrangement associated with the exploitation of waged labor. It is perhaps telling that even on the right of the political spectrum, Marx is invoked to promote the ostensibly revolutionary power of the Internet. Conservative blogger Andrew Sullivan (2002), for example, once claimed that one of the most important things blogs do "is—to invoke Marx—seize the means of production. It's hard to underestimate what a huge deal this is." In a similar vein, Futurist William Wriston triumphantly proclaimed that "the force of microelectronics will blow apart all monopolies hierarchies, pyramids, and power grids of established industrial society" (as quoted in Barney, 2000, p. 19).

Direct references to Marx do not make it into the corporate promotional literature, but promises to overcome alienation, revitalize community, and empower citizen-consumers are recurring themes. Thus, for example, Facebook's company overview simply states: "Facebook's mission is to give people the power to share and make the world more open and connected" (Facebook, 2009b). Likewise, YouTube is "empowering" users "to become the broadcasters of tomorrow" (YouTube, 2009). The promise, in other words, is to overcome the separation that lies at the core of capitalist alienation—the separation enacted by private control over productive resources that compels workers to surrender control over their own activity. The commercial digital solution borrows from the familiar spear-that-heals-the-wound-it-caused logic of advertising: separation can be remedied by further separation.

According to such an account, community and creativity can be fostered by commercial sites that store our data—everything from the details of our social networks to our shared musings, pictures, videos, and music. These can be circulated so easily because they are separated from us, stored and distributed (increasingly) on commercially owned and operated servers and networks, and administered by commercial applications. The conditions of access to this infrastructure for social networking and communication include submission to forms of surveillance, data-mining, and target marketing that support the emerging logic of online commerce: data-driven mass customization and target marketing.

According to the standard market account, the logic at work here is analogous to that of free exchange. Sites like Facebook and Gmail provide users with a service, and in exchange they extract some form of payment. Just as there is a "cost" associated with free-to-air TV, namely submission to marketing appeals, so too there is a cost associated with the services provided by commercial Internet services: submission to monitoring and targeted advertising. If, on this account, the logic of *free* exchange underlies e-commerce—if we willingly submit to the conditions set by commercial websites—then the common-sense notion of exploitation is no longer in play; exploitation entails coercion. The contribution of critical political economy is to discern the ways in which relations of power and hence forms of coercion structure the terms of so-called free exchange. Such a critique is crucial to any analysis of exploitation within the context of so-called "free" labor. The coercion inherent in "free" submission to the forms of monitoring, control, and payment associated with wage labor contracts is relatively straightforward: control over productive resources provides owners with disproportionate power in setting the terms of access to them (especially in conditions when there is a surplus labor force). If they are to provide for themselves, those with nothing to sell but their labor power must do so under terms structured by unequal power relations. In the case of social networking, the situation is different: access to the privately owned means of sociality is not (yet?) inseparable from the ability to earn a livelihood. For the most part, people aren't earning their living by using such resources, so they can go without them and still survive (though one might assume differently to hear some users describe how reliant they have become on their Facebook pages or their mobile phones).

The standard Marxist critique of exploitation combines the humanist concerns outlined above with an economic critique. The extraction of surplus value is based on the labor commodity—whose value in use differs from its value in exchange. Viewed within the context of market relations, workers are not underpaid for labor *qua* commodity (this is central to Marx's account of exploitation in Volume I of Capital). In the wage–labor exchange, labor receives its accurate market price: the (historically determined) cost of its replacement. However, because its value in use exceeds its exchange value— because labor *produces* value—its economic worth to those who own and control it is greater than its market price. Absent coercion, it would be preferable to control such power rather than to sell it. This account lines up with the Marxist account of alienation outlined by Holmstrom (1997)—one that equates the loss of control over creative activity and collective productive life with a loss of freedom. At the heart of both accounts is the ability to retain control over one's creative activity. As Marx puts it in the 1844 Manuscripts:

> Man makes his life activity itself an object of his will and consciousness. . . . Only because of that is his activity free activity. Estranged labour reverses the relationship so that man, just because he is a conscious being, makes his life activity, his *essential being*, a mere means for his *existence*.
>
> (2009)

Exploitation does not merely deprive the individual of the full value realized from his or her creative activity, but crucially of the freedom to make this activity an object of will and consciousness. Estrangement occurs when our own activity appears as something turned back against us as "an alien power" over and against oneself (Marx, 2009).

With this somewhat richer conception of exploitation, we might develop a set of criteria for discerning its relevance to "free" online labor. First, exploitation entails some form of coercion—even if this lurks only in the background conditions that structure "free" exchange. Second, exploitation obtains when there is loss of control over one's creative, productive activity—a loss that results in the re-appearance of one's own activity in the form of an alien force turned back upon oneself.

Drawing on this definition of exploitation, we can revisit the example of Appirio's workplace application. Online social networking apparently fits neatly into the category of those freely given activities exercised under neither the compulsion of necessity nor the threat of force. It is worth noting, however, that social networking takes place against the background of forms of estrangement associated with industrial capitalism—the very alienation for which new media promise an antidote, according to the marketing hype. Thus, the offer of a modicum of control over productive resources as well as the promise to resuscitate extended forms of community and to challenge central-ized control over collective representations all gain their appeal against the background of the depredations of industrial capitalism. Viewed in this context, the exchange that characterizes interactive sites (willing submission to monitoring and advertising in exchange for access to communication resources) might be understood as a second-order result of capitalist appropri-ation. The promise is that, thanks to interactive technology, workers can regain some of the control over their own activity that is surrendered in the wage–labor contract. Individuals are offered a modicum of control over the product of their creative activity in exchange for the work they do in building up online community and sociality upon privately controlled network infra-structures. Their free participation is redoubled as a form of productive labor captured by capital. In a self-generating cycle, the offer to overcome estrange-ment or alienation produces a second-order form of separation: that of users from the data they generate.

The case of Appirio makes the analogy to the workplace more direct. The request by employers to piggyback market research applications onto the social networks built by employees takes place within the power relations that struc-ture submission to workplace conditions more generally. In this instance the appeal to old-school, retro-Marxist accounts of workplace exploitation remains relevant. Workers submit to the forms of monitoring and control exerted by employers precisely because the alternative is to lose their jobs. In the case of Appirio, the same power relations that govern the appropriation of control over labor are brought to bear upon "autonomous" forms of activity like the creation and maintenance of online social networks.

However, the capture and use of social network information does not entail the capture of control over the productive activity of employees: they are not (yet?) being told *how* to conduct this activity, merely to make the results available for marketing purposes. We might then argue that even if conditions of coercion exist ("accept Appirio's application or face workplace consequences"), estrangement does not. Such is the standard rejoinder to the charge of exploitation in the context of sites like Facebook: people continue to enjoy the benefits of online social networking so why shouldn't Facebook and the applications it runs on its platform benefit as well, since their profits do not detract from the benefits that accrue to users?

But the appropriation of social networking activity, Appirio-style, may result in estrangement after all, not least if it becomes an expected part of what might be described as extra-workplace labor, something to be done on one's own time for the sake of building connections and collecting data for employers. Direct control in the form of explicit orders regarding what to do online can be replaced by indirect forms of governance in the name of maximizing one's marketable assets. Once social networks become part of a worker's assets to employers, they are subject to indirect forms of governance: maximize the productivity of one's network for the company or face workplace consequences.

A further test of exploitation is whether a form of appropriation results in the return of the fruit of one's own labor in the form of an alien force: the fact that one's own online social network activity will—in the scenario envisioned by Appirio and other applications—return in the form of an ongoing barrage of custom-tailored marketing appeals and strategies to influence behavior. Although built from the raw material of our own productive activity and the myriad forms of experimentation and data-mining exercised upon it by marketers, this activity will return to us in ways that make it difficult to discern the traces of our own contributions. The promise of interactivity, channeled through commercial websites, is to enlist the participatory public in the process of marketing to itself. The resulting opacity of representation—the inability to trace our own contributions in the forms of cultural suasion visited upon us by dint of our own activity recapitulates the estrangement that the digital "revolution" promised to overcome. The world envisioned by the operators of the data-mine, the owners of the databases, and the developers of marketing algorithms is one in which ever greater participation by the public will be transformed into increasingly exclusive forms of proprietary knowledge, available to the few for use upon the many.

Conclusion

Appirio is just one example of emerging attempts to put the activity of online social networking to work. Because it is a workplace application, one whose use is requested by employers, it brings into play the power relations that structure "free" submission to workplace requirements. But what about other uses of user-generated data—such as that of Facebook in the absence of Appirio's applications? Is it possible to discern the workings of exploitation without the coercion associated with workplace social relations? There is no external compulsion to use Facebook or other similar applications—such decisions are generally portrayed as a matter of choice, convenience, and personal pleasure. However, conditions of estrangement may still obtain since the commercial character of online social networking sites means that users will still be subject to detailed forms of data-gathering and ongoing controlled experiments in target marketing designed to more effectively influence their behavior without their knowledge. Their own activities will be turned back upon them in complex and opaque forms with the express purpose of channeling and directing their behavior.

In signing up to use such services, however, users arguably knowingly agree to submit to such forms of monitoring and manipulation and there is no law that says they *have to* join sites like Facebook or MySpace. Set aside for the moment the fact that by all accounts only a tiny fraction of users both read and understand the terms of use to which they ostensibly agree. Set aside even the fact that the terms themselves—subject to change at any time *without notice*—can hardly serve as the basis for either "fully informed" consent or enforceable claims on behalf of users. What would it mean to take seriously the notion that access to online communities facilitated by social networking sites comprised a productive resource in the emerging information economy? That is to say, what if we were to describe such sites not just as consumer services or entertaining novelties for the informated class, but as crucial information resources in the network era? This is a perspective that some of the more digitally advanced companies in the information economy are starting to embrace—one in which social networking sites serve, as one employer put it, as "a fundamental communication tool to probably more than half our workforce" (Moscaritolo, 2007). If this sounds absurd, a similar historical progression took place in the use of email, a popular communication-enhancing novelty that developed into an indispensable communication tool for a range of workers in the information-age workplace. It is not hard to imagine a world in which those who eschew networking sites will seem as outdated, hard-to-reach, and perhaps overly protective of their privacy as those who don't have an email account or carry mobile phones. In the social factory, the boundaries between spheres of labor and leisure, domesticity, and consumption upon which the distinction between consumer choice and workplace coercion relies, become blurred. To the extent that our communicative, educational, and social lives are folded into the social factory and become the resources that we draw upon and sell to employers, access to resources for online networking becomes a crucial component of generating value.

One of the constitutive half-truths about the character of immaterial or affective labor in the digital era is that, as Banks and Humphreys (2008), echoing Sullivan (2002) and De Kerckhove (in Barney, 2000) put it, "the means of knowledge and cultural production are now in the hands of the consumers" (p. 406). The formulation blurs the important line between *access* to the means of online content production and *ownership or control* over these resources. Consumers may own computers and software, but not the networks and vast server farms that make possible the creation and maintenance of online social networks and the forms of content sharing that characterize the emerging online economy.

Thus, any comparison of industrial-era production to information-age creativity needs to take into account not just the fact that productive resources are in the hands of consumers, but also that the means of communication and distribution are *not*. That the privatization of network infrastructures and the commercialization of online applications lies at the core of emerging online business models is obscured by a narrow focus on user-generated content.

This chapter's premise is that the new forms of communication, transaction, consumption, and interaction made possible by digital technologies need to be situated within their larger economic context, namely, the creation of a privately owned and operated commercial media structure. When we explore what people do on Facebook or MySpace and the forms of community such sites enable, we must also keep in mind what gets done with the products of this activity, who controls its use and re-use, who profits from its transformation into commercial commodities and marketing campaigns, as well as who is targeted by these campaigns and to what end. Contrary to conventional wisdom, social networking sites don't publicize community, they *privatize* it. Commercial social networking sites are ostensibly collaborative productions, except when it comes to structuring terms-of-use agreements, and, of course, allocating the profits they generate.

This is not to discount the real forms of satisfaction and communion that users get out of participating in such sites—rather, it is to situate these within the larger economic context whereby value-generating activity is exchanged according to terms structured by those who own and operate the means of their production. The fact that third parties may benefit from the collection and use of our personal information does not in itself constitute exploitation, at least according to the definition proposed by this chapter. Nor does the fact that we may enjoy and benefit from our social networking practices exempt such activities from being subject to exploitation, any more than the fact that some forms of wage labor may be enjoyable and rewarding. The capture and use of user-generated information for commercial purposes—its reconstitution in forms of suasion, manipulation, and control turned back upon those who created it—recapitulates the logic of separation and estrangement.

In the broadest sense, the promise of access to sites of online creativity and sociability takes place against a background already structured by separation (of the great majority of individuals from control over productive resources) and resulting forms of estrangement. Moreover, as the example of Appirio suggests, as interactive technologies facilitate forms of extra-workplace productivity, workplace relations help determine the capture and "monetization" of this activity. The case of Appirio represents the more general logic behind attempts to piggyback on commercial forms of social networking. Facebook markets itself as a platform for a broad range of applications designed to capitalize on the information generated by its members.

Consider, for example, the use of add-on applications (one of which is suggestively named Encompass) by universities to build alumni networks for marketing and fundraising. As one press release put it:

> When looking to engage young alumni, you have to become part of their conversation, and many of those interactions start on Facebook. . . . Using Facebook Connect, Encompass just became more social by allowing member activity, like an event RSVP or a donation, to be published on members' Facebook News Feeds. . . . Facebook Connect is what our market needs to achieve their development and advancement goals.
>
> (*Science Letter*, 2008)

Perhaps access to educational resources will one day be conditional upon sharing information about (and via) one's social networks.

In the end, theoretical approaches to commercial social networking applications that treat them as a site of free choice paradoxically recapitulate the distinction between production and consumption they profess to undermine. If, indeed, such sites are productive ones, if they erode the distinction between consumer and producer, audience and author, user and creator, then they become amenable to critiques of the conditions that structure access to the means of productive resources. The lens of consumer choice then becomes a flawed one for examining the workings of social networking. It ignores the productive aspect of such sites and thus overlooks both the value-generating work done by consumers and the logic of enclosure whereby this value is captured. Second, it naturalizes the process whereby private ownership of productive resources structures the terms of exchange whereby users exchange their value-generating activity for access to resources for communication, information sharing, and sociability. Third, it backgrounds the forms of coercion that may contribute to willing submission to detailed forms of monitoring. Finally, it concedes that, in the information age, our communal life will be permeated by comprehensive monitoring and tightly targeted advertising while assuming that the natural form community takes in the digital era is one based on privately owned resources. It should be possible, by contrast, to envision forms of online community and sociability that do not entail submission to increasingly detailed forms of monitoring and sophisticated target marketing.

Social networking needn't be constituted as a commercially supported activity. Indeed, the sites lend themselves to the collaborative peer-to-peer logic described by Bauwens (2009), in which use value is produced directly,

> through the free cooperation of producers who have access to distributed capital. . . . Its product is not exchange value for a market, but use-value for a community of users (for example in the sharing of film and music). It is governed by the community of producers (and users) themselves, and not by market allocation or corporate hierarchy.

There is a longstanding history of groups creating not-for-profit modes of sociality in a range of spaces and contexts, and, as Facebook itself demonstrates, people are willing to contribute the necessary work in exchange for the non-monetary and collective benefits they receive. Nor is it the case that users are unwilling or unable to pay the cost of supporting online social networks—indirectly they already do so in the form of the advertising costs passed on to them in the purchase price of the products they consume. Such costs would likely be much lower if they were directly incorporated into user fees for a not-for-profit online infrastructure. The Internet didn't start as a privately owned and commercially operated communication system, and it needn't remain so. However, it is perhaps a symptom of the triumph of market logic that it sounds outlandish even to suggest the possibility of a non-commercial Internet—as if it had always been primarily a privately owned and commercially operated system. Perhaps one way to trouble the seemingly intractable assumption of the naturally commercial basis of new forms of sociability is to highlight alternative forms of production, as Bauwens does, and to highlight the exploitative character of online commerce. The reduction of our notion of community to one structured by marketing interests and built upon the exploitation of user labour represents not a limitation of the technology, but of our conception of community and our grasp of the potential of networked interactivity.

References

Arvidsson, A. (2007). Creative class or administrative class? On advertising and the "underground." *Ephemera, 1*, 2007.

Banks, J. & Humphreys, S. (2008). The labour of user co-creators. *Convergence, 14*(4), 401–418.

Barney, D. (2000). *Prometheus wired: The hope for democracy in the age of network technology*. Chicago: University of Chicago Press.

Bauwens, M. (2009). "Technological alternatives." *Red Pepper*, January 3. Online, available at: www.redpepper.org.uk/Technological-alternatives (accessed October 10, 2009).

De Angelis, M. (2001). Marx and primitive accumulation: The continuous character of capital's "enclosures." *The Commoner*, September 2. Online, available at: www.commoner.org.uk/02deangelis.pdf (accessed October 10, 2009).

Facebook. (2009a). Friends for sale: Info. Online, available at: www.facebook.com/friendsforsale?v=info&viewas=0 (accessed July 8, 2009).

Facebook. (2009b). Info. Online, available at: www.facebook.com/facebook?ref=pf#/facebook?v=info&viewas=0&ref=pf (accessed June 12, 2009).

Facebook. (2009c). Terms. Online, available at: www.facebook.com/terms.php (accessed June 10, 2009).

Facebook. (2009d). Policy. Online, available at: www.facebook.com/policy.php (accessed June 10, 2009).

Hardt, M. (1999). Affective labor. *Boundary 2, 2*, 89–100.

Hesmondhalgh, D. (2008). Neoliberalism, imperialism and the media. In D. Hesmondhalgh & J. Toynbee (Eds.) *The media and social theory*. London and New York (pp. 95–111): Routledge.

Holmstrom, N. (1997). Exploitation. In Kai Nielsen & Robert Ware (Eds.) *Exploitation: Key concepts in critical theory*. Atlantic Highlands (pp. 81–102): Humanities Press International.

Independent, the. (2007). Battle for Facebook, September 26, p. B1.

Ippolita, Lovink, G. & Rossiter, N. (2009). The digital given: 10 Web 2.0 theses. *Fibreculture*, 14. Online, available at: http://journal.fibreculture.org/issue14/issue14_ippolita_et_al_print.html (accessed October 12, 2009).

Lazzarato, M. (1996). Immaterial labour. In P. Virno & M. Hardt (Eds.) *Radical thought in Italy: A potential politics* (pp. 133–150). Minneapolis: University of Minnesota Press.

Market Wire. (2009). Appirio referral management solution connects social networks with business applications to encourage, manage and measure word-of-mouth referrals. February 2.

Marx, K. (2009). *The economic & philosophic manuscripts of 1844*. Online, available at: www.marxists.org/archive/marx/works/1844/manuscripts/preface.htm (accessed July 20, 2009).

Moscaritolo, M. (2007). Facebook is a valuable and enjoyable social networking site but it is not without pitfalls. *The Advertiser*, December 6, p. 19.

Mosco, V. (1989). *The pay-per society*. Toronto: Ablex.

MySpace. (2008). Terms & conditions. Online, available at: www.myspace.com/index.cfm?fuseaction=misc.terms (accessed June 20, 2008).

Science Letter. (2008). iModules Software Inc. iModules connects alumni using Facebook platform. November 25.

Sullivan, A. (2002). The blogging revolution: Weblogs are to words what Napster was to music. *Wired*, 10(5) (May). Online, available at: www.wired.com/wired/archive/10.05/mustread.html?pg=2 (accessed June 25, 2009).

Terranova, T. (2000). Free labor: Producing culture for the digital economy. *Social Text*, 63(18): 33–57.

Weed, J. (2009). Finding new employees, via social networks. *New York Times*, May 30. Online, available at: www.nytimes.com/2009/05/31/jobs/31recruit.html?_r=1&scp=2&sq=appirio&st=cse (accessed June 1, 2009).

YouTube. (2009). *Company history*. Online, available at: www.youtube.com/t/company_history2 (accessed September 2, 2009).

Part II

Social Textures

Emerging Patterns of Sociability on Social Network Sites

Chapter 5

Social Network Sites as Virtual Communities

Malcolm R. Parks

> Virtual communities are social aggregations that emerge from the Net when enough people carry on ... public discussions long enough, with sufficient human feeling, to form webs of personal relationships in cyberspace.
>
> (Rheingold, 1993, p. 5)

In 1993, Howard Rheingold brilliantly captured the zeitgeist of the emerging Internet with his book entitled *Virtual Communities: Homesteading on the Electronic Frontier*. Although the image of online settings as communities can be traced to the Internet's founding documents (e.g., Licklider & Taylor, 1968), Rheingold's characterization captured the imagination just as Internet use began to enter the mainstream of public consciousness. The community metaphor was so successful that it effectively banished alternative metaphors of the day (e.g., "information superhighway"). More importantly, the community metaphor continues to influence the way we think about and study the social Internet. Nowhere is this more apparent than with contemporary social networking sites (SNSs) such as MySpace and Facebook.

My goal in this chapter is to assess the status of online settings like MySpace as sites for virtual communities. MySpace and other SNSs such as Facebook are not communities in any singular sense, but rather function as social venues in which many different communities may form. Thus I seek to determine what conditions are necessary for the formation of communities, as well as how often and where they form. My approach is decidedly eclectic, drawing from the historic literature on community, a large observational study of MySpace, and on analyses of select cases. I begin by revisiting the community metaphor in contemporary discourse about SNSs, MySpace in particular, and then ground the discussion in the more traditional sociological literature on community. From there, we may assess the requirements for virtual communities, ask how frequently SNS users are involved in community activity, and explore the conditions that most facilitate the development of communities. All of this will, I hope, leave us at chapter's end with a renewed, but more cautious, appreciation of the concept of "virtual community."

Social Network Sites as Virtual Communities

Today's social network sites are direct heirs to the community metaphor Rheingold and others popularized nearly 20 years ago. Like many of their Internet predecessors, SNSs carry expectations of sociability, meaningful connection to others, conviviality, perhaps even empathy and support. Whether the actual interaction on these venues reaches the level of a "virtual community" depends on one's perspective and definition, but there can be no question that "community," with all its affective and historical complications, will continue to frame popular understanding of MySpace, Facebook, QQ, and other SNSs. MySpace, for example, has been described as "an imagined egocentric community" (boyd, 2006). And *Time* magazine hailed MySpace as a powerful technology enabling individuals to take control of the Information Age and proclaimed it to be an "online metropolis" that promotes "community and collaboration on a scale never seen before" (Grossman, 2006, p. 40).

The internal rhetoric of social network sites often valorizes communal language and imagery as well. Facebook.com's log in page proclaims, "Facebook helps you connect and share with the people in your life." MySpace.com describes itself as a place to "find old friends" and "make new friends," as a place to "connect," and, in a word, as a "community." The rhetoric of community resonates among MySpace users as well. At this writing, for instance, an internal search of MySpace returns approximately 317,000 references to "community."

Debates about whether people can find community or community-like experiences online continue to reverberate in academic discourse. Some of these debates take extreme, almost Manichean, forms (Wellman & Gulia, 1999). Some hotly reject the concept of virtual community as a "confused oxymoron" (Lockard, 1997, p. 224), while others, including Wellman and Rheingold, advocate viewing online communities in terms of networks of personal relationships (Rheingold, 2000; Wellman & Gulia, 1999). Still others draw on the notion that SNSs may enhance community by increasing participants' "social capital" (Ellison, Steinfield, & Lampe, 2007; see also Ellison et al., this volume, Chapter 6). For many, the community metaphor appears to be accepted uncritically and used without further elaboration (e.g., Chua, 2009; Fogel & Nehmad, 2008; Johnson, 2008; Sohn, 2008), and yet it is difficult to think of a social scientific concept in greater need of careful use and critical elaboration.

What Constitutes "Community?"

The concept of community has an unsettled intellectual history dating back nearly 200 years. Attention waxes and wanes with changes in scholarly fashion, political conditions, and technology, but the term continues to resonate in our lives. It does so, in part, because it feels good; it evokes feelings of friendliness, trust, and belonging that are often deemed lacking in ruthless, individualistic times (Bauman, 2001). This nostalgic element has deep roots. In classic treatises, Tönnies (1887/1957) and later Wirth (1938) argued that traditional, densely-knit communities had been undermined by urbanization and industrialization so that most people now experienced their social ties as transitory, disconnected, and impersonal. Although there have been powerful responses to these images of lost community (Bernard, 1973; Wellman, 1979; Wellman, Carrington, & Hall, 1988), yearnings for the assumedly deeper connections and greater belonging of the past still emanate from contemporary discussions of virtual community. Rheingold (1993, p. 62), for example, speculated that the popularity of online communities is a "response to the hunger for community that has followed the disintegration of traditional communities."

Conceptualizations of community are further complicated by tensions between descriptive and prescriptive approaches, and by tensions between what might be called "strong" and "weak" requirements. Social network theorists tend to approach the concept descriptively, delineating the nature of social ties within physical and mediated settings (Hampton & Wellman, 2003; Wellman & Gulia, 1999; Wellman et al., 1988). But, as Willson (2006, p. 22) observed, others lay down "rigorous outlines of what a community is and how it should behave." Chief among the prescriptivists are scholars calling for community renewal and greater civic engagement (e.g., Putnam, 2000; Putnam & Feldstein, 2003). Those who favor a "strong" conceptualization usually restrict the term to groups of people who share physical space, are relatively self-sufficient within that space, and who are linked by ties that include kinship (Bell & Newby, 1974; Kinton, 1975; Weinreich, 1997). Over time, however, theorists have moved away from conceptualizing community as a geographic entity to conceptualizing it in psychological terms or as quality of sociality (Amit, 2002). In this "weak" sense, community is viewed as a culture, a set of ideas and interpersonal sentiments rather than as a physical place (Anderson, 1991; Bender, 1978; Calhoun, 1980). Within this framework, "virtual communities" are defined as social groups that display the psychological and cultural qualities of strong community without physical proximity (Willson, 2006).

Given these tensions, it is not surprising that nearly every scholar who has surveyed the literature on community over the last half century has lamented the conceptual turmoil (Bell & Newby, 1974; Hillery, 1955; Willson, 2006).

In spite of this, a number of themes regularly reappear in definitions of community and are, to varying degrees, relevant for the evaluation of SNSs as locations for virtual communities. These are summarized Table 5.1, along with the behaviors of SNS users that would be required in order to participate in a virtual community. The defining characteristics of community are discussed below and the behaviors required of SNS users are discussed in the section that follows. The first two requirements, sharing geographic space and self-sufficiency, represent the traditional "strong community" perspective and are generally viewed as less relevant for virtual communities in which members, almost by definition, do not share physical space or depend on one another for the satisfaction of basic needs to any great degree.

Five recurrent themes in the literature on community can, I believe, serve as criteria for evaluating the extent to which online groups function as virtual communities. The ability to engage in collective action is generally considered to be an essential test of the authenticity of any community, including virtual communities (Jones, 1995). Acting collectively both reflects and reinforces two other common requirements for community, namely, that the group think of itself as a community and that the members identify with the community (Bell & Newby, 1974; Willson, 2006). Communities are also created through the ritualized sharing of information (Carey, 1989; Jones, 1995). To be sustained, a community must engage in such information-sharing rituals on a regular basis.

Community is also constituted in the larger patterns of interaction that grow out of regularized information exchange (Bell & Newby, 1974). Although the resulting interactive and relational structures are most evident in the public or common areas of the community, there is little agreement regarding the role and importance of a "public commons" in the life of communities. Public areas may be sites for behavior that enhances community cohesion, but behavior in

Table 5.1 Recurring themes in definitions of community and associated requirements on SNSs

Defining elements of community	Associated social requirements on SNSs
Less relevant for virtual communities • Sharing geographic space • Self-sufficiency	
More relevant for virtual communities • Ability to engage in collective action • Shared rituals, social regulation	• Users must create and visit their profiles with some regularity
• Patterned interaction among members	• Users must personalize their profiles
• Identification, a sense of belonging and attachment	• Users must make social contacts and respond to other users
• Self-awareness of being a community	

public areas may threaten cohesion when shared resources are exploited by "free-riders" who do not contribute to the commonweal (e.g., Bonacich, 1990; Kollock, 1998). Cohesion and positive sentiment may thus depend as much on private ties among community members as on their behavior in public space (Bender, 1978). Consistent with this view, researchers investigating online communities have suggested that distributed network structures can take the place of a public commons (Sohn, 2008). That is, interlinked private networks, such as those found on social network sites, may take the place of a public forum. Indeed, rates of participation may actually be higher in these more diffuse networks than in the shared public areas of online communities.

Finally, definitions of community typically specify that members exhibit attachments to one another and to the community more generally (Kantor, 1972; Willson, 2006). "Communities are defined as shared, close, and intimate" (Jensen, 1990, p. 71). These emotional bonds need not be experienced toward every member of the community, but it is generally assumed that the majority of members have personal attachments to at least some other members.

Community and the Social Affordances of MySpace

Although these characteristics of community provide a useful framework for thinking about the constitutional requirements of virtual communities, they are difficult to observe directly. Even if agreement could be reached on how these characteristics might be measured, it is likely that the range and complexity of data required for their assessment would create a major impediment to research. An alternative strategy is to ask if the various elements of community depend on a smaller, underlying set of social affordances that could be assessed more directly.

By "social affordances" I refer to the possibilities for action that are called forth by a social technology or environment. Thus, pencils "call forth" writing; telephones call forth talking; and photocopier stations in offices call forth informal interaction among the employees who gather around them. The theory of affordances originated in work on visual perception (Gibson, 1979), but has since been applied to texts, social technologies, and social settings more generally (e.g., Fayard & Weeks, 2007; Graves, 2007; Hutchby, 2001). It provides a framework for identifying the characteristics of SNSs like MySpace that facilitate or "call forth" the constitutive elements of community. I argue that three types of social affordances are required for the formation of virtual communities on social network sites: affordances of membership, expression, and connection (Table 5.1). The discussion of these affordances below focuses on MySpace because I will be presenting research findings from a study of MySpace later in the section that follows. This research sought to determine how many MySpace users actually took advantage of each type of affordance, and thus how many might have engaged in the foundational activities essential for the higher-order experience of community.

Affordances of Membership

The ease and durability of membership in MySpace are its chief social affordances. Membership is open to all who state that they are aged 14 or older, click affirmatively on a user agreement, and who have not been identified as convicted sexual offenders. Two aspects of membership may be directly observed. The length of time since the user last logged in can be determined from the date of the member's most recent visit, which is automatically displayed. MySpace also allows users over the age of 15 to set their profile to "private" or "public." Private profiles display only basic demographic information, a photo (if given), and the date of the most recent visit to the public. The full profile is available only to those the user has accepted as "friends." Public profiles display the full range of content regardless of whether one is on the user's friend list. Because the choice of private/public display has a fundamental effect on how others might relate to an individual, it represents a significant communicative affordance. Public profiles facilitate the formation of weak ties among unacquainted people to a greater degree than private profiles and therefore encourage community formation and cohesion.

Affordances of Personal Expression

MySpace, perhaps more than other SNSs, is rich in affordances for personal expression. Two basic affordances of personal expression were examined in this study. The first was whether or not the user had customized his or her profile page. Customization allows users to express themselves more individually by altering their profile's standard fonts and background colors, by embedding new elements such as music or video, and by rearranging the page layout. The second category of expressive choice examined in this study was whether or not users provided a personal picture. Visual images express individuality and open users to more individualized responses in return. Although MySpace affords a variety of more specific mechanisms for self-expression, the opportunity to customize content and to upload personal pictures are two of the most basic.

Affordances of Connection

MySpace enables users to establish connections with one another using a variety of tools—direct messages, creation of groups, "friending," instant messaging, bulletins, and comments posted on the recipient's site. Of these, the two most visible are the linkages between friends and the posting of comments. Although "friending" enables a variety of relationships on MySpace (boyd, 2006), with some exceptions, the number of individual friends one has would appear to be an obvious indicator of social connectivity. Social connectivity is also enhanced when users post comments on each other's profiles. Users who take advantage of these two affordances of connectivity are more likely to experience the involvement, identification, attachment, and sense of belonging characteristic of community. Those with little social connectivity are unlikely to experience MySpace as a community.

To summarize in more general terms, although "community" and "virtual community" have enduring rhetorical and cultural appeal, the concept of community is notoriously slippery. However, by extracting the most common themes running through the previous literature, we may get at least a general sense of what is necessary if we are to designate a social group as a "community." For online settings such as social network sites, the most relevant of these requirements are engaging in shared rituals, social regulation, and collective action through patterned interaction and the creation of relational linkages among members that promote emotional bonds, a sense of belonging, and a sense of identification with the community. While this complex of actions and sentiments is difficult to observe directly, we can directly observe the extent to which participants utilize the basic social affordances of a venue like MySpace— social affordances that constitute the raw materials for the higher-order elements of community. Wide utilization of the affordances of membership, personal expression, and connectivity would suggest that MySpace provides fertile grounds for the development of virtual communities, while limited utilization would suggest that MySpace is, whatever its other social and commercial functions, not living up to its billing as a site rich in virtual communities. In the next section, I present the results of an observational study intended to assess just how commonly these affordances are used by the members of MySpace.

How Often Do Members Utilize the Social Affordances of MySpace?

Study Description

A large-scale observational study was conducted in the summer of 2007 to determine the extent to which people who created profiles on MySpace also utilized the affordances of membership, personal expression, and connection. The initial sample of 2,000 profiles was randomly selected based on MySpace profile identification numbers. The final sample was reduced to 1,500 by the exclusion of invalid or deleted profiles (20.5%) and by the exclusion of commercial sites belonging to entertainers, celebrities, businesses, and sites belonging to groups rather than individuals (4.5%). Reported age in the final sample ranged from 14 to 84, but 75% were aged 25 or younger. Males and females were almost equally represented among subjects aged 21 or younger, but males significantly outnumbered females among members over the age of 21.

Seven aspects of MySpace use were coded for each profile. To assess membership activity, we calculated the number of days since the most recent log in and noted whether the profile was public or private. To assess personal expression, we coded whether or not the user had customized his or her profile page in some fashion, and whether or not the user had provided a personal profile picture. Pictures that did not obviously include the individual were excluded. Finally, to assess connectivity, we counted the number of friends listed, the number of comments received from others, and the number of days since the most recent comment had been received. These latter measures were available only for public profile pages. Friendship counts were corrected by excluding "friends" who appeared to represent music groups, celebrities, politicians, fan sites, business-oriented sites, or MySpace administrators (e.g., "Tom"). Any profile whose primary function was to promote a person or product for commercial or political gain rather than to describe an individual and his/her interests was excluded on the grounds that these linkages were less likely to trigger the interpersonal feelings and behaviors associated with the concept of community. Reliabilities for these measures were calculated using 20% of the final sample and ranged from 0.82 to 0.99.

Membership Activity

Our initial analyses revealed that MySpace contained a large number of profiles belonging to individuals who had not used MySpace recently. Of the 1,500 profiles examined, 569 (37.9%) had not been visited by their owners in the past six months. In order to avoid biasing the results by including subjects who essentially no longer used MySpace, the remaining analysis was limited to people who had logged in within the previous six months ($n = 931$). Although the average number of days since the last visit was over a month for this group, 52.4% had logged in within the past week ($M = 34.17$ days, $Mdn = 5.00$, $SD = 50.75$).

There were few demographic differences in how often people visited their profiles. Visits by males and females were equally recent. People who self-classified as Whites, Blacks, or Hispanics had logged in equally recently. Older users had not logged in quite as recently as younger users, but the correlation was quite small ($r = 0.10$, $p < 0.05$) and the fact that most users were aged between 15 and 22 should be kept in mind. Very few people classified themselves as divorced or as "swingers." But users who were married ($M = 20.98$

days, $SD = 39.33$) or "in a relationship" ($M = 20.98$ days, $SD = 37.34$) had logged in significantly more recently than people who were single ($M = 45.57$ days, $SD = 55.08$, $F_{2,570} = 12.21$, $p < 0.001$).

Another fundamental affordance of membership is the ability to regulate access to the information others may view. Most users (63.8%) made their sites public—allowing any other member to view them. The proportion of private sites (36.2%) reflects MySpace policy that automatically sets the sites of all users under the age of 16 to private. A majority of 16 year olds kept their sites private as well (59.4%), but 77.3% of the sites of older users were public. Thus most users make their profiles public as soon as or shortly after they are allowed to do so. Although the majority of men and majority of women made their sites public, more females than males set their profiles to private (34.8% vs. 17.4%, $\chi^2 = 31.04$, $df = 1$, $p < 0.0001$).

Personal Expression

If MySpace supports communities of engaged users, we might expect to see that most of its members actively express themselves as individuals. This may be done either by customizing the standard format of one's profile page or by adding personal content. We found that over two-thirds of users (69.4%) did not customize their profile pages in spite of the fact that tools and templates for doing so are widely available. Customization was unrelated to gender, self-reported education, sexual orientation, or ethnicity. The relational status of the user, however, was associated with customization. Married users (59.6%) and users "in a relationship" (65.3%) customized their profiles significantly more often than single users (41.3%, $\chi^2 = 21.33$, $df = 2$, $p < 0.001$). Customization rates also differed by age group ($\chi^2 = 13.02$, $df = 5$, $p < 0.05$). Younger users were more likely to customize their pages than older users, with the highest rate of customization (41.6%) observed among those aged 19–21 and the lowest rate (24.3%) observed among those over the age of 33.

Displaying a photograph of oneself represents one of the most basic forms of personal expression in online settings. Photographs convey a personal presence that textual material does not. Slightly over half of MySpace members (54.9%) included a photograph of themselves as part of their profile, but many did not (38.3%), and some (6.9%) included a photo that was either ambiguous or contained too many other persons to allow identification. The likelihood of posting a personal picture did not differ by gender or by self-reported education level, ethnicity, and sexual orientation. Married users (74.5%) and users in relationships (73.4%) were significantly more likely than single users (49.7%) to display a photo of themselves ($\chi^2 = 26.70$, $df = 4$, $p < 0.001$). The likelihood of displaying a personal picture varied across age groups

($\chi^2 = 52.61$, $df = 12$, $p < 0.0001$). The lowest rates of display were among the youngest and oldest users—only 42% of 14–15 year olds and 38.8% of those over the age of 33 displayed a personal picture. The highest rates of display, ranging from 66.2% to 66.9%, were among those aged 19–24.

Connection

Being connected to others fosters a sense of purpose, belonging, and attachment that is central to the concept of community. To evaluate how frequently such connections occurred on MySpace, we evaluated the size of users' "friend" lists and the number of comments they had received from others. While we did not attempt to differentiate friends in terms of function or relational strength, we did exclude links to musical groups, political figures, celebrities, and others with whom an individual was unlikely to have an actual social relationship. Even among those who had logged into MySpace within the previous six months, the number of friends varied dramatically, ranging from 0 to 4,039. The mean number of friends was 46.61 ($SD = 179.08$), but most had fewer. Half listed seven or fewer friends and just over one-third (33.7%) listed no friends at all.

Connections with others are also reflected in the comments friends post to the user's profile. These comments reflect more personally directed, but still public, communication between users. The number of comments users had received ranged from 0 to 3,067. Although the average was 81.10 ($SD = 266.22$), the majority of users had received far fewer comments. The median was five comments and mode was zero. Nearly 40% of the public profiles had no comments from friends. It is possible that users have deleted comments that were no longer current, but we saw little evidence of this. Among those receiving at least one comment ($n = 355$), the average length of time since the most recent comment had been received was 37.21 days ($SD = 75.32$). Although just over half had received a comment in the past week, one-quarter (26.2%) had not received a comment in the previous 30 days.

There were few demographic differences in the number of friends MySpace users listed, the number of comments they received from friends, or in how recently the latest comment had been received. Age was modestly, but negatively, associated with the number of friends ($r = -0.12$, $p < 0.01$) and the number of comments ($r = -0.19$, $p < 0.001$), but not with how recently the latest comment had been received. There were no significant gender differences. Blacks, Hispanics, and Whites did not significantly differ in terms of the number of friends listed, the number of comments received, and how recently the last comment had been received. There were also no differences between those who reported their relational status as single, "in a relationship," or married.

Looking across these analyses, it appears, first of all, that a substantial portion of those who have created MySpace profiles use them rarely, if ever. Even if we restrict consideration to those who have visited their profiles within the past six months, no more than one-third to a half utilize the various social affordances of MySpace. Only about half log in on a weekly basis. Only about one-third of users customize their profiles and only slightly over half provide a picture of themselves. Thus, while the majority made their profiles publicly accessible, the information available to others was often quite limited. Social contacts between users also appeared to be limited. Half of users listed fewer than seven friends, one-third listed no friends at all, and 40% had received no comments from others. It is possible that users rely on other less visible social connections such as private messaging, but the overall picture emerging from this survey is one in which the majority of users have relatively low levels of activity, personal expression, and connectivity. Moreover, although there are noteworthy demographic variations in this pattern, utilization of the social affordances of MySpace appears to be low regardless of gender, age, relational status, and ethnicity.

The levels of activity, personal expression, and connectivity found in this study are much lower than those found in two previous studies of MySpace (Jones, Millermaier, Goya-Martinez, & Schuler, 2008; Liu, 2007). Closer inspection of these studies, however, reveals that each utilized a sampling frame that biased results in favor of finding unrepresentatively high levels of user engagement by focusing either on members with a specified number of friends or on users who had logged in recently. Two other studies that employed random samples of the full spectrum of MySpace users have reported levels of member activity, personal expression, and connectivity consistent with those found here (Parks, 2009; Thelwall, 2008).

Together with the results of those studies, the results of the present study suggest that the majority of MySpace members do not utilize the rudimentary social affordances necessary for the formation of virtual communities. This does not mean that members do not experience community in this online setting, but it does imply that the qualities of community are experienced by only a small portion of MySpace users. In the next section we attempt to specify how big that group might be and identify the conditions under which communities are most likely to form.

How Often Do Communities Form on MySpace and What Encourages Community Formation?

It appears that virtual communities are relatively rare on MySpace. That is, the portion of users who are active enough, express themselves in individuating ways often enough, and who interact with others frequently enough to generate the higher-order characteristics of community is quite small. But how small is it?

The answer obviously depends on how criteria are set, but we can at least get a sense of the possibilities by specifying both a set of minimal parameters and a set of more demanding, but not overly restrictive, parameters. What is the minimum set of requirements for membership in a virtual community on MySpace? I propose, somewhat arbitrarily, that in order for an individual to qualify as a member of a virtual community, he or she must have logged in within the past three months, have a personal picture, have at least two friends, and have received at least two comments from friends. A more robust set of requirements might insist on higher levels of engagement—say, logging in within the past seven days, displaying a personal picture, having 10 or more friends, and receiving 10 or more comments.

We returned to our data to see how many users actually satisfied these minimal or more robust criteria for community. Out of the original sample of 1,500 profiles, 16.5% met our minimal criteria and 13.5% met our more robust criteria. The proportion meeting these criteria increases if we exclude those who have not logged in within the past six months. In this restricted sample of 931 profiles, 26.7% met our minimal criteria and 21.7% met our more robust criteria. Again, one should not conclude that roughly a quarter of MySpace users are active in virtual communities—only that a maximum of approximately one-quarter are potentially eligible for membership in a virtual community by virtue of their membership activity, creation of an online identity, and social connections to others.

Who are these more engaged users? Those who met and failed to meet our criteria did not differ in age. Blacks, Whites, and Hispanics were equally likely to meet both the minimal and more robust criteria. On the other hand, a greater proportion of women met the criteria. Married subjects or subjects in relationships were more likely to meet the criteria than single people. However, case analyses of several highly engaged users revealed another characteristic that may be essential for the formation of virtual community. Two cases, randomly selected from among the most active users, are offered by way of illustration.

Case 1: Mike—20-Year-Old Male

At the time of data collection, Mike was 20 years old, had completed high school, and was living in his hometown of Texarkana, a city of approximately 80,000 people split between the states of Texas and Arkansas. Mike indicated that he was currently involved in a relationship and prominently displayed pictures of himself, his girlfriend, and his car. Mike's friends list included 79 people. Females slightly outnumbered males, but the most striking feature of Mike's social network was revealed when we examined each of the friends' profiles. Of the 67 who gave location information, approximately 66% lived within 10–15 miles of Mike. His MySpace network was therefore essentially a local network.

Case 2: Anjoli—17-Year-Old Female

At the time of data collection, Anjoli was a 17-year-old high school student living in Mesquite, a suburb of Dallas with a population of approximately 136,000. She described herself in this way: "basically I'm a woman who can handle her own, smart, got a lot going for myself." She appeared to log in regularly, displayed a playful picture of herself with a friend, and listed a total of 105 friends. Each friend profile was examined and, when available, location information was used to calculate how far each person lived from Anjoli. Of the 86 who gave location information, 76% lived in Mesquite itself. An additional 14% lived within approximately 15 miles of Mesquite. Thus it appeared that 90% of Anjoli's MySpace friends lived within a relatively short distance of Anjoli herself.

While hardly a definitive analysis, these and several other cases suggest that local, geographically shared connections may form a foundation for high levels of activity on social network sites like MySpace. It would seem that those who have rich sets of offline connections that can be transported to MySpace are more likely to become active users and to have rich sets of online connections.

Virtual Communities in Perspective

The rise of online discussion groups and other social venues in the early 1990s renewed interest in the concept of community and introduced the concept of a virtual community. Today's social network sites such as MySpace and Facebook are simply the latest, and arguably most complete, online social venues where virtual communities might form. The purpose of this chapter was to explicate the concept of virtual community and to determine how often and under what conditions the underlying requirements for community formation were being met in the behavior of typical MySpace users.

Although scholars have never settled on a single definition of community, there are nonetheless a small number of themes that recur in the literature and which can be used to think about the nature and requirements of virtual communities. Based on common themes in community literature, I suggested that a group might qualify as a virtual community if its members engaged in collective action, shared in rituals, had a variety of relational linkages, and were emotionally bonded to others in a way that conferred a sense of belonging and group identification. Social network sites certainly provide the functionality, the social affordances, necessary to satisfy these requirements. MySpace, like many other SNSs, provides easy access to diverse people, offers a rich set of options for users to express and address their personal interests, and is structured so as to facilitate communication and relational formation among members. Moreover, those who design and market SNSs have emphasized the relational and communal potential of these sites. It is therefore not surprising that both academic and popular observers have described SNSs like MySpace as virtual communities.

The community metaphor, however, merits close examination, particularly because it resonates so deeply with individual and cultural aspirations. Although it is difficult to assess each of the components of community in a large, diverse setting like MySpace, it was possible to explore how many users met a set of underlying requirements for activity, personal expression, and connectivity. Just as astrobiologists search for life in extraterrestrial environments indirectly by looking for chemical and molecular signatures, my approach was to search for evidence of the building blocks of community rather than for the more elusive communities themselves.

The results of an observational study of randomly selected MySpace profiles indicate that these building blocks of community occur much less often than is commonly assumed. Substantial numbers of users visit their profiles only very rarely, if at all—indeed nearly 40% visit so infrequently as to raise doubts about their continued membership. Rates of site personalization and social connectivity were generally low, even among users who had logged into MySpace within the past six months. The majority of people who create MySpace accounts clearly fail to visit them enough, interact enough, or make enough contacts to meet even the most minimal requirements of a "virtual community."

Perhaps it is well to remember that social networking sites like MySpace are commercial enterprises. Although they may have been originally constructed with the hope of building community, they are increasingly viewed as "monetization opportunities" by developers and investors (Virgin, 2007). As these sites grow in size and commercial value, the community metaphor may come to refer more to marketing appeals than to the actual quality of interaction and social engagement among members. MySpace, for example, markets itself as "a place for friends," but many members have few or no friends there. At some point, the disjunction of market image and member experience may cause people to turn away from social networking sites. Indeed, the large number of seemingly abandoned profiles we found suggests that more than a few users have already turned away.

Perhaps the fault lies not in our sites but in ourselves. Users may bring unrealistic expectations for the level of social connection and community that can be created with social networking applications like MySpace. In other cases, users may exhibit an inflated sense of technological agency. That is, they may expect that creating a profile will, more or less on its own, lead to friendships and meaningful social connections. When the technology fails to produce the expected social result, users become disenchanted and drift away.

Alternatively it could be that, although social networking sites are touted as sites for community, users themselves are really seeking theater, or at least something much more akin to a mass medium. The behavior of large portion of participants more closely resembles that of passive viewers or audience members than that of active participants in a community. This is consistent with the perspective that SNSs function as a form of theater (Mathias, 2007). The entertainment element is further illustrated by the fact that MySpace celebrities are beginning to cross over to more traditional mass media and by the growing number of advertisements, movie trailers, and other material that is typically associated with traditional mass media. More research is needed to determine if the content on social networking sites is becoming more standardized and users are becoming more passive, but MySpace does appear to be transitioning from a social network to a "social portal" for the delivery of television programming, music, and complex promotions linking advertisers with entertainment content (McGirt, 2008).

Although virtual communities do not materialize on MySpace as often as is generally assumed, we did find that between 15%–25% of members were active enough, had established a sufficient identity, and had forged enough social ties to at least meet the minimal requirements for the formation of virtual communities. The biggest difference between these users and less engaged users, I believe, is that they draw more extensively on pre-existing offline networks, especially their local networks. The evidence supporting this speculation is still largely anecdotal, but it is consistent with the "critical mass" theory of interactive media (e.g., Hiltz, 1984; Markus, 1987; Rogers, 1986). This theory argues that people are more likely to adopt a new interactive medium when others they know have also adopted it. This implies that new users will become active, committed users of an SNS only when they find that a sizable number of their existing contacts are already using it. Compared to MySpace users who discover few of their existing friends online, users who discover that many existing friends are using MySpace will become more active users, be more motivated to flesh out their online identities, and will list more people as friends.

This speculation suggests a new line of research and a very different perspective on the concept of virtual community. Specifically it reinforces calls for research on "mixed-mode" relationships that exist in both online and offline settings (Walther & Parks, 2002). Recent research, for instance, indicates that people who use SNSs to learn more about people they have met or observed in offline settings may feel more a part of and more connected to their offline communities (Ellison, Steinfield, & Lampe, 2009). A recent study of Teen Second Life suggests that adolescents tend to make friends with users who live in the same area offline than with users who do not (Foucault, Zhu, Huang, Atrash, & Contractor, 2009). It appears, then, that offline and online communities are linked in ways that we are only beginning to understand.

Importantly, these findings imply that virtual communities are not so virtual after all. If our case studies and the findings on friendship choices on Teen Second Life (Foucault et al., 2009) are correct, then geographically proximal offline communities are frequently the foundation for "virtual" online communities. Although it is widely assumed that computer-mediated communication frees individuals from the limits of physical proximity, it appears social connections in online settings may depend on offline contact. It is revealing that the WELL, the virtual community that Howard Rheingold (1993, 2000) elevated to iconic status, actually depended on regular face-to-face gatherings of its San Francisco-based members (for a history of the WELL, see Hafner, 2001). Willson (2006, p. 16) defined virtual communities as "communities without propinquity," but it may be more accurate to say that virtual communities are often simply the online extension of geographically situated offline communities.

References

Amit, V. (2002). Reconceptualizing community. In V. Amit (Ed.), *Realizing community: Concepts, social relationships and sentiments* (pp. 1–20). London: Routledge.

Anderson, B. (1991). *Imagined communities: Reflections on the origin and spread of nationalism* (rev. ed.). London: Verso.

Bauman, Z. (2001). *Community: Seeking safety in an insecure world*. Cambridge: Polity Press.

Bell, C., & Newby, H. (1974). *The sociology of community*. London: Frank Cass & Company, Ltd.

Bender, T. (1978). *Community and social change in America*. New Brunswick, NJ: Rutgers University Press.

Bernard, J. (1973). *The sociology of community*. Glenview, IL: Scott Foresman.

Bonacich, P. (1990). Communication dilemmas in social networks: An experimental study. *American Sociological Review, 55*, 448–459.

boyd, d. (2006). Friends, friendsters, and MySpace top 8: Writing community into being on social network sites. *First Monday, 11*(12). Online, available at: http://firstmonday.org/htbin/cgiwrap/bin/ojs/index.php/fm/article/view/1418/1336 (accessed June 15, 2009).

Calhoun, C. J. (1980). Community: Toward a variable conceptualization for comparative research. *Social History, 5*, 105–129.

Carey, J. (1989). *Communication as culture*. Boston, MA: Unwin-Hyman.

Chua, C. E. H. (2009). Why do virtual communities regulate speech? *Communication Monographs, 76*(2), 234–261.

Ellison, N. B., Steinfield, C., & Lampe, C. (2007). The benefits of Facebook "friends": Social capital and college students' use of online social network sites. *Journal of Computer-Mediated Communication, 12*(4), 1143–1168.

Ellison, N. B., Steinfield, C., & Lampe, C. (2009). Connection strategies: Relationship formation and maintenance on social network sites. *International Communication Association*. Chicago, IL.

Fayard, A. L., & Weeks, J. (2007). Photocopiers and water-coolers: The affordances of information interaction. *Organization Studies, 28*, 605–634.

Fogel, J., & Nehmad, E. (2008). Internet social network communities: Risk taking, trust, and privacy concerns. *Computers in Human Behavior, 25*, 153–160.

Foucault, B., Zhu, M., Huang, Y., Atrash, Z., & Contractor, N. (2009). Will you be my friend? An exploration of adolescent friendship formation online in Teen Second Life. *International Communication Association*. Chicago, IL.

Gibson, J. J. (1979). *The ecological approach to visual perception*. Boston: Houghton Mifflin.

Graves, L. (2007). The affordances of blogging: A case study in culture and technological effects. *Journal of Communication Inquiry, 31*(4), 331–346.

Grossman, L. (2006). Person of the year. *Time*, December 25, 40–41.

Hafner, K. (2001). *The WELL: A story of love, death, and real life in the seminal online community*. New York, NY: Carroll & Graf.

Hampton, K., & Wellman, B. (2003). Neighboring in Netville: How the Internet supports community and social capital in a wired suburb. *City & Community, 2*(4), 277–311.

Hillery, G. A. (1955). Definitions of community: Areas of agreement. *Rural Sociology, 20*(2), 111–123.

Hiltz, S. R. (1984). *Online communities: A case study of the office of the future*. Norwood, NJ: Ablex.

Hutchby, I. (2001). Technologies, texts and affordances. *Sociology: The Journal of the British Sociological Association, 35*(2), 441–456.

Jensen, J. (1990). *Redeeming modernity*. Newbury Park, CA: Sage.

Johnson, N. (2008). Using Facebook to find sources. *Media, 13*(3), 27.

Jones, S. (1995). Understanding community in the information age. In S. Jones (Ed.), *CyberSociety: Computer-mediated communication and community* (pp. 10–35). Thousand Oaks, CA: Sage.

Jones, S., Millermaier, S., Goya-Martinez, M., & Schuler, J. (2008). Whose space is MySpace? A content analysis of MySpace profiles. *First Monday, 13*(9). Online, available at: www.uic.edu.offcampus.lib.washington.edu/htbin/cgiwrap/bin/ojs/index.php/fm/article/viewArticle/2202/2024 (accessed June 10, 2009).

Kantor, R. M. (1972). *Commitment and community: Communes and utopias in sociological perspective*. Cambridge, MA: Harvard University Press.

Kinton, J. F. (1975). *The American community: Creation and revival.* Aurora, IL: Social Science and Sociological Resources.

Kollock, P. (1998). Social dilemmas: The anatomy of cooperation. *Annual Review of Sociology, 24*, 183–214.

Licklider, J. C. R., & Taylor, R. W. (1968). The computer as a communication device. *Science & Technology, 76*(21–31).

Liu, H. (2007). Social network profiles as taste performances. *Journal of Computer-Mediated Communication, 13*(1), 252–275.

Lockard, J. (1997). Progressive politics, electronic individualism and the myth of the virtual community. In D. Porter (Ed.), *Internet culture* (pp. 219–232). New York, NY: Routledge.

McGirt, E. (2008). MySpace, the sequel. *Fast Company*, September, 92–102.

Markus, M. L. (1987). Toward a "critical mass" theory of interactive media: Universal access, interdependence and diffusion. *Communication Research, 14*(5), 491–511.

Mathias, A. (2007). Facebook generation leaps into reality. *New York Times*, October 6.

Parks, M. (2009). Explicating and applying boundary conditions of online social network theories in MySpace. *International Communication Association*. Chicago, IL.

Putnam, R. D. (2000). *Bowling alone: The collapse and revival of American community.* New York, NY: Simon & Schuster.

Putnam, R. D., & Feldstein, L. M. (2003). *Better together: Restoring the American community.* New York, NY: Simon & Schuster.

Rheingold, H. (1993). *The virtual community: Homesteading on the electronic frontier.* Reading, MA: Addison-Wesley.

Rheingold, H. (2000). *The virtual community: Homesteading on the electronic frontier* (rev. ed.). Cambridge, MA: MIT Press.

Rogers, E. M. (1986). *Communication technology: The new media in society.* New York, NY: Free Press.

Sohn, D. (2008). *Social network structures and the Internet: Collective dynamics in virtual communities.* Amherst, NY: Cambria Press.

Thelwall, M. (2008). Social networks, gender, and friending: An analysis of MySpace member profiles. *Journal of the American Society for Information Science and Technology, 59*(8), 1321–1330.

Tönnies, F. (1887/1957). *Community & society (Gemeinschaft und Gesellschaft)* (C. P. Loomis, Trans.). East Lansing, MI: Michigan State University Press.

Virgin, B. (2007). An elusive search for the new mass medium. *Seattle Post-Intelligencer*, October 30, pp. 1 & 6.

Walther, J. B., & Parks, M. (2002). Cues filtered out, cues filtered in: Computer mediated communication and relationships. In M. L. Knapp, J. A. Daly, & G. R. Miller (Eds.), *The handbook of interpersonal communication* (3rd ed., pp. 529–563). Thousand Oaks, CA: Sage.

Weinreich, F. (1997). Establishing a point of view toward virtual communities. *Computer-Mediated Communication*, 3(2). Online, available at: www.december.com/cmc/mag/1997/feb/wein.html.

Wellman, B. (1979). The community question: The intimate networks of East Yorkers. *American Journal of Sociology, 84*, 1201–1231.

Wellman, B., & Gulia, M. (1999). Virtual communities as communities: Net surfers don't ride alone. In M. A. Smith & P. Kollock (Eds.), *Communities in cyberspace* (pp. 167–194). London: Routledge.

Wellman, B., Carrington, P. J., & Hall, A. (1988). Networks as personal communities. In B. Wellman & S. D. Berkowitz (Eds.), *Social structure: A network approach* (pp. 130–184). Cambridge: Cambridge University Press.

Willson, M. A. (2006). *Technically together: Rethinking community within techno-society*. New York, NY: Peter Lang.

Wirth, L. (1938). Urbanism as a way of life. *American Journal of Sociology, 44*, 3–24.

Chapter 6

With a Little Help From My Friends

How Social Network Sites Affect Social Capital Processes

Nicole B. Ellison, Cliff Lampe,
Charles Steinfield, and Jessica Vitak

Introduction

In this chapter, we will describe two related strands of research—social capital gains and online/offline interaction patterns—to explicate the mechanisms by which social capital is generated and maintained on social network sites (SNSs). This chapter reviews a series of studies we have conducted investigating college undergraduates' use of Facebook, one of the most popular SNSs among undergraduate students in the United States. This body of research explores two primary questions. First, what are the social capital implications, if any, of Facebook use by students, specifically in relation to bridging and bonding social capital? Second, how is Facebook integrated into the daily communication practices of its users? Specifically, are users articulating existing relationships in Facebook, or are they using the site to discover and interact with strangers? We review extant literature examining these questions, and then summarize our studies over the last four years. Finally, we describe the mechanisms by which we believe these two sets of findings are related.

Facebook shares a set of characteristics with hundreds of other SNSs, defined as:

> web-based services that allow individuals to (1) construct a public or semi-public profile within a bounded system, (2) articulate a list of other users with whom they share a connection, and (3) view and traverse their list of connections and those made by others within the system.
>
> (boyd & Ellison, 2007, p. 211)

After creating a profile, SNS users typically add contacts (called "Friends" on Facebook) who are bi-directionally linked, meaning that both users must approve of the connection before it is valid. These Friends can usually see one another's full profile by default (although privacy settings are available to control who sees what).[1] Facebook facilitates communication among these network ties; it contains a suite of communication tools, such as instant messaging, wall posts, and comments, and allows users to share photos, short essays ("notes") and Web links with one another. Since its introduction in 2004, Facebook has been very popular among college under-graduates. The site is highly used by undergraduate students: among the 94% of students ages 18–24 who report using any SNSs, 94% use Facebook, compared with just 45% who report using MySpace (Salaway, Caruso, & Nelson, 2008).

This chapter focuses on college students' use of Facebook, both because it is deeply integrated into the daily communication practices of the popula-tion we study and because of the special role that SNSs play during this crit-ical time of life. Arnett (2000) argues that the period between the ages of 18 and 25, which he calls "emerging adulthood," is critical to an individual's social and psychological development. He writes, "Emerging adulthood is a time of life . . . when the scope of independent exploration of life's possibil-ities is greater for most people than it will be at any other period of the life course" (p. 469). It is also a time of transition, when young people are likely to be leaving their hometowns and established social networks for a new environment. Examining how they form new relationships and maintain old ones—and the role of SNSs like Facebook in this process—is critical for understanding how social capital is accumulated and maintained for this population.

Theoretical Frameworks: Online/Offline Communication and Social Capital

Online and Offline Communication

Like other communication technologies, Internet-enabled communication tools such as email allow users to reshape temporal and spatial constraints on communication. It should come as no surprise, then, that much of the early research on computer-mediated communication (CMC) focused on instances in which online tools were used to connect those who did not otherwise share time and space. Popular narratives and formative research on early online communities assumed that users of these systems would be connecting with others based on shared interests, as opposed to shared geography (Rheingold, 1993), thus producing communities that were sometimes limited to online communication. Often, these online connections resulted in face-to-face meetings, but when this happened, the directionality was *online* connections that resulted in *offline* meetings. For instance, Parks and Floyd (1996) report that one-third of their respondents later met their online correspondents face-to-face. As they write, "These findings imply that relationships that begin on line rarely stay there" (n.p.). Online-to-offline interaction is still a core part of many online contexts. For instance, online dating sites such as Match.com, which began gaining popularity in the mid-1990s, function to bring together individuals who have never met. Of course, in organizational and other settings, CMC tools such as email were used for communication among people who were co-located or had previous face-to-face interactions (an "offline-to-online" interaction pattern).

Because interaction patterns among individuals and the ways they employ face-to-face and mediated communication are complex, researchers face a challenging task when they attempt to assess and describe these practices. Many instances are not as clear-cut as two co-located colleagues who use instant messaging for quick exchanges during the day, or two strangers who encounter one another in an online gaming environment and then arrange to meet face-to-face. Designing measures for accurately assessing these interaction patterns is difficult for many reasons. Terminology is not widely agreed on (e.g., definitions of "online" and "offline"), and users may have different understandings of what they mean. Survey questions about "where" an individual first "met" a communication partner can be both ambiguous and leading. Additionally, the complex communication ecology many of us inhabit is not reflected by questions that assume "online" and "offline" to be dichotomous spaces—for instance, how would one categorize a situation in which someone uses information from a Facebook profile to initiate a face-to-face conversation? Because of the way in which Facebook is integrated into the complex communication ecologies of its users, it is critical that SNS researchers acknowledge and meet these measurement challenges.

There is some evidence that SNSs are more often used to articulate previously established relationships than to meet strangers. boyd and Ellison (2007) argue that the term "social network sites" reflects actual usage patterns, in that individuals typically use the sites to articulate and reflect offline social relationships, and are generally not trying to meet strangers on the site (as might be suggested by the term "social networking sites"). Pew data suggest that nearly all (91%) teens who use SNSs do so to connect with current friends (Lenhart & Madden, 2007), and other research generally supports this perception (e.g., Mayer & Puller, 2008).

In summary, although SNSs enable users to connect with strangers, this is not typically the norm, and more work is needed to develop instruments that capture nuances of hybrid (online/offline) interaction patterns and their impact on relationship development and maintenance.

Social Capital

Overview

Social capital as a theoretical framework is rooted in the work of Bourdieu (1985) and Coleman (1988), with subsequent development by Burt (1992), Putnam (1995, 2000), and Lin (2001), among others. Broadly conceived, social capital refers to the benefits that can be attained from connections between people through their social networks (Putnam, 2000). More specifically, it can be considered as "the aggregate of the actual or potential resources which are linked to possession of a durable network of more or less institutionalized relationships of mutual acquaintance and recognition" (Bourdieu, 1985, p. 248). Definitions and measurement of social capital consider the role of social structure (Burt, 2000; Coleman, 1988; Portes, 1998), social norms (Adler & Kwon, 2002; Putnam, 2000), trust (Burt, 2000; Putnam, 2000; Woolcock, 1998), reciprocity (Lin, 2001; Putnam, 2000; Woolcock, 1998), flow of information (Lin, 2001; Adler & Kwon, 2002), and solidarity (Putnam, 2000; Adler & Kwon, 2002). Definitions of social capital also vary in their focus on the substance, sources, or effects of social capital, as well as their focus on internal or external ties (Adler & Kwon, 2002). More recently, scholars have distinguished between offline social capital and online—or sociotechnical—capital (Resnick, 2001; Wellman & Gulia, 1999; Williams, 2006), based on the unique affordances online tools provide for communicating with a wide range of people.

Social capital evokes many dimensions of financial and human capital, but focuses on the relationships between individuals. Through this network of relationships, the individual in turn receives opportunities to obtain or use other forms of capital (Burt, 1992). Members of one's social network can be categorized according to the strength of the tie, which Granovetter (1973) defines as a combination of the amount of time, emotional intensity, intimacy, and reciprocity involved in the relationship. One component of network structure relates to the concepts of bridging and bonding social capital, each of which are associated with different kinds of ties and network structures. Putnam (2000) refers to bridging social capital as inclusive and better suited for information diffusion; it is created through exposure to heterogeneous networks, with the majority of connections representing weak ties. Bonding social capital, on the other hand, can be exclusive and aids in creating group solidarity. Bonding social capital is created among groups of strongly connected individuals such as one's family and closest friends. Whereas bridging social capital provides access to a wider range of information and diverse perspectives, bonding social capital is linked to social support and more substantive support, such as financial loans.

Granovetter (1973) argues that weak ties often serve as bridges, connecting otherwise disparate groups of individuals. Burt (1992) calls these gaps between groups "structural holes" and suggests that individuals whose networks span these holes are at an advantage because they have access to a more diverse set of information and can better control the flow of that information between groups, thus garnering more bridging social capital. As will be discussed below, the Internet provides individuals with increased opportunities to locate and interact with members outside of their network, subsequently increasing opportunities for bridging social capital outcomes.

The Internet's Impact on Social Capital

The Internet provides individuals with new ways to interact with members of their existing social networks and to make new connections through a variety of synchronous and asynchronous forms of communication, thus reshaping social networks and the ability of members to draw social capital from them. However, there has been a long-standing debate over whether the Internet plays a positive or negative role in people's social lives, relationships, sense of community and, subsequently, their social capital. Early ethnographic research on virtual communities portrayed the Internet as a space where individuals could overcome the constraints of space and time to form close and meaningful relationships with others who shared common interests (e.g., Baym, 1997; Rheingold, 1993; Wellman & Gulia, 1999). Empirical research has also found that the level of interaction over the Internet is positively related to indicators of social capital, such as generalized trust (Best & Krueger, 2006). Likewise, Hampton and Wellman (2002) found that Internet users were more connected to their community offline than non-users, as indicated by their greater knowledge of and interaction with their neighbors.

On the other hand, several researchers suggest the Internet may be having the opposite effect, isolating and alienating people from their communities, which would in turn negatively impact social capital. In an early longitudinal study of Internet users during their first one to two years online, Kraut, Patterson, Lundmark, Kiesler, Mukopadhyay, and Scherlis (1998) found small negative effects of Internet use on people's social involvement and psychological well-being; a follow-up study found that these effects dissipated over time, but that those with strong support networks experienced more benefits than those with weaker support networks (Kraut, Kiesler, Boneva, Cummings, Helgeson, & Crawford, 2002a). Nie (2001) argues that the Internet does not make people more sociable, as the types of people who use the Internet are already highly sociable, and that time spent using the Internet implies less time for face-to-face relationships. Although they primarily advocate that positive social outcomes are associated with Internet use, Wellman, Quan-Haase, Witte, and Hampton (2001) note that it may also reduce individuals' commitment to community.

A third perspective suggests that the Internet should not be defined in such extreme terms, but rather considered as a supplement to other forms of interaction. For example, in their study of technology use and interaction among members of a Toronto suburb, Hampton and Wellman (2002) found that the Internet did not replace other methods of communication, such as telephone or face-to-face interaction, but filled the gap when other methods of interaction were unavailable. Likewise, Wellman et al. (2001) found that the Internet neither increased nor decreased other forms of communication, and that it supplemented organizational and political participation. In other words, the Internet neither diminishes nor transforms social capital, but instead serves an additive role when combined with other methods of communication (Quan Haase & Wellman, 2004; Uslaner, 2000).

In line with this third approach to viewing social capital on the Internet, Resnick (2001) suggests the construct of sociotechnical capital as a subset of social capital in order to highlight the ways in which social and technical components "jointly influence the ability of people to act together" (p. 249). He points to six technological affordances that may affect social capital online, including the ability to: remove barriers to interaction such as distance and time; expand one's reach (e.g., sending an email to hundreds of recipients); restrict information flows via access controls, which may lower the risks of participation; manage dependencies (e.g., calendar programs); maintain a history of interactions (e.g., email archives); and reify roles or create a group identity through naming. A number of outcomes derived from these capabilities have the potential to enhance the individual's bridging social capital; for example, it may be easier to maintain relationships with members of one's social network with a smaller investment of time, provide coordination and support for large groups, and make new connections outside of one's social network through the Internet. As with Wellman et al.'s (2001) findings, these affordances appear to serve a supplemental role, working with other forms of communication to create and maintain social capital.

Resnick points to a need for new measures of sociotechnical capital, as traditional measures of social capital may not reflect the affordances of the technology. One example of this is Williams' (2006) Internet Social Capital Scales (ISCS), which measure bridging and bonding social capital outcomes in online and offline environments. Williams notes that there are many forms of online interaction which can often be in conjunction with offline interactions that occur in person or via other media, making it difficult to assess the role that the Internet plays in social capital development. He proposes new scales that explicitly measure social capital formation in both online and offline settings in order to better assess the tradeoffs between these two contexts.

Social Network Sites and Social Capital

One question emerging from Williams' (2006) research on online social capital measurement considers whether the Internet is more conducive to creating bridging or bonding social capital. He notes that because of the low cost of entry and relative anonymity in many online communities, the Internet may allow for greater bridging outcomes than do offline interactions. However, SNSs' unique features and uses may encourage both bridging and bonding outcomes. In contrast to the anonymous interactions between strangers on public forums, the majority of connections on SNSs comprise pre-existing relationships (Ellison, Steinfield, & Lampe, 2007). Furthermore, users are able to provide very detailed identity information in their profiles, which are rarely anonymous. SNSs provide for public displays of connections between users via Friend lists, which may help users expand their networks through shared connections (Donath & boyd, 2004).

While the ability to maintain pre-existing relationships may be a strong motivation for using SNSs, they also enable users to transform latent ties, or ties which are "technically possible but not yet activated socially" (Haythornthwaite, 2005, p. 137), into weak or strong ties. Latent ties arise whenever a new medium is introduced that allows for individuals to connect with each other. SNSs open up new pathways of communication between individuals who otherwise might not have the opportunity to interact with one another. The importance of transforming latent ties into weak ties is especially relevant for college students, who are also among the heaviest users of SNSs. For many students, the undergraduate experience is an opportunity to interact with more and different kinds of individuals than they might have encountered before college. SNS scholars suggest that technological tools such as SNSs may assist people in maintaining relationships with more individuals (e.g., Donath, 2007; Donath & boyd, 2004), as these sites simplify the process of communicating with and keeping updated on the lives of hundreds—even thousands—of "Friends." Maintaining a large network of weak ties, and especially bridging weak ties, has been shown to result in positive outcomes stemming from the increased access to a diverse set of information (Granovetter, 1983).

College students who use Facebook may reap the developmental benefits of this expanded social network (with more bridges to other networks) in the form of exposure to new and diverse ideas, information, and people. At the same time, SNSs may also supplement relationships between close friends by allowing for additional modes of communication, thus expanding bonding social capital. Ellison et al. (2007) found that intensity of Facebook use predicted bonding social capital, and 20% of the SNS users in one study of college undergraduates believed that their SNS use made them closer to their friends (Subrahmanyam, Reich, Waechter, & Espinoza, 2008). SNS research tends to focus on bridging outcomes over bonding outcomes, perhaps because SNSs' impact on bonding social capital is likely not as strong due to media multiplexity effects (Haythornthwaite, 2005). In other words, close friends are probably more likely to make use of multiple methods of interaction (e.g., face-to-face, phone, texting, Internet) to maintain their relationship than weak ties.

Ties vs. Friends in Social Capital and SNSs

On Facebook, all of a user's contacts are labeled as "Friends" and there is little opportunity within the standard profile for users to differentiate between close friends and casual acquaintances. This differs from other SNSs, such as MySpace, which enable users to demarcate their "top 8" contacts. In December 2007, Facebook introduced a feature which enabled users to group Friends into categories, but prior to this all contacts were undifferentiated: casual acquaintances, best friends, co-workers, romantic partners—all were labeled globally as "Friends." As Fono and Raynes-Goldie (2006) write:

> Our findings indicated that the understandings of friendship on the service were multiple, not just across users, but within individual understandings as well . . . it is often difficult for two users who both call each other a friend to know if they are talking about the same thing.
>
> (p. 94)

danah boyd (2006) similarly notes that a wide range of reasons exist for Friending, thus disputing the notion that users view all "Friends" as actual friends. Donath (2007) notes that the lack of explicit relationship definitions on SNSs is not necessarily a problem to be solved, and that oftentimes this ambiguity is preferred in that it can preserve face and reduce social discomfort. Skeptics have expressed concern about the vernacular of friendship that infuses the site, and the high number of friends reported on these sites is concerning to some. As Brian Boyd (2006) writes, "What does it mean, then, to be on someone's 'Buddy List,' or to be 'friended,' by contrast to what it means to be a friend? And will the rising generation be able to tell the difference?" (p. 125).

When considering Friendship and social capital on SNSs, it is important to note that the concept of social capital is not contingent upon close friendships and requires only that a connection exist between two individuals in a network. Some types of social capital, like bridging, are difficult to generate from close friends and depend on a heterogeneous set of ties in a social network. Hence, even though SNS users are most likely not close friends with all of their Friends, especially when connections can number in the hundreds or even thousands, these ties are likely to provide social capital benefits.

A Summary of Facebook Research at MSU

Online/Offline Communication and Facebook

Like many SNSs, Facebook provides users with features that support existing relationships as well as the ability to randomly browse one's "network" (those that share a geographical or institutional affiliation) and initiate contact. Some studies argue that relatively few Facebook connections begin online. Mayer and Puller (2008) found that only 1% of their sample reported relationships that exist purely online. Subrahmanyam et al. (2008), however, report that 73% of their participants only connected with people they knew in person—implying that more than one-quarter of respondents do connect with strangers. Pew data have shown that 44% of teens with a SNS profile report being contacted by someone who had no connection to themselves or their friends (Smith, 2007).

A series of studies at Michigan State University has investigated the issue of how connections in Facebook originate. Lampe, Ellison, and Steinfield (2006) conducted a survey of first-year undergraduates ($n = 1,210$) to determine their attitudes, reported behaviors, and perceived audience regarding Facebook. As this was early in Facebook's history, we were interested in probing the extent to which Facebook use adhered to a Rheingoldian (1993) narrative of online interaction in which online interactants were largely pseudonymous and used online tools to find others like them. Facebook was different in that it was rooted in a network structure, which grouped those who self-selected into geographical or institutional networks, used real names as a default, and employed a set of standardized and searchable profile fields. Lampe et al. (2006) found that students reported on Likert scales low agreement with statements like, "I use Facebook to meet new people" and "I use Facebook to find people to date." However, students reported high levels of agreement with statements like, "I use Facebook to keep in touch with old friends" and "I use Facebook to check out someone I met socially." In addition to these reported behaviors, respondents were asked about who they thought had looked at their profiles. People who were unlikely to share an offline connection with the respondent, such as strangers, the police, or university administrators were seen as unlikely to have looked at a profile. However, friends from high school, people from one's classes, and people one might have met at a party were all seen as likely to have looked at the respondent's profile. We interpreted these findings as support that undergraduate Facebook users were more likely to be connecting to people with whom they had a previous connection (usually because of a shared experience like a high school or class) than meeting new people based on shared interest.

Lampe et al. (2007) analyzed undergraduate profiles ($n = 30,773$) and found that Facebook profile fields that were hard to fake and that allowed users to create common ground in offline environments (e.g., hometown and high school vs. preferences like favorite books and movies) were most important in creating large networks of connections on the site. We interpreted this as suggesting that users were seeking cues about each other to create common ground, and the profile fields of Facebook reduced the cost of finding these commonalities between users. This suggests that Facebook users may be more likely to use online information to find others with whom they share some kind of offline connection, as opposed to finding others based on common interests like music or movies. In addition, it could be that simply knowing you are from the same town as someone else provides common context and reference points that create common ground, even if you have not previously interacted with that person in that context. Knowing that you have easy conversation topics like local landmarks or shared acquaintances or events may lower the barriers to future interaction.

The empirical question of how Facebook undergraduates used the site was probed further in Ellison et al. (2007). In this survey of a random sample of MSU undergraduates ($n = 286$), we used a simple measure of online to offline communication and offline to online communication, finding that our survey respondents engaged in significantly more Facebook use involving people with whom they shared an offline connection, such as an existing friend, a classmate, someone living near them, or someone they met socially (mean = 3.64 on a scale ranging from $1 =$ very unlikely to $5 =$ very likely), than use that involved meeting new people (mean = 1.97).

In a recent study, we used longitudinal data to explore changes in these patterns of interaction over time. Lampe, Ellison, and Steinfield (2008) surveyed random samples of MSU's undergraduate student population from 2006 through 2008 regarding their use of and attitudes toward Facebook. In each of the cross-sectional surveys, we found that respondents showed similar behaviors and attitudes over time. Specifically, in each year respondents reported low agreement with statements like, "I use Facebook to meet new people" or "I use Facebook to find people to date" and high agreement with statements like, "I use Facebook to keep in touch with old friends" and "I use Facebook to check out people I meet socially." Also, the sense of audience for one's profile remained constant. Peers, such as friends from high school and people in classes, were seen as likely to have viewed the respondent's profile, and non-peers like professors and law-enforcement were seen as unlikely to have done so. Between 2006 and 2007 we saw strong increases in numbers of friends and number of minutes per day on Facebook, as well as increases in reports of satisfaction with Facebook. We attribute at least part of this increase to the News

Feed, which reduced the cost of maintaining large, dispersed networks of friends by providing users with a continually updating stream of their Friends' actions on the site. Hence, the evidence from our studies strongly supports the notion that Facebook is used predominantly to articulate connections that have some basis offline.

The Role of Facebook in Generating Social Capital

A second prominent theme of our research has been the social capital implications of Facebook use. We've conducted a series of studies examining how Facebook use relates to various forms of social capital among students, attempting to tease out whether the effect is specifically related to Facebook, or Internet use in general, as well as whether the evidence supports a causal explanation or is more consistent with the argument that those having more social capital simply have more reason to use Facebook.

Ellison et al. (2007) assessed levels of social capital and Facebook use in an undergraduate student population, finding that students' Facebook use was significantly related to their levels of social capital. We examined three kinds of social capital—bridging, bonding, and maintained. Bridging social capital, as described above, describes the benefits associated with weak ties, such as access to novel information, and was measured using five items derived from Williams (2006), as well as three additional items intended to assess outcomes of bridging social capital in the MSU context. Bonding social capital is associated with close ties and was measured using five items developed and validated by Williams (2006). Maintained social capital was assessed using an original scale, which included items such as, "I'd be able to find information about a job or internship from a high school acquaintance" and "If I needed to, I could ask a high school acquaintance to do a small favor for me." These items were constructed in light of pilot interview data that suggested one of the primary uses of Facebook for undergraduates was keeping in touch with people from high school.

Ellison et al. (2007) report regression analyses showing that, after controlling for demographic variables and general Internet use, Facebook Intensity[2] emerged as a significant predictor of all three forms of social capital, with the largest effect demonstrated on bridging social capital. We also found an interesting interaction effect with self-esteem, such that those with low self-esteem seemed to accrue more bridging social capital from their Facebook use than those with higher self-esteem.

This question was revisited, using panel data, in order to gain more insight into the directionality of the relationship between Facebook use and social capital (Steinfield, Ellison, & Lampe, 2008). Based on a panel of 92 cases surveyed in April of 2006 and again in April 2007, we investigated the lagged relationships between Facebook Intensity (FBI) and bridging social capital. The within-year relationships remained strong from one year to the next ($R_{FBI\_2006-BSC\_2006} = 0.46$; $R_{FBI\_2007-BSC\_2007} = 0.35$), but these do not reveal directionality. The difference in lagged relationships was telling, however ($R_{FBI\_2006-BSC\_2007} = 0.48$; $R_{BSC\_2006-FBI\_2007} = 0.14$). Those with greater social capital in 2006 did not necessarily use Facebook more intensively a year later, while those who used Facebook more intensively in 2006 reported higher bridging social capital a year later. These results held up in lagged regression analyses, even after controlling for demographic factors and general Internet use.

These two studies establish an empirical relationship between Facebook use and social capital. A further finding in both studies was the heightened impact of Facebook use on bridging social capital for students who scored lower on self-esteem scales. Interaction analyses in both studies revealed that those lower in self-esteem reported greater benefit in terms of bridging social capital from their Facebook use than those with higher self-esteem. Moreover, this effect held up over time in the second study. This suggests to us that the affordances of a SNS like Facebook may be helping those who might otherwise have difficulty connecting with diverse others.

Communication Patterns and Social Capital

In order to better assess the relationship between online/offline interaction patterns and outcomes of use—specifically social capital—we attempted to develop a series of scales that measured how various individuals used the site to learn more about others. In Ellison, Steinfield, and Lampe (2009), we report on survey data ($n = 450$) that explicitly address the question of how undergraduates are using the site, and the social capital implications of these communication practices. The instrument includes a series of items asking respondents to indicate how likely they were to engage in a range of possible behaviors (browse the Facebook profile, contact via Facebook, add as a Facebook friend, and meet face-to-face) with three types of individuals: a total stranger, someone from one's residence hall, and a close friend. Our instrument also included several items gauging the extent to which Facebook was used for various social purposes, derived from items used in Ellison et al. (2007). Through factor analysis, we identified three distinct sets of behaviors:

- *Initiating*: This scale assessed the use of Facebook to meet strangers or make new friends. Items include all four of the online/offline behaviors (browsing, contacting, Friending, and meeting face-to-face) in relation to MSU strangers, as well as one other item, "I use Facebook to meet new people."

- *Maintaining*: This scale refers to the use of Facebook to maintain existing close ties. It includes all four of the online/offline behaviors in relation to close friends.
- *Information-seeking*: This scale measures use of the site for learning more about people with whom the user has some offline connection. It includes three items about how the site is used ("I have used Facebook to check out someone I met socially"; "I use Facebook to learn more about other people in my classes"; "I use Facebook to learn more about other people living near me") and one item probing the likelihood of browsing the profile of someone in their residence hall.

With a mean of 1.87 on a five-point Likert scale (where $1 =$ very unlikely and $5 =$ very likely), initiating was the least common strategy reported by respondents, while maintaining, with a mean of 4.67, was the highest, thus providing additional support for earlier work that suggested using the site to connect with existing or latent ties was more common than using it to meet strangers. Notably, regression analyses revealed that only the information-seeking connection strategy was a significant predictor of bridging and bonding social capital. Additionally, for this work we asked about what percentage of the respondents' total Facebook "Friends" were actual friends. The number of "actual" friends on the site was predictive of the existence of social capital, but the total number of friends was not. These findings suggest that individuals who used Facebook to discover information about latent ties, rather than engage in indiscriminate "friend collecting," were more likely to accrue social capital from their use of the site. We will continue to explore these relationships in future work.

Mechanisms of Social Capital Generation in Social Network Sites

Taken as a whole, our research suggests two trends. First, use of Facebook by undergraduate students in our samples is associated with higher levels of bridging and bonding social capital, and Facebook use appears to precede these gains in social capital, suggesting a causal relationship. Second, users are more likely to use the site to connect with existing friends, distant acquaintances, or latent ties than they are to use the site to meet new people. Additionally, using the site to research or find out about people with whom they have some kind of offline connection (but don't already know well) is a significant predictor of social capital. In this final section, we describe the mechanism by which we believe these sets of findings are related.

As Burt (2005) argues, social capital is embedded in the structure of social networks and the location of individuals within these structures. Social networks are not all shaped alike, and the shape of the network affects the promulgation of social capital. Social networks that are comprised of small clusters of people who all know one another are going to accrue different benefits than networks where individuals have more diffuse connections with a large set of distant ties. We believe the key way in which Facebook serves to support the generation of social capital is through reshaping the social network of individuals and by lowering the costs of communicating with (and thus contributing to and extracting benefits from) this social network.

One way of conceptualizing the effect of Facebook use on social capital is by considering the relationship between physical proximity and relationship development. Research on proximity has long suggested that proximity between two individuals increases the chances that a relationship will form.[3] Friendships often form based on where one lives, works, attends school, or spends leisure time, in part because there are more opportunities for communication (Kraut, Fussell, Brennan, & Siegel, 2002b; Neckerman, 1996) and because proximity decreases the effort required to initiate a relationship (Kraut et al., 2002b). Facebook extends these proximity-based social processes in two ways. First, it allows those who formed a relationship through physical proximity, but subsequently lost that proximity, to maintain the relationship. High school students moving to college, people shifting jobs, or families moving are all examples of this. Second, Facebook can reinforce relationships formed through proximity that would be too ephemeral to survive otherwise. For example, two students who meet through a class may connect for the duration of the class because of the forced proximity. However, when that proximity is removed, the relationship may not survive the sudden increased cost of maintenance. Facebook makes it easy to keep lightweight contact with each other even when the benefits of proximity are no longer available.[4]

Facebook enables individuals to maintain a larger set of weak ties. As described by Donath (2007) and Donath and boyd (2004), SNSs can be "social supernets" in that they increase the number of weak ties a user can maintain, thus expanding the range of available information sources. This kind of social network, which consists of casual acquaintances and close friends, is well suited for supporting ad-hoc advice-seeking. Larger heterogeneous networks of strong and weak ties are more likely to include diverse individuals who share a tangential connection, but can also serve as resources for new information. Additionally, some SNSs enable "friends of friends" to interact, thus exposing users to an even more diverse set of weak ties. In addition to the access to new information and perspectives these weak ties may provide, learning how to manage, speak to, and engage with the conflicting opinions that diverse others represent is a valuable skill set which may result in social capital outcomes (Burt, 2009).

Facebook allows individuals to make ephemeral connections persistent. In our everyday lives, we frequently encounter people with whom we might want to reconnect at some point in the future, but often the social or logistical barriers to do so are too high. The potential benefits of staying in touch are overwhelmed by the costs of coordination, making it unlikely that the connection persists. In the professional realm, proximity in workspaces leads to successful collaborations because repeat chance encounters encourage individuals to develop common ground and thus nurture a nascent relationship (Kraut et al., 2002b). But for chance encounters, especially when there are no immediate and significant perceived benefits, we often don't make the effort to coordinate re-connecting once the encounter is over. For example, participants at a workshop, members of a club, students in a class, or parents at a playground are all examples of connections that in the face-to-face context, bounded by limitations of proximity, are ephemeral and often lost.

SNSs can help ameliorate this problem. Using SNSs, a profile can be located and reconnections made possible. SNSs facilitate interaction, both at that moment and (assuming a friend request is initiated) in the future. The connection between two individuals can be digitally reconstituted at any time, should the need or desire arise. When both parties use an SNS to connect, the coordination costs become lower because these tools enable active (e.g., messaging) and passive (e.g., status updates) communication with very little effort.

Facebook lowers the cost of maintaining (or re-engaging) weak ties. A similar process occurs when we use SNSs to connect with people from our past, a dominant strategy in SNS use. For example, college students often use Facebook to maintain contact with high school friends. Increasingly, older populations coming to Facebook reconnect with high school and college friends with whom they've lost touch, but have found again using the features of Facebook. These acquaintances and friends or contacts from the past are likely to be different from us and thus provide us with valuable new information, ideas, and perspectives. The affordances of SNSs, namely the ability to easily track changes in the lives of these individuals and to inform them of one's own activities, helps with relationship maintenance and lowers the barriers for future contact. By being connected to people less likely to be like us, and by maintaining lightweight (weak) social ties with those individuals, opportunities to generate bridging social capital increase.

Facebook profiles can lower the barriers to initial interaction and facilitate formation of common ground. The fields included in the profile vary from SNS to SNS, but typically include the ability to display photographs, list contact information, and to describe personal characteristics such as music preferences and other taste indicators (boyd & Ellison, 2007; Liu, 2007). Access to personal identity information can support relationship-formation. For instance, in the workplace, profile information can help people engage in "people sensemaking," the process of understanding "who someone is and to determine how and why that user should interact with someone" (DiMicco & Millen, 2008, p. 1). Personal information such as updates about family members or travel plans may spark conversations, replicating the spontaneous exchanges of information associated with proximity (Kraut et al., 2002b).

The identity information in the profile assists individuals in finding common ground and thus facilitates communication and coordination processes (Olson & Olson, 2001). Clark and Brennan (1991) write that individuals "cannot even begin to coordinate on content without assuming a vast amount of shared information or common ground—that is, mutual knowledge, mutual beliefs, and mutual assumptions. . . . All collective actions are built on common ground and its accumulation" (p. 127). Among distributed individuals, the lack of visual cues can make establishing common ground more challenging (Kiesler & Cummings, 2002); for these individuals, profile content can help broker interactions, reduce friction, and facilitate more effective communication processes. Previous scholarship on SNSs suggests that profile information in Facebook may help users find common ground with one another (DiMicco & Millen, 2007; Lampe et al., 2007). SNS profiles are less likely to contain the deceptive self-presentation sometimes found in other online contexts, such as online dating sites (Toma, Hancock, & Ellison, 2008), because the visible social network serves as a warrant for users' profile content (Walther, Van Der Heide, Hamel, & Shulman, 2009) and increases the trustworthiness of self-presentation in SNSs (Donath, 2007).

Facebook makes it easier to seek information and support from one's social network, and to provide these resources to others. Communication between Facebook Friends is facilitated by the site, and the transaction costs (Williamson, 1981) associated with online and offline interaction are lowered due to the communication features of the site and because offline contact information is often included in profiles. It is unlikely that individuals use Facebook to discover large numbers of new close friends, but the site effectively facilitates the ability to ask for (and receive) emotional support from strong and weak ties and supports acts of "social grooming" (Donath, 2007; Tufekci, 2008). In our own use of Facebook, we've seen individuals suffering from chronic health problems update their status with explicit statements marking pain or depression, and receiving public comments of support and sympathy (and, most likely, private notes as well).

Future Research Directions

In the future, we plan to extend this line of inquiry to other populations and contexts, in order to discover how generalizable these findings are. Preliminary work suggests that social capital benefits can result in work settings outside the university. In a survey of IBM employees using Beehive, an internal

SNS, we found that greater SNS use was associated with such outcomes as greater bonding social capital, more access to both new people and expertise in the company, a greater willingness to contribute to the company in terms of citizenship, and a stronger interest in global connections (Steinfield, DiMicco, Ellison, & Lampe, 2009). Recent Pew survey data reinforce the notion that SNS use is associated with more diverse social networks among the general U.S. population (Hampton, Sessions, Her, & Rainie, 2009). In short, while many of the practices and outcomes we've identified are likely to be seen in other populations, more work needs to be done to understand how these social capital mechanisms operate among older populations and younger people outside the college undergraduate population.

We also plan to refine our measurement of social capital and communication practices. Social capital is notoriously hard to measure, and while our scales are reliable, they are limited in that they assess psychological orientation and feelings, not actual outcomes of use. We plan to develop additional scales that include other dimensions of social capital. Additionally, we plan on using other methods for assessing social capital that are based on behavioral data, such as content analysis of actual site postings that display characteristics of social capital in action (e.g., requests for advice or assistance). Analysis of server-level data is another necessary step for making claims about the extent to which Facebook or other SNSs support social capital and the mechanisms by which this might happen.

Another area we intend to explore is the measurement of social ties. There is a range of relationships that are currently enacted on SNSs, and we need to develop measures to capture these nuances and go beyond notions of weak and strong ties. Our "information-seeking" strategy may be the first step in understanding the ways in which latent ties are exploited on these sites, but these variables should be subjected to more rigorous testing. For instance, because we didn't include measures of offline, traditional information-seeking in our instrument, we cannot rule out the possibility that individuals who score higher on our Facebook information-seeking measures also engage in this activity in other contexts, and that this, rather than Facebook-specific behavior, is responsible for the social capital changes we have observed. Future research should address these limitations.

Finally, a promising line of future research could explore the ways in which specific features and the design of SNSs affect social capital and other outcomes. Friendship in Facebook is bi-directional (both parties must agree), whereas other sites enable relationships that are asymmetrical. For example, Twitter enables individuals to "follow" others who may not follow them. While this design may encourage individuals to access content from a broader network (thus increasing bridging social capital), it may have implications for the ways in which reciprocity norms are enacted if information flow is one-directional. One hypothesis is that greater use of Twitter can build bridging social capital due to the increased exposure to new information, but would be less likely to impact bonding social capital. Hence the design of the site may result in different types of relational interaction, and subsequent social capital outcomes. More research is needed into the way in which design features, such as asymmetrical ties, affect social capital outcomes.

Conclusion

We do not mean to suggest that all SNS activity is positive or results in social capital. There are potential negative outcomes of many of the processes and features we mention above. For instance, personal information about others may be used to broker productive interaction, but it could also reinforce existing stereotypes, making them more intractable, or may be misused by marketing agents or used for nefarious purposes such as stalking, bullying, and identity theft. There are many who may not be taking advantage of the opportunities provided by these sites, as has been illustrated by work on digital inequities (Hargittai, 2008).

Overall, however, we believe there is potential for positive social outcomes resulting from SNS use, and Facebook is a tool that facilitates specific types of connections between people that can generate social capital. The technical and social affordances of these sites allow users to maintain broader, more diverse social networks, keep social ties they may have lost in other situations, and interact with a diverse set of contacts using online tools. These outcomes of SNS use will have benefits we can only guess at in the long run, but already we've seen positive effects on social capital among both university students and workers in an enterprise setting (Steinfield et al., 2009). SNSs are continuously reshaping our social networks and the communication practices we use to maintain them, and thus constitute a vibrant, important, and challenging context for studying communication practices and their social capital outcomes.

Notes

1. Following boyd and Ellison (2007), we capitalize Friends when we are referring to online connections in order to distinguish them from colloquial notions of traditional friendship.
2. The Facebook Intensity measure (Ellison et al., 2007) combines psychological and usage items in order to assess how integrated Facebook is into the daily routines of a user and other indications of psychological affiliation. FBI consists of the following six items as well as number of friends and daily minutes on the site:

   • Facebook is part of my everyday activity.
   • I am proud to tell people I'm on Facebook.
   • Facebook has become part of my daily routine.
   • I feel out of touch when I haven't logged on to Facebook for a while.

- I feel I am part of the Facebook community.
- I would be sorry if Facebook shut down.

3. Verbrugge (1977) notes that spatial proximity is one of the likely prerequisites of friendship formation among adults. Similarly, research on friendship patterns among adolescents has reaffirmed the important role of proximity in shaping these social relationships (Neckerman, 1996) and campus residential location affects friendship formation patterns among college students (Foster, 2005).

4. Other SNSs may function as a kind of proxy for proximity because, like shared spaces, they allow individuals to come together based on shared interests or demographics. SNSs like BlackPlanet and AsianAvenue have long been places where individuals with shared cultural backgrounds gather. Sites like Ning now allow for the creation of "micro-SNSs," where people with shared interests ranging from trout fishing to band appreciation to alumni groups can gather. The ability to include interests and characteristics in the SNS profile may allow for a type of "proximity" that also extends the physical environment and enables distributed groups to form. Although our research on Facebook suggests that it is not typically used to make connections purely on shared interest, other SNSs have different social and technical features that may promote these kinds of formations.

References

Adler, P. S., & Kwon, S.-W. (2002). Social capital: Prospects for a new concept. *Academy of Management Review, 27*, 17–40.

Arnett, J. J. (2000). Emerging adulthood: A theory of development from the late teens through the twenties. *American Psychologist, 55*, 469–480.

Baym, N. K. (1997). Interpreting soap operas and creating community: Inside an electronic fan culture. In S. Kiesler (Ed.), *Culture of the Internet* (pp. 103–120). Mahweh, NJ: Lawrence Erlbaum.

Best, S. J., & Krueger, B. S. (2006). Online interactions and social capital. *Social Science Computer Review, 24*, 395–410.

Bourdieu, P. (1985). The forms of capital. In J. G. Richardson (Ed.), *Handbook of theory and research for the sociology of education* (pp. 241–258). New York, NY: Greenwood.

Boyd, B. (2006). The Dotcomrade: The many faces of online friendship. *The New Atlantis, 14*.

boyd, d. (2006). Friends, Friendsters, and MySpace Top 8: Writing community into being on social network sites. *First Monday, 11*(12).

boyd, d., & Ellison, N. (2007). Social network sites: Definition, history, and scholarship. *Journal of Computer-Mediated Communication, 13*, 210–230.

Burt, R. S. (1992). *Structural holes: The social structure of competition.* Cambridge, MA: Harvard University Press.

Burt, R. S. (2000). The network structure of social capital. In B. M. Staw & R. I. Sutton (Eds.), *Research in organizational behavior* (vol. 22, pp. 345–423). Greenwich, CT: JAI Press.

Burt, R. S. (2005). *Brokerage and closure: An introduction to social capital.* Oxford: Oxford University Press.

Burt, R. S. (2009). *Neighbor networks: Competitive advantage local and personal*. Oxford: Oxford University Press.

Clark, H. H., & Brennan, S. E. (1991). Grounding in communication. In L. B. Resnick, J. M. Levine, & S. D. Teasley (Eds.), *Perspectives on socially shared cognition* (pp. 127–149). Washington, DC: American Psychological Association.

Coleman, J. S. (1988). Social capital in the creation of human capital. *The American Journal of Sociology, 94*, 95–120.

DiMicco, J. M., & Millen, D. R. (2007). Identity management: Multiple presentations of self in Facebook. In *Proceedings of the 2007 International ACM Conference on Supporting Group Work* (pp. 383–386). New York, NY: ACM.

DiMicco, J. M., & Millen, D. R. (2008). *People sensemaking with social network sites*. Paper presented at the Sensemaking Workshop, CHI '08, Florence, Italy, April.

Donath, J. (2007). Signals in social supernets. *Journal of Computer-Mediated Communication, 13*, 231–251.

Donath, J. S., & boyd, d. (2004). Public displays of connection. *BT Technology Journal, 22*(4), 71–82.

Ellison, N. B., Steinfield, C., & Lampe, C. (2007). The benefits of Facebook "friends": Exploring the relationship between college students' use of online social networks and social capital. *Journal of Computer-Mediated Communication, 12*, 1143–1168.

Ellison, N. B., Steinfield, C., & Lampe, C. (2009). *Connection strategies: Patterns of social network use on campus and their social capital implications*. Paper presented at the annual meeting of the American Sociological Association, San Francisco, CA.

Fono, D., & Raynes-Goldie, K. (2006). Hyperfriends and beyond: Friendship and social norms on LiveJournal. In M. Consalvo & C. Haythornthwaite (Eds.), *Internet research annual Volume 4: Selected papers from the Association of Internet Researchers Conference* (pp. 91–103). New York, NY: Peter Lang.

Foster, G. (2005). Making friends: A nonexperimental analysis of social pair formation. *Human Relations, 58*, 1443–1465.

Granovetter, M. (1973). The strength of weak ties. *American Journal of Sociology, 78*, 1360–1380.

Granovetter, M. (1983). The strength of weak ties: A network theory revisited. *Sociological Theory, 1*, 201–233.

Hampton, K. N., & Wellman, B. (2002). The not so global village of Netville. In B. Wellman & C. Haythornthwaite (Eds.), *The Internet and everyday life* (pp. 345–371). Oxford, UK: Blackwell.

Hampton, K., Sessions, L., Her, E. J., & Rainie, L. (2009). Social isolation and new technology: How the Internet and mobile phones impact Americans' social networks. Pew Internet & American Life Project.

Hargittai, E. (2008). The digital reproduction of inequality. In D. Grusky (Ed.), *Social stratification* (pp. 936–944). Boulder, CO: Westview.

Haythornthwaite, C. (2005). Social networks and Internet connectivity effects. *Information, Communication & Society, 8*, 125–147.

Kiesler, S., & Cummings, J. N. (2002). What do we know about proximity in work groups? A legacy of research on physical distance. In P. Hinds & S. Kiesler (Eds.), *Distributed work* (pp. 57–80). Cambridge, MA: MIT Press.

Kraut, R. E., Fussell, S. R., Brennan, S. E., & Siegel, J. (2002b). Understanding effects of proximity on collaboration: Implications for technologies to support remote collaborative work. In P. J. Hinds & S. Kiesler (Eds.), *Distributed work* (pp. 137–161). Cambridge, MA: MIT Press.

Kraut, R., Kiesler, S., Boneva, B., Cummings, J., Helgeson, V., & Crawford, A. (2002a). Internet paradox revisited. *Journal of Social Issues, 58*, 49–74.

Kraut, R., Patterson, M., Lundmark, V., Kiesler, S., Mukopadhyay, T., & Scherlis, W. (1998). Internet paradox. A social technology that reduces social involvement and psychological well-being? *American Psychologist, 53*, 1017–1031.

Lampe, C., Ellison, N., & Steinfield, C. (2006). A Face(book) in the crowd: Social searching vs. social browsing. In *Proceedings of the 2006 20th Anniversary Conference on Computer Supported Cooperative Work* (pp. 167–170). New York, NY: ACM.

Lampe, C., Ellison, N., & Steinfield, C. (2007). A familiar face(book): Profile elements as signals in an online social network. In *Proceedings of the SIGCHI conference on human factors in computing systems* (pp. 435–444). New York, NY: ACM.

Lampe, C., Ellison, N. B., & Steinfield, C. (2008). Changes in use and perception of Facebook. In *Proceedings of the ACM 2008 Conference on Computer Supported Cooperative Work* (pp. 721–730). New York, NY: ACM.

Lenhart, A., & Madden, M. (2007). Social networking websites and teens. Pew Internet & American Life Project.

Lin, N. (2001). Building a network theory of social capital. In N. Lin, K. S. Cook, & R. S. Burt (Eds.), *Social capital: Theory and research* (pp. 3–29). New York, NY: Aldine de Gruyter.

Liu, H. (2007). Social network profiles as taste performances. *Journal of Computer-Mediated Communication, 13*, 252–275.

Mayer, A., & Puller, S. L. (2008). The old boy (and girl) network: Social network formation on university campuses. *Journal of Public Economics, 92*, 329–347.

Neckerman, H. J. (1996). The stability of social groups in childhood and adolescence: The role of the classroom social environment. *Social Development, 5*(2), 131–145.

Nie, N. H. (2001). Sociability, interpersonal relations, and the Internet. *American Behavioral Scientist, 45*, 420–435.

Olson, G. M., & Olson, J. S. (2001). Distance matters. In J. Carroll (Ed.), *HCI in the New Millennium* (pp. 139–179). New York, NY: Addison-Wesley.

Parks, M. R., & Floyd, K. (1996). Making friends in cyberspace. *Journal of Computer-Mediated Communication, 1*(4).

Portes, A. (1998). Social capital: Its origins and applications in modern sociology. *Annual Review of Sociology, 24*, 1–24.

Putnam, R. D. (1995). Bowling alone: America's declining social capital. *Journal of Democracy, 6*, 65–78.

Putnam, R. (2000). *Bowling alone: The collapse and revival of American community*. New York, NY: Simon & Schuster.

Quan-Haase, A., & Wellman, B. (2004). How does the Internet affect social capital? In M. Huysman & V. Wulf (Eds.), *Social capital and information technology* (pp. 113–135). Cambridge, MA: MIT Press.

Resnick, P. (2001). Beyond bowling together: Socio-technical capital. In J. Carroll (Ed.), *HCI in the new millennium* (pp. 647–672). New York, NY: Addison-Wesley.

Rheingold, H. (1993). *The virtual community: Homesteading on the electronic frontier*. Cambridge, MA: MIT Press.

Salaway, G., Caruso, J. B., & Nelson, M. R. (2008). *The ECAR study of undergraduate students and information technology, 2008*. Educause Center for Applied Research.

Smith, A. (2007). Teens and online stranger contact. Pew Internet & American Life Project.

Steinfield, C., Ellison, N. B., & Lampe, C. (2008). Social capital, self-esteem, and use of online social network sites: A longitudinal analysis. *Journal of Applied Developmental Psychology, 29*, 434–445.

Steinfield, C., DiMicco, J. M., Ellison, N. B., & Lampe, C. (2009). Bowling online: Social networking and social capital within the organization. In *Proceedings of the Fourth International Conference on Communities and Technologies* (pp. 245–254). New York, NY: ACM.

Subrahmanyam, K., Reich, S., Waechter, N., & Espinoza, G. (2008). Online and offline social networks: Use of social networking sites by emerging adults. *Journal of Applied Developmental Psychology, 29*, 420–433.

Toma, C. L., Hancock, J. T., & Ellison, N. B. (2008). Separating fact from fiction: An examination of deceptive self-presentation in online dating profiles. *Personality and Social Psychology Bulletin, 34*, 1023–1036.

Tufekci, Z. (2008). Grooming, gossip, Facebook and MySpace: What can we learn about these sites from those who won't assimilate? *Information, Communication & Society, 11*, 544–564.

Uslaner, E. M. (2000). Social capital and the Net. *Communications of the ACM, 43*, 60–64.

Verbrugge, L. M. (1977). The structure of adult friendship choices. *Social Forces, 56*, 577–597.

Walther, J. B., Van der Heide, B., Hamel, L. M., & Shulman, H. C. (2009). Self-generated versus other-generated statements and impressions in computer-mediated communication. *Communication Research, 36*, 229–253.

Wellman, B., & Gulia, M. (1999). Net surfers don't ride alone: Virtual communities as communities. In P. Kollock & M. Smith (Eds.), *Communities and cyberspace* (pp. 167–194). New York, NY: Routledge.

Wellman, B., Quan-Haase, A., Witte, J., & Hampton, K. (2001). Does the Internet increase, decrease, or supplement social capital? *American Behavioral Scientist, 45*, 436–455.

Williams, D. (2006). On and off the 'Net: Scales for social capital in an online era. *Journal of Computer-Mediated Communication, 11*, 593–628.

Williamson, O. E. (1981). The economics of organization: The transaction cost approach. *American Journal of Sociology, 87*, 548–577.

Woolcock, M. (1998). Social capital and economic development: Toward a theoretical synthesis and policy framework. *Theory and Society, 27*, 151–208.

Chapter 7

From Dabblers to Omnivores

A Typology of Social Network Site Usage[1]

Eszter Hargittai and Yu-li Patrick Hsieh

Introduction

Social network sites (SNSs) have become some of the most popular online destinations in recent years (comScore, 2009) and accordingly have started to attract the attention of academic researchers (see boyd & Ellison, 2007, for a review of related literature, as well as other chapters in this volume). Despite the upsurge in related work, most current investigations tend to look at SNS usage as an either-or phenomenon by focusing on the use of just one such site or, alternatively, investigating the use of any such site at any level of engagement (e.g., Jones, Millermaier, Goya-Martinez, & Schuler, 2008; Ross, Orr, Sisic, Arseneault, Simmering, & Orr, 2009; Steinfield, Ellison, & Lampe, 2008; Tong, Van Der Heide, Langwell, & Walther, 2008). But is it justifiable to assume that there is no difference among users in intensity of their SNS usage or that such variation is inconsequential for questions exploring the implications of SNS uses? It is this gap in the literature that this chapter addresses both theoretically and empirically. We put forward a typology of SNS usage that takes into consideration both frequency and diversity of SNS uses, the combination of which we refer to as "SNS use intensity." We then apply this framework to an empirical example of SNS usage intensity in a community.

How do users differ in their engagement with SNSs? Are there systematic differences among frequent and occasional users of such sites? Is there a difference among those who are loyal to one SNS only compared to those who are actively involved with several? The lack of data on details of SNS usage has made it difficult for researchers to ask such nuanced questions about this topic. Here, thanks to a unique data set based on a survey administered to a diverse group of young adults with sufficiently detailed information about their SNS uses, we are able to explore answers to these questions. Findings suggest that intensity of SNS use varies among the group. While some people use only one site and do so only occasionally, others use one SNS often while yet others engage with numerous sites regularly. Moreover, level of engagement is not randomly distributed across the sample. Rather, a person's gender, context of Internet use and online experiences are all associated with level of SNS use intensity. The results suggest the importance of more nuanced approaches to the study of SNS uses than has been traditionally the case.

Research on Social Network Site Uses

Social network sites have become some of the most popular online services since the early 2000s (comScore, 2009). Users create an online profile on these sites by listing personal information and interests, linking up with other users of the site, and sharing, often daily, updates about their thoughts and activities with those in their networks (boyd & Ellison, 2007). Given their significant rise in popularity, it is not surprising that these sites and how people use them has attracted much scholarly attention in recent years. Several papers were published in a special issue of the *Journal of Computer-Mediated Communication* in 2007 dedicated to investigating various aspects of SNSs. Its editors, boyd and Ellison (2007), review early scholarship in this domain, identifying four main research areas: (1) impression management, friendship perform- ance, and identity construction; (2) networks and network structure; (3) online/offline social networks and social capital; and (4) concerns about privacy. This body of work finds that many people who use SNSs have started to integrate them into their everyday lives as a common daily practice. Con- sequently, SNS use may start to challenge some existing social conventions such as approaches to privacy, the way some people construct their self- identity, and how people interact with one another in their daily lives. Accord- ingly, it is important to have a better understanding of the possible variation in the extent to which different people use such sites for an appreciation of how their different uses may influence social practices.

In the past few years, there has been continued rapid growth in SNS research exploring earlier questions in more detail, asking new questions, and doing so through the use of an increasingly diverse set of methodologies. In studies of computer-mediated communication (CMC), some scholars have employed various perspectives to conceptualize and empirically investigate impression management and identity construction on SNSs (e.g., Goodings, Locke, & Brown, 2007; Walther, Van Der Heide, Hamel, & Shulman, 2009; Walther, Van Der Heide, Kim, Westerman, & Tong, 2008; Zhao, Grasmuck, & Martin, 2008). For example, Walther and colleagues found that the content on one's Facebook friends' profiles rather than the content on one's own profile affects how others perceive a user on Facebook. Empirical analyses of profiles on MySpace (Goodings, Locke, & Brown, 2007) and Facebook (Zhao, Grasmuck, & Martin, 2008) have found that, due to some relatively unique features of SNSs compared to previous online spaces, the practices of identity construction on them are different from anonymous online environments. Unlike in some other online spaces, on SNSs, users' identities are often anchored in physical proximities, institutions, and shared personal relationships in daily life, thereby often mirroring offline aspects of people's lives.

Researchers have also started to look at the properties of Facebook users' friendship networks and their implications (e.g., Lewis, Kaufman, Gonzalez, Wimmer, & Christakis, 2008; Seder & Oishi, 2009; Tong et al., 2008). For example, in their experimental study of online impression formation, Tong and colleagues found a complex non-linear relationship between the total number of friends on an individual's profile (i.e., network size) and the person's perceived attractiveness and perceived extraversion. Racial and ethnic homogeneity of personal networks on these sites is another question that has attracted scholarly attention. Researchers have found that White Facebook users may have more ethnically and racially homogeneous friendship networks than others on the site (Lewis et al., 2008; Seder & Oishi, 2009).

Some scholars have directly addressed moral panics introduced in mainstream media about the possible detrimental consequences of using SNSs (Bahney, 2006; Hope, 2009; Leake & Warren, 2009; Nussbaum, 2007; Roush, 2006). Such academic research tends to suggest that empirical evidence rarely supports overarching fears about the social and psychological implications of using such sites (Hinduja & Patchin, 2008; Jones et al., 2008; Livingstone, 2008; Pasek, more, & Hargittai, 2009). Other researchers in this domain have focused on exploring the factors that explain different patterns in SNS use and adoption such as gender, personality, and motivations (Barker, 2009; Joinson, 2008; Lampe, Ellison, & Steinfield, 2008; Pfeil, Arjan, & Zaphiris, 2009; Ross et al., 2009; Seder & Oishi, 2009; Steinfield et al., 2008; Zywica & Danowski, 2008). While some of the more recent work has started to consider level of engagement with SNSs (e.g., Barker, 2009; Joinson, 2008; Steinfield et al., 2008), no systematic approach has so far been put forth to address the question of use intensity despite the fact that level and types of usage likely have repercussions for how SNS usage fits into and impacts people's lives.

Frequency and Diversity of Social Network Site Uses

As noted above, the academic literature on SNS uses has covered considerable ground despite being a relatively new area of inquiry. Here, we are especially interested in work that has considered frequency and diversity of SNS usage. These aspects of use may reflect actual differences in how people are incorporating these services into their lives and possible consequences resulting from their uses. Accordingly, they may be problematic to ignore in studies of SNSs.

Some recent scholarship has started to look at SNS usage in more nuanced ways by considering such factors as frequency of use. One example of work that has considered frequency of use is Joinson's (2008) two-stage approach to studying motivations for, and interest in, using Facebook. The researcher was interested in explaining different levels of Facebook use and operationalized the concept in the following two ways: the amount of time spent on and the frequency of visits to the site during an average week. Joinson found that female respondents, on average, visited Facebook more often than males, but once on the site, there was no gender difference in how much time people spent on it.

While Joinson (2008) was interested in explaining frequency of use, i.e., this was the dependent variables in his study, others have considered this aspect of usage as an explanatory factor, i.e., as independent variables, while focusing on other outcomes in their analyses (Barker, 2009; Steinfield et al., 2008). For example, in her study of college students' motivations for using SNSs, Barker (2009) included frequency of SNS use in her analyses measured by a variable constructed from answers to questions about both number of visits to SNSs and amount of time spent on such a site (measures similar to those employed by Joinson, 2008, cited above). Barker defined this latter measure, however, as a global estimate of SNS usage, not accounting for any specific information about particular sites visited. She found a gender difference in motivations of SNS usage with female students and those possessing stronger group identity using SNSs more frequently for communicative and entertainment motivations than others. Despite having included the frequency measure in her survey of first-year college students, she did not analyze it or interpret its association with other variables in the paper, so we do not know whether this measure is related to the outcomes of interest in her project.

In their study of social-capital formation through Facebook use, Steinfield and colleagues (2008) developed a "Facebook Intensity scale" as an important explanatory variable when looking at how Facebook use may predict changes in users' social capital. This measure is based on data about daily time spent on the site, total number of Facebook friends, and a series of attitudinal items assessing "the degree to which the respondent felt emotionally connected to Facebook and the extent to which Facebook was integrated into daily activities" (Steinfield et al., 2008, p. 439). The authors found that intensity of use leads to increases in bridging social capital. This finding lends support to the central idea of this chapter: that it is limiting to consider SNS usage as a simple binary variable separating users from non-users; rather, it is important to look at level of engagement with such sites when considering their implications.

As the above studies suggest, some scholars have started to consider frequency of SNS usage in their work. However, neither the studies reviewed in this section nor other research in this domain has looked at the diversity of social network site usage (i.e., the number of different such sites respondents use). The prevailing approach seems to be to look at the use of just one such service (e.g., see Pfeil et al., 2009, for MySpace and Steinfield et al., 2008, for Facebook) with a possible underlying implication that findings about their uses are interchangeable. However, work has shown that these sites attract different communities (Hargittai, 2007), they also have different designs, they allow for varied functionality and affordances, and so generalizing findings from one to others may be problematic. For example, while some sites are mainly used for social relationship maintenance (e.g., Facebook), others are more likely for the cultivation of professional networks (e.g., LinkedIn). Given the increasing number and prevalence of SNSs and differences in how much time people spend online on various activities more generally speaking (e.g., Fallows, 2004; Howard & Jones, 2004; Wellman & Haythornthwaite, 2002), it seems problematic to collapse all SNS users into one group. It may pose a challenge to generalize findings about one site's usage to another and thereby ignore specifics about types of site uses in investigations. To address this shortcoming of the literature, we propose a typology of SNS usage that takes the diversity of SNSs used into account.

Typology of Social Network Site Uses

To refine scholarly approaches to the study of SNS uses, we propose taking into consideration both the frequency with which users visit such sites and the number of SNSs with which people engage on a regular basis. This approach yields a two-by-two matrix of SNS engagement presented in Figure 7.1. Those who only use one such site and do so only sometimes are Dabblers. Those who visit more than one SNS, but none of them often, are Samplers. Users who are active often on one such site only are Devotees. Finally, those who are visitors to more than one such site and use at least one of them often are Omnivores. Dabblers are the least engaged group of the four. Samplers are not active on any particular SNS, but spend time on more than one so their engagement is likely higher than that of Dabblers. Devotees only engage with one such service, but do so often. Omnivores have embraced SNSs the most by using a diversity of them and spending considerable time on at least one such service.

Number of SNSs used

		One SNS only	More than one SNS
Use frequency	Sometimes	Dabbler	Sampler
	Often	Devotee	Omnivore

Figure 7.1 Typology of social network site usage.

Methods

Data Collection

College students in the U.S. constitute an ideal population for studying differences in digital media uses given their high Internet connectivity levels. Accordingly, the analyses presented here are based on data representing a diverse group of mainly 18- and 19-year-old college students. The data collection was conducted in February and March of 2007 at the University of Illinois, Chicago, which is a U.S. urban public research university.[2] *U.S. News and World Report* (2006) ranked this campus among the top-10 national universities regarding campus ethnic diversity, suggesting that this school offers an ideal location for studying how different kinds of people use online sites and services.

There is one course on this campus that is required of all students: the First-Year Writing Program. Surveying students based on enrollment in this course ensures that there is no selection bias among study participants. Out of the 87 sections offered as part of this course, the survey was administered in 85 sections, constituting a 98% participation rate on the part of course sections. Overall, there was a final response rate of 82% based on all of the students enrolled in the course. In order to control for time in the program, this article focuses on the 1,060 students in the first-year class.[3]

The survey was administered on paper instead of online. Relying on an online questionnaire when studying Internet uses could create a bias toward people who spend more time on the Web, given that they may be more inclined to fill out the questionnaire and also, perhaps, more inclined toward higher rates of participation on the sites of research interest. The survey included detailed questions about respondents' Internet uses (e.g., experience, types of sites visited, and online activities) as well as people's demographic background in addition to a number of other questions.

Independent Variables

We measure basic demographic information using standard modes of opera-tionalization. Students were asked their year of birth and this information is used to calculate their age, which is included in the models as a continuous vari-able. Male is the base gender category (male = 0, female = 1). Information about race and ethnicity was collected using the U.S. 2000 Census Bureau ques-tionnaire format (U.S. Census Bureau, 2001), and dummy variables are used in the statistical models, with White as the base category. Consistent with work by others, parental education is used as a measure of socioeconomic status (e.g., Carlson, Uppal, & Prosser, 2000). This information is included in the model as dummy variables, with some high school education or less as the base.

We collected data about students' living situation as well as the context of their Internet uses given that social context of use has been shown to matter in how people use the medium (Frohlich & Kraut, 2003; Hassani, 2006). Both the question about living at home with parents and the question about having access to the Internet at a friend's or family member's home is included as a binary vari-able, where 1 signals affirmative and 0 stands for negative. Regarding Internet experiences, we asked about how much time respondents spend online and calcu-lated hours spent on the Web per week, excluding time spent on email, chat, and voice services. We also asked how long they have been using the Internet and have a measure with number of years online. Figures for both of these are logged in the analyses given that an additional hour or year, respectively, likely has dimin-ishing returns as the values increase. Also, following Hargittai (2005, 2009), we construct an Internet skill measure from 27 items asking about respondents' level of understanding of Internet-related terms. With the exclusion of missing values on these measures, the valid responses to these five-point Likert-scale questions are averaged to generate a global measure of Internet skill level.

Dependent Variables

To measure SNS usage, the survey asked respondents first to indicate their familiarity with various sites and then their experiences with using them. The six SNSs included on the questionnaire—based on their popularity at the time—were: Bebo, Facebook, Friendster, MySpace, Orkut, and Xanga. To measure familiarity, we asked respondents to indicate whether they had ever heard of the site. To measure experience, participants were asked to choose one of the following options: "No, have never used it," "Tried it once, but have not used it since," "Yes, have tried it in the past, but do not use it nowadays," "Yes, currently use it sometimes," and "Yes, currently use it often." We construct our measures of use from answers to this latter question.

Usage is measured by two dummy variables. The first considers whether the respondent uses the site *sometimes* and the second accounts for using it *often*. We then use these binary variables to construct measures of where users fall in the typology of SNS usage described in the previous section. In addition to constructing this five-category variable of typology, we further create two binary dependent variables for SNS users. First, we construct a variable for frequency of SNS use by collapsing Dabblers and Samplers (denoted as 0) versus Devotees and Omnivores (denoted as 1). Second, we construct a variable measuring the diversity of SNS use by collapsing Dabblers and Devotees (denoted as 0) versus Samplers and Omnivores (denoted as 1).

Methods of Analysis

We first report descriptive statistics about variation in SNS usage (i.e., the aforementioned typology), and how this variation may differ by students' demographic background. Next, given that our dependent variable, the typology of SNS usage, is a categorical variable, we employ multinomial logistic regression models in order to investigate further the differences in frequency and diversity of SNS use, with controls for various factors. The multinomial logistic regression is appropriate for our analyses, because it is developed for modeling categorical dependent variables (Long, 1997).[4] We also employ two separate logistic regression models to analyze whether demographic factors, Internet user context and experiences, and online skills exhibit any systematic relationship with either frequency or diversity of SNS usage among participants.

Sample Descriptives

The 1,060 first-year students included in these analyses represent a diverse group of young adults. Table 7.1 shows descriptive statistics about the group. In total, 56% of the respondents are female, 44% are male. Almost all are 18 or 19 years old, with a mean age of 18.4 and a median of 18. Fewer than half are White and non-Hispanic. Slightly fewer than 8% claim African or African American descent, almost 30% are of Asian or Asian American ancestry, and just under one-fifth are of Hispanic origin. Students come from varied family backgrounds. Over one-quarter of respondents have parents whose highest level of education is no more than a high school degree, an additional 20% have parents without a college degree (i.e., some college education). While it may seem that sampling from a college population assumes a highly educated group, 25% of first-years at this university leave the institution by their second year (Ardinger et al., 2004) and fewer than half (43.6%) will graduate from this school within six years of enrollment (University of Illinois-Chicago, 2004).[5] Over half of the students at this university commute from home and live with their parents (53.1%).

Baseline Internet access and use statistics (Table 7.2) for the sample suggest that being online is not a novel concept in most of these students' lives. On average, participants have access to the Internet at over six locations and have been users for over six years. When asked how often they go online, the vast majority report doing so several times a day. They estimate spending 15.5 hours visiting websites weekly (excluding email, chat, and voice services). While there is certainly variation in levels of access and use among particip-ants, there are no basic barriers standing in the way of these young adults to accessing the Internet. Limits may be put on their uses due to other factors (e.g., the need to share resources at home, limited hours of access due to employment, commuting or parental controls), but they all have basic access. This suggests that traditional concerns about the so-called digital divide do not apply to these students regarding basic Internet availability. Thus, looking at such a wired group of users allows us to hold basic access constant and focus on differences in details of use instead.

Variation in Social Network Site Usage

As reported in earlier work based on this data set (Hargittai, 2007), overall, 88% of respondents in this sample are SNS users. Only one student claimed

Table 7.1 Descriptive statistics about the sample

	Percent
Women	55.8
Age	
18	64.8
19	32.2
20–29	3.0
Race and ethnicity	
White, non-Hispanic	42.7
Hispanic	18.8
African American, non-Hispanic	7.7
Asian/Asian American, non-Hispanic	29.6
Native American, non-Hispanic	1.2
Highest level of parental education	
Less than high school	7.4
High school	19.0
Some college	20.1
College	34.4
Graduate degree	19.1
Lives with parents	53.1

Table 7.2 Internet experiences of sample participants

	Mean	Standard deviation
Number of Internet access locations	6.2	(2.1)
Number of Internet use years	6.4	(2.0)
Number of hours on the Web per week*	15.5	(10.0)

Note
*This figure excludes time spent on email, chat, or online telephony (VoIP).

not to have heard of any of the six SNSs included on the survey (i.e., Bebo, Facebook, Friendster, MySpace, Orkut, Xanga), so non-use is not a result of not being familiar with these services. Rather, despite knowing about such sites, over 12% of the sample does not use any of them. Table 7.3 presents more details about what proportion of respondents has heard about and has used or currently uses the six SNSs discussed here. Facebook is the most popular service among these students (78.8%), followed by MySpace (54.6%). Almost two-thirds of the overall sample use Facebook frequently, but just over one-third use MySpace often. The other four sites are considerably less popular among respondents.

Table 7.4 presents the prevalence of each type of SNS use among participants. As previously defined, "Dabbler" refers to those who only use one SNS and do so only sometimes. Students who report using only one of the six sites sometimes at the time of the study, we categorize as "Dabblers." Just under one-tenth of the sample (9.2%) fits this description. Students who currently visit more than one of these sites, but none of them often, we categorize as

Table 7.3 Familiarity and experience with social network sites among participants (percentages)

	Uses it*	Has heard of it	Has never used it	Tried it once, but no more	Used to use it, no longer
Facebook	78.8 (62.8)	99.4	14.2	3.6	3.4
MySpace	54.6 (38.4)	99.5	20.8	9.4	15.2
Xanga	6.2 (1.9)	76.4	61.7	11.8	20.3
Friendster	3.3 (1.0)	43.3	84.7	5.6	6.4
Orkut	1.6 (0.6)	5.8	97.1	0.5	0.9
Bebo	0.6 (0.0)	9.6	95.4	2.8	1.2

Note
*Figures in parentheses refer to percent of students who visit the site often.

Table 7.4 Prevalence of social network site usage type among respondents*

	Full sample	Among SNS users only
Non-users	12.31	
Dabblers	9.19	10.48
Samplers	4.45	5.08
Devotees	28.79	32.83
Omnivores	45.27	51.62

Note
*These figures are based on 1,056 respondents due to missing data for four respondents that make it impossible to classify their level of SNS engagement.

"Samplers." This is the smallest category in the group with only 4.4% of students classified as such. Students who currently use only one of the six sites, but do so often, are categorized as "Devotees." They make up almost one-third of the sample at 32.9%. Finally, we classify those who visit more than one of these six sites with at least one of them visited often as "Omnivores." This is by far the biggest category, with almost half of our respondents (45.3%) exhibiting such behavior. These students are quite familiar with social network sites and many of them use SNSs quite a bit.

Table 7.5 reports descriptive statistics by user background for SNS usage in general, and for the various categories of users in particular (Dabbler, Sampler, Devotee, and Omnivore). While women are more likely to use SNSs than men, once we break down usage by frequency and diversity of use, women are only more likely to be Omnivores than are men, and there is no gender difference regarding being a Dabbler, Sampler, or Devotee. There is no sharp contrast between students with different racial and ethnic backgrounds. We only find that non-Hispanic African American students are significantly less likely to be Dabblers and non-Hispanic Asian American students are significantly more likely to be Devotees than their counterparts. Regarding parental education, the most pronounced finding is that students whose parents have at least one parent with a college education are significantly less likely to be Dabblers and more likely to be Omnivores. In addition, students whose parents have less than a high school education are significantly more likely to be Dabblers and those whose parents have some college education are significantly more likely to be Samplers than others.

As found in earlier work (Hargittai, 2007), however, there is a relationship between SNS usage and other factors such as context of use and experience with the Internet, so it is best to further examine the differences in frequency and diversity of SNS usage employing more advanced statistical techniques that allow us to control for various factors simultaneously in our models. Given the

Table 7.5 Percentage of different groups of people who use SNSs at all and by SNS level of engagement

	Any SNS	Dabbler	Sampler	Devotee	Omnivore
Gender					
Male	86	10.0	4.7	29.2	41.2
Female	90*	8.5	4.2	28.3	48.2*
Race/ethnicity					
White, non-Hispanic	89	9.5	3.6	27.0	47.6
Hispanic	86	11.7	5.4	25.4	43.9
African American, NH	84	3.8*	3.8	26.3	50.0
Asian American, NH	89	8.2	5.6	33.7*	41.2
Native American, NH	83	8.3	0.0	25.0	50.0
Parental education					
Less than high school	88	15.4*	7.7	24.4	41.0
High school	85	10.0	4.5	26.4	43.8
Some college	85	7.6	7.1*	30.2	40.1
College	90*	6.9*	3.0	29.1	50.8*
Graduate degree	88	11.9	3.0	30.2	42.6

Notes
1. The figures in the columns of Dabbler, Sampler, Devotee, and Omnivore are the breakdown of the percentage of "Any SNS use" and thus do not add up to 100%.
2. Chi-square test for statistical significant difference between groups. $*p < 0.1$; $**p < 0.01$; $***p < 0.001$.

categorical nature of our typology of SNS use, in the next section we employ multinomial logistic regression analyses to investigate what may explain people's propensity to exhibit a particular type of SNS usage.

Explaining Different Levels of Social Network Site Engagement

In this section, using multinomial logistic regression analyses, we look at the relationship of several factors and intensity of SNS usage.[6] In Table 7.6, we summarize all 10 comparisons between different types of SNS users in our model. For example, the second column (O–N), refers to the odds comparing the likelihood of being an Omnivore versus a Non-User. Likewise, we compare the odds of being an Omnivore to the odds of being a Dabbler in the third column, and so on moving down the rest of the columns. The estimates listed in Table 7.6 are the odds ratios generated from the multinomial logistic regression models. Odds ratios larger than one favor the category on the left-hand side, whereas the odds smaller than one favor the category on the right-hand side. For example, looking at the row labeled "Female," the number in the "O–N" column is 2.49. This means that women are considerably more likely to be Omnivores versus Non-Users than are men. Likewise, if we go down a few rows, the figure for those living with parents in the same "O–N" column is 0.530, suggesting that the respondents who currently live with their parents are less likely to be Omnivores versus Non-Users than are those who are not living with their parents. In order to facilitate interpretation of the results, we derive the predicted probabilities from the models and explain these probabilities regarding the relationship between our explanatory factors and SNS user type. Figures that are statistically significant are highlighted in bold typeface.

User Background Variables

Figure 7.2 summarizes the gender difference in the predicted probabilities of SNS user type while holding other variables at their mean. In particular, female students are more likely to be Omnivores versus Non-Users, Dabblers, or Devotees than are male students once we control for race/ethnicity, parental education, context of use, Internet experience, and skill. Females are also more likely to be Devotees or Samplers versus Non-Users than are males. While earlier work (Hargittai, 2007) has already shown that female students in this sample have a higher likelihood of using various SNSs, the current analysis further indicates that they also have a higher likelihood of using such sites more intensely than their male peers. In other words, we find a significant gender difference in level of SNS user intensity.

As the next rows in Table 7.6 suggest, the odds of being different types of SNS users do not differ by students' race and ethnic background except for one case: Asians and Asian Americans are more likely to be Devotees or Samplers versus Omnivores than are White students. None of the comparisons are statistically significant regarding parental education, suggesting that socioeconomic background does not relate to level of SNS engagement on the part of the student when we take user context, as well as Internet experience and skill, into consideration.

Context of Use

Variables measuring context of use were more likely to be significant predictors of SNS user type than users' demographic characteristics. The results show that students who have Internet access at the homes of those in their social networks are more likely to be Omnivores and Devotees versus Non-Users than those who do not have Internet access at such locations. Those who have access at such places are also more likely to be Omnivores versus Dabblers than are those who do not have such access. The most pronounced

Table 7.6 Comparison of odds ratios between different types of social network site user types (n = 1,010)

	Odds comparing being type A to alternative type B									
	O–N	O–Db	O–Dv	O–S	Dv–N	Dv–Db	Dv–S	S–N	S–Db	Db–N
Age	0.883	0.885	0.863	0.756	1.023	1.026	0.877	1.167	1.170	0.997
Female	2.499*	1.811*	1.470*	1.175	1.700*	1.231	0.799	2.127	1.541	1.380
Race/ethnicity (as compared to White)										
Hispanic	1.027	0.824	0.949	0.786	1.083	0.865	0.828	1.308	1.047	1.250
African American	0.738	2.320	1.043	0.878	0.708	2.224	0.842	0.840	2.640	0.318
Asian/Asian American	0.804	0.869	0.608*	0.448*	1.322	1.430	0.737	1.793	1.939	0.925
Parental education (as compared to high school degree and lower)										
Some college	0.817	1.082	0.790	0.591	1.035	1.370	0.748	1.383	1.831	0.755
College degree	1.429	1.385	1.090	1.916	1.310	1.270	1.757	0.746	0.723	1.032
Advanced degree	0.894	0.600	0.845	1.285	1.058	0.709	1.521	0.696	0.467	1.492
Living with parents	0.530*	0.508*	0.857	0.319*	0.618*	0.593*	0.372*	1.663	1.594	1.043
Net access at friends'/family's home	2.291*	2.041*	1.050	1.525	2.182*	1.945	1.453	1.502	1.338	1.122
Years online	0.807	1.690	0.870	0.800	0.928	1.942	0.929	1.009	2.113	0.478
Hours on Web/week (logged)	1.570*	2.509*	1.250	1.209	1.256	2.007*	0.967	1.299	2.075*	0.626*
Internet skills (standardized)	1.429*	1.137	1.269*	1.003	1.126	0.896	0.791	1.424	1.133	1.257

Notes
1. O: Omnivore; Db: Dabbler; Dv: Devotee; S: Sampler; N: Non-user.
2. In this table, values are odds ratios (ORs) from multinomial logistic regression. The odds larger than 1 favor type A (left-hand side), whereas the odds smaller than 1 favor type B (right-hand side).
3. *$p < 0.05$.

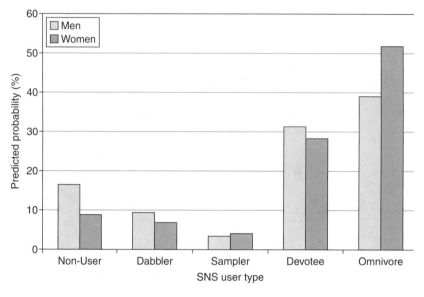

Figure 7.2 Probability of social network site user types by gender.

finding concerns the living context of participants. Respondents who live with their parents are less likely to be Omnivores versus Non-Users, Dabblers, or Samplers than those who do not live with their parents (see Figure 7.3). Respondents who live with their parents are less likely to be Devotees versus Samplers. These comparisons suggest that there is a significant relationship between living condition and intensity of SNS usage, where students who live with their parents have a lower likelihood of engaging with SNSs intensely.

Internet Experience

Perhaps not surprisingly, we observe a statistically significant relationship between some Internet experience variables and SNS usage type. Understandably, students who spend more time online weekly are more likely to be Omnivores versus Non-Users and Dabblers than those who spend less time online. Additionally, students who spend more time online are more likely to be Devotees, Samplers, and Non-Users versus Dabblers than are those who spend less time online. The figures in Table 7.7 illustrate the relationship between intensity of SNS usage and hours spent online weekly. Taken all together, we find that, for the students who spend 30 hours or more on the Web per week, the likelihood of being Non-Users and Dabblers is lower by 5.2 and 11.4 percentage points respectively than for those who only spend five

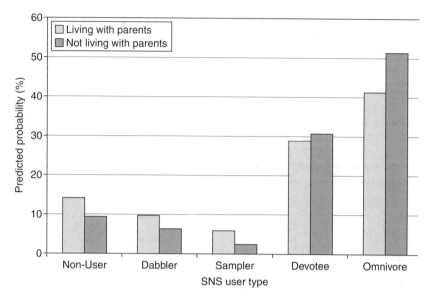

Figure 7.3 Probability of social network site user types by living context.

hours or less on the Web. At the same time, a frequent Web user's likelihood of being an Omnivore is 16.9 percentage points higher than an infrequent user's likelihood. In contrast to the importance of time spent online regarding SNS usage type, years of being an Internet user is not associated with variation in SNS use intensity.

Regarding online skills, students who exhibit higher levels of Internet know-how are more likely to be Omnivores versus Non-Users or Devotees than are those who possess lower-level skills, once we control for students' demographic and socioeconomic backgrounds, context of use, and Internet experiences. In order to demonstrate the magnitude of probability change associated with Internet skills, we present the predicted probability for the

Table 7.7 Probability (%) of being each type of social network site user for an infrequent (5 hours per week) versus frequent (30 hours per week) Web user

| | Time spent online per week | |
	5 hours	30 hours
Non-Users	14.7	9.5
Dabblers	15.9	4.5
Samplers	3.6	3.8
Devotees	29.5	29.0
Omnivores	36.3	53.2

minimum and the maximum skill level in Table 7.8. As the figures reported in Table 7.8 suggest, the predicted probability of being a Non-User for respondents who report minimal levels of Internet skill is 19.3% and these students have a 33.6% chance of using SNSs intensely. However, for respondents with the maximum level of Internet skill, the predicted probabilities of being a Non-User and an Omnivore, respectively, are 6.5% and 59.1%. In other words, highly skilled users are much more likely to be in the Omnivore user category than lower-skilled users.

Diversity and Frequency of Social Network Site Usage Among SNS Users

In order to examine further whether the various explanatory variables exhibit any systematic relationship with either diversity or frequency of SNS usage among SNS users, we look at the results of two separate logistic regression models including only SNS users. As the figures in the "Diversity of use" column in Table 7.9 show, women as well as students who spend more time online per week, and those who have higher Internet skills, are more likely to be more diverse SNS users than their counterparts. In addition, compared to White students, Asian and Asian American students have a lower likelihood of being diverse SNS users. The results presented in the "Frequency of use" column suggest that no demographic factors influence how regularly respondents use SNSs. However, context of use and Internet experiences do seem to make a difference. Students who do not live with their parents, who have Internet access at a friend's or family member's home, and who spend more time online per week are more likely to use SNSs often.

Tables 7.10 and 7.11 illustrate the predicted probabilities of diverse and frequent SNS usage among SNS users in the sample, respectively. Here, we only report figures for factors that exhibit a statistically significant relationship with the outcome variables as per the results in Table 7.9. We find that hours

Table 7.8 Probability (%) of being each type of social network site user by Internet skill level (minimum versus maximum skill)

	Internet skills (Standardized)	
	Minimum	Maximum
Non-Users	19.3	6.5
Dabblers	7.7	7.6
Samplers	2.8	4.9
Devotees	37.2	21.9
Omnivores	33.0	59.1

Table 7.9 Logistic regressions predicting diversity and frequency of SNS use

	Diversity of use	Frequency of use
	Odds ratios (Standard errors)	
Age	0.90	0.88
	(0.08)	(0.09)
Female	**1.54****	1.37
	(0.24)	(0.29)
Race/ethnicity (as compared to White)		
Hispanic	0.91	0.82
	(0.18)	(0.22)
African American	1.16	1.44
	(0.34)	(0.68)
Asian/Asian American	0.71*	0.85
	(0.12)	(0.20)
Parental education (as compared to high school and lower)		
Some college	0.89	0.92
	(0.19)	(0.26)
College degree	1.08	1.48
	(0.21)	(0.39)
Advanced degree	0.74	0.78
	(0.17)	(0.23)
Living with parents	0.85	**0.47*****
	(0.13)	(0.10)
Net access at friends'/family's home	1.17	**1.75***
	(0.28)	(0.49)
Years online	1.05	1.36
	(0.27)	(0.47)
Hours on Web/week (logged)	**1.46*****	**1.79*****
	(0.16)	(0.27)
Internet skills (standardized)	**1.25****	0.99
	(0.11)	(0.11)
n	884	884
Pseudo R^2	0.0327	0.0681

Notes
1. The odds ratios (ORs) larger than 1 means more diverse or intense SNS use respectively, whereas the odds ratios smaller than 1 suggest that less diverse or intense SNS use.
2. *$p < 0.05$; **$p < 0.01$; ***$p < 0.001$.

spent online per week can explain both diversity and frequency of SNS usage, suggesting that the more time an individual spends online, the more likely this person is to use different types of SNS often. At the same time, the variables concerning context of use only affect the frequency of SNS usage, whereas gender, being Asian or Asian American, and level of Internet skill are related to diversity of SNS usage, but not frequency of use.

Table 7.10 Probability (%) of diverse social network site usage

	Diverse SNS usage	
Gender	Male 50.9	Female 61.5
Race/ethnicity	Asians 51.1	Whites 59.4
Internet skills	1 standard deviation below mean 51.4	1 standard deviation above mean 62.2
Time spent online per week	5 hours 47.4	30 hours 63.9

Conclusion

Drawing on a unique data set with unprecedented granularity about the use of social network sites coupled with detailed demographic background information, this study has looked at what types of user characteristics (from among a diverse group of first-year students at an urban public university) are most likely to be associated with different levels of SNS use intensity. Findings suggest that level of engagement is not randomly distributed among the group. Gender is an important factor when it comes to explaining intensity of SNS usage, with women more likely to be intense users of SNSs than men. We also find that context of Internet use may explain one's level of engagement with SNSs; namely, students who do not live with their parents and have more access points in their personal networks have a higher likelihood of using SNSs intensely. Additionally, we find that there is a systematic relationship between hours spent online weekly as well as Web user skills and intensity of SNS usage, suggesting that students who have more Internet experiences and higher online abilities are more likely to be more engaged with SNSs. We are unable to speak to the direction of causality here based on the data set we have. It may well be that more skilled users are more likely to integrate SNSs into their daily routines. However, it may also be that those who spend more time on such sites develop a better understanding of the Internet. There is a good chance that both of these processes are at work, reinforcing each other long term.

While our nuanced data set has allowed us to explore some questions that previous literature has been unable to consider, there are other issues our data are not suited to examine. In particular, the information available here does not allow us to distinguish between the importance of different site designs, affordances and memberships for why some people are more or less likely to become intense users of one SNS over another. However, it is reasonable to

Table 7.11 Probability (%) of frequent social network site usage

	Frequent SNS usage	
Living with parents	No 90.2	Yes 81.3
Have Net access at friends'/family's home	No 79.1	Yes 86.8
Time spent online per week	5 hours 77.5	30 hours 90.7

expect that such divergences across these services result in different levels of engagement on behalf of users. In particular, if the designs and affordances support certain types of outcomes at varying levels (e.g., civic organizing is easier on one as compared to another), then people will likely embrace the sites that are most supportive of their particular interests. A user who is especially focused on political engagement may expend more energies on building networks on a site that encourages related activities, while a user more intrigued by following the latest artistic trends will spend time on the site that caters to that particular interest best. Future work in this area can apply our proposed SNS usage typology to investigate what factors may lead users to engage with different sites at varying levels of intensity.

In addition to its substantive contributions, this study also has important methodological implications. When examining SNS usage, researchers must be careful to take the extent to which users are engaged with the sites under consideration. Rather than assume that all SNS usage is interchangeable, it is important to recognize that some people have incorporated use of such sites into their everyday lives much more than others. Accordingly, when considering the various social, cultural, political, and psychological implications of time spent on such sites, it is important to establish where people fall in the typology of social network site usage, recognizing that varying levels of usage intensity are not necessarily synonymous.

Notes

1. The authors thank Jeremy Freese, Zizi Papacharissi, Klaus Weber, and the anonymous reviewers for helpful comments. They appreciate the support of faculty and staff at the University of Illinois-Chicago for making this study possible, namely, Mary Case, Ann Feldman, Tom Moss, and Karen Mossberger. Additionally, they are grateful for the generous support of the John D. and Catherine T. MacArthur Foundation through its Digital Media and Learning initiative. They thank the following people for their assistance with data collection and entry: Waleeta Canon, Gina Walejko, Soo An, Dan Li, and the group of undergraduate research assistants

in the Web Use Project group during the 2006–2007 academic year. The first author is also indebted to the Berkman Center for Internet & Society at Harvard University, the Center for Advanced Study in the Behavioral Sciences at Stanford University, and The Lenore Annenberg and Wallis Annenberg Fellowship in Communication. She thanks the support offered by Northwestern University's Research Grants Committee, the School of Communication Innovation Fund, and the Department of Communication Studies Research Fund.

2. The Principle Investigator of this project is not now nor has ever been affiliated with this university in any way other than in the context of this study. Focus on this campus is not due to convenience; rather, it is the result of careful consideration about what type of student population would be most helpful in addressing questions of interest in the overall research project.

3. The survey included a question verifying students' attentiveness to the questionnaire. A small portion of students (3.4%) were identified as not paying attention to question wording, suggesting that they were checking off responses randomly instead of replying to the substance of the questions. The responses of these students have been excluded from the data and analyses presented here so as to minimize error introduced through such respondents.

4. Multinomial logistic regression estimates the likelihood of being in a certain category versus the likelihood of being in another category (i.e., baseline category), while holding all the explanatory variables constant. Researchers can switch the baseline category and repeat the comparison process in order to acquire the estimates of every possible pair of comparisons. Based on the estimated coefficients, we can then generate the predicted probabilities of being a member of each category and interpret the results.

5. Some of those who leave UIC will transfer to other schools and end up graduating elsewhere. Data are not available to establish what percentage of UIC first-years end up leaving college altogether.

6. Students of Native American background have been excluded from these analyses, due to their small number. We also excluded respondents from our regression models if they were missing values on any of the variables used in the analyses.

References

Ardinger, Nick, Pat Inman, Bob Lees, Tony Martin, Agnes Roche, Kim Savage, Julian Szucko, Flecia Thomas, & Lee Willis. (2004). *UIC freshman—One year later: A report on the one-year retention of the UIC freshman class*. University of Illinois-Chicago, Chicago.

Bahney, Anna. (2006). Don't talk to invisible strangers. *New York Times*.

Barker, Valerie. (2009). Older adolescents' motivations for social network site use: The influence of gender, group identity, and collective self-esteem. *CyberPsychology & Behavior* 12: 209–213.

boyd, danah & Nicole Ellison. (2007). Social network sites: Definition, history, and scholarship. *Journal of Computer-Mediated Communication* 13: 11.

Carlson, Cindy, Sarika Uppal, & Ellie C. Prosser. (2000). Ethnic differences in processes contributing to the self-esteem of early adolescent girls. *The Journal of Early Adolescence* 20: 44–67.

comScore. (2009). *comScore Media Metrix ranks top 50 U.S. Web properties for April 2009.* Reston, VA.

Fallows, Deborah. (2004). The Internet and Daily Life. Pew Internet and American Life Project, Washington, DC.

Frohlich, David M. & Robert Kraut. (2003). The social context of home computing (pp. 127–162). In R. Harper (Ed.), *Inside the smart home.* London: Springer-Verlag.

Goodings, Lewis, Abigail Locke, & Steven D. Brown. (2007). Social networking technology: Place and identity in mediated communities. *Journal of Community & Applied Social Psychology* 17: 463–476.

Hargittai, Eszter (2005). Survey measures of web-oriented digital literacy. *Social Science Computer Review 23*(3), 371–379.

Hargittai, Eszter. (2007). Whose space? Differences among users and non-users of social network sites. *Journal of Computer-Mediated Communication* 13: 14.

Hargittai, Eszter. (2009). An update on survey measures of Web-oriented digital literacy. *Social Science Computer Review* 27: 130–137.

Hassani, Sara Nephew. (2006). Locating digital divides at home, work, and everywhere else. *Poetics* 34: 250–272.

Hinduja, Sameer & Justin W. Patchin. (2008). Personal information of adolescents on the Internet: A quantitative content analysis of MySpace. *Journal of Adolescence* 31: 125–146.

Hope, Jenny. (2009). Twitter can make you immoral, claim scientists. *Daily Mail.*

Howard, Philip N. & Steve G. Jones. (2004). *Society online: The Internet in context.* Thousand Oaks, CA: Sage Publications.

Joinson, Adam N. (2008). Looking at, looking up or keeping up with people? Motives and use of Facebook. *Proceeding of the twenty-sixth annual SIGCHI conference on human factors in computing systems.* Florence, Italy: ACM.

Jones, Steve G., Sarah Millermaier, Mariana Goya-Martinez, & Jessica Schuler. (2008). Whose space is MySpace? A content analysis of MySpace profiles. *First Monday* 13.

Lampe, Cliff, Nicole B. Ellison, & Charles Steinfield. (2008). Changes in use and perception of Facebook. *Proceedings of the ACM 2008 conference on computer supported cooperative work.* San Diego, CA: ACM.

Leake, Jonathan & Georgia Warren. (2009). Facebook fans do worse in exams. *The Times.*

Lewis, Kevin, Jason Kaufman, Marco Gonzalez, Andreas Wimmer, & Nicholas Christakis. (2008). Tastes, ties, and time: A new social network dataset using Facebook.com. *Social Networks* 30: 330–342.

Livingstone, Sonia. (2008). Taking risky opportunities in youthful content creation: Teenagers' use of social networking sites for intimacy, privacy and self-expression. *New Media & Society* 10: 393–411.

Long, J. Scott (1997). *Regression models for categorical and limited dependent variables* (Advanced quantitative techniques in the social sciences). Thousand Oaks, CA: Sage Publications.

Nussbaum, Emily. (2007). Say everything. *New York Magazine,* February 12.

Pasek, Josh, eian more, & Eszter Hargittai. (2009). Facebook and academic performance: Reconciling a media sensation with data. *First Monday* 14.

Pfeil, Ulrike, Raj Arjan, & Panayiotis Zaphiris. (2009). Age differences in online social networking—A study of user profiles and the social capital divide among teenagers and older users in MySpace. *Computers in Human Behavior* 25: 643–654.

Ross, Craig, Emily S. Orr, Mia Sisic, Jaime M. Arseneault, Mary G. Simmering, & R. Robert Orr. (2009). Personality and motivations associated with Facebook use. *Computers in Human Behavior* 25: 578–586.

Roush, Wade. (2006). The moral panic over social-networking sites. *Technology Review*, August 7.

Seder, J. Patrick & Shigehiro Oishi. (2009). Ethnic/racial homogeneity in college students' Facebook friendship networks and subjective well-being. *Journal of Research in Personality* 43: 438–443.

Steinfield, Charles, Nicole B. Ellison, & Cliff Lampe. (2008). Social capital, self-esteem, and use of online social network sites: A longitudinal analysis. *Journal of Applied Developmental Psychology* 29: 434–445.

Tong, Stephanie Tom, Brandon Van Der Heide, Lindsey Langwell, & Joseph B. Walther. (2008). Too much of a good thing? The relationship between number of friends and interpersonal impressions on Facebook. *Journal of Computer-Mediated Communication* 13: 531–549.

University of Illinois-Chicago. (2004). *Graduation Rate Disclosure Statement*.

U.S. Census Bureau. (2001). *Technical Documentation: Race and Hispanic or Latino Summary File*. U.S.C. Bureau.

U.S. News and World Report. (2006). Campus ethnic diversity: national universities. *America's Best Colleges 2007*.

Walther, Joseph B., Brandon Van Der Heide, Lauren Hamel, & Hillary Shulman. (2009). Self-generated versus other-generated statements and impressions in computer-mediated communication: A test of warranting theory using Facebook. *Communication Research* 36:229–253.

Walther, Joseph B., Brandon Van Der Heide, Sang-Yeon Kim, David Westerman, & Stephanie Tom Tong. (2008). The role of friends' appearance and behavior on evaluations of individuals on Facebook: Are we known by the company we keep? *Human Communication Research* 34: 28–49.

Wellman, Barry & Caroline Haythornthwaite. (2002). *The Internet in everyday life*. Oxford: Blackwell Publishers.

Zhao, Shanyang, Sherri Grasmuck, & Jason Martin. (2008). Identity construction on Facebook: Digital empowerment in anchored relationships. *Computers in Human Behavior* 24: 1816–1836.

Zywica, Jolene & James Danowski. (2008). The faces of Facebookers: Investigating social enhancement and social compensation hypotheses; Predicting Facebook™ and offline popularity from sociability and self-esteem, and mapping the meanings of popularity with semantic networks. *Journal of Computer-Mediated Communication* 14: 1–34.

Chapter 8

Exploring the Use of Social Network Sites in the Workplace

Mary Beth Watson-Manheim

Introduction

There is considerable interest in the use of social media in organizations today. In this chapter I explore the potential for use of social network sites (SNSs) for performing organizational work activities. I focus on the use of SNSs in the workplace for communication and collaboration between employees (either in the same or different organizations), which is directed toward the range of firm activities supporting the production and distribution of products and services. In other words, this chapter is not focused on customer interactions primarily directed toward the marketing of products and services or the management of the firm's brand.

The question I explore is what value a new set of communication media tools can bring to organizations where employees already have a plethora of media to choose from to perform work activities, and under what conditions is it likely that these tools will be adopted. In particular, I discuss the use of SNSs to perform collaborative work activities. There are a wide variety of different types of SNS available to users which have had varying degrees of success (boyd & Ellison, 2008). However, I do not focus on a particular site, i.e., LinkedIn or MySpace, but in software applications that enable similar functionalities. In this chapter, I base my discussion of SNSs on the general definition offered by boyd and Ellison (2008):

> web-based services that allow individuals to (1) construct a public or semi-public profile within a bounded system, (2) articulate a list of other users with whom they share a connection, and (3) view and traverse their list of connections and those made by others within the system.
>
> (p. 211)

In line with Grudin (2006), I argue that a significant benefit of social media in organizations will likely be for knowledge management, which includes "acquiring or creating knowledge, transforming it into a reusable form, retaining it, and finding and reusing it" (Grudin, 2006, p. 1). A number of different types of software products have been developed to support organizational knowledge management, e.g., document management systems, other information repositories, expertise location systems. However, these products have generally not been as successful as expected; they are often cumbersome to use while providing limited benefit, and are expensive to implement and maintain (Grudin, 2006). Social media, on the other hand, require much fewer resources to implement, e.g., equipment, maintenance, and user training. Moreover, they are self-organizing and make information and networks of activity highly visible.

The adoption of a new communication medium in organizations is complicated. Organizations have become more and more geographically distributed with increasing dependence on electronic media for communication and collaboration. Employees have a wide variety of communication media to use in performing work activities, from email to instant messaging to pagers to groupware applications to the telephone, in addition to new social media such as wikis and blogs. The variety of devices and applications in use has increased the complexity of the communication environment. Multiple communication media are used both separately and in combination with usage patterns varying across different teams and different work processes (Watson-Manheim & Belanger, 2007). The introduction of any new communication medium into an organization disrupts existing communication practices. New usage structures and routines must be developed for the new medium and integrated into the overall communication patterns of the user community (Rennecker & Godwin, 2003; Orlikowski, 2000).

Hence, while the use of social media may offer a number of benefits for organizations, when and under what conditions adoption will take place is not clear. In this chapter, I explore this question. I first present a brief example (based on a summary of several conversations with senior IT executives) of a company that expects to receive benefits from the organizational use of a specific social media tool, SNSs, but sees considerable barriers in the actual adoption of the medium. I then explore more generally the unique capabilities of SNSs and the benefits use of this medium may offer to today's organization. I introduce the notion of communication media repertoire to investigate the introduction of a new medium into the existing array of communication media used in an organization (Watson-Manheim & Belanger, 2007).

SNSs at GenCo

GenCo is a large multinational corporation with approximately 75,000 employees and offices in more than 100 countries. GenCo is very decentralized with autonomous business units focused on specialty products and services for the healthcare industry. Because of the focus on different products with different customer needs and different levels and types of product complexity, the units operate differently. Yet, there are potential synergies across product lines. Co-marketing and co-development of product lines and services is a potential growth area. For example, drugs and services developed and marketed for different diseases may be co-branded to provide a broader range of services for a healthcare patient with multiple needs.

The challenge faced by management is how to foster connections between individuals across autonomous business units of a highly distributed company in a complex and rapidly changing industry. A common management practice to address this problem is to create customer-facing cross-functional teams across different areas of the firm and providing groupware, e.g., WebEx^{TM}, or other electronic communication platforms to support collaboration between these individuals. However, management at GenCo believes that it is difficult to predetermine the members of these teams. The rapidly changing environment, both in discovery of new treatments and in the regulation of treatments, means that it is difficult to ascertain the next innovation or the individuals with the knowledge to develop the innovation. Instead, the firm wants to focus on creating social connections to support the emergence of collaborative relationships that will lead to innovation.

GenCo IT managers report that they have been unable to find one tool that supports the development of social connections between disparate individuals. The emergence of effective teams that can work together to produce a product or service innovation requires not only that members have the necessary expertise but also that they can work cohesively together. As one manager said, "There is a difference between finding an expert and finding a 'trusted' expert." Thus, the challenge is two-fold. There is the challenge of finding and connecting people with the needed expertise, but also providing a social context for trusting relationships to emerge. Managers feel that SNSs add important context to information such as: how is this person related to me? Who do they know that I know? Is their background similar to mine? This social context is especially critical to the working relationships of distant employees.

Finally, management expects that SNSs can offer intangible benefits that would be valuable to GenCo. First, in an increasingly discontinuous work environment, SNSs offer a platform for creating a social community within the workplace. Second, management feels that young people, who have deeply integrated SNS use into their personal life, will be more likely to work at firms that support this communication platform.

This GenCo example does not represent one particular firm but an aggregation of comments made by IT managers at a number of firms with employees, and hence knowledge, distributed across many geographic locations. GenCo, like many firms, is competing in an industry marked by rapid change, global competition, and the need for continuous innovation. I next discuss in more detail the changes that are taking place in the workplace and the possible limitations of current communication media used in these firms.

Connecting in a Discontinuous Work Environment

The ability of an organization to assess and respond rapidly to the competitive environment is a necessity in a hypercompetitive environment. Communication with colleagues is critical to performing work activities in this environment. This is particularly true in the complex and knowledge-intensive environment of a company such as GenCo. The expertise of employees is a critical capability of the firm. Leveraging that expertise to bring new innovative products and services to market faster than the competition is a core competitive advantage of the firm.

Performing work activities often involves the application of individuals' knowledge or expertise to generate new knowledge (O'Leary, Wooley, & Mortensen, 2008). New knowledge is created as individuals exchange and combine knowledge through communication events (Nonaka, 1994). Although ranging in degree, knowledge work tasks are inherently ill-structured (Quinn, 2005). As seen at GenCo, it is not always predictable what particular expertise is needed in a project. For example, an employee with expertise in nutrition may see an opportunity in the market for co-marketing cholesterol-lowering drugs with nutrition advice. After putting together a team with expertise in both areas and surveying the market, the group may decide that they also need someone with understanding of diabetic needs. In other words, the combination of expertise needed to develop an innovative product or service may evolve over the life of the project.

A critical component of knowledge work, then, is to be able to identify individuals with needed expertise in a timely manner and communicate with them at a productive level. For example, the GenCo team may simply need information about the possibility of swelling or weight gain in diabetic patients with abnormal cholesterol. Communication in this instance may involve finding relevant resources and gathering information. On the other hand, the team may actually need an expert to contribute as a member of the team which could require a different set of skills and a different working relationship. To effectively perform work activities, knowledge workers invest significant time and effort to develop and maintain personal social networks of contacts to fit the specific needs of a situation. "These networks are a significant organizing principal for work and information" (Nardi et al., 2002, p. 89).

Although hierarchical organizations still provide important efficiencies in the global economy, organizations are flatter and more decentralized, often spread across a number of geographic locations. Organizational borders are more and more porous; integration across the supply chain, alliances with both customers and competitors, and other types of partnerships mean that an employee's network of contacts often includes members from the same and different organizations who work at various locations which can be spread across one or many different countries.

While necessary, it is complicated and expensive for employees to use their networks of personal relationships to get the resources they need to perform work activities (Nardi et al., 2002). Maintaining a personal network requires significant effort when compared to hierarchical or formal organizational relationships, which are pre-determined and role-based. For example, employees must remember identities of and details about individuals who are not contacted frequently, connections between people, and what information or documents have previously been exchanged. Whereas in formal organizational relationships, such specific information is not required: knowing the formal role of the person would provide sufficient information to acquire the needed resources (Nardi et al., 2002).

Thus, while the use of electronic communication makes it easier to engage in communication with colleagues regardless of location, the complexity of work relationships and communication practices is increasing. The speed at which connections between people are configured and reconfigured has increased dramatically, as has the number of connections an employee may have. Workers increasingly communicate electronically to work with colleagues at distant locations, often without actually meeting colleagues face-to-face. Work activities must be dynamically allocated across people or subgroups depending on environmental demands, resulting in increased switching of tasks, roles, and work assignments.

A key characteristic of these situations is that connected individuals are working across boundaries which create discontinuities, i.e., gaps or lack of coherence in aspects of work (Watson-Manheim, Chudoba, & Crowston, 2002). Boundaries can include the temporal work location (e.g., working asynchronously across time zones), geographic work location, work group membership (e.g., who you work with), and cultural backgrounds, either national or professional. Workers may collaborate across organizational boundaries, e.g., teams in supply chain, or boundaries in national or professional background, e.g., cross-functional teams, global software development teams (Espinosa, Cummings, Wilson, & Pearce, 2003).

Working across boundaries can highlight a lack of shared context that can lead to difficulties performing collaborative work activities. Individuals can have differing priorities, norms of behavior, communication practices, and understanding of problems that can create a lack of coherent work practices. For example, a team with members primarily in the US which adds a member from a work unit in China may suddenly face discontinuities in time zone and language. Established communication norms and work practices will need to be adjusted if the team is to collaborate effectively. Similarly, a manager of a team in an inter-organizational global alliance described the following difficulties that members faced:

> Dissimilar market conditions and customer acceptance expectations led to different understanding of the product, and complicated the selling process. In Europe, standards are a big issue. Everything has to meet the particular government's environmental, electrical, etc. standards and this makes selling the product more complicated than in the US.
>
> (Personal conversation with management)

Thus, differences in the political and regulatory environments in the respective countries can also create significant challenges to distributed workers.

An increasingly common feature of today's work environment is multi-teaming, where an employee is a member of multiple teams at any one time (Chudoba, Wynn, Lu, & Watson-Manheim, 2005; O'Leary et al., 2009). This can amplify the effect of discontinuities as individuals may not only face a discontinuous team environment but also discontinuities across teams. Chudoba et al. (2005) found that employees at Intel were members of an average of five teams/person, with a number of employees reporting membership on as many as 12 teams. Team membership can change rapidly (O'Leary et al., 2009) to respond to shifting requirements or environmental changes; members move in and out depending on current priorities. New members can be added as skills are needed without consideration of geographic location. These members may be core, i.e., active participants who are integral to the overall work of the team, or they may be peripheral, i.e., less-active participants who only attend meetings when their particular area is being addressed or when their skill is needed (Crowston & Howison, 2005).

Paradoxically, the dramatic increase in information and resources available to knowledge workers and the ease with which connections can be formed has increased the complexity of the work environment. Electronic communication media is becoming deeply integrated into knowledge work activities, while the work environment employees face is often disconnected.

More Ways to Connect but Less Connectedness

At GenCo, management does not believe current electronic communication platforms provide the support for connecting individuals in an increasingly fragmented and discontinuous environment. On the surface, this seems to be a surprising assessment as there are an increasing number of communication media available in the workplace for individuals to use in performing collaborative activities and sharing information. Email is ubiquitous, available on an individual's desktop, laptop, or mobile device. Employees can also use instant messaging and text messaging via these devices. Employees report that synchronous voice conversations via telephone at the desk, over landline or VOIP, or the mobile phone, are still some of the most commonly used media. In general, this set of communication media allows directed communication between a sender and an unlimited, but pre-determined, number of recipients. The conversation is generally available only to those who are participating.

Other applications such as electronic bulletin boards, discussion forums, and online communities allow individuals to share, request, or discuss information in a more public manner. Conversations are open to all members of the community. Any message can be read (and responded to) by anyone else who is a member. Members of the community may be predefined by organizational role or they may emerge based on interest. These conversations can be organized and archived in document databases although this archiving does not always happen.

The increasing digitization of information and the increase in electronic communication has led to an explosion of explicit organizational knowledge available to be transmitted and reused or combined to create new knowledge. Despite the ease of communicating electronically, actually finding relevant information in a timely manner is a continuing problem in the workplace (Grudin, 2006). Grudin cites the following example of a typical problem: "a pharmaceutical company found that although clinical tests of a compound are expensive, searching for possible past test results of a compound would be more expensive than retesting some of them" (2006, p. 1).

Despite the proliferation of document management systems to catalog structured documents, organized discussions archived in document databases, and other electronic storage and retrieval devices, applicable knowledge remains difficult to find. Moreover, the social context surrounding the knowledge is often not available, e.g., who created it under what circumstances. Stripped of its context, the knowledge becomes even more difficult to reuse.

As compared to other electronic media, SNSs offer a number of advantages for organizations. SNSs facilitate the emergent formation of new relationships and support the maintenance of existing relationships (Ellison, Lampe, Steinfield, & Vitak, 2010). Importantly, SNSs enable users to articulate and make visible their social networks (boyd & Ellison, 2008). After joining an SNS, users are prompted to identify others in the system with whom they have a relationship. The unique nature of SNSs allows users to more quickly establish contextual information about contacts—for example, situating new acquaintances within their existing network of contacts, e.g., are any of their friends also my friends or belong to the same group that I belong to?

While SNSs are organized around individuals, their value comes from the social capital created within the community. The information on the SNS is user generated and propagated through the users' network of contacts. More personally relevant information is spread faster and more easily. Users of SNSs acquire, evaluate, and disseminate information, e.g., comparing movie preferences, with their network of contacts. In addition, they are developing methods of leading and influencing others toward collective goals, e.g., use of SNSs for political activity was especially prominent in the recent US Presidential election (Kaye, 2010). These actions and the understanding of using the capabilities of media to carry them out are similar to the skills required of knowledge workers in distributed organizations.

Despite the potential of significant benefit for GenCo, management is skeptical of the actual adoption of this medium by employees. The benefits of SNSs to an individual user, such as a feeling of community or the ability to connect with colleagues with common interests, are difficult to realize until the medium has an adequate critical mass of users. Like any communication medium, the benefits increase dramatically as the number of users increase. However, it is unclear what benefit users will find in the medium until a large number of people are using the site.

I suggest that this difficulty is compounded by the fact that the adoption of any new communication medium requires a change in an individual's communication practices. If this change is to be sustained, the practices of the individual's communication partners must also change and new norms of communication develop. I propose that the adoption of SNSs will be more likely to be pushed into the organization as they become more widely established in external social practices instead of being pulled into the organization as previous knowledge management applications or most other communication media. I next use the concept of a communication media repertoire as a lens to view the adoption of SNSs in organizations.

Communication Media Repertoire

Watson-Manheim and Belanger (2007) put forth the notion of a communication media repertoire to investigate the use of multiple communication media in organizations. They define a communication media repertoire as "the collection of communication channels and identifiable routines of use for specific communication purposes within a defined community" (p. 268). The general framework they propose is shown in Figure 8.1. I have modified the framework by elaborating their original description of institutional conditions to include both organizational and social components.

The framework links institutional conditions and norms of communication usage with individual perceptions of different media and with usage patterns. It emphasizes the dynamic nature of the communication media repertoires. Individuals within a work community use different media for different purposes. Through usage, they develop rules or norms for communicating, thereby forming communication media repertoires. A community's communication media repertoire is reflexively constructed through media usage in the performance of work activities. Thus, use of a medium (or combination of media) plays a central role in understanding the repertoires in the community. In a specific situation, media usage is influenced by:

1. the existing repertoire of practices,
2. structuring conditions, and
3. perceived consequences of use.

Structuring conditions include both institutional and situational conditions. Institutional conditions shape the set of possibilities of media usage that a user perceives as appropriate. Institutional conditions can include physical structure, organizational culture, and incentive structures (Watson-Manheim & Belanger, 2007). For example, employees in the two organizations they studied worked in different physical structures. In one organization the employees were in a "hoteling" environment, where there were no permanent offices. Employees came to work in an office at intermittent times during the week, spending the rest of the time in a client office or at home. In the second organization, employees had collocated permanent offices at a large customer location. Not surprisingly, employees in the two different organizations had different preferences for the use of face-to-face meetings for various communication processes, e.g., knowledge sharing, coordination, etc.

More importantly, the employees reported very different perceptions of the capabilities of the media to support the same communication processes. At the first organization, employees did not simply report that FTF meetings were convenient so they did not use electronic media for meetings, they stressed the value of capabilities of FTF meetings (e.g., the ability to look someone in the eye) as a reason for using this medium. On the other hand, individuals in the "hoteling" organization stressed capabilities of electronic media that made it most suitable for accomplishing the same communication process.

Through routine use of media and the perceived consequence of usage, employees in the work unit developed perceptions of the capabilities of the media and appropriateness of use (Watson-Manheim & Belanger, 2007;

Yates & Orlikowski, 1992). For example, trying to hold FTF meetings at the "hoteling" organization required employees to restructure their entire day while electronic media did not. In this framework, institutional conditions shape the set of possibilities, while situational conditions can have more influence over which practice is invoked at a particular point in time. These variations are based on individuals' interpretations of the situation and their perception of the capabilities that the media afford in a given situation. It is through situational variances that new media practices are developed and adopted in the user community as suggested in the following example.

> An example from our research illustrates the improvisational nature of media usage practices. At IntOrg, the pager was described as the primary medium for urgent communications. In practice, understanding of what exactly was meant by "urgent" and when to actually use the pager varied significantly. While most employees agree that the pager was to be used when there was an immediate need to respond to a customer request or concern, the pager was also seen as a way to insure a timely response under a variety of circumstances. Consequently, some employees report that the pager was overused making it difficult to get a timely response and often causing them to use an alternative medium in combination with the pager. These isolated examples did not emerge as an alternate norm of media usage in urgent situations; however, this case provides an example of the dynamic nature of the repertoires and how actual usage practices and observations of consequences can ultimately lead to changes in norms of usage.
>
> (Watson-Manheim & Belanger, 2007, p. 285)

Communication media repertoires are constituted and reconstituted through media usage in the performance of ongoing, routine work activities. Situational variations can lead to the emergence of new norms. It is clear that the introduction of a new communication medium will also disrupt existing work practices and communication norms. For this reason, even when the use of a new medium can bring benefit to those who use it, there is often resistance to changing established patterns of behavior. For individuals to change existing communication practices requires them to envision some benefit that will offset the effort required to learn to use a new medium. In addition, the repertoire of the communication must be adapted to encompass the new medium.

Many software applications have been developed and implemented in organizations to help users find and reuse knowledge, and make connections with individuals who have expertise in a particular domain. However, these applications have met with little success due to limited use by organizational members. In many cases, knowledge workers have not found that these applications actually provide sufficient advantage in their search for resources, either information or people, to integrate them into their media repertoire (Grudin, 2006).

Influence of External Communication Practices

A communication media repertoire is defined to exist with a particular user community. As use of the Internet has become more wide-spread and more integrated into the communication practices of individuals across the multiple spheres of their lives, organizational users belong to different communities with different understandings and expectations of communication media use. It is reasonable to expect that social practices external to the organization can influence the development of a repertoire in an organization (Markus, 1994; Yates & Orlikowski, 1992).

SNSs represent an electronic communication medium where social norms are rapidly being developed outside of the organization. For example, a large number of entry-level employees, who entered college after 2004 when Facebook began to spread across college campuses, have integrated the medium into their methods of meeting new people and building relationships. In general, boyd and Ellison (2008) argue that through regular use SNSs become "deeply embedded in people's lives." Users can "gather" with their friends even when they are not geographically collocated, thereby potentially strengthening relationships that may have weakened due to inactivity. Contrary to some popular perceptions, SNSs are not primarily used by people to meet strangers but to deepen and extend offline connections (Ellison et al., 2010). Thus, people who use SNSs routinely will develop communication norms that include SNS usage practices. These individuals will bring an understanding of capabilities of SNSs into the organization. Increasingly they will expect to use similar strategies and technologies to develop relationships and gather information for job performance.

To capture this phenomenon, I extend the communication media repertoire framework by elaborating the notion of institution as put forth by Watson-Manheim and Belanger (2007). They categorize physical structure, the social structure, and incentive structure (for use of different media) as institutional factors. These three structural dimensions are located within the organizations they were studying. The authors did not consider the influence of technology usage practices developed outside of the organization. In Figure 8.1, I suggest that institutional structuring conditions and norms of usage are composed of an organizational aspect and a social aspect. The social aspect includes the normative use of media by an employee referent group outside of the organization.

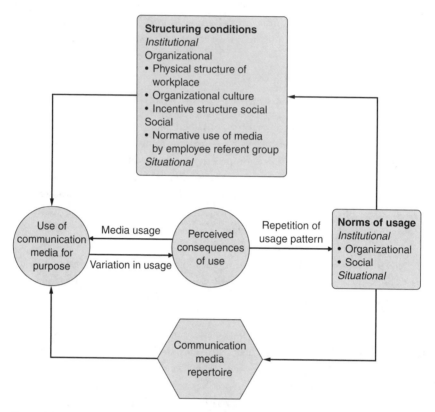

Figure 8.1 Framework for investigating communication media repertoire (source: adapted from Watson-Manheim & Belanger, 2007).

The intangible benefit of community building may become a significant motivating factor for many users if the use of SNSs becomes more accepted across society. SNSs will likely become places to connect with others with similar interests or backgrounds. This may be a powerful motivator in an increasingly dispersed organization where people are commonly separated from their work group, e.g., they are members of a geographically distributed team. Physical separation from co-workers, or isolation in the case of telecommuters, can cause feelings of isolation and loss of identity, which can be detrimental to organizational cohesion.

I contend that the adoption of SNSs may be primarily a grass-roots effort, pushed into the organization by external social norms initially, rather than largely pulled through a formal implementation. This does not mean, however, that management in the organizations will not exercise control over the process. It is not clear how the process will evolve, but management still must align use of the medium and the work activities people engage in with the overall goals of the organization. New types of incentives may be needed, not individual, group, or organization, but some motivation to stimulate development of self-organized networks, e.g., encourage people to collaborate to solve complex problems where the expertise needed is not immediately clear.

In addition, management must address issues of security and privacy. There are likely long-term implications stemming from the adoption of SNSs for organizational use. Since SNSs by design enable users to construct an identity within a community, there will be implications for security of information in an organization. For example, self-organized teams of employees will need some way to insure that co-workers they have never met are in fact who they say they are; that their profile and connections are an accurate representation.

References

boyd, d. m., & Ellison, N. B. (2008). Social network sites: Definition, history, and scholarship. *Journal of Computer-Mediated Communication, 13*(1), 210–230.

Chudoba, K., Wynn, E., Lu, M., & Watson-Manheim, M. B. (2005). How virtual are we? Measuring virtuality and understanding its impact in a global organization. *Information Systems Journal, 15*(4), 279–306.

Crowston, K., & Howison, J. (2005). The social structure of free and open source software development. *First Monday, 10*(2).

Ellison, N., Lampe, C., Steinfield, C., & Vitak, J. (2010). With a little help from my friends: How social network sites affect social capital processes. In Z. Papacharissi (Ed.), *A networked self: Identity, community, and culture on social network sites* (pp. 124–145). New York, NY: Routledge, Taylor and Francis.

Espinosa, J. A., Cummings, J. N., Wilson, J. M., & Pearce, B. M. (2003). Team boundary issues across multiple global firms. *Journal of Management Information Systems, 19*(4), 157–190.

Grudin, J. (2006). Enterprise knowledge management and emerging technologies. *Proceedings of the 39th Annual Hawaii International Conference on System Sciences*, vol. 3.

Kaye, B. K. (2010). Between Barack and a net place: Motivations for using social network sites and blogs for political information. In Z. Papacharissi (Ed.), *A networked self: Identity, community, and culture on social network sites* (pp. 208–231). New York, NY: Routledge, Taylor and Francis.

Markus, M. L. (1994). Electronic mail as the medium of managerial choice. *Organization Science, 5*(4), 502–527.

Nardi, B. A., Whittaker, S., Isaacs, E., Creech, M., Johnson, J., & Hainsworth, J. (2002). Integrating communication and information through ContactMap. *Communications of the ACM, 45*(4), 89–95.

Nonaka, I. (1994). A dynamic theory of organizational knowledge creation. *Organization Science, 5*(1), 14–37.

O'Leary, M., Wooley, A., & Mortensen, M. (2009). Multiple team membership: Productivity and learning effects for individuals, teams, and organizations. MIT working paper: http://papers.ssrn.com/.

Orlikowski, W. J. (2000). Using technology and constituting structures: A practice lens for studying technology in organizations. *Organization Science, 11*(4), 404–428.

Quinn, R. W. (2005). Flow in knowledge work: High performance experience in the design of national security technology. *Administrative Science Quarterly, 50*(4), 610–641.

Rennecker, J., & Godwin, L. (2003). *Theorizing the unintended consequences of instant messaging (IM) use.* Presented at Academy of Management OCIS Division, Seattle, WA.

Watson-Manheim, M. B., & Belanger, F. (2007). Communication media repertoires: Dealing with the multiplicity of media choices. *MIS Quarterly, 31*(2), 267–293.

Watson-Manheim, M. B., Chudoba, K., & Crowston, K. (2002). Discontinuities and continuities: A new way to understand virtual work. *Information, Technology, and People, 15*(3), 191–209.

Yates, J. A., & Orlikowski, W. J. (1992). Genres of organizational communication: A structurational approach to studying communication and media. *Academy of Management Review, 17*(2), 299–326.

Part III

Convergent Practices

Intuitive Appropriations of Social Network Site Affordances

Chapter 9

United We Stand?

Online Social Network Sites and Civic Engagement

Thomas J. Johnson, Weiwu Zhang,
Shannon L. Bichard, and Trent Seltzer

The 2008 election marked a seismic shift in how candidates, particularly Barack Obama, campaigned for the presidency. Pundits have touted 2008 as the Facebook Election where the top-down style of political campaigning was replaced by the grass-roots dynamics of online social networks, particularly Facebook and YouTube. Obama used his huge advantage in number of Facebook members over challengers Hillary Clinton and John McCain to mobilize an army of volunteers and to amass a huge campaign war chest through his legion of small, individual donors (Fraser & Dutta, 2008; Stelter, 2008). YouTube provided a way for both candidates to get their message directly to the voter and for citizens to create videos and become part of the campaign conversation (Grove, 2008).

Most of the work on social network sites (SNSs) has focused on user characteristics and user motives for accessing these sites (e.g., boyd, 2004; Kaye, 2010; Papacharissi & Mendelson, 2008; Postelnicu & Cozma, 2007, 2008; Royal, 2008; Sweetser & Weaver-Lariscy, 2007). Less attention has been paid to the effects of social network sites on users' political attitudes and behaviors. The few studies that have examined the connection between social network sites and political attitudes suggest that, in general, these sites may not have much influence on political attitudes and behavior (Polstelnicu & Cozma, 2008; Zhang, Johnson, Seltzer, & Bichard, in press), although political users of SNSs may do a much better job of predicting political attitudes and behaviors (Kim & Geidner, 2008; Utz, 2009; Valenzuela, Park, & Kee, 2009; Vitak, Zube, Smock, Carr, Ellison, & Lampe, 2009).

This study uses a national online panel of 533 Internet users to explore the degree to which relying on social network sites and YouTube will predict offline political participation, online political participation, intent to vote, and reliance on face-to-face discussion for political information.

Social Network Sites and Political Engagement

Most of the studies examining the effects of social networks on political atti-tudes and behavior have centered on social capital (Ellison, Lampe, Steinfield, & Vitak, 2010; Ellison, Steinfield, & Lampe, 2007; Leiner, Hohlfeld, & Quiring, 2009; Royal, 2008; Steinfield, Ellison, & Lampe, 2008; Valenzuela, Park, & Kee, 2009) because studies suggest that people primarily use social network sites to remain in contact with existing friends and learn more about individuals they meet offline (boyd & Ellison, 2007; Lampe, Ellison, & Stein-field, 2006). Less attention has been paid to whether social network sites influ-ence political attitudes and behavior, and that evidence has been mixed.

Studies suggest that social network site users score high on political atti-tudes and behaviors such as political interest, campaign interest, and political efficacy (Kaye, 2010; Kim & Geidner, 2008; Postelnicu & Cozma, 2008; Vitak et al., 2009), but social network use in general does not seem strongly related to political attitudes and behaviors. Postelnicu and Cozma (2008) found that motivations for using social network sites had little influence on campaign involvement, interest, and efficacy. Similarly, Zhang and associates (in press) found social network use linked to civic participation, but not political partici-pation or confidence in government. Zhang and associates suggested that because social network sites are designed to connect individuals, it is not sur-prising that it is more connected to civic participation such as volunteering for local organizations.

However, studies that look specifically at political uses of social network sites indicate they can have a much greater influence on political attitudes and behav-iors (Kim & Geidner, 2008; Utz, 2009; Valenzuela et al., 2009; Vitak et al., 2009). For instance, Kim and Geidner (2008) found that time spent with social network sites had little influence on increasing the benefits of voting and was negatively related to perceptions of civic duty. On the other hand, political online social network use (i.e., measures of visiting candidate profiles on a social network site and sending messages to the candidate) both increased the per-ceived benefits of voting as well as some of the variables linked to the perception that voting is rewarding, such as self-efficacy, bridging social capital, and civic duty. Similarly, while Vitak and associates (2009) found that both political activ-ity on Facebook and exposure to Facebook political activity predicted offline and online political behavior, the intensity of Facebook activity was actually nega-tively related. The researchers also found that political knowledge, political interest, and political participation predicted political activity on Facebook.

These results suggest that, among general social network users, reliance on these sites does not greatly boost political involvement, although it could increase civic involvement because of the social nature of these sites. But, among those already interested in election campaigns, reliance on social network sites may increase the likelihood that they seek out political information. As Vitak and associates (2009) suggest, Facebook may also provide a comfortable environment for those not normally engaged in politics to explore political activity because they see their friends engaged in political behavior on Facebook, which, in turn, translates into offline political participation.

YouTube and Political Engagement

The relationship between the use of YouTube and political participation bears some further discussion due to the characteristics of YouTube that set it apart from other social network sites. First and foremost, YouTube is focused on video sharing while other social network sites, although capable of video sharing, focus more on relationship building and maintaining interaction with other users; this includes sharing multimedia, but is not limited to videos. Second, sites such as Facebook and LinkedIn require the user to have their own account (i.e., to create a profile in the networked space) in order to view and interact with other users and user content. YouTube is different in that, while users may create a profile on their site to *manage* content (i.e., upload, favorite, rate, and comment on videos), other Internet users can visit the site and *view* content without creating a YouTube profile. Additionally, visitors to YouTube who do not have accounts can still share content off-site by copying and pasting the URLs of YouTube videos into emails along with commentary in the body of the message that contextualizes the video much in the same way registered users can share and comment on videos on the YouTube site itself. Therefore, YouTube acts both as a space for establishing and maintaining a social network as well as a channel for consuming video content without directly taking part in the site's social network. This makes the content on YouTube accessible to a broader online audience beyond only Internet users who have YouTube accounts.

A third important distinction between YouTube and other social network sites is that the networks on sites such as Facebook and MySpace often (though not exclusively) feature interactions between users who also have interpersonal connections offline, potentially resulting in homogeneous networks of likeminded individuals interacting with one another in the networked space (boyd & Ellison, 2007; Lampe, Ellison, & Steinfield, 2006). This is relevant to our study because political discussion that takes place with likeminded individuals within homogeneous networks serves to reinforce pre-existing political positions (Cho, 2005). However, the openly accessible content on YouTube means that site visitors could be more likely to be exposed to a heterogeneous online network where other users, content, and opinions reflect a diversity of political perspectives. This is important in that exposure to heterogeneous discussion networks has been linked to increased levels of political participation and political knowledge (Scheufele, Hardy, Brossard, Waismel-Manor, & Nisbet, 2006), nurturing dialogue and deliberation (MacKuen, 1990), and fostering understanding and tolerance (Mutz & Mondak, 2006).

These findings would suggest that social network sites that expose users to diverse political opinions might result in positive political outcomes such as increased political participation, knowledge, and discussion with others both online and offline. However, Zhang et al. (in press) found that social network sites, including YouTube, did not influence political participation or confidence in government, although it did have a positive effect on civic engagement. While their study did not differentiate between YouTube and other social network sites, this study does, and may help identify whether or not YouTube influences political participation in a different manner than social network sites. Such a distinction takes into account (a) the potential demographic and motivational differences in the types of users who frequent social network sites versus those that visit YouTube and (b) the differences in the degree of network integration required of users seeking to access and share content on those sites.

Social Network Sites and Interpersonal Discussion

Interpersonal discussion is key to a functioning democracy because of the role discussion plays in sound political deliberation (Brundidge, 2006, 2008; De Tocqueville, 1965). Discussion plays a major role in political learning, attitude formation, and behavior (Huckfeldt & Sprague, 1995; MacKuen & Brown, 1987). Studies have revealed that interpersonal discussion about politics is related to an increase in political involvement (Calhoun, 1988; McLeod, Scheufele, & Moy, 1999).

Political conversation often facilitates an increased desire to participate in political affairs (Katz, 1992) because the very act of interacting with one another helps to solidify opinions. Deliberation also serves to empower citizens (Warren, 1992). Political conversation contributes to the development of higher-quality opinions because of the refinement inherent in dialogue (Price, Nir, & Cappella, 2002).

Communication with others can stimulate political activity. This is especially true for local political engagement. Stamm, Emig, and Hesse (1997) suggest a key role of interpersonal discussion as "the primary mechanism for community integration." Interpersonal communication networks serve to promote political participation by providing information regarding how to get involved, and by conveying a sense of duty and obligation to serve the local community (Verba, Schlozman, Brady, & Nie, 1995).

Research indicates that the development of homogeneous social networks reinforces existing political dispositions, often leading to more actively empowered political behavior (Carey, 1989; Walsh, 2003). On the other hand, a more diverse social network stimulates discussion of controversial topics. Past analyses have found that citizens with more heterogeneous discussion networks are more likely to participate in community forums and assorted political activities (McLeod et al., 1999; Scheufele et al., 2006). It is apparent that interpersonal discussion with those of similar and different viewpoints is related to political activity at many levels.

While few studies have examined whether or not discussion on social network sites specifically boosts offline political discussion, several social capital studies have focused on social network sites' ability to enhance a sense of community, specifically by bridging and bonding social capital. Bonding social capital is found between individuals in more tightly knit, homogeneous communities such as family and friends, and may provide emotional support. Bridging social capital involves connecting more heterogeneous groups of people to bring about social and political change (Putnam, 2000).

Studies suggest that social network sites may increase both bonding and bridging social capital (Ellison et al., 2007, 2010; Royal, 2008; Stevens, Chattopadhyay, & Rill, 2008). Social network users are significantly more likely to use the sites to connect with someone they already know offline than meeting new people (Ellison et al., 2010; Mendelson & Papacharissi, 2010). They also perceive that the primary audience for their SNS profile is people they know offline, suggesting social network sites increase bonding social capital (Ellison et al., 2007, 2010). Social network sites also allow users to join groups and causes that could potentially connect them with a diverse group of people. Nearly 80% of Facebook and MySpace users in one survey had joined a group (Royal, 2008), suggesting that social network sites can also create bridging capital.

Past research would suggest that social networking behavior allows users access to diverse political opinions that might stimulate political behavior such as increased interpersonal engagement about politics offline. The increased social nature of social network sites when compared with YouTube would suggest that reliance on SNSs may even prove a stronger predictor of face-to-face interpersonal discussion about political matters.

Social Network Sites in the 2008 Presidential Campaign

While social network sites may not appear to be a source of political news because of their focus on connecting friends, more than half (52%) of social network users relied on these sites for political information. In keeping with the social nature of network sites, the main reasons individuals relied on social network sites were to discover which candidates their friends voted for (41%) and one-third posted political information for their friends to see. However, nearly a quarter (23%) used the sites to get campaign information and 16% started or joined a political cause or group. Young voters, not surprisingly, used social network for political purposes (65%) almost twice as much as those over 45 (36%) (Smith, 2009). Young voters may also use social network sites differently than older ones, as most see themselves as more than consumers of news but conduits, emailing friends links and videos, and receiving them in return (Stelter, 2008).

Political observers have credited Obama's understanding of social network sites as not only key to his election, but also in changing the way elections are conducted. Obama relied on both mainstream (MySpace and Facebook) and niche sites (redandblueamerica, blackplanet) to raise funds, attract volunteers, and publicize campaign events (Fraser & Dutta, 2008; Stelter, 2008). Obama created his own social network site, Mybarackobama.com (MyBO), which allowed voters to create their own blog, join groups of likeminded individuals (such as Texans for Obama), create or find out about Obama-related events, as well as make phone calls to potential supporters in their neighborhood or adjoining states (Fraser & Dutta, 2008; Sanchez, 2008). Political observers also credited Obama's huge advantage in attracting campaign funds and volunteers for defeating Hillary Clinton in the primaries and John McCain in the general election campaign in part to his skilled use of social network sites. Obama signed up 2.4 million Facebook users as supporters, compared with just 624,000 for McCain. Facebook helped attract new, young voters who provided Obama with his margin of victory. The number of voters under 30 rose by 3.4 million from 2004 to 2008 and about 66% of those voters supported Obama (Sanchez, 2008).

The use of social network sites represented a change from the usual top-down campaign style to a much more grass-roots campaign that empowered voters by focusing more on putting volunteers in contact with each other than with the Obama campaign. As CNN analyst Leslie Sanchez (2008) noted, "Web-based political social networking requires empowerment—introducing well-trained, highly motivated local supporters to one another and then turning the campaign over to them."

Obama's SNS strategy allowed him to raise about 50% more than McCain in the first six months of 2008, with almost 88% coming online and with two million donations of less than $200. Thus, Obama could spend more time on the campaign trail and less time on the phones begging for donations (Holahan, 2008).

Social network sites not only served as a campaign tool for candidates. Social networks, both alone and partnered with media organizations, also worked to involve and inform voters. For instance, Facebook launched a forum to encourage online debates and partnered with ABC for election coverage and political forums. On Election Day, Facebook posted an online virtual ticker that urged users to go to the polls (Sanchez, 2008).

Mainstream news organizations are increasingly relying on social network sites to attract younger readers to their websites (Emmett, 2008). Several media organizations have created a strong online presence through advertising and by creating fan pages where members can access news, photos, features, quizzes, and blogs. Many other media sites, such as CNN, ABC, CBS, and CNET, have registered for Facebook Connect, which allows users to log onto participating websites using their Facebook identification to see their friends' activities on the site as well as broadcast their own actions on those sites to their Facebook friends (Emmett, 2008).

Scholars suggest that SNSs are successful in stimulating political activity because they lower the cost of seeking out political information and sharing it with friends (Vitak et al., 2009; Wu, 2009). Vitak and associates (2009), in their study of Facebook use during the 2008 presidential election, note that Facebook easily allows people to connect with politics as they can become a fan of the candidate, download candidate applications to their profile page, share political views through wall posts and status updates, and join various politically oriented groups and causes. Also, SNSs like Facebook add a social element to politics as the site's news feeds allow users to quickly share information or links, or promote political events with members of one's network.

YouTube and the 2008 Elections

Political observers did not have to wait until the 2008 presidential election to understand the importance of YouTube to political campaigns. In the 2006 midterm election, Virginia Senator George Allen saw his re-election chances evaporate after a video captured him using the racial epithet "macaca" in referring to one of his aides (Topcik, 2008).

In the 2008 campaign, online videos became major sources of information for Internet users. A Pew Internet study found that 45% of American Internet users and 60% of those who sought out political information online watched online videos during the campaign, watching videos produced both by the candidate or news organizations (50%) as well as user-generated content (43%). While online video use was highest among those under 30 (67%), still four in 10 online political users over the age of 65 viewed online videos. Furthermore, one-quarter of online political users forwarded the videos to friends (Smith, 2009).

YouTube allowed candidates to post speeches and campaign ads directly to the public, unfiltered by the traditional media (Gueorguieva, 2007; May, 2008). Each of the 16 candidates was given a YouTube channel, and seven candidates (including Barack Obama and Hillary Clinton) announced their candidacy on YouTube (Grove, 2008).

But while YouTube provided candidates a platform to present their message unvarnished to the public, the site also allowed average citizens to create their own political content. Two YouTube videos, "Crush on Obama" by Obama Girl and Will.i.am's "Yes We Can" video clip introduced Obama at the beginning of his campaign, with both getting more than 10 million hits (Fraser & Dutta, 2008). On the other hand, videos about Obama's minister Jeremiah Wright condemning America and about Obama's "adviser and mentor" William Ayers threatened to derail his campaign (Grove, 2008).

YouTube made everyone with a video camera a potential citizen journalist. Campaign gaffes were often captured by citizens attending campaign events (May, 2008). John McCain undoubtedly rued the decision to sing "Bomb Iran" at a campaign event, a video viewed by more than 1.2 million people (Topcik, 2008).

Candidates could decide what campaign ads and speeches they would post online. However, they lost control over the content once it was posted. Hillary Clinton's ad about the telephone ringing in the White House may have helped her capture the popular vote in Texas, but it also became fodder for video parodies. In fact, so many people spoofed the ad that CNN thought the parodies worth a story.

The media helped bring YouTube politics into the mainstream by partnering with the video-sharing site. YouTube combined with CNN to sponsor a debate for both parties, with the public submitting video questions. This debate attracted a 10% larger audience of 18–34 year olds than any other debate (Topcik, 2008). On Election Day, YouTube partnered with PBS for Video the Vote, where more than 3,700 volunteers documented both the voting process in their community as well as looking to document cases of voter fraud (Video the Vote, 2008).

Research Questions

This study examines how YouTube and social network sites influenced political attitudes and behaviors in the 2008 election campaign. More specifically, this study will address the following questions:

RQ1: How will the profile of users of social network sites such as Facebook and MySpace compare to that of users of YouTube in terms of demographic and political characteristics?

RQ2: How well will (a) reliance on social network sites and (b) YouTube for political information predict offline and online political participation, intent to vote, and reliance on face-to-face discussion after controlling for demographic and political variables?

RQ3: Will reliance on social network sites or YouTube for political information be a stronger predictor of political attitudes and behaviors?

Method

Data Collection

An online survey investigating the effects of reliance on YouTube and social network sites such as Facebook and MySpace on political attitudes and behaviors was posted from October 23 to November 3, 2008. Politically interested Internet users were solicited from an online panel operated by a major Western survey research firm. Email invitations were received by 2,309 panel members encouraging them to participate if they used the Internet to search for political information and were eligible to vote in the United States. Respondents were also offered an incentive in the form of a cash drawing. This sample yielded 533 completed surveys with a 23.9% cooperation rate.

Measures

Demographic Variables

This study treated demographics (gender, age, education, income, and race) as exogenous measures.[1] The researchers found that 70.5% of the sample respondents were female. The median age was 48 years old ($SD = 12.8$). On average, respondents reported having "some college" ($SD = 1.2$). Respondents also reported a median household income between $40,001 and $55,000. Also, 87.7% of the respondents were Caucasians, 1.0% Hispanics, 4.5% African Americans, 3.9% Asians, and 2% Native Americans. The race variable was recoded as a dummy variable where Caucasians were "1" and non-Caucasians "0."

Political Antecedent Variables

The strength of party affiliation was measured with a 10-point scale where 1 meant "very weak party affiliation" and 10 meant "very strong party affiliation." Respondents showed fairly strong party affiliation, with an average of 6.6 ($SD = 2.8$). Overall, 39.1% considered themselves moderate, 40.1% conservative, and 20.8% liberal.

Interest in politics was an additive measure of two items: (1) interest in politics in general and (2) interest in the presidential election on a 10-point scale ranging from 1 "absolutely not interested" to 10 "absolutely interested in politics." Respondents are moderately interested in politics in general ($M = 7.0$, $SD = 2.7$).

Efficacy was an additive measure of six Likert-type items adapted from the National Election Studies. Respondents were asked the extent to which they disagreed or agreed with three statements on a five-point scale where 1 meant "strongly disagree" and 5 meant "strongly agree": (1) people like me don't have any say about what the government does (reverse coded); (2) most of our leaders are devoted to the service of our country; (3) every vote counts in an election; (4) politicians never tell us what they really think (reverse coded); (5) I don't think public officials care much about what people like me think (reverse coded); and (6) sometimes politics and government seem so complicated that a person like me can't really understand what is going on (reverse coded) (Cronbach's alpha = 0.70).

Reliance on New Media

On a five-point scale where 1 meant "don't rely on at all" and 5 meant "heavily rely on," respondents were asked the extent to which they relied on social network sites (e.g., Facebook or MySpace) and also the extent to which they relied on YouTube.

Dependent Variables

Respondents were also asked their likelihood of voting in the 2008 presidential election on a 10-point scale where 1 meant "not at all likely" and 10 meant "very likely."

Reliance on face-to-face discussion for political information was a single item measured on a five-point scale where 1 meant "don't rely on at all" and 5 meant "heavily rely on." Respondents were asked the extent to which they relied on face-to-face discussion for political information.

Offline participation was measured by an index of five items adapted from the National Election Studies, where 1 meant "never" participated and 5 meant "very often." Respondents were asked how often they had engaged in a variety of political activities (such as wearing a campaign button, helping a political candidate, giving money to a candidate, attending political meetings, and persuading others to support a candidate) during the past two years.

On the same five-point scale, online political participation was an additive measure of seven items taken from the Pew Research Center. The items were: register your own opinions by participating in an online poll; get information about a candidate's voting record; sent or received emails about the candidates or campaigns; contribute money online to a candidate running for public office; look for more information online about candidates' positions on the issues; find out about endorsements or ratings of candidates by organizations or individuals online; and check the accuracy of claims made by or about the candidates online (Cronbach's alpha $= 0.93$).

Data Analysis Strategies

Data analysis for this study proceeded in two steps. First, crosstabs and means were run to answer the first research question. Second, hierarchical regression analyses were conducted to answer the second and third research questions. Demographics were entered as the first block, followed by political antecedents (political efficacy, political interest, strength of party affiliation, and ideology). Reliance on social network sites and reliance on YouTube were entered as the final block. The results are shown in Tables 9.1–9.6.

Results

The first research question compared and contrasted demographic and political characteristics of the users of social network sites and those of the users of YouTube. Those who never relied on social network sites and YouTube were dropped from the analysis, which left 189 for users of social network sites and 204 for users of YouTube. According to Tables 9.1–9.3, users of social network sites and users of YouTube shared similar demographic and political profiles with few differences. For instance, females relied more heavily on social network sites (72.5%) and YouTube (71.6%), and users were overwhelmingly Caucasian for both social network sites (80.4%) and YouTube (83.3%). Means and standard deviations were almost the same for users of social network sites and those of YouTube in terms of age, education, income, efficacy, political interest, strength of party affiliation, and ideology.

The second research question examined the effects of reliance on social network sites and reliance on YouTube on online and offline political participation, intention to vote, and reliance on face-to-face discussion for political

Table 9.1 Reliance on SNSs and YouTube: Gender crosstabulations

	Males (%)	Females (%)	Total (%)
Users of social network sites	52 (27.5)	137 (72.5)	189 (100)
Users of YouTube	58 (28.4)	146 (71.6)	204 (100)

Table 9.2 Reliance on SNSs and YouTube: Race crosstabulations

	Non-Caucasians (%)	Caucasians (%)	Total (%)
Users of social network sites	37 (19.6)	152 (80.4)	189 (100)
Users of YouTube	34 (16.7)	170 (83.3)	204 (100)

information after controlling for demographic variables and political antecedent variables. As seen in Tables 9.4 and 9.5 after controlling for influences of
demographic variables and political antecedent variables, both reliance on
social network sites ($\beta = 0.30$, $p < 0.001$) and reliance on YouTube ($\beta = 0.15$,
$p < 0.001$) were significant predictors of online political participation; both
were also significant predictors of offline political participation. The more one
relied on YouTube, the less likely one intended to vote, but reliance on social
network sites did not have a significant influence on one's intention to vote.
Reliance on social network sites was also a significant predictor of reliance on
face-to-face discussion for political information ($\beta = 0.29$, $p < 0.001$), while
reliance on YouTube was not ($\beta = 0.02$, n.s.).

In terms of political antecedent variables, people's political interest was a
significant predictor of all dependent variables. The more interest people had
in politics, the more they would participate in politics online ($\beta = 0.44$,
$p < 0.001$) and offline ($\beta = 0.31$, $p < 0.001$); the more they possessed political
knowledge ($\beta = 0.22$, $p < 0.001$), the more likely they would vote ($\beta = 0.42$,
$p < 0.001$), and the more they would rely on face-to-face discussion for political information ($\beta = 0.33$, $p < 0.001$). The stronger people were affiliated
with their political parties, the more they would be active in politics offline
($\beta = 0.08$, $p < 0.05$), the more likely they would vote ($\beta = 0.27$, $p < 0.001$),
and the more they would rely on face-to-face discussion for political information ($\beta = 0.10$, $p < 0.05$). However, strength of political affiliation did not
have significant influence on online political participation. As for the influence
of ideology, the more conservative people were, the more likely they would
vote ($\beta = -0.09$, $p < 0.05$). However, ideology did not have significant impact
on online and offline political participation or reliance on face-to-face discussion for political information. People's political efficacy was not a significant
predictor of any dependent variable.

Table 9.3 Means and standard deviations

	Age	Education (6-point scale)	Income (8-point scale on $10,000 increments)	Efficacy (5-point scale, 1 = strongly disagree, 5 = strongly agree)	Political interest (10-point scale)	Strength of party affiliation (10-point scale)	Ideology (5-point scale; 1 = very conservative, 5 = very liberal)
Users of social network sites	43.9 (14.1)	3.3 (1.1)	4.0 (2.2)	3.0 (0.6)	7.3 (2.6)	6.7 (2.5)	2.8 (1.2)
Users of YouTube	45.1 (14.0)	3.3 (1.2)	4.0 (2.1)	3.0 (0.6)	7.3 (2.6)	6.9 (2.4)	2.7 (1.2)

Table 9.4 Hierarchical regression analyses predicting online and offline participation

	Online political participation	Offline political participation
Demographics		
Gender (female coded higher)	−0.09**	−0.09*
Age	−0.01	0.05
Education	0.09*	0.05
Income	0.06	0.07
Race (Caucasian coded higher)	0.08*	0.04
R^2 (%)	7.6***	5.7***
Political antecedents		
Efficacy	−0.04	0.01
Political interest	0.44***	0.31***
Strength of political affiliation	0.04	0.08*
Ideology (liberal coded higher)	−0.04	0.06
Incremental R^2 (%)	25.2***	17.9***
Reliance on new media		
Reliance on social network sites	0.30***	0.30***
Reliance on YouTube	0.15**	0.22***
Incremental R^2 (%)	16.5***	20.4***
Total R^2 (%)	49.3***	44.0***

Note
*$p < 0.05$; **$p < 0.01$; ***$p < 0.001$.

In regards to demographic variables, male respondents were more likely to participate in politics online ($\beta = -0.09$, $p < 0.01$, female coded higher) and offline ($\beta = -0.09$, $p < 0.01$, female coded higher). Gender was not a significant predictor of intention to vote or reliance on face-to-face discussion for political information. People with more education were more likely to participate in political activities online ($\beta = 0.09$, $p < 0.05$) but not offline; however, education did not have an influence on intention to vote or reliance on face-to-face discussion for political information. More-wealthy people relied on face-to-face discussion for political information ($\beta = 0.10$, $p < 0.05$); however, income was not a significant predictor of any of the remaining dependent variables. Caucasians were more likely to participate in politics online ($\beta = 0.08$, $p < 0.05$), but did not appear to influence any of the remaining dependent variables.

The third research question examined whether reliance on social network sites or reliance on YouTube was a stronger predictor of political attitudes and behaviors. As seen in the semi-partial correlations between reliance on social network sites and YouTube and the five dependent variables, with the exception of voter intention, reliance on social network sites had larger semi-partial correlation coefficients with all other dependent variables than reliance on YouTube

Table 9.5 Predicting intention to vote, and reliance on face-to-face discussion for information

	Intention to vote	Reliance on face-to-face discussion for information
Demographics		
Gender (female coded higher)	−0.03	0.04
Age	0.04	−0.02
Education	0.05	0.01
Income	0.04	0.10*
Race (Caucasian coded higher)	0.06	0.04
R^2 (%)	**9.1***	**3.9**
Political antecedents		
Efficacy	−0.003	0−.04
Political interest	0.42***	0.33***
Strength of political affiliation	0.27***	0.10*
Ideology (liberal coded higher)	−0.09*	0.02
Incremental R^2 (%)	**30.5***	**16.0***
Reliance on new media		
Reliance on social network sites	0.04	0.29***
Reliance on YouTube	−0.15**	0.02
Incremental R^2 (%)	**1.5***	**8.5***
Total R^2 (%)	**41.1***	**28.4***

Note
*$p < 0.05$; **$p < 0.01$; ***$p < 0.001$.

(Table 9.6). For instance, reliance on social network sites was significantly related to online political participation ($\beta = 0.21$, $p < 0.001$) as opposed to reliance on YouTube ($\beta = 0.10$, $p < 0.01$); reliance on social network sites was also significantly related to offline political participation ($\beta = 0.20$, $p < 0.001$) compared with reliance on YouTube ($\beta = 0.15$, $p < 0.001$). Reliance on social network sites was significantly related to reliance on face-to-face discussion for political information ($\beta = 0.20$, $p < 0.001$) as opposed to reliance on YouTube ($\beta = 0.02$, n.s.). Furthermore, those with greater reliance on YouTube were less likely to vote ($\beta = -0.10$, $p < 0.001$), while reliance on social network sites was not significantly related to voting intentions. Overall, reliance on social network sites was a stronger predictor of political attitudes and behavior than reliance on YouTube.

Overall, then, studies suggest that while SNS users and YouTube users were similar on demographic measures, they differed more substantially on their ability to influence political attitudes and behaviors. Reliance on social network sites proved to be more strongly related to political measures than YouTube in four of five cases. YouTube was a stronger predictor of intention to vote than SNS reliance, but the relationship between YouTube and intention to vote was negative.

Table 9.6 Semi-partial correlations between reliance on social network sites and reliance on YouTube and five dependent variables

	Online political participation	Offline political participation	Intention to vote	Reliance on face-to-face discussion
Reliance on SNSs	0.21***	0.20***	0.03 n.s.	0.20***
Reliance on YouTube	0.10**	0.15***	−0.10**	0.02 n.s.

Note
$*p < 0.05$; $**p < 0.01$; $***p < 0.001$.

Discussion

Several pundits declared 2008 the Facebook election because of how Barack Obama skillfully used a variety of social network sites as well as YouTube to engineer a successful grass-roots movement to attract the volunteers and funds necessary to win the election (Fraser & Dutta, 2008; Grove, 2008; Stelter, 2008). However, few scholars have examined whether social network sites and YouTube predict political attitudes and behaviors necessary for a democracy to function.

Researchers often lump YouTube in with social network sites such as MySpace and Facebook because it meets many of the characteristics of a social network site. Specifically, YouTube, like social network sites, allows you to construct a public or semi-public profile as well as connect with friends (boyd & Ellison, 2007; Lange, 2007). However, this study separated YouTube from SNSs because it focused on one network activity, video sharing, and because most sites such as Facebook, MySpace, and LinkedIn require people to create an account. Internet users can visit YouTube, view its content, and share it with others without creating an account. While YouTube and social network sites may function differently, this study found that they attract a very similar audience. Those who relied on both YouTube and social network sites were overwhelmingly female, had attended some college, and had earned an average annual income of $40,001–$55,000. Both were moderately efficacious and reported fairly high political interest. The respondents only differed slightly on other measures. YouTube users were marginally more likely to be Caucasian (83.3% to 80.4%), were somewhat older (45.1 to 43.9 years old) and reported slightly higher support for their political parties (6.9% to 6.7%). Thus, while YouTube may function differently from other types of social network sites, it attracts similar types of people.

This finding is not surprising due to the conceptual overlap between the activities of both users of Facebook and YouTube. Convergent media use has become the norm online, with many users cross-posting and seamlessly communicating in multiple platforms. Links are often present connecting one site to the next, and in many cases accounts can be managed that allow singular status updates to appear on multiple profiles. This thrust toward user integration of varied sites will likely perpetuate the similarity of users among all types of social network sites. Future study will be needed to further understand convergent social media consumption and the motivations for such behavior.

Research on political uses of social network sites has focused on its ability to create social capital (Ellison et al., 2007, 2010; Royal, 2008; Steinfield et al., 2008; Valenzuela et al., 2009) because studies suggest that people employ social network sites primarily to remain in contact with existing friends and to learn more about people they meet both offline and online (boyd & Ellison, 2007, Ellison et al., 2010; Lampe et al., 2006). Indeed, in the current study, both reliance on YouTube and social networks predicted civic political behaviors, namely offline political activity (e.g., helping a political candidate, attending political meetings, and persuading others to support a candidate), online political activity (e.g., contacting candidates online, sending and receiving campaign emails, and making online contributions), and getting information about the campaign through face-to-face communication. This parallels results from an earlier study (Zhang et al., in press) that found social network use was more closely linked to civic participation (e.g., volunteering for a local government board, working with others in the community to solve community problems, or helping to form a group to solve community problems). This study also supported a Pew Internet study that found of those who used social network sites for campaign information, most used it for social purposes such as to discover which candidates their friends voted for and to post political information for their friends to see. Fewer social network users employed the sites to get campaign information (Smith, 2009).

Surprisingly, in the current study reliance on social network sites did not boost intention to vote. Political observers indicated that Obama had a dominating presence on social network sites and used them as a mechanism to get people involved in his campaign (Fraser & Dutta, 2008; Grove, 2008; Stelter, 2008). Most political groups in social networks voice a clear perspective, such as Barack Obama ("One Million Strong for Barack") or LIFE: "Let's see how many pro-life people are on Facebook?" Just as studies suggest that, increasingly, people are seeking out political websites and blogs that support their political views (Johnson, Bichard, & Zhang, 2009; Johnson, Zhang, & Bichard, 2008; Stroud 2006, 2007, 2008), perhaps people who already know who they are going to vote for join Facebook groups sympathetic to that candidate so that they can be in discussions with likeminded individuals and get involved in the campaign itself. Social networking sites appear to attract more homogeneous interaction and are less likely to predict intention to vote. The current

findings suggest that voting behavior is more likely predicted by political variables such as ideology, strength of party affiliation, offline political participation, and political knowledge.

The results for intention to vote were even more disheartening with respect
to YouTube. In fact, the more you watched YouTube, the *less* you were
inclined to vote. YouTube may have reduced the intent to vote because, while
each candidate was allowed to post their videos promoting their candidacy
(Gueorguieva, 2007; May, 2008), YouTube also made it easier to attack a
political opponent, as one does not have to approve the message as is required
on television. Also, while some videos posted by others outside the campaign
praised the candidate (e.g., Williams' "Yes We Can Video"), often such out-
sider videos attacked the candidate, captured their gaffes on the campaign trail
or parodied the candidates' ads and campaign message (Grove, 2008; Topcik,
2008). This abundance of divergent messages may have frustrated viewers to
the point of inaction or simply provided entertainment to those with no intention to vote in the first place.

This study found that social network sites consistently proved a better predictor of political attitudes and behaviors than YouTube, even though more
people relied on YouTube for information about the election than social
network sites (204 vs. 189), and the demographic and political profiles of the
two types of site users were similar. Differences were particularly acute for
online political participation and reliance on face-to-face discussion. Social
network sites may have had a greater influence on political behavior than
YouTube because social network sites focus on building and maintaining personal relationships through online discussion. Studies suggest that political discussion plays a major role in political learning, attitude formation, and
behavior (Huckfeldt & Sprague, 1995; MacKuen & Brown, 1987), including
an increase in political involvement (McLeod et al., 1999).

Not surprisingly, political measures, particularly political interest and
strength of party affiliation, generally dwarfed reliance on social network sites
and YouTube as predictors of political attitudes and behaviors. However, reliance on social network sites and YouTube proved a more powerful predictor
of offline political participation than political antecedents, demonstrating the
need for continued study on the link between social network sites and political
measures, particularly measures that involve civic engagement.

Limitations and Future Studies

This study relied on an online panel of Internet users from a leading Western
research firm. While such a panel holds advantages to a convenience sample
of online users, such as knowing the demographic characteristics of the

population, this is still a self-selected group of Internet users. Therefore, results cannot be generalized to Internet users in general or social network users in particular. Less than half of the respondents said they used social network sites for political information. Future studies may want to survey social network users directly to better understand how social network reliance influences political attitudes and behaviors.

Papacharissi and Mendelson (2008) found that motives for visiting Facebook influenced social capital measures. Such a study could be expanded to look at how motives for using social network sites influence political attitudes and behaviors. Motives for using multiple social media platforms at the same time could also be measured in an effort to understand convergent media activity. It would be interesting to discover the underlying gratifications for social behavior online and the implications in the offline world. This study focused on political attitudes and behaviors, but an earlier study by Zhang and associates (in press) suggested that social network sites had a greater influence on civic participation than political participation. Because of the social nature of social network sites, future studies could include measures of local civic engagement.

Finally, this study looked at reliance on social network sites in general, although studies suggest that different social network sites attract different audiences, with some social networks (e.g., AsianAve, LDS Linkup for Mormons) geared to very specific audiences. Therefore, future studies might want to further examine how specific social network sites have differing influences on political attitudes and behaviors.

Note

1. For gender, the research lab panel demographics were 47.1% male and 52.9% female. However, our sample yielded 29.5% male and 70.5% female. The education profile for the majority of respondents on the Media Research Lab panel indicated some college up to a four-year degree. The majority of our sample also reported some college up to a four-year degree. Therefore, our sample closely resembled the population on gender and level of education, but is older than the panel population as a whole.

References

boyd, d. m. (2004). Friendster and publicly articulated social networks. *Proceedings of ACM Conference on Human Factors in Computing Systems (CHI 2004)* (pp. 1279–1282). New York, NY: ACM Press. Vienna, April 24–29.

boyd, d. m. & Ellison, N. B. (2007). Social network sites: Definition, history, and scholarship. *Journal of Computer-Mediated Communication, 13*(1), 11. Online, available at: http://jcmc.indiana.edu/vol.13/issue1/bod.ellison.html.

Brundidge, J. (2006). *The contribution of the Internet to the heterogeneity of political discussion networks: Does the medium matter?* Paper presented at the International Communication Association Annual Conference, Dresden, Germany, June.

Brundidge, J. (2008). *The contemporary media environment and breadth of communication: The contribution of the Internet to the heterogeneity of political discussion networks.* Paper presented at the International Communication Association Conference, Montreal, CN, May.

Calhoun, C. (1988). Populist politics, communications media, and large scale social integration. *Sociological Theory, 6*, 219–241.

Carey, J. W. (1989). *Communication as culture: Essays on media and society.* Boston, MA: Hyman.

Cho, J. (2005). Media, interpersonal discussion and electoral choice. *Communication Research, 32*, 295–322.

De Tocqueville, A. ([1830] 1965). *Democracy in America.* New York, NY: Mentor Books.

Ellison N., Lampe, C., Steinfield, C., & Vitak, J. (2010). With a little help from my friends: How social network sites affect social capital processes. In Z. Papacharissi (Ed.), *A networked self: Identity, community, and culture on social network sites* (pp. 124–145). New York, NY: Routledge.

Ellison, N., Steinfield, C., & Lampe, C. (2007). The benefits of Facebook "friends": Social capital and college students' use of online social networks. *Journal of Computer-Mediated Research, 12*(4), 1. Online, available at: http://jcmc.indiana.edu/vol.12/issue4/ellison.html.

Emmett, A. (2008). *Networking news: Traditional news outlets turn to social networking Web sites in an effort to build their online audiences.* Online, available at: from http://findarticles.com/p/articles/mi_hb3138/is_6_30/ai_n31163066? tag=content;col1.

Fraser, M. & Dutta, S. (2008). *Barack Obama and the Facebook election.* Online, available at: www.usnews.com/articles/opinion/2008/11/19/barack-obama-and-the-facebook-election.html.

Grove, S. (2008). *YouTube: The flattening of politics.* Online, available at: www.nieman.harvard.edu/reportsitem.aspx?id=100019.

Gueorguieva, V. (2007). Voters, MySpace and YouTube: The impact of alternative communication channels on the 2006 election cycle and beyond. *Social Science Computer Review, 25*, 1–13.

Holahan, C. (2008). *Has Obama already won in online fund-raising?* Online, available at: www.businessweek.com/technology/content/.aug2008/tc20080825_761567.htm?chan=top+news_top+news+index_technology.

Huckfeldt, R. & Sprague, J. (1995). *Citizens, politics, and social communication: Information and influence in an election campaign.* New York, NY: Cambridge University Press.

Johnson, T. J., Bichard, S. L., & Zhang, W. (2009). *Communication communities or "cyberghettos?" A path analysis model examining factors that explain selective exposure to blogs.* Paper presented to the International Organization of Internet Researchers, Copenhagen, October.

Johnson, T. J., Zhang, W, & Bichard, S. L. (2008). *Voices of convergence or conflict? A path analysis investigation of selective exposure to political websites.* Paper presented to the

Association for Education in Journalism & Mass Communications annual conference, Chicago, IL, August.

Katz, E. (1992). On parenting a paradigm: Gabriel Tarde's agenda for opinion and communication research. *International Journal of Public Opinion Research, 4*, 80–85.

Kaye, B. K. (2010). Between Barack and a Net place: Motivations for using social network sites and blogs for political information. In Z. Papacharissi (Ed.), *A networked self: Identity, community, and culture on social network sites* (pp. 208–231). New York, NY: Routledge.

Kim, Y. M. & Geidner, N. (2008). *Politics as friendship: The impact of online social networks on young voters; political behavior.* Paper presented at the annual convention of the International Communication Association, Montreal, Canada, May.

Lampe, C., Ellison, N., & Steinfield, C. (2006). A Face(book) in the crowd: Social searching vs. social browsing. *Proceedings of the 2006 20th Anniversary Conference on Computer Supported Cooperative Work* (pp. 167–170). New York, NY: ACM Press.

Lange, P. G. (2007). Publicly private and privately public: Social networking on YouTube. *Journal of Computer-Mediated Communication, 13*(1), 18. Online, available at: http://jcmc.indiana.edu/vol.13/issue1/lange.html.

Leiner, D. J., Hohlfeld, R., & Quiring, O. (2009). *What people make of social capital online: An empirical study on the conversion of capital via network sites.* Paper presented at the annual meeting of the International Communication Association, Chicago, IL, May.

MacKuen, M. (1990). Speaking of politics: Individual conversational choice, public opinion, and the prospects for deliberative democracy. In J. Ferejhon & J. Kuklinski (Eds.), *Information and democratic process* (pp. 59–99). Urbana, IL: University of Illinois Press.

MacKuen, M. & Brown, C. (1987). Political context and attitude change. *American Political Science Review, 81*(2), 471–490.

McLeod, J. M., Scheufele, D. A., & Moy, P. (1999). Community, communication and participation: The role of mass media and interpersonal discussion in local political participation. *Political Communication, 16*, 315–336.

May, A. L. (2008). Campaign 2008: It's on YouTube. *Nieman Reports*, Summer. Online, available at: www.nieman.harvard.edu/reports.aspx?id=100006.

Mendelson, A. L. & Papacharissi, Z. (2010). Look At Us: Collective Narcissism in College Student Facebook Photo Galleries. In Z. Papacharissi (Ed.), *A networked self: Identity, community, and culture on social network sites* (pp. 251–273). New York, NY: Routledge.

Mutz, D.C . & Mondak, J. J. (2006). The workplace as a context for cross-cutting political discourse. *The Journal of Politics, 69*, 140–155.

Papacharissi, Z. & Mendelson, A. L. (2008). *Friends, networks and zombies: The social utility of Facebook.* Paper presented at the Association of Internet Researchers annual convention, Copenhagen, Denmark, October.

Postelnicu, M. & Cozma, R. (2007). *Social network politics: A content analysis of MySpace profiles of political candidates from the 2006 U.S. mid-terms.* Paper presented to the annual meeting of the National Communication Association, Chicago, IL.

Postelnicu, M. & Cozma, R. (2008). *Befriending the candidate: Uses and gratifications of candidate profiles on MySpace.* Paper presented to the National Communication Association annual meeting, San Diego, CA, November.

Price, V., Nir, L., & Cappella, J. (2002). Does disagreement contribute to more deliberative opinion? *Political Communication, 19,* 95–112.

Putnam, R. D. (2000). *Bowling alone: The collapse and revival of American community.* New York, NY: Simon & Schuster.

Royal, C. (2008). *User-generated content: How social networking translates to social capital.* Paper presented to the Association for Education in Journalism and Mass Communication annual convention, Chicago, IL, August.

Sanchez, L. (2008). *Commentary: Obama's high-tech edge in presidential politics.* Online, available at: www.cnn.com/2008/TECH/09/01/sanchez.obama/index.html?eref=rss_topstories.

Schuefele, D. A., Hardy, B. W., Brossard, D., Waismel-Manor, I. S., & Nisbet, E. (2006). Democracy based on difference: Examining the links between structural heterogeneity, heterogeneity of discussion networks, and democratic citizenship. *Journal of Communication, 56,* 728–753.

Smith, A. (2009). *The Internet's role in campaign 2008.* Online, available at: www.pewinternet.org/Reports/2009/6–The-Internets-Role-in-Campaign-2008.aspx.

Stamm, K. R., Emig, A. G. & Hesse, M. B. (1997). The contribution of local media to community involvement. *Journalism and Mass Communication Quarterly, 74,* 97–107.

Steinfeld C., Ellison, N., & Lampe, C. (2008). Social capital, self-esteem, and use of online social network sites: A longitudinal analysis. *Journal of Applied Developmental Psychology, 29,* 434–445.

Stelter, B. (2008). Politics via the Internet spreads with new force. *The International Herald Tribune,* March 26, p. 5.

Stevens Aubrey, J., Chattopadhyay, S., & Rill, L. A. (2008). *Are Facebook friends like face-to-face friends? Exploring relations between the use of social network websites and social capital.* Paper presented at the annual convention of the International Communication Association, Montreal, Canada, May.

Stroud, N. J. (2006). *Selective exposure to partisan information.* Unpublished dissertation, University of Pennsylvania.

Stroud, N. J. (2007). Media effects, selective exposure, and *Fahrenheit 9/11. Political Communication, 24,* 415–432.

Stroud, N. J. (2008). Media use and political predispositions: Revisiting the concept of selective exposure. *Political Behavior, 30,* 341–366.

Sweetser, K. D. & Weaver-Lariscy, R. (2007). *Candidates make good friends: An analysis of candidates' use of Facebook.* National Communication Association, Chicago, IL, November.

Topcik, J. (2008). The election year that was . . . on YouTube. *Broadcasting & Cable,* November 3, p. 6.

Utz, S. (2009). The (potential) benefits of campaigning via social network sites. *Journal of Computer-Mediated Communication, 14,* 227–243.

Valenzuela, S., Park, N., & Kee, K. F. (2009). Is there social capital in a social network site? Facebook use and college students' life satisfaction, trust and participation. *Journal of Computer-Mediated Communication, 14*, 875–901.

Verba, S., Schlozman, K. L., Brady, H. E., & Nie, N. H. (1995). *Voice and equality: Civic volunteerism in American politics.* Cambridge, MA: Harvard University Press.

Video the Vote. (2008). Online, available at: http://videothevote.org/.

Vitak, J., Zube, P., Smock, A., Carr, C., Ellison, N., & Lampe, C. (2009). *"Poking" people to participate: Facebook and political participation in the 2008 election.* Paper presented at the annual meeting of the International Communication Association, Chicago, IL, May.

Walsh, K. C. (2003). *Talking about politics: Informal groups and social identity in American Life.* Chicago, IL: University of Chicago Press.

Warren, M. (1992). Democratic theory and self-transformation. *American Political Science Review, 86*, 8–23.

Wu, J. (2009). *Facebook politics: An exploratory study of American youth's political engagement during the 2008 presidential election.* Paper presented at the annual meeting of the International Communication Association, Chicago, IL, May.

Zhang, W., Johnson, T. J., Seltzer, T., & Bichard, S. (in press). The revolution will be networked: The influence of social network sites on political attitudes and behaviors. *Social Science Computer Review.*

Chapter 10

Between Barack and a Net Place

Motivations for Using Social Network Sites and Blogs for Political Information

Barbara K. Kaye

Introduction

Blogs emerged as 2004 election season must-reads, with bloggers leading the charge for and against candidates and issues. Recognizing the need to use the Internet to connect to his supporters, Senator Howard Dean was the first presidential candidate to create a blog. Dean's blog and his strategy of using the blogosphere to raise money, mobilize supporters, generate excitement, and spread the word about his campaign was so successful in boosting his popularity that the mainstream media heralded it as a campaign revolution (Nagourney, 2008; Stromer-Galley & Baker, 2006).

By the 2008 presidential election, online politics had changed. Most notable was the emergence of social network sites (SNSs)[1] such as Facebook and MySpace. Not only were these new venues social gathering spaces, they were also used by campaigners as a means of connecting to political constituents and creating political links among SNS users. Presidential hopeful Senator Barack Obama was heralded for his clever campaigning on blogs, social network sites and YouTube to organize supporters, raise money, and get his message out to voters (Nagourney, 2008). In contrast, Senator John McCain was dubbed the "analog candidate" for minimizing the importance of blogs and SNSs. Strategists mused whether his scant digital presence alienated the younger, online-savvy voters (Leibovich, 2008).

Even though the campaign of 2008 is long over, blogs and SNSs continue as the newest and hottest online arenas for scrutinizing political happenings (Stelter & Perez-Pena, 2008). But the creation of online content is of small matter without a large, enthusiastic audience to use the technology to its full potential. The number of SNS and blog users alone begs the question of what draws them to online sources, especially for political information. The percentage of adults who sought online information about politics or a presidential election jumped from 4% in 1996 to 29% in 2004 to 44% in 2008 (Smith,

2009). Much of that increase is attributed to blogs, which took hold as a strong political presence in 2004, and SNSs, which caught on in 2008.

Who are these users and why do they long for social network interactions and eagerly swig down blog content? This study sets out to answer these questions within the uses and gratifications framework. Specifically, this chapter explores the motivations for using SNSs and blogs for political information and compares the demographic and political characteristics of SNSs and blog users who completed an online survey during the two weeks before and the two weeks after the 2008 presidential election.

Using Social Network Sites and Blogs to Disseminate Political Information

Candidates for political office were experimenting with their own blogs in 2004. By the 2006 mid-term elections, and certainly by the 2008 presidential campaign, candidate blogs were commonplace. Senator John McCain, a rare Internet holdout among major candidates, told reporters that, "I don't expect to set up my own blog" (Leibovich, 2008). Some candidates, such as Senator Hillary Clinton, hired prominent political bloggers to build an online image campaign (Hernandez, 2006). The necessity to set up blogs and bring political bloggers into the campaign camp signifies the growing importance of the influence of both candidate- and blogger-hosted blogs.

Campaigners also relied on social network sites and other Web 2.0² applications to drum up support. Barack Obama led the way with his heavy use of SNSs, which pundits claim contributed to his victory in what they dubbed the "Facebook Effect" (Fraser & Dutta, 2008). Obama's new communication media team, led by Facebook founder Chris Hughes, masterminded an online crusade on Facebook, MySpace, YouTube, Twitter, and other social network sites, and established connections from these sites to mybarackobama.com (Fraser & Dutta, 2008) also known as MyBo (Stelter, 2008b). The success of the Obama team's online strategies is evidenced by the number of users: one million Facebook and MySpace friends; 112,000 Twitter followers; 18 million views of 1,800 videos on the BarackObama.com channel; 3.4 million YouTube views of Obama's speech about race; 900,000 MyBo members (Fraser & Dutta, 2008; Stelter, 2008a, 2008b). Senator McCain also deployed an online campaign, but it was not as successful as Obama's. The JohnMcCain.com channel held only about 300 videos and attracted just over 28,000 subscribers and eked out slightly more than two million visits. McCain's weaker numbers could be an indication that Web 2.0 use is influenced by user characteristics and political attitudes, with younger, more liberal voters connecting online.

What is a Social Network Site? What is a Blog? Who Uses Them?

Social network sites are typically used as one-stop venues for sending email, photos, and videos to "friends," who are those who have been allowed access to someone's SNS page. These friends then may interact with each other, thus creating and expanding existing social ties. Blogs are diary-styled venues that offer news and information posted by a blogger and to which readers may add their own opinions and begin discussion on new topics.

SNSs and blogs share similar characteristics: they offer news and opinion, promote discussion and community, are online venues for communicating with others and for making new online friends, and connect users with similar interests and viewpoints. Yet SNSs and blogs differ in their structure and perhaps in their purposes. Blogs tout themselves as providers of information and opinion, whereas SNSs tend to be perceived as places to widen social circles, to make friends, and to find personal information. Blogs promote cognitive processes while SNSs are more emotional and social. More importantly, user participation on blogs is not crucial. Blog users may participate heavily by commenting and sending links to more information sources, or they may simply read blog postings and not interact at all. The purpose of SNSs, however, is to connect with others; therefore, user participation is paramount. Without two-way communication there is not much point to social network sites (boyd & Ellison, 2007; Joinson, 2008; Lampe, Ellison, & Steinfield, 2006; Lange, 2007; Murchu, Breslin, & Decker, 2004).

Blogs splashed into cyberspace after the 9/11 attacks and the war in Iraq as people sought personal and in-depth accounts of the events. As blog readership jumped to about 50% of those living in the U.S., the number of blogs exploded from about 50 in 1999 (Levy, 2002) to an estimated 70 million worldwide in 2007 (The State of the News Media, 2008), to 133 million only one year later, as tracked by Technorati (Internet 2008 in Numbers, 2009).

Social network use also surged. The percentage of adult Internet users with an SNS profile quadrupled from 8% in 2005 to 35% by the end of 2008 (Lenhart, 2009). But more astounding than percentages is the sheer number of SNS users. MySpace boasts of over 100 million users (Joinson, 2008) and Facebook claims 400 million registrants (Facebook Statistics, 2010). These numbers translate into about 65 million unique visitors per month on MySpace and a staggering 93 million stopping in on Facebook (Shapira, 2009; Sydell, 2009).

Demographic and Political Characteristics of Users of SNSs and Blogs

As with other Web 2.0 applications, SNSs are dominated by young people—between 75%–83% of those between the ages of 18–24 have a profile. Two-thirds of those with a profile also engaged in some form of political activity or discussion on SNSs during the 2008 campaign (Lenhart, 2009; Smith, 2009).

Young people also dominate the blogosphere, with just over three-quarters of those between the ages of 18–24 reporting they have read blogs (The State of the News Media, 2008), but more specifically, 42% of those between the ages of 18–29 read political/campaign blogs (Pew Research Center, 2008b).

Men are more likely than woman to seek political information from blogs (Rainie & Horrigan, 2005; Salwen, Garrison, & Driscoll, 2005). About half of men visit political blogs compared to one-third of women (Connelly, 2007). Male blog users tend to be young and highly educated with high incomes (Eveland & Dylko, 2007; Graf, 2006; Johnson, Kaye, Bichard, & Wong, 2007; Kaye & Johnson, 2004a, 2004b; Perlmutter, 2008; Rainie, 2005).

Political attitudes have been linked to using SNSs and blogs. Although liberals and conservatives are equally likely to go online (Horrigan, Garrett, & Resnick, 2004; Kohut, 2004), SNSs seem to be inhabited by more liberal users. Those affiliated with the Democratic party are more likely than Republicans to have created an online profile—36% vs. 21% (Smith & Ranie, 2008).

Studies of the political ideology of blog users show inconsistent results. Some studies indicate that blog users are Republican and conservative (Johnson & Kaye, 2004; Johnson et al., 2007; Kaye & Johnson, 2004b, 2006), some find they are equally liberal and conservative (Eveland & Dylko, 2007; State of the News Media, 2007), and others suggest that blog users are more likely to be liberal (Blogads, 2006; Blog Reader, 2007) by a two-to-one margin (43% to 22%) (Pew Research Center, 2008b).

Those who read blogs tend to distrust the government and media (Graf, 2006; Johnson & Kaye, 2007b; Kaye & Johnson, 2004b), but they also report high levels of self-efficacy, the belief that they have the power to bring about governmental change (Johnson & Kaye, 2004, 2007b), as do SNS users (Postelnicu & Cozma, 2007). SNS users were also very interested in the 2008 presidential campaign (Postelnicu & Cozma, 2007), and those who use social network tools are also more likely to read blogs (Smith, 2009). A study conducted during the time of the 2004 presidential campaign found that nine of 10 blog users were very interested in and knowledgeable about the election. Three-quarters reported very high interest in politics and two-thirds claimed they were very knowledgeable about politics in general (Kaye & Johnson, 2006).

Using Social Network Sites and Blogs for Political Information

During the 2008 presidential election, the Internet captured almost as many U.S. adult users as newspapers for campaign news (26% vs. 28%) (Smith,

2009). Moreover, almost three-quarters (74%) of Internet users connected to online sources specifically to get news and information about the 2008 campaign (Smith, 2009).

Underscoring the importance of blogs and social network sites for political information is the percentage of online users who rely on these sites—26% visit blogs that cover news, politics, or media and 40% read someone else's commentary about the campaign on an online news group, website, or blog (Smith, 2009), even though only about one in 10 blogs is politically-oriented (Horrigan, 2007). Additionally, almost one in five (18%) of online users posted opinions, comments, or questions about the 2008 campaign on SNSs or blogs (Smith, 2009), and 10% have used SNSs such as Facebook or MySpace to gather political information or to become politically involved (Smith & Rainie, 2008).

Applying Uses and Gratifications to Social Network Sites and Blogs

As a significant percentage of online users turn to blogs and SNSs for political information, the question of why they do so arises. Since the early 1990s, academic researchers have been studying the uses and gratifications for using the Internet as a whole. As new online components emerge (e.g., chat, blogs, SNSs), attention turns toward understanding the motivations for using these new sources. The basic premise of uses and gratifications theory is that users are active and goal-directed, thus they are aware of the needs that they are attempting to satisfy (Lin & Jeffres, 1998; Palmgreen, 1984). The approach is from a user perspective—what people do with the media, not what the media do to people.

Academic research indicates that, although different components of the Internet (Web, chat, bulletin boards, email, blogs) satisfy many of the same needs, each also gratifies needs unique to a particular online resource. Users are motivated to connect to websites in general to pass the time, to be entertained, to escape, and to make social connections (Charney & Greenberg, 2001; Eighmey, 1997; Ferguson & Perse, 2000; Kaye, 1998; Papacharissi & Rubin, 2000). Chatrooms serve social contact, personal identity, and expression needs (Fuentes, 2000; Kaye & Johnson, 2006; Turkle, 1999), bulletin boards/electronic mailing lists tend to gratify information/education and social needs (James, Wotring, & Forrest, 1995; Kaye & Johnson, 2004a, 2006), and email satisfies interpersonal needs (Dimmick, Kline, & Stafford, 2000; Stafford, Kline, & Dimmick, 1999) and convenience needs (Papacharissi & Rubin, 2000). Just as different online components serve unique needs, the same may be true of SNSs and blogs.

Motivations for Using Social Network Sites

Research has identified uses and gratifications of most Internet components, but because SNSs and blogs are relatively new, the reasons people seek information from them requires further study.

New SNS users typically set up individual profiles and then identify and display names, photos, and videos of others with whom they have a relationship. Displaying the "friends" list establishes one's popularity and motivates users to email or otherwise connect to their friend's friends, thus expanding their own networks (boyd & Ellison, 2007). Researchers have found that SNSs are used mainly to keep in touch with friends, to make new friends (Raacke & Bonds-Raacke, 2008), for social surveillance, and for tracking those within their group (Joinson, 2008; Lampe et al., 2006).

Newer research has found that social network sites are also used to gather political information. This shift was especially predominant during the 2008 election campaign. A study conducted by the Pew Research Center disclosed that 40% of all social network users and 50% of those under the age of 30 used SNSs to obtain or share information about politics and the campaigns. Specifically, 29% of SNS users purposively sought out their friends' political interests or affiliations, and 22% looked for information about a candidate or campaign (Smith & Rainie, 2008).

Motivations for Using Blogs

Blogs began as online diaries used to keep in touch with friends and family, a role since assumed by SNSs. Blogs have evolved from simple diaries read only by an inner circle of contacts to powerful forums that address many issues. Blogs are now used for a multitude of reasons, such as to share opinions and become politically involved (Haigh & Pfau, 2007; Hebert, 2004; Reynolds, 2004). Blogs are also used because they are a convenient way to become informed, for political, social, and media surveillance, for personal fulfillment and expression/affiliation, and because they offer different and more insightful perspectives on events than traditional media, which is held in distain by many blog readers (Johnson & Kaye, 2006, 2007b, 2009; Johnson et al., 2007; Kaye, 2005, 2007, 2008; Kaye & Johnson, 2006).

Study Goals

This study examines the users and uses of SNSs and blogs for political information. Because these two online sources differ on their purposes and levels of interactivity, they are likely to satisfy different gratifications and draw users for different purposes. Therefore, this study explores the following two questions:

1. What are the demographic and political characteristics of individuals who heavily use only SNSs and blogs for political information?
2. What motivates individuals to heavily rely only on SNSs and blogs for political information?

Method

A survey targeted to politically interested Internet users was posted online during the two weeks before and the two weeks after the 2008 presidential election. Following the same method used in other published studies (Johnson & Kaye, 2004, 2007a, 2009; Kaye, 2005, 2007; Kaye & Johnson, 2004b), politically interested Internet users were solicited to fill out the survey by placing an announcement containing the survey URL on hundreds of politically oriented websites, blogs, and social network sites that represented a cross section of political ideologies.[3]

After completion of the survey, respondents were encouraged to "snowball" it (Babbie, 2002; Witte, Amoroso, & Howard, 2000) to politically interested friends and family by clicking on a link that automatically forwarded it. This convenience sample of politically interested Internet users yielded 4,241 completed surveys.[4] The survey software allowed computation of a cooperation rate[5] by recording the number of individuals who accessed the survey and the number who completed it. For this survey, the cooperation rate was 26.2%.

Survey questions assessed respondent demographics (gender, age, income, education) and political characteristics including political party, strength of party ties, political ideology, trust in the government, self-efficacy, political knowledge, political interest, knowledge of the 2008 presidential campaign, and interest in the 2008 political campaign. (Detailed operationalization is available in the "Notes" section of this chapter.[6])

Data Analysis

First, responses to the reliance question ("How much do you rely on . . . ?") for social network sites and blogs were re-coded into two separate categories. Those who "relied" or "heavily relied" on a component were classified as "high reliance," and those who marked "sometimes rely on," "rarely rely on," and "don't rely on at all" were classified as "low reliance."

Next, two-step cluster analysis was conducted to define groupings of users based on reliance on SNSs and blogs, and to assess characteristics within and among each user segment. Two-step cluster analysis allows segmenting of continuous and categorical variables. Cases are assigned to clusters according to Schwarz's Bayesian Inference Criterion (BIC) (Table 10.1). Past research has employed cluster analyses to segment online shoppers (Bhatnagar & Ghose, 2004) and cell phone users (Jih & Lee, 2003) by gratifications and demographics, thus this method was appropriate for the current study.

Chi-square analysis was used for *between* cluster comparisons for the categorical variables (gender, education, political party). Frequencies and mean scores were computed for *within* cluster analysis of demographics, political party affiliation, and political ideology. ANOVA was performed to ascertain differences among the clusters for the continuous variables (age, income, political ideology, political party ties, interest and knowledge of politics, interest and knowledge of the 2008 presidential election, trust in government, and self-efficacy). Tukey's HSD test for unequal sample sizes was applied to determine which means were significantly different.

Lastly, mean scores were calculated for each of the 35 motivations for using SNSs and blogs. Comparisons were made on two of the four clusters—Social Networkers (those who heavily rely only on SNSs) and Blogophiles (those who heavily rely only on blogs).

Results

The main purpose of this study is to examine the demographic and political characteristics of those who use SNSs and blogs for political information. Additionally, the motivations for using SNSs and blogs are compared.

The 4,241 respondents who completed the survey are predominately male (66.7%). The respondents are highly educated, have a yearly income of $92,500, with three-quarters (76.5%) having completed college and higher. Almost all (91.8%) are white and they average 46.4 years of age. The respondents closely

Table 10.1 Cluster model (Schwarz's Bayesian Inference Criterion (BIC))

Auto-clustering				
Number of clusters	Schwarz's Bayesian Criterion (BIC)	BIC change[a]	Ratio of BIC changes[b]	Ratio of distance measures[c]
1	6,934.520			
2	2,042.880	−4,891.639	1.000	2.814
3	315.558	1,727.323	0.353	6.569
4	66.731	−248.826	0.051	d.

Notes
a. The changes are from the previous number of clusters in the table.
b. The ratios of changes are relative to the change for the two-cluster solution.
c. The ratios of distance measures are based on the current number of clusters against the previous number of clusters.
d. Since the distance at the current number of clusters is zero, auto-clustering will not continue.

match the typical politically interested online user (well-educated, white, males) found in other studies (Pew Research Center, 2008a).

Ideologically, four in ten (39.2%) of the respondents assert that they are conservative/very conservative, 38.7% liberal/very liberal, and 22.9% moderate. Political party affiliation closely mirrors ideology, with 35.6% Republicans, 38.4% Democrats, and 18.1% Independents.

To get a clear look at those who use SNSs and those who use blogs, a two-step cluster analysis categorized four groups of users. Cluster 1 (Dabblers) is made up of 1,308 respondents (31.1% of the overall sample) who do not rely heavily on SNSs or blogs for political information. Cluster 2 (Social Networkers) contains 78 respondents (1.9%) who heavily access SNSs but not blogs. Cluster 3 (Ambi-textrous) consists of 120 respondents (2.9%) who heavily use SNSs and blogs when seeking political information, and Cluster 4 (Blogophiles) holds the majority of respondents (2,688, 64.1%) who heavily connect only to blogs to find political information[7] (Table 10.2). This study is primarily interested in those who heavily use only SNSs (Social Networkers) and those who heavily use only blogs (Blogophiles) for political information, and therefore the results are presented with a focus on these two groups.

Demographics and Political Characteristics

Within-cluster analysis shows that males make up a larger percentage (71.1%) of Blogophiles (C4) (those who heavily use blogs) than any other cluster, whereas females dominate Cluster 2, those who heavily use only SNSs for political information (68.0%). Further, almost six of ten (57.7%) Social Networkers are affiliated with the Democratic party, whereas Blogophiles are more evenly divided, with just over one-third (38.3%) belonging to the Republican party and the slightly fewer (37.1%) to the Democratic party. A look at political ideology shows that 20.7% of Social Networkers consider themselves conservative/very conservative compared to 42.7% of Blogophiles. Ambi-textrous (C3), those who rely on SNSs and blogs, consists of the largest percentage (64.2%) of liberals than any other cluster (Table 10.2).

Between-cluster comparisons of frequencies on the categorical variables are based on expected values. The findings show that Cluster 2, Social Networkers, has the largest percentage of females than the other cluster ($\chi^2 = 86.718$, $df = 3$, $p < 0.000$), whereas a greater percentage of males are found in C4, those who rely heavily only on blogs for political information. Further, Social Networkers are significantly younger (m = 34.0 years) than Blogophiles (m = 46.6 years) ($F[3,3895] = 35.368$, $p < 0.000$). Levels of education do not significantly vary among the clusters, nor does income, even though Social Networkers report a lower income ($38,500) than Blogophiles ($97,500) (Table 10.3).

Table 10.2 Demographic profile within clusters

Cluster	C1 Dabblers (31.1%) n = 1,308 (Do NOT heavily use SNSs or Blogs)	C2 Social networkers (1.9%) n = 78 (Heavily uses only SNSs)	C3 Ambi-textrous (2.9%) n = 120 (Heavily uses SNSs and Blogs)	C4 Blogophiles (64.1%) n = 2,688 (Heavily uses only Blogs)
Male	(61.0%) 750	(32.0%) 24	(55.8%) 63	(71.1%) 1,772
Female	(39.0%) 479	(68.0%) 51	(44.2%) 50	(28.9%) 719
Age (mean)	46.9	34.0	39.6	46.6
Income (mean)	$89,000	$38,500	$57,000	$97,500
High school grad or less	(1.7%) 21	(1.3%) 1	(5.3%) 6	(2.2%) 56
Some college/degree	(53.8%) 662	(64.0%) 48	(47.8%) 54	(56.6%) 1,408
Graduate degree	(44.5%) 547	(34.7%) 26	(46.9%) 53	(41.2%) 1,024
Political party				
Republican	(33.0%) 426	(19.2%) 15	(17.6%) 21	(38.3%) 1,019
Democrat	(37.7%) 486	(57.7%) 45	(60.5%) 72	(37.1%) 987
Independent	(21.1%) 271	(15.4%) 12	(14.3%) 17	(16.9%) 450
Other	(8.2%) 106	(7.7%) 6	(7.6%) 9	(7.7%) 205
Political ideology				
Very liberal/Liberal (1)	(36.3%) 473	(44.2%) 24	(64.2%) 77	(38.7%) 1,031
Moderate	(29.3%) 383	(35.1%) 27	(15.8%) 19	(18.6%) 495
Very conservative/Conservative (5)	(34.4%) 450	(20.7%) 16	(20.0%) 24	(42.7%) 1,148
Mean (range 1–5)	2.9	2.68	2.18	2.95

Notes
Numbers and percentages run vertically to equal 100%.

Table 10.3 Political and demographic profile between clusters

Cluster	C1 Dabblers (31.1%) n=1,308 (Do NOT heavily use SNSs or Blogs)	C2 Social networkers (1.9%) n=78 (Heavily uses only SNSs)	C3 Ambi-textrous (2.9%) n=120 (Heavily uses SNSs and Blogs)	C4 Blogophiles (64.1%) n=2,688 (Heavily uses only Blogs)
Gender (χ^2=86.718, df=3, p<0.000)				
Male	(28.7%) 750	(0.9%) 24	(2.4%) 63	(71.1%) 1,772
Female	(36.9%) 479	(3.9%) 51	(3.8%) 50	(55.4%) 719
Age (mean) (F[3.3895]=35.368, p<0.000)	46.9A	34.0C	39.6B	46.6A
Income (mean) N.S.	$89,000	$38,500	$57,000	$97,500
Education N.S.				
High school grad or less 1	(21%) 25	(1.2%) 1	(7.1%) 6	(66.6%) 56
Some college/degree	(30.5%) 662	(2.2%) 48	(2.5%) 54	(64.8%) 1,408
Graduate degree	(33.1) 547	(1.6%) 26	(3.2%) 53	(62.1%) 1,024
Political party χ^2=58.182, df=9, p<0.000				
Republican	(28.8%) 426	(1.0%) 15	(1.4%) 21	(68.8%) 1,019
Democrat	(30.6%) 486	(2.8%) 45	(4.5%) 72	(62.1%) 987
Independent	(36.1%) 271	(1.6%) 12	(2.3%) 17	(60.0%) 450
Other	(32.5%) 106	(1.8%) 6	(2.8%) 9	(62.9%) 205
Political ideology				
Very liberal/Liberal (1)	(29.3%) 473	(2.1%) 34	(4.8%) 77	(63.8%) 1,031
Moderate	(41.5%) 383	(2.9%) 27	(2.1%) 19	(53.6%) 495

	(27.5%) 450	(1.0%) 16	(1.5%) 24	(70.1%) 1,148
Very conservative/Conservative (5)				
Mean (range 1–5) (F[3,4177]=24.083, p<0.000)	2.90A	2.68A	2.18B	2.95A
Political party ties (range 0–10) (F[3,4192]=14.908, p<0.000)	6.18C	6.77AB	7.28A	6.71AB
Trust in government mean (range 3–15) (F[3,4172]=7.459, p<0.000)	8.10B	8.87A	8.87A	7.99B
Self-efficacy mean (range 4–20) (F[3,4167]=50.114, p<0.000)	16.27B	15.65C	17.15A	17.14A
Interest in politics (mean range 0–10) (F[3,4189]=84.176, p<0.000)	7.91B	8.00B	8.94A	8.65A
Knowledge of politics (mean range 0–10) (F[3,4192]=55.479, p<0.000)	7.92B	7.64B	8.49A	8.42A
Interest in 2008 election (mean range 0–10) (F[3,4188]=44.452, p<0.000)	8.87C	9.03BC	9.44A	9.24AB
Knowledge of 2008 election (mean range 0–10) 8.49B (F[3,4191]=56.465, p<0.000)	8.31B	9.14A	8.94A	

Notes

Numbers and percentages run horizontally to equal 100%. Significance by Pearson chi-square. Mean scores with capital letters = horizontal comparisons – differ by p < 0.05 ANOVA. Some cells have expected count less than 5.

Of all Republican respondents, more than expected are Blogophiles; whereas, of all Democrats, more than expected are Social Networkers as well as Dabblers (those who do not rely heavily on SNSs or blogs). A comparison of mean scores indicates a significant difference in political ideology among the clusters, but not between Social Networkers and Blogophiles. Cluster 3 respondents (Ambi-textrous), those who access SNSs and blogs, are significantly more liberal (m = 2.18, range 1–5) than those in the other clusters ($F[3,4177] = 24.083$, $p < 0.000$) (Table 10.3).

Between-cluster analysis indicates significant differences between Social Networkers (heavy use of only SNSs) and Blogophiles (heavy use of only blogs) in interest and knowledge about politics. Social Networkers are significantly less interested in (m = 8.00, range 0–10) and perceive themselves as less knowledgeable about (m = 7.64, range 0–10) politics than Blogophiles (m = 8.65, m = 8.42, respectively) ($F[3,4189] = 84.176$, $p < 0.000$). Further, those who do not heavily rely on SNSs or blogs (Dabblers) report statistically similar levels of political interest (m = 7.91) and knowledge (7.92) as Social Networkers, whereas the Ambi-textrous, who heavily rely on both SNS and blogs, are similar to Blogophiles (political interest m = 8.94, political knowledge m = 8.49). In general, all four clusters report moderate to high levels of interest and knowledge in politics.

Social Networkers (C2) state significantly lower levels of knowledge about the 2008 presidential election (m = 8.31, range 0–10) than Blogophiles (C4) (m = 8.94) ($F[3,4191] = 56.465$, $p < 0.000$); however, there was no difference between the two clusters in levels of interest in the election. However, significant differences were found among the four clusters ($F[3,4188] = 44.452$, $p < 0.000$). Dabblers, those who do not heavily rely on SNSs or blogs, were significantly less interested (m = 8.87) in the election than those who heavily rely on both resources (Ambi-textrous) (m = 9.44). Overall, respondents reported high levels in interest and knowledge of the 2008 election.

When examining trust and self-efficacy, the findings indicate that Social Networkers are more trusting of the government (m = 8.87, range 3–15) than Blogophiles (m = 7.99) ($F[3,4172] = 7.459$, $p < 0.000$). Ambi-textrous (rely heavily on SNSs and blogs) express similar levels of trust (m = 8.87) as Social Networkers, whereas Dabblers (do not heavily rely on SNSs or blogs) are closely aligned (m = 8.10) with Blogophiles. In general, all clusters report low to moderate trust. Additionally, Social Networkers assert significantly lower self-efficacy (m = 15.65, range 4–20) than Blogophiles (m = 17.14) ($F[3,4191] = 56.465$, $p < 0.000$). In comparison, Social Networkers are more trusting of the government but are lower in self-efficacy, whereas Blogophiles are lower in trust but higher in self-efficacy.

Regarding the strength of ties to a political party, Social Networkers and Blogophiles are statistically similar (m = 6.77, m = 6.71, respectively, range 0–10). Differences occur among Dabblers (C1) who do not heavily rely on SNSs or blogs and who report weaker ties to a political party (m = 6.18) than the other clusters ($F[3,4192] = 14.908$, $p < 0.000$) (Table 10.3).

This study also investigates the top-10 motivations for using SNSs and blogs for political information. Specifically, comparisons are made between Social Networkers who seek political information from SNSs, and Blogophiles who turn to blogs. In all, 56 motivations were examined and the top-10 reasons by mean score were identified for each of the two clusters.

Four of the top-10 motivations are common to each cluster: "because it's interesting," "because I want to learn something new," "to keep up with political issues," and "to access political information at any time." Politically interested users are motivated to use SNSs and blogs for political information, convenience, and personal fulfillment, both emotional and cognitive (Table 10.4).

Apart from those four motivations, clear differences in the reasons for using SNSs and blogs emerged. Social Networkers who mostly go to SNSs for political information tend to do so mainly for social reasons. For example, this cluster that is made up primarily of younger females who are Democrats, with lower levels of self-efficacy but higher trust than Cluster 4, and who report lower interest in and knowledge about politics and less knowledge of the election, find SNSs "entertaining," they "enjoy the excitement of the election race," they gravitate to SNSs to "be in contact with like-minded people," "for the ongoing political debates," and to "have something to talk about with others." On the other hand, Blogophiles (C4), who tend to be older Republican males, are drawn to blogs for political information, for anti-traditional media, and cognitive reasons. They access blogs for information not found in traditional media and because blogs are independent of mainstream media sources. They also turn to blogs for "links to more political sources," "for political news analysis," "for depth of political information," and "to keep up with the issues of the day." None of the top-10 reasons were socially oriented.

The mean scores themselves indicate a difference in the strength of the motivations within each cluster. Nine of the ten reasons for using SNSs for political information were rated less strongly (range 1–5) than all of the motivations for using blogs. In other words, the strength of agreement for reasons for using SNSs ranges from a high of 4.38 to a low of 3.79, whereas the reasons for using blogs ranges from a high of 4.50 to a low of 4.29. These mean scores indicate that the reasons for seeking political information are more strongly associated with blogs than with SNSs (Table 10.4).

Table 10.4 Top-10 motivations for heavily using political blogs and social networking
sites for political information

Social networking sites (C2. Social networkers. Heavily use only SNSs)	Mean (range 1–5)
1. Because it's interesting	4.38
2. Because it is entertaining	4.15
3. To give me something to talk about with others	4.12
4. Because I want to learn something new	3.94
5. To keep up with political issues	3.88
6. Because information is easy to obtain	3.88
7. To be in contact with like-minded people	3.86
8. For ongoing political debates and arguments	3.85
9. To access political information at any time	3.82
10. To enjoy the excitement of an election race	3.79
Political Blogs (C4. Blogophiles. Heavily use only blogs)	
1. For information I can't get from traditional media	4.50
2. Because it's interesting	4.45
3. For links to more political information sources	4.44
4. To access political information at any time	4.37
5. To keep up with political issues	4.36
6. Because they are independent from traditional media	4.35
7. For political news analysis	4.34
8. Because I want to learn something new	4.31
9. For depth of political information	4.30
10. To keep up with the main issues of the day	4.29

Discussion

The primary purpose of this study is to examine the users and uses of SNSs and
blogs for political information within the uses and gratifications framework.
Two-step cluster analysis identified four clusters of users: Cluster 1 (Dabblers)—
those who do not heavily use SNSs or blogs for political information; Cluster 2
(Social Networkers)—those who heavily use only SNSs; Cluster 3 (Ambi-
textrous)—those who heavily use SNSs and blogs; and Cluster 4 (Blogophiles)—
those who heavily use only blogs. This study also investigated how the four
clusters of users differ in terms of demographic and political characteristics. The
primary comparisons are between Cluster 2 (Social Networkers) and Cluster 4
(Blogophiles) on demographic and political characteristics, and on their reasons
for using SNSs and blogs for political information. Focusing on these two groups
of users opens the potential for sharp differences among personal and political
characteristics and motivations to emerge.

Overall, this study found those who heavily rely on only SNSs (Social Networkers) or a combination of SNSs and blogs (Ambi-textrous) tend to be
younger females, whereas those who rely heavily on only blogs (Blogophiles) or
rarely use blogs or SNSs (Dabblers) for political information tend to be older

males. These results may have emerged in part because females of low socio-economic status were more likely to vote for Obama, who had a stronger online presence than McCain (CNN.com, 2008). These gender and age differences are similar to those found in other studies (Johnson, Zhang, Bichard, & Seltzer, 2010; Lenhart, 2009; Pew Research Center, 2008b; Rainie, 2005; Rainie & Horrigan, 2005; Salwen et al., 2005; Smith, 2009), but they do not account for all differences between blog and SNS users. Therefore this study also examined the political characteristics of SNS and blog users.

In general, this study found that demographic, political, and motivational differences among online users influence the online components they rely on most heavily (blogs or SNSs) for political information. Analysis of political party affiliation found that Social Networkers tend to belong to the Democratic party, whereas Blogophiles favor the Republican party. This finding is not surprising given that Democrats are more likely to use and to have created an online SNS profile than Republicans (Smith & Ranie, 2008). From these party differences, it would be expected that liberals would be more likely to inhabit Cluster 2 and conservatives Cluster 4, but that is not the case in this study. Instead, there was no difference between these two clusters in whether respondents were liberal, moderate, or conservative. The results on ideology further confound the questions of whether liberals are more likely to use blogs (Pew Research Center, 2008b), or whether blogs are the domain of the right wing (Johnson et al., 2007; Kaye & Johnson, 2004b), and if SNS users are indeed more liberal (Johnson et al., 2010; Smith, 2009).

It is curious that party affiliation is tied to SNS and blog use, but political ideology is not, especially when party ties tend to be based on ideological agreement. Perhaps in the case of this study when data were collected during the height of the presidential campaign and subsequent election, respondents were seeking political information mainly from party- and candidate-supported SNSs and blogs, which generally follow more closely the mainstream perspective of a party, leaving the ideologues (party fringe) to look elsewhere for like-minded information. Also, because the Obama campaign had such a high online profile and there was little voter crossover (10% Democrats voted for McCain, 9% Republicans voted for Obama; CNN.com, 2008), online users (especially Democrats) may have connected to SNSs and blogs as a show of party support, rather than out of ideological concerns.

Other political characteristics also distinguish Social Networkers from Blogophiles. Significant differences emerged in degree of trust in the government, self-efficacy, interest in and knowledge about politics, and knowledge about the 2008 election. Blogophiles are less trusting of the government, more self-efficacious, more interested in politics, more knowledgeable about politics, and more interested in the 2008 presidential election than Social

Networkers. Presumably, those who use blogs often do so to get behind a cause and to rally support for a blogger or issue, thus these users harbor stronger confidence in their power to bring about political change than those who rely only on SNSs. Additionally, the findings that levels of interest in and knowledge about politics and the election are higher among those who rely heavily on blogs accords with other research that indicates that blogs are used for more cognitive, informational reasons (Haigh & Pfau, 2007; Hebert, 2004; Johnson & Kaye, 2006, 2007b, 2009; Johnson et al., 2007; Kaye, 2005, 2007, 2008; Kaye & Johnson, 2006), while SNSs are used for more emotional or social purposes (boyd & Ellison, 2007; Joinson, 2008; Lampe et al., 2006; Raacke & Bonds-Raacke, 2008).

There are several demographic and political overlaps among Social Networkers, Blogophiles, and Ambi-textrous. Similar to Social Networkers, the Ambi-textrous tend to be females who belong to the Democratic party and trust the government. The Ambi-textrous also resemble Blogophiles—both groups report high levels of education, are self-efficacious, interested in politics and in the 2008 election, and are knowledgeable about politics and the election. The ambidextrous see value in both SNSs and blogs. As blogs and social network sites evolve and are seen less as alternative sources and more as mainstream suppliers of news and political information, the Ambi-textrous may become the more typical Web 2.0 user.

This study also assessed the motivations for using SNSs and blogs for political information, and compared those reasons between Social Networkers (heavily use only SNSs) and Blogophiles (heavily use only blogs). The findings indicate several key differences in the motivations for using SNSs and blogs. SNSs are primarily used for political purposes but with a social spin, whereas blogs are used for information and because users do not like or trust traditional media. For example, SNS users are motivated "to be in contact with like-minded people," and "to give me something to talk about with others." Blog users, on the other hand, are motivated "for political news analysis," and "for information not found in traditional media."

These differences in motivations between Social Networkers and Blogophiles supports previous studies which suggest that those who connect to blogs do so for information and as an alternative source to distrusted mainstream media (Johnson & Kaye, 2006, 2007b, 2009; Johnson et al., 2007; Kaye, 2005, 2007, 2008; Kaye & Johnson, 2006). Early blogs were online diaries that were used to keep in touch with family and friends, but they have since evolved into multifaceted sites that are primarily used for information. Instead of helping to form online social connections, perhaps blogs now foster issue-oriented communities. The motivations found in this study also support the general conclusion that users are drawn to SNSs to belong to social communities and for social surveillance (boyd & Ellison, 2007; Joinson, 2008; Lampe et al., 2006; Raacke & Bonds-Raacke, 2008). Although users seek political information on SNSs, they may be looking for more personal political information (i.e., who friends are voting for) rather than for general political analysis. In general, this study indicates that users turn to blogs to obtain political information from the blogging community, whereas SNS users show party support and form political social circles. As unique purposes for using SNSs and blogs emerge, perhaps they will each attract a more homogeneous, but more engaged, niche audience.

Although it is still too soon to know how SNSs will evolve, and how and whether they will supplement or supplant other online sources, blogs are in flux. They have since morphed into online venues for expression of any type, be it thoughtful analysis or impulsive ranting, about any topic imaginable. But the number of active blogs is fading. An estimated 95% lie dormant. As bloggers tire of the burden of frequent updates and of responding to anonymous others, they are moving on to SNSs for more personal interactions of their choosing (Quenqua, 2009).

As new Web 2.0 resources are created, they open new ways for users to be both content providers and content receivers. Rather than holding to one or two older and favored sources (e.g., listservs), online users are expanding their repertoire and embracing updated and new technologies (e.g., blogs, SNSs). In doing so, users are changing their online behaviors and are shifting among sources that gratify their needs more readily. It will be interesting to see if, by the 2012 presidential election, a larger percentage of users rely on SNSs for political news and information, and if users of blogs and SNSs still differ on key political characteristics. It would also be interesting to find whether users supplement or supplant political information found on blogs with that found on SNSs, and whether distinct motivations draw them to each of the sources for political information.

Notes

1. Although often called "Social *Networking* Sites" this chapter uses the term "Social *Network* Sites" as defined by boyd & Ellison (2007), who assert that networking is not the only reason for using such sites.
2. SNSs and blogs are considered part of the second generation of online resources collectively known by the term "Web 2.0," which is defined as any online source that involves consumer activity such as posting videos, writing blog content, and networking (The State of the News Media, 2008).
3. The primary problem with online surveys is the absence of public central registries from which to randomly select online users. Therefore, this study relied on a self-selected convenience sample of users who were solicited by online announcements to fill out the survey. Posting surveys online, however, is an efficient and low-cost

way to attract respondents and the method has become fairly common—most market research these days is conducted using online convenience samples (Keeter, 2009). Further, in situations where random probability sampling is not possible, non-probability sampling is acceptable (Babbie, 2002, Web Center for Social Research Methods, 2008; Witte et al., 2000). Although researchers must be mindful of the limitations of online purposive sampling, such samples can produce results that may be representative of a specific subset of Internet users such as politically interested ones. Additionally, this study followed procedures used in other published studies (Johnson & Kaye, 2004, 2007a, 2009; Kaye, 2005, 2007).

4. The survey's first question asked respondents to enter their email addresses; all but 17 (99.1%) complied. The respondents' email addresses, together with a computer-generated ID, were used to delete duplicated surveys. Additionally, after sending the completed survey a Web page would immediately appear thanking the respondents for their participation and verifying that the survey had been sent so respondents would not retransmit the survey.

5. Cooperation Rate: As defined by AAPOR "Standard Definitions": "The proportion of all cases interviewed of all eligible units ever contacted."

6. Survey Variables: reliance on blogs and social networks was assessed by asking respondents whether they "heavily rely," "rely," "sometimes rely," "rarely rely," or "don't rely" on political websites, blogs, bulletin boards/lists, and chat/instant messaging as sources of political information. Respondents were asked with which political party they were registered and how strongly they are affiliated with their party of choice (0–10 scale, ranging from no party ties to very strong ties). They were also asked to mark their political ideology (very liberal, liberal, neutral, conservative, very conservative). Respondents rated their levels of political knowledge, political interest, and knowledge and interest in the 2008 political campaign on a 0–10 scale, ranging from not at all interested to very interested. Lastly, they were asked to assess their levels of trust in the government and self-efficacy.

This study also includes four demographic measures: gender, age, education, and income. Respondents were asked to indicate whether they are male or female and their age as of their last birthday. Respondents marked the highest grade completed from the following list: "less than high school," "high school graduate," "some college," "four year college degree," "master's degree," "Terminal degree (PhD, MD, JD, Ed.D)," and "other," and they estimated their 2008 income.

Motivations for using blogs and SNSs for political information were comprised of 35 statements derived from past uses and gratification studies (Johnson & Kaye, 2007b; Kaye, 2007, 2008; Kaye & Johnson, 2004a, 2006). Respondents were asked to mark their level of agreement along with the reasons for accessing each of the four Internet components. Responses ranged from (1) strongly disagree to (5) strongly agree.

7. Totals: 4,194 respondents—47 did not fill out the reliance question.

References

Babbie, E. (2002). *The basics of social research*. Belmont: Wadsworth.

Bhatnagar, A., & Ghose, S. (2004). A latent class segmentation analysis of e-shoppers. *Journal of Business Research, 57*, 758–767.

Blog Reader (2007). Blog reader project. Online, available at: www.blogreader-project.com (accessed May 8, 2008).

Blogads (2006). Political blogs reader survey 2006. Online, available at: http://blogads.com/survey/2006/2006_political_blogs_reader_survey.html   (accessed January 18, 2008).

boyd, D. M., & Ellison, N. B. (2007). Social networking sites: Definition, history, and scholarship. *Journal of Computer-Mediated Communication, 13*(1), 210–230.

Charney, T., & Greenberg, B. S. (2001). Uses and gratifications of the Internet. In C. A. Lin & D. J. Atkin (Eds.), *Communication technology and society: Audience adoption and uses of the new media* (pp. 379–407). Cresskill, NJ: Hampton.

CNN.com (2008). Election Center 2008. Online, available at: www.cnn.com/ELECTION/2008/results/polls/#USP00p1 (accessed October 13, 2009).

Connelly, M. (2007). The Caucus: The blogs. *New York Times*, March 13. Online, available at: www.nytimes.com (accessed March 18, 2009).

Dimmick, J., Kline, S., & Stafford, L. (2000). The gratification niches of personal e-mail and the telephone. *Communication Research, 27*(2), 227–248.

Eighmey, J. (1997). Profiling user responses to commercial web sites. *Journal of Advertising Research, 37*, 59–66.

Eveland, W. P., & Dylko, I. (2007). Reading political blogs during the 2004 election campaign: Correlates and political consequences. In M. Tremayne (Ed.), *Blogging, citizenship, and the future of media* (pp. 105–125). New York, NY: Routledge.

Facebook Statistics (2010). Facebook. Online, available at: www.facebook.com/press/info.php?statistics (accessed June 9, 2010).

Ferguson, D. A., & Perse, E. M. (2000). The World Wide Web as a functional alternative to television. *Journal of Broadcasting & Electronic Media, 44*, 155–174.

Fraser, M., & Dutta, S. (2008). Barack Obama and the Facebook election. *U.S. News & World Report*, November 19. Online, available at: www.usnews.com/articles/opinion/2008/11/19/barack-obama-and-the-facebook-election (accessed March 31, 2009).

Fuentes, A. (2000). Won't you be my neighbor? *American Demographics, 22*, 60–62.

Graf, J. (2006). *The audience for political blogs: New research on blog readership*. Washington, DC: Institute for Politics Democracy & The Internet.

Haigh, M., & Pfau, M. (2007). *Don't tread on my blog: A study of military web logs.* Paper presented to the Association for Education in Journalism & Mass Communication, Washington, DC, August.

Hebert, J. (2004). Troop blogs offer voices, visions from Iraq. Copley News Service, August 2.

Hernandez, R. (2006). A well-known political blogger is hired by the Clinton campaign. *New York Times*, June 27. Online, available at: www.nytimes.com (accessed March 21, 2009).

Horrigan, J. (2007). Broadband: What's all the fuss about? *Pew Internet & American Life Project*, October 18. Online, available at: www.pewinternet.org/Reports/2007/Broadband-Whats-All-the-Fuss-About.aspx (accessed April 12, 2009).

Horrigan, J., Garrett, K., & Resnick, P. (2004). *The Internet and democratic debate: Wired Americans hear more points of view about candidates and key issues than other citizens.* Pew Research Center. Online, available at: www.pewinternet.org/reports (accessed October 27, 2004).

Internet 2008 in numbers. Royal Pingdom.com, January 22. Online, available at:

http://royal.pingdom.com/2009/01/22/internet-2008-in-numbers (October 28, 2009).

James, M. L., Wotring, C. E., & Forrest, E. J. (1995). An exploratory study of the perceived benefits of electronic bulletin board use and the impact on other communication activities. *Journal of Broadcasting & Electronic Media, 39*, 30–50.

Jih, W. J. K., & Lee, S. F. (2003). An exploratory analysis of relationships between cellular phone users' shopping motivators and lifestyle indicators. *Journal of Computer Information Systems, 44*(2), 65–73.

Johnson, T. J., & Kaye, B. K. (2004). Wag the blog: How reliance on traditional media and the Internet influence perceptions of credibility of blogs among blog users. *Journalism & Mass Communication Quarterly, 81*(3), 622–642.

Johnson, T. J., & Kaye, B. K. (2006). Blog day afternoon: Are blogs stealing audiences away from traditional media sources? In Ralph Berenger (Ed.), *Cybermedia go to war* (pp. 316–333). Spokane, WA: Marquette Books.

Johnson, T. J., & Kaye, B. K. (2007a). Blog readers: Predictors of reliance on warblogs. In M. Tremayne (Ed.), *Blogging, Citizenship, and the Future of Media* (pp. 165–184). New York, NY: Routledge.

Johnson, T. J., & Kaye, B. K. (2007b). *Choosing is believing? How Web gratifications and reliance affect Internet credibility among politically interested users.* Paper presented to the Association for Education in Journalism and Mass Communication annual conference. Washington, DC, August.

Johnson, T. J., & Kaye, B. K. (2009). In blog we trust? Deciphering credibility of components of the Internet among politically interested Internet users. *Computers in Human Behavior, 25*, 175–182.

Johnson, T. J., Kaye, B. K., Bichard, S. L., & Wong, W. J. (2007). Every blog has its day: Politically interested Internet users' perceptions of blog credibility. *Journal of Computer-Mediated Communication, 13*, 6. Online, available at: http://jcmc.indiana.edu/vol.13/issue1/johnson.html.

Johnson, T. J., Zhang, W., Bichard, S. L., & Seltzer, T. (2010). United we stand? Online social network sites and civic engagement. In Z. Papacharissi (ed.), *A networked self: Identity, community, and culture on social network sites* (pp. 185–207). New York, NY: Routledge.

Joinson, A. N. (2008). *"Looking at", "looking up" or "keeping up with" people? Motives and uses of Facebook.* Paper presented to the conference on Human Factors in Computing Systems. Proceedings of the twenty-sixth annual SIGCHI conference, Florence, Italy.

Kaye, B. K. (1998). Uses and gratifications of the World Wide Web: From couch potato to Web potato. *New Jersey Journal of Communication, 6*, 21–40.

Kaye, B. K. (2005). It's a blog, blog, blog, blog world: Users and uses of blogs. *Atlantic Journal of Communication, 13*(2), 73–95.

Kaye, B. K. (2007). Blog use motivations: An exploratory study. In M. Tremayne (ed.), *Blogging, citizenship, and the future of media* (pp. 127–148). New York, NY: Routledge.

Kaye, B. K. (2008). *Going to the blogs: Exploring the uses and gratifications of blogs.* Paper presented to the Association for Education in Journalism and Mass Communication annual conference, Chicago, IL, August.

Kaye, B. K., & Johnson, T. J. (2004a). A Web for all reasons: Uses and gratifications of Internet resources for political information. *Telematics and Informatics, 21*(3), 197–223.

Kaye, B. K., & Johnson, T. J. (2004b). Blogs as a source of information about the 2003 Iraq War. In R. D. Berenger (Ed.), *Global media goes to war: Role of news and entertainment media during the 2003 Iraq War* (pp. 291–301). Spokane, WA: Marquette Books.

Kaye, B. K., & Johnson, T. J. (2006). The Age of reasons: Motives for using different components of the Internet for political information. In A. P. Williams & J. C. Tedesco (Eds.), *The Internet election: Perspectives on the role of the Web in campaign 2004* (pp. 147–167). Lanham, MD: Rowman & Littlefield.

Keeter, S. (2009). *New tricks for old—and new—dogs.* Keynote address to the 31st Annual Research Symposium, University of Tennessee, Knoxville, TN, February.

Kohut, A. (2004). *Cable and Internet loom large in fragmented political news universe: Perceptions of partisan bias seen as growing, especially by Democrats.* Pew Research Center. Online, available at: www.pewinternet.org/reports (accessed January 1, 2004).

Lampe, C., Ellison, N., & Steinfield, C. (2007). *A Face(book) in the crowd: Social searching vs. social browsing.* Paper presented to the proceedings of the twentieth-anniversary conference of the Association for Computing Machinery, Banff, Vancouver, Canada.

Lange, P. G. (2007). Publicly private and privately public: Social networking on YouTube. *Journal of Computer-Mediated Communication, 13*(1), 361–380.

Leibovich, M. (2008). McCain, the analog candidate. *New York Times*, August 3. Online, available at: www.nytimes.com (March 28, 2009).

Lenhart, A. (2009). Social networks grow: Friending Mom and Dad. *Pew Internet & American Life Project*, January 14. Online, available at: http://pewresearch.org/pub/1079/social-networks-grow (March 20, 2009).

Levy, S. (2002). Living in the blog-osphere. *Newsweek,* 140, August 26, pp. 42–45.

Lin, C. A., & Jeffres, L. (1998). Predicting adoption of multimedia cable service. *Journalism Quarterly, 75*, 251–275.

Murchu, I. O., Breslin, J. G., & Decker, S. (2004). Online social and business networking communities. *Digital Enterprise Research Institute*. Technical Report, August 11.

Nagourney, A. (2008). The '08 campaign: Sea of change for politics as we know it. *New York Times*, November 8. Online, available at: www.nytimes.com (accessed March 28, 2009).

Palmgreen, P. (1984). Uses and gratifications: A theoretical perspective. In R. N. Bostrom (Ed.), *Communication Yearbook 8* (pp. 61–72). Beverly Hills, CA: Sage Publications, Inc.

Papacharissi, Z., & Rubin, A. M. (2000). Predictors of Internet use. *Journal of Broadcasting & Electronic Media, 44*, 175–196.

Perlmutter, D. A. (2008). *Blog wars.* New York, NY: Oxford University Press.

Pew Research Center. (2008a). *Key news audiences now blend online and traditional sources*. Online, available at: http://people-press.org/report/444/news-media (accessed March 16, 2009).

Pew Research Center. (2008b). *More than a quarter of voters read political blogs*. Online, available at: http://people-press.org/report/464/campaign-engagement (accessed March 30, 2009).

Postelnicu, M., & Cozma, R. (2007). *Social network politics: A content analysis of MySpace profiles of political candidates from the 2006 U.S. mid-terms*. Paper presented at the annual meeting of the National Communication Association, Chicago, IL.

Quenqua, D. (2009). Blogs falling in an empty forest. *New York Times*, June 7, Styles, pp. 1, 7.

Raacke, J., & Bonds-Raacke, J. (2008). Applying the uses and gratifications theory to exploring friend-networking sites. *CyberPsychology & Behavior, 11*, 170–174.

Rainie, L. (2005). The state of blogging, *Pew Internet and American Life Project*. Pew Research Center. Online, available at: www.pewinternet.org/ (accessed February 1, 2005).

Rainie, L., & Horrigan, J. (2005). *A decade of adoption: How the Internet has woven itself into American life*. Pew Research Center. Online, available at: www.pewinternet. org/reports (accessed January 25, 2005).

Reynolds, G. H. (2004). The blogs of war. *National Interest, 75*, 59–64.

Salwen, M. B., Garrison, B., & Driscoll, P. D. (2005). The baseline survey projects: Exploring questions. In M. B. Salwen, B. Garrison, & P. D. Driscoll (Eds.), *Online news and the public* (pp. 121–145). Mahwah, NJ: Lawrence Erlbaum Associates.

Shapira, I. (2009). In a generation that friends and tweets, they don't. *Washington Post*, October 15, pp. A1, A11.

Smith, A. (2009). The Internet's role in campaign 2008. *Pew Internet & American Life Project*, April 15. Online, available at: www.pewinternet.org/Reports/2009/6–The-Internets-Role-in-Campaign-2008/3–The-Internet-as-a-Source-of-Political-News/5–Long-tail.aspx?r=1 (accessed April 19, 2009).

Smith, A., & Rainie, L. (2008). The Internet and the 2008 election. *Pew Internet & American Life Project*, June 15. Online, available at: www.pewinternet.org/Reports/2008/The-Internet-and-the-2008-Election.aspx (accessed April 8, 2009).

Stafford, L., Kline, S. L., & Dimmick, J. (1999). Home e-mail: Relational maintenance and gratification opportunities. *Journal of Broadcasting & Electronic Media, 43*(4), 659–669.

State of the News Media. (2007). An annual report on American Journalism. *Project for Excellence in Journalism/Pew Research*. Online, available at: www.stateofthemedia. org/2007/narrative_overview_intro.asp?media=1 (accessed March 15, 2008).

State of the News Media. (2008). Citizen media: An annual report on American journalism. *Project for Excellence in Journalism/Pew Research*. Online, available at: www.stateofthemedia.org/2008/narrative_online_citizen_media.php (accessed March 1, 2009).

Stelter, B. (2008a). Finding political news online, the young pass it on. *International News Herald*, March 27. Online, available at: www.iht.com/articles/2008/03/27/america/27voters.php (March 28, 2009).

Stelter, B. (2008b). Obama draws on social network of support. *International News*

Herald, July 7. Online, available at: www.iht.com/articles/2008/07/06/business/hughes07.php (accessed March 28, 2009).

Stelter, B., & Perez-Pena, R. (2008). U.S. media outlets still looking for campaign bounce. *International News Herald*, August 4. Online, available at: www.iht.com/articles/2008/08/04/business/ratings.php (March 28, 2009).

Stromer-Galley, J., & Baker, A. B. (2006). Joy and sorrow of interactivity on the campaign trail: Blogs in the primary campaign of Howard Dean. In A. P. Williams & J. C. Tedesco (Eds.), *The Internet election: Perspectives on the Web in campaign 2006* (pp. 111–131). Lanham, MD: Rowman & Littlefield.

Sydell, L. (2009). Facebook, MySpace divided along social lines. *National Public Radio*, October 21. Online, available at: www.npr.org/templates/story/story.php.?storyID=113974893 (October 21, 2009).

Turkle, S. (1999). Cyberspace and identity. *Contemporary Sociology, 28*, 643–648.

Web Center for Social Research Methods (2008). *Nonprobability samples*. Online, available at: www.socialresearchmethods.net/kb/sampnon.php (May 19, 2008).

Witte, J., Amoroso, L., and Howard, P. E. N. (2000). Method and representation in Internet-based survey tools: Mobility, community, and cultural identity in Survey2000. *Social Science Computer Review, 18*(2), 179–195.

Chapter 11

Working the Twittersphere

Microblogging as Professional Identity Construction

Dawn R. Gilpin

Public relations professionals are called upon to forge and maintain relationships with vast networks of stakeholders, colleagues, and contacts. These relational networks are fluid, adjusting to constantly changing needs. The growth of online communication environments has been seen by many scholars and practitioners as an opportunity to extend the reach of public relations efforts to a larger number of current and potential organizational stakeholders. To manage these networks of relationships, many practitioners have become active users of social media. One outlet that is rapidly growing in popularity is Twitter: a Web 2.0 service that allows users to perform "micro-blogging," or communicate in messages of no more than 140 characters (known as "tweets").

This chapter approaches Twitter as a window into the complex processes of professional identity construction employed by public relations practitioners today. Analyzing some of the most prominent Twitter feeds among the online professional public relations community in the United States, the study described here used social and semantic network analysis to examine use of the microblogging site among public relations practitioners. Findings indicate that Twitter serves multiple purposes for practitioners, such as information sharing, networking, and establishing professional expertise. Finally, Twitter itself emerges as a boundary-blurring tool that links multiple online spheres and spans the divide between offline and virtual professional domains. Twitter illustrates the ways in which social media are encouraging patterns of self-organization among public relations practitioners seeking new ways to adapt to a turbulent professional environment.

Literature Review

The use of Twitter by public relations professionals can be situated within a context of extant research on identity construction, co-creational processes in public relations practice, and the rise of "reality" media across multiple platforms.

Constructing a Professional Identity

Identity construction can be seen as the sense-making process by which people selectively organize their experiences into a coherent sense of self (Fisher, 1987; Giddens, 1991; Ricoeur, 1985; Somers, 1994). Recent literature on identity shifts attention away from subject attributes to dialogic processes of negotiation and performance constructed through interaction over time (Somers, 1994; Wiley, 1994). Polillo (2004) expands on Wiley's (1994) concept of the "semiotic self" by incorporating contemporary understanding of social networks. In this view, identity is constructed as the result of structural and power dynamics, and subject to constant negotiation of boundaries.

Online interactive media further complicate the question of boundaries. Giddens (1991) reflected at length on the role of mediated experience in constructing identity and organizing social relationships disembedded from space and time. Several scholars have remarked in particular on the blurring between professional and personal identities in electronically mediated environments (Andrejevic, 2004; Lüders, 2008; Papacharissi, 2009). Online interactions take place in a space that is neither distinctly professional nor distinctly personal. Lüders (2008) noted that the relative personal or professional nature of digital media can only be determined through a case-by-case review of both structure and content. A television program may allow viewer call-ins, but still takes place in an institutionalized context, whereas a blog may be created and maintained by an individual, but emphasize professional content. Unless users adopt multiple online profiles, social networking sites represent a confluence of identity roles, spaces where users "must adjust their behavior so as to make it appropriate for a variety of different situations and audiences" (Papacharissi, 2009, p. 207). The message is now as important, or even more important, than the medium, and yet it is constrained by the multiplicity of contexts in which it will be received.

Public professional identities are constructed through a combination of social ties and relational content. This process can be facilitated through social networking sites which, as Papacharissi (2009) observed, "operate on enabling self-presentation and connection-building" (p. 201). The role of social ties has been explored by numerous scholars. Connections to other users on such sites have been described as "public displays of connection" (boyd & Heer, 2006, p. 73) that add value and validity to an individual's identity performance. Unlike other social networking sites such as Facebook or MySpace, the primary site for this performance on Twitter is not the individual's own profile space, however loosely bounded. Twitter leaves little room for visual cues or sidebars of taste (Papacharissi, 2009). Twitter user profiles are very short, and provide minimal information about the account holder. While the profiles do list both the users followed and the account holder's own followers, many users participate via third-party applications rather than the Twitter.com page itself, bypassing profiles altogether and operating almost exclusively in the common space of social exchange.

Twitter's emphasis on public interaction makes active interlocutors a more significant indicator of social capital than follower counts. This is also the case since public Twitter profiles allow any user to follow any other, without the "walled garden" effect of relatively enclosed social networking sites such as Facebook. A so-called "at-reply" or "mention," a directed message prefaced by the @ symbol and an individual's user name, is instead a marker of a stronger tie between users. Interaction thus plays an especially strong role in identity construction in a conversational medium such as Twitter, as followers will primarily draw conclusions based on the contents of tweet messages as well as indications of the intended recipients of those messages (see also Papacharissi, 2009).

Most research on constructing professional identity has focused on individuals. For example, in a study of Russian public relations practitioners, Tsetsura (2007) described the importance of exploring processes of constructing and negotiating professional identities as twofold: helping to distinguish professional roles and understand the individual communication strategies employed. However, she also noted that "such identity negotiations influence the way public relations is practiced" (p. 2). Thus, constructing a professional identity also means constructing the identity of the profession, especially a profession in a state of flux such as contemporary public relations.

Co-Creational Public Relations and Social Media in the Professional World

Recent trends in public relations scholarship and practice have distanced the field from one-way publicity and press agentry models (Grunig, 1989) to emphasis on the relationship-building function of public relations (Ledingham & Bruning, 2000). This shift away from an organization-centric perspective also leads to conceptualizing issues and publics as dynamic, contextually situated, co-creational processes rather than objectively defined entities (Botan & Taylor, 2004; Curtin & Gaither, 2006). An issue, in this case, is defined as any publicly discussed matter that may constitute either a threat or an opportunity from the perspective of those discussing it (Bridges & Nelson, 2000; Heath, 1997). Publics are groups of stakeholders that emerge and coalesce based on their objective or subjective interest in a given issue (Botan & Taylor, 2004).

The emergence of new and social media may be viewed as an issue for public relations practitioners, since they require adaptation to new tools and challenge practices that previously relied on traditional mass media. A recent survey of practitioners found that blogs had become part of the accepted toolbox (used by nearly 42% of those surveyed), whereas social networking sites such as Facebook and MySpace, social bookmarking, and microblogging were far less commonly adopted (Eyrich, Padman, & Sweetser, 2008). The same study found that practitioners' personal adoption of tools correlated to a significant degree to their perception of industry-wide adoption. In other words, practitioners are more likely to use a tool if they see it as an important part of professional practice. Thus, the more the profession is seen to rely on social media, the more its members will turn to these tools for their own communication purposes. Early adopters therefore have the opportunity to significantly influence the identity of the profession and the shape of future practice through their use of new forms of communication and the way they construct the role of these tools in public relations work.

The constitution of social media as an issue among public relations practitioners also ties into Giddens' (1991) observation of the role of expert knowledge in modern abstract systems, and in the construction of what he termed "self-identity," or "the self as reflexively understood by the person" (p. 53) and based on the ability to maintain some sort of coherent self-narrative over time. The modern emphasis on constant self-improvement and development of ever-more specialized and narrow forms of expertise creates pockets of knowledge that become disembedded from other spheres of activity, and may lead to unintended consequences. If practitioners who establish their identity on the basis of expertise in these new forms of digital communication become too insular, then, they are likely to lose sight of the potential ramifications of their activities on the profession and on their client organizations. This risk may be exacerbated by the tendency to view socially mediated relations as more transparent than those of traditional media, given the erosion of boundaries and pressure to offer one's work up to public surveillance (Holtz & Havens, 2008). This pressure emerges from the larger trend toward mediated reality.

The Reality of New Media and Mediated Reality

In today's communication environment, and in particular the professional realm, there is "a premium on the ability to see through public façades by relying on strategies of detection and verification facilitated by interactive communication technologies that allow users to monitor one another" (Andrejevic, 2006, p. 391). Active users of public discussion technologies voluntarily expose themselves to observation by peers, clients, potential clients, and others. Media scholars who have studied reality television programming have noted how the medium emphasizes the sharing of mundane life events, information, and advice (Ouellette & Hay, 2008). This content is geared toward an entrepreneurial ethos of self-directed information-seeking and the need for "highly dispersed and practical techniques for reflecting on, managing, and improving the multiple dimensions of our personal lives with the resources available to us" (Ouellette & Hay, 2008, p. 2).

The Internet is another domain that offers such a range of techniques, particularly the rise of social media and personal publishing. Like television, the Internet can be described as a cultural technology that serves to inform and influence people while sitting at an intersection of regulatory, cultural, and economic interests (Bennett, 1995; Ouellette & Hay, 2008). Bennett (1995) described the "new logic" of cultural technologies as "a set of exercises through which those exposed to its influence were to be transformed into the active bearers and practitioners of the capacity for self-improvement that culture was held to embody" (p. 24). In this vein, Twitter has been cited as the emerging marketplace for "the new gurus" (*Rolling Stone*, 2009), a place where readers can find and share information (Palser, 2009), and even a tool for empowering citizens to organize large-scale protests and enact social change (Grossman, 2009). Twitter can thus be seen, alongside other social networking sites and online communication tools, as part of the new reality media landscape.

Similar trends extend beyond the personal realm to the professional. The progressive blurring of lines between entertainment and labor was observed by Andrejevic (2004), who noted that the Internet offers unprecedented opportunities for the atomization and surveillance of work-related activities. Ouellette and Hay (2008) pointed out that, in reality television programming, "[t]he assumption that we must all maximize our greatest asset—ourselves— has accelerated" (p. 7) as world economies and job markets become increasingly turbulent and uncertain. Reputation is a central concept of public relations (see Carroll & McCombs, 2003; Williams & Moffitt, 1997). Current definitions of reputation hinge on its dynamic, co-constructed nature as a process dependent on both direct and symbolic experiences between individuals or between individuals and organizations (Gioia, Schultz, & Corley, 2000; Gotsi & Wilson, 2001). Public relations professionals seek to develop positive associations on behalf of client organizations through both direct and indirect communication, and organizations are urged to use social networking to help improve their reputation with key stakeholders (Maddock & Vitn, 2008).

Online tools such as Twitter are therefore a logical extension of existing and emerging public relations practices, a site where professionals can engage in reputation management for themselves while gaining skills that will serve them in their capacity as consultants. These practices effectively expand professional public relations activities to include *public relating*, in which professionals conduct interactions under open surveillance. In doing so, it is argued here, they construct their own public and professional identity, contribute to shaping the identity of public relations as a whole, and perform in a new media reality context. The purpose of this study is to take a first step in examining some of the processes by which these identities and performances take place, and suggest avenues of future research.

Data and Methods Used

Data for this study were gathered starting with a core of three subjects, identified using the blog search engine at technorati.org. Technorati calculates an "authority index" intended to reflect the number of linkages between each blog and others, as an approximation of social capital. The focal subjects for this study were selected by identifying the three most authoritative blogs tagged (by their authors) as concerning the topic of "public relations," written by individual practitioners and with links to a Twitter account from the blog itself. Using the Twitter search function at search.twitter.com (then a separate service, but later incorporated into the Twitter homepage), a search conducted on each focal subject's moniker produced all messages, or tweets, sent and received by that person. These tweets were saved for a four-week period, from April 4 through May 1, 2008, to provide sufficient data for analysis. Another advantage of the period chosen was that both the Society for New Communication Research (SCNR) Forum and the Web 2.0 Expo were held during the third week, April 22–25, and provided the opportunity to observe any changes in network dynamics based on offline interactions among the individuals observed. Table 11.1 provides a summary of the data gathered.

Around 17% of the tweets contained links, which are a primary form of information and resource sharing among Twitter users. Undirected tweets are those without an @ symbol, a Twitter convention signifying that a tweet is addressed to or contains a mention of another Twitter user. Undirected tweets are intended for the public at large, and often respond to the Twitter.com question, "What are you doing?" Directed tweets are those containing the @ symbol, and are indicative of interaction between Twitter users. These tweets therefore form the basis of the network analyses.

Table 11.1 Summary of data gathered

Total tweets logged	1,854
Links	316
Undirected	427
Directed	1,427

Social and Semantic Network Analysis

Communication networks have been defined as "patterns of contact that are created by the flow of . . . data, information, knowledge, images, symbols, and any other symbolic forms that can move from one point in a network to another or can be cocreated by network members" (Monge & Contractor, 2003, p. 5). Interactions conducted via social networking tools such as Twitter represent an accessible terrain for analysis of both the structure of communication networks and the symbolic forms, or language, used by network members.

As mentioned already, identity is publicly constructed through a combination of associative patterns and communication content. This study therefore used two forms of network analysis, or the study of linkage patterns among actors or other elements—including lexical units—in an identified group (Borgatti & Foster, 2003; Carley & Kaufer, 1993; Kadushin, 2004; Kilduff & Tsai, 2003), to examine both dimensions of this process. Social network analysis produces a map of connections between the Twitter users examined here, to identify groupings and form a starting point for theorizing about basic power dynamics. The study design, which focused on three central users and recorded their interactions with others, does not offer a complete picture of all relationships within the network: the focal subjects will emerge as the most important figures in the network, simply because interactions that did not involve them were excluded from the study. It is therefore impossible to draw firm conclusions about the position of each within the public relations "Twittersphere" as a whole. However, the interaction patterns that emerge from this study can provide clues about more general trends and suggest lines of future inquiry.

Social network analysis can identify the key players in a given domain, the relationships among them, and patterns of change. The main software package used to conduct these analyses was Pajek (de Nooy, Mrvar, & Batagelj, 2005), which offers a number of advanced computational functions that can help identify structural patterns in data. In this case, Pajek was used to identify aggregate social formations among the users studied.

Groups develop their own habits, customs, and even linguistic references. The term "idioculture" refers to "a system of knowledge, beliefs, behaviors and customs shared by members of an interacting group" (Gunawardena et al., 2009). Idioculture can also be studied as a network property: semantic network analysis uses network theories and methods to identify patterns in language, and was employed in this study to give a sense of the overall idioculture of the group identified. The tweet texts were analyzed using a process known as centering resonance analysis (CRA), which relies on theories of language processing and network measures to identify the most influential nouns and noun phrases within a text or set of texts (Corman, Kuhn, McPhee,

& Dooley, 2002). Crawdad software (Corman & Dooley, 2006) was used for this purpose. Crawdad does not simply count word frequency, but can also calculate ties between non-adjacent words to reveal more fully developed concepts. This is done using the network concept of betweenness centrality, which measures how many ties within the text must pass through a given term (Corman et al., 2002). The software does not require the researcher to input prepared dictionaries or prepare drop lists of potentially confounding words such as definite and indefinite articles. This approach thus reduces the risk of instrumental or researcher bias compared to some forms of content analysis. At the same time, the resulting data provide only a starting point for analysis, and the researcher must interpret the output based on context. Since CRA only focuses on noun phrases, it is best suited for exploratory analysis to identify general topics and themes within a text or set of texts.

Findings and Analysis

Although the relational patterns and semantic content of the tweet texts are closely intertwined, this section will describe the findings for each type of analysis carried out. The discussion in the following section will then contextualize and explore the significance of the combined semantic and social network analyses.

Social Network Analysis

The social network analysis revealed a two-tiered pattern of interaction: a core group of users who exchanged at least 20 tweets with the central figures in the space of a week, and a slightly larger group with whom the latter exchanged at least 10 tweets. These tiers represent levels of relational interaction within a subnetwork, a group of people whose members communicate with one another via Twitter on a relatively regular basis. Table 11.2 shows the nodes and ties for each week as well as the aggregate figures.

Table 11.2 Weekly colloquy composition

	Total nodes	Total core nodes	Total core ties (%)	Total extended nodes	Total ties
Week 1	27	3 + 9	236 (54)	15	435
Week 2	35	3 + 11	268 (51)	21	521
Week 3	40	3 + 12	306 (54)	25	569
Week 4	45	3 + 14	316 (50)	28	629
Aggregate	51	3 + 15	334 (48)	33	691

Figure 11.1 shows the network diagram for the aggregate subnetwork. As indicated in Table 11.2, this subnetwork consisted of 51 individuals: the three central figures, and those belonging to the two highest tiers of interaction. The size of the nodes in Figure 11.1 represents their degree, or the total number of tweets exchanged. Arrows represent the existence and direction of tweets exchanged between users. Thus the three largest nodes are the three central practitioners; the black nodes represent the core group with whom at least one user exchanged 20 or more tweets in at least one week of the period examined; and the smaller, white nodes are the second tier of interaction, with at least 10 messages exchanged in a week.

Table 11.3 shows the total number of interlocutors and directed messages for each central subject, week by week. User M1 was far more densely connected to start with, interacting with 88 other users the first week compared to 58 for M2 and just 37 for F1. He exchanged a total of 188 directed messages with those interlocutors. All three of the focal users increased their total number of contacts during the period studied, but the patterns of growth differed markedly: users F1 and M2 showed large spikes in both contacts and messages during weeks 3 and 4, coinciding with the two major social media events held that week and attended by both. User M1, on the other hand, interacted with just over half the number of contacts in week 3 as in week 4 (67 compared to 119). The number of directed messages, however, did not drop to the same degree: M1 exchanged 212 directed tweets in week 3, down from 265 in week 2. By week 4 he returned to similar levels as week 2, exchanging 264 directed tweets with 111 users (compared to 265 and 119, respectively, in week 2).

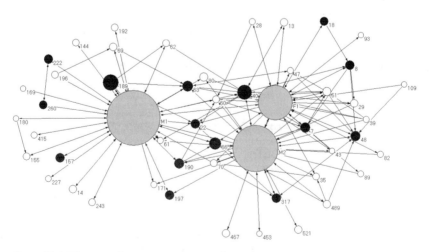

Figure 11.1 Diagram of aggregate subnetwork.

Table 11.3 Colloquy composition per focal user

	Total interlocutors	Total ties (directed messages)
F1		
Week 1	37	110
Week 2	31	112
Week 3	52	179
Week 4	58	187
M1		
Week 1	88	188
Week 2	119	265
Week 3	67	212
Week 4	111	264
M2		
Week 1	58	134
Week 2	66	158
Week 3	85	208
Week 4	112	247

A closer review of M1's tweeting patterns indicates that he took the opportunity to live-tweet the events. As a highly visible figure in the social media community among public relations and marketing practitioners, he continued to receive a relatively large number of directed tweets (203, compared to 156 for the first two weeks), but sent more undirected tweets during this period (176, compared to 85 for the first two weeks). At the same time, being already well embedded in these communities, the events did not apparently serve the same function of expanding his circle of professional contacts as it did for the other two focal users.

These patterns suggest that practitioners use Twitter for a variety of purposes at offline events: to expand and reinforce professional contacts; to serve as a "broadcasting voice" reporting events as they occur, and expressing opinions on them; and to construct or cement an identity of membership in the social media community.

Semantic Network Analysis

The semantic network analysis revealed a total of 31 individual words with a betweenness centrality (a measure of influence, see Corman et al., 2002) of 0.013 or greater, and 31 word pairs with a betweenness centrality of 0.01 or greater. Since network measures take place within a specific circumscribed domain, there is no universal threshold of significance; values must be assessed relative to others within the same context. Table 11.4 lists these words and word pairs along with their relative centrality values for comparison.

Table 11.4 Influential words and word pairs

Word	Betweenness centrality	Word pair	Betweenness centrality
Twitter	0.14226	Twitter – good	0.053
good	0.12376	Twitter – great	0.048
great	0.08464	good – time	0.047
time	0.06365	Twitter – time	0.036
new	0.06142	Twitter – new	0.035
blog	0.06011	Twitter – blog	0.034
thanks	0.05973	great – post	0.030
post	0.05128	Twitter – post	0.029
today	0.04071	Twitter – thanks	0.025
day	0.037378	good – thing	0.024
PR	0.03213	good – post	0.019
social media	0.03189	good – people	0.019
people	0.03052	new – post	0.019
nice	0.02817	Twitter – PR	0.018
thing	0.02409	Twitter – nice	0.016
client	0.02352	great – time	0.016
retweet	0.2216	good – new	0.015
way	0.02214	good – blog	0.015
session	0.02165	good – thanks	0.015
social	0.01863	good – today	0.015
big	0.01841	new – thanks	0.015
week	0.01746	Twitter – thing	0.014
SNCR	0.01735	Twitter – people	0.013
bad	0.0158	Twitter – today	0.012
SEO	0.1526	good – PR	0.012
same	0.0151	good – social media	0.012
media	0.0147	blog – post	0.012
guy	0.01424	good – great	0.010
cool	0.01407	great – blog	0.010
interesting	0.01375	new – social media	0.010
tool	0.01343	Twitter – social media	0.010

Several surface trends are evident from these data. The most immediately evident is that Twitter and other digital media tools and concepts constituted a primary topic of discussion within the group. "Twitter" itself is the most influential single word in the aggregate text, with "social media" (treated as a single term) also ranked highly. "SEO" (the common abbreviation for "search engine optimization," or the design of online content to permit effective indexing by search engine crawlers and, therefore, visibility to users seeking information about a given topic) appears relatively low but still influential. This ranking suggests that practitioners active in online environments such as Twitter are attentive to the role of SEO in the dissemination of messages and reach measurement, and is another indicator of conscious attention to reputation.

Second, Twitter was often used to express positive opinions, particularly about these tools, or to recommend and discuss specific instances of good practice by others ("Twitter great" and "Twitter good" were the two most influential word pairs; other examples include "great post," "great blog," "good social media," and "good PR"). "Good," "great," "nice," "cool," and "interesting" all appeared among the most influential words, with a single negative term "bad" appearing toward the bottom of the influence rankings. Since the centering resonance analysis technique used to examine the tweets only identifies noun phrases, it does not perfectly capture aspects such as tone and valence: for instance, the term "good" may appear as a question ("Is this an example of good practice?") or even in the negative ("This is not a good tool to use with clients"). Neither instance would be reflected in the analysis, and requires qualitative study. That said, the high prevalence of terms such as "good" and "great" indicate a generally positive tone of most discussions in the data set—praising colleagues, social media tools, articles, and blog posts about professional topics, and so on. This pattern makes sense if Twitter is seen as, at least in part, an instrument for disseminating links, information, or reflections one believes will be useful to fellow professionals.

Finally, the profession itself was also a common topic of discussion among those studied: "PR" was in the top one-third of individual terms, and appeared in conjunction with both "Twitter" and "good" in the list of influential word pairs. "Media" and "tool" suggest further discussion of public relations practice. Although the content of links shared is not accessible through the semantic analysis of the tweets, the numerous references to blog posts in this context implies pointers to more in-depth discussion of professional topics outside the restrictive Twitter milieu. Word pairs such as "Twitter–new" and "new–social media" also indicate discussions about the expanding boundaries of public relations practice as the media environment evolves to include new communication channels.

Discussion

Although the analyses provide some interesting findings when viewed separately, combining semantic and social network data depicts patterns of interaction more comprehensively. The aggregate analysis conducted here does not allow for fine-grained review of individual identity construction strategies, but the wide lens does allow a useful perspective from which to contextualize future research in this area.

Colloquys: Knowledge Communities of Parallel Experience

The people with whom we associate help to shape and reinforce our identity, and network scholars have noted that people tend to aggregate based on shared characteristics (homophily), and can mutually influence one another in areas such as innovation adoption if they hold similar positions, even if they are not directly linked (structural equivalence) (see Burt, 1982; McPherson, Smith-Lovin, & Cook, 2001). Connections forged directly at offline social media events or via Twitter can therefore influence the professional choices and behaviors even of those who do not directly participate in these activities. The social groupings observed in the data are therefore worthy of careful examination.

Describing groups based on shared attributes can pose particular conceptual and methodological challenges in online media, since not all users can be identified by gender, age, professional affiliation, education, socioeconomic status, or other typical markers. If we view social networking as "the practice of expanding knowledge by making connections with individuals of similar interests" (Gunawardena et al., 2009, p. 3), then we need to examine the groupings constituted by those connections as phenomena unto themselves, quite separate from any specific attributes shared by individual members.

Numerous types of emergent professional groups are described in organizational literature. Communities of practice are social networks that may combine online or offline means of communication and collaboration (Cox, 2008; Wenger, 1998; Wenger, McDermott, & Snyder, 2002). Communities of practice typically share a common purpose and have a sense of their group as directed toward a specific work goal, to be achieved by sharing resources and deepening knowledge through ongoing interaction (Wenger et al., 2002). A dispersed group formed in an informal setting rarely has a directed focus, however. Cox (2008) described occupational communities as assemblages of individuals who share the same occupational role, hold similar values, observe common norms, and frequently overlap with personal relationships. While some or all of these features may apply to the core grouping identified in this study, there is no way to accurately verify them.

The stronger the social ties, the more likely a group is to see itself as a bounded entity, creating an in-group/out-group dynamic that may also affect the sharing of information and resources among members (McGraw & Tetlock, 2005). However, if these distinctions are too blurry to be meaningful identifiers of group membership, then individuals may be less inclined to participate in electronic word-of-mouth sharing, as they "may become relatively more sensitive to the personal gains/losses from giving information, which would make them pay more attention to the traits/value of information" (Sohn, 2009, p. 355). This tendency suggests that information shared in fluid, public, online venues such as Twitter is frequently the result of a more or less conscious decision to share only that information which brings the greatest gain, in terms of social capital or professional reputation, at the least cost to the individual.

The data used in this study were gathered in early 2008, approximately one year after the service was first launched (http://twitter.com/about). The users tracked were therefore fairly early adopters of this new technology. Cox (2008) suggested that "parallel experiences of work" (p. 329) can produce a sense of community among people with otherwise loose ties. The experience of being an active user of this new social networking site may be considered a form of parallel experience in and of itself. Combined with the parallel work experience shared by public relations professionals by virtue of their practice, the ties formed in an atmosphere of community that fostered a desire to share knowledge, information, and experiences.

The central grouping that emerged from the data may therefore be viewed as a form of *colloquy*, an ongoing discussion of interested professionals who congregate to discuss specific topics of interest and collectively negotiate definitions, applications, norms, and professional identities. The existence of tiers beyond the colloquy suggest that public relations professionals on Twitter find core homophilous groups for ongoing conversation, while taking advantage of the extended reach provided by a channel such as Twitter to seek information and a wider range of perspectives on topics of interest. The aggregate semantic network analysis indicates that professionals who closely associate with each other in this context share central concerns. These central concerns largely focus on the role of Twitter itself in professional public relations practice.

Professional Twittering: Working On Being Watched

Situating the findings in the theoretical frameworks of the new reality media, modernity, and co-creational public relations, the social and semantic network data suggest the following patterns of professional identity construction among the individuals studied.

Social Media as a Significant Professional Issue

The prevalence of discussion about Twitter—and, more generally, the broader area of social media—over the four-week period constitutes these topics as an issue according to the co-creational approach favored by recent scholarship (Botan & Taylor, 2004). The emergence of a core colloquy also constitutes participants as a key public in relation to this issue; in particular, since the focal subjects are public relations professionals, at least some of the participants represent a burgeoning cluster of opinion leaders on the subject. At the same time, one's own habits can influence perceptions: researchers have found that "more advanced users of social media ... have a greater feeling that social media has been integrated widely into the industry" (Eyrich et al., 2008, p. 414) than those who use only more common digital forms of communication such as blogs and Intranets. There is thus the risk of active online practitioners inaccurately generalizing their experience to the profession as a whole, and exaggerating the importance of social media or specific tools in public relations activities. These factors, along with social network scholarship on the effects of social equivalence (Burt, 1982), suggest that these conversations can influence the direction and identity of the public relations profession as a whole, even beyond the confines of Twitter and other social networking sites.

Professional Embeddedness

Although this study examines Twitter participation in isolation from other forms of social media such as blogging, Facebook, discussion forums, or others, the prevalence of retweeting, links, and mentions of terms such as "blog post" confirm that Twitter users typically partake of a broad menu of social media offerings. Activity on Twitter can be seen as a means of increasing one's professional visibility, as well as driving traffic to one's presence in other online venues. Public interaction with others, including posts about offline professional events and social interaction with other practitioners, contributes to building an identity as an entrenched professional.

Public Relations as Publicly Relating

In keeping with the profession's emphasis on building relationships rather than relying on media reports for publicity and image enhancement, the public relations practitioners at the core of this study publicly engaged in the practice of using social media tools to construct professional relationships. In this way, they move the profession as a whole further in the relational direction, and take the opportunity to publicly experiment with new media tools for professional purposes. These skills and connections can then be used on behalf of client organizations.

Performing the Professional Self

As noted in the analysis, there was a high prevalence of positive terms in the tweets, particularly in relation to Twitter itself and social media practices in general, as well as praising the comments and actions of other users. It seems likely that negative opinions are typically expressed elsewhere, either offline or in formats such as blog posts, which allow more nuanced exposition of opinions and may appear less confrontational. It is not surprising that communication professionals should show such awareness of the potential pit-falls inherent in various communication channels, but it does highlight the performative nature of professional conversations that take place in public channels such as Twitter. This is not to say that the opinions expressed are not sincere, only that one must be cautious in accepting social media conversations as wholly representative of a person's or group's opinions. Furthermore, these positive expressions reinforce group membership in the colloquy or may indicate a desire to enter the core group from a peripheral tier. Further research at the individual and dyadic levels can offer further insight into the role of expressive valence in professional performance via social media.

Conclusion

Social media, or interactive online media, exist as conduits for relationships and information. These are also the basis for public expressions of individual and collective professional identity. Public relations practitioners active on Twitter voluntarily enter what Andrejevic (2006) referred to as the digital enclosure, or "the process whereby activities and transactions formerly carried out beyond the monitoring capacity of the Internet are enfolded into its virtual space" (p. 35). Twitter, with its signature question, "What are you doing?," is the latest embodiment of the digital enclosure, an extension of the larger world of reality media.

It is within this world that practitioners construct their own professional identity, and influence the larger identity of the public relations profession. They do so by "publicly relating": organizing into colloquys of peers who share an interest in social media, and engaging in strategic online reputation management. These strategies have implications for the individual and collective professional futures of the participants as well as those who do not actively take part in Twitter conversations or social media events. If indications that practitioners using Twitter focus considerable attention on social media persist, and are found to apply more generally, it is possible that an increasingly sharp dichotomy will emerge between traditional and socially mediated public relations. Practitioners who construct their professional identity primarily through their "public relating" are highly visible in search engine rankings and online professional social networks, but this visibility is not necessarily a reliable indicator of overall expertise. It is possible that overemphasis on the public discussion of social media tactics, to the exclusion of other forms of relationship-building communication and traditional media relations, may exaggerate the perceived importance of these tools within the public relations profession. Taken to extremes, this could create a reputational hierarchy in which those practitioners heavily engaged in Twitter discussions of social media are viewed as having greater overall professional capabilities, at least by those who accept the constructed identity of public relations as a field largely reliant on social media skills.

These observed patterns among Twitter users are also a reflection of larger societal trends, since the fragmentation of online interactive channels as well as reality programming in mainstream media have reinforced the notion that "the applied art and science of self-presentation is something we are all increasingly expected to draw from, to various degrees" (Ouellette & Hay, 2008, p. 7). As boundaries between personal and professional identities continue to blur and erode, questions of self-presentation become increasingly complex. The manner in which groups of individuals negotiate these questions, and voluntarily engage in public practices aimed at "personal branding"—establishing a constructed identity for themselves and for the groups or categories to which they belong—is emerging as an important form of social interaction facilitated by digital media. Thus the patterns of interaction within the professional Twittersphere of public relations practitioners are of significance beyond the confines of the field, and are worthy of further inquiry to understand new directions in professional communication across fields.

References

Andrejevic, M. (2004). *Reality TV: The work of being watched.* Lanham, MA: Rowman & Littlefield.

Andrejevic, M. (2006). The discipline of watching: Detection, risk, and lateral surveillance. *Critical Studies in Media Communication, 23*(5), 391–407.

Bennett, T. (1995). *The birth of the museum: History, theory, politics.* New York, NY: Routledge.

Borgatti, S. P., & Foster, P. C. (2003). The network paradigm in organizational research: A review and typology. *Journal of Management, 29*(6), 991–1013.

Botan, C. H., & Taylor, M. (2004). Public relations: State of the field. *Journal of Communication, 54*(4), 645–661.

boyd, d., & Heer, J. (2006). *Profiles as conversation: Networked identity performance on Friendster.* Paper presented at the Hawai'i International Conference on System Sciences (HICSS-39), Kaui, HI.

Bridges, J. A., & Nelson, R. A. (2000). Issues management: A relational approach. In J. A. Ledingham & S. D. Bruning (Eds.), *Public relations as relationship management* (pp. 95–115). Mahwah, NJ: Lawrence Erlbaum Associates.

Burt, R. S. (1982). *Toward a structural theory of action.* New York, NY: Academic.

Carley, K. M., & Kaufer, D. S. (1993). Semantic connectivity: An approach for analyzing symbols in semantic networks. *Communication Theory, 3*(3), 183–213.

Carroll, C. E., & McCombs, M. (2003). Agenda-setting effects of business news on the public's images and opinions about major corporations. *Corporate Reputation Review, 6*(1), 36–46.

Corman, S. R., & Dooley, K. J. (2006). *Crawdad Text Analysis System 2.0.* Chandler, AZ: Crawdad Technologies, LLC.

Corman, S. R., Kuhn, T., McPhee, R. D., & Dooley, K. J. (2002). Studying complex discursive systems: Centering resonance analysis of communication. *Human Communication Research, 28*(2), 157–206.

Cox, A. M. (2008). An exploration of concepts of community through a case study of UK university Web production. *Journal of Information Science, 34*(3), 327–345.

Curtin, P. A., & Gaither, T. K. (2006). Contested notions of issue identity in international public relations: A case study. *Journal of Public Relations Research, 18*(1), 67–89.

de Nooy, W., Mrvar, A., & Batagelj, V. (2005). *Exploratory social network analysis with Pajek* (27). New York, NY: Cambridge University Press.

Eyrich, N., Padman, M. L., & Sweetser, K. D. (2008). PR practitioners' use of social media tools and communication technology. *Public Relations Review, 34*(4), 412–414.

Fisher, W. R. (1987). *Human communication as narration: Toward a philosophy of reason, value, and action.* Columbia, SC: University of South Carolina Press.

Giddens, A. (1991). *Modernity and self-identity: Self and society in the late modern age.* Stanford, CA: Stanford University Press.

Gioia, D. A., Schultz, M., & Corley, K. G. (2000). Organizational identity, image, and adaptive instability. *Academy of Management Review, 25*(1), 63–81.

Gotsi, M., & Wilson, A. M. (2001). Corporate reputation: Seeking a definition. *Corporate Communications: An International Journal, 6*(1), 24–30.

Grossman, L. (2009). The moment. *Time*, June 29.

Grunig, J. E. (1989). Symmetrical presuppositions as a framework for public relations theory. In C. H. Botan & V. Hazleton (Eds.), *Public relations theory* (pp. 17–44). Hillsdale, NJ: Lawrence Erlbaum Associates.

Gunawardena, C. N., Hermans, M. B., Sanchez, D., Richmond, C., Bohley, M., & Tuttle, R. (2009). A theoretical framework for building online communities of practice with social networking tools. *Educational Media International, 46*(1), 3–16.

Heath, R. L. (1997). *Strategic issues management: Organizations and public policy challenges.* Thousand Oaks, CA: Sage Publications.

Holtz, S., & Havens, J. C. (2008). *Tactical transparency: How leaders can leverage social media to maximize and build their brand.* San Francisco, CA: Jossey-Bass.

Kadushin, C. (2004). Some basic network concepts and propositions. *Introduction to social network theory* (pp. 1–60). Online, available at: http://stat.gamma.rug.nl/snijders/Kadushin_Concepts.pdf.

Kilduff, M., & Tsai, W. (2003). *Social networks and organizations.* Thousand Oaks, CA: Sage.

Ledingham, J. A., & Bruning, S. D. (Eds.). (2000). *Public relations as relationship management.* Mahwah, NJ: Lawrence Erlbaum Associates.

Lüders, M. (2008). Conceptualizing personal media. *New Media & Society, 10*(5), 683–702.

McGraw, A. P., & Tetlock, P. E. (2005). Taboo trade-offs, relational framing, and the acceptability of exchanges. *Journal of Consumer Psychology, 15*(1), 2–15.

McPherson, M., Smith-Lovin, L., & Cook, J. M. (2001). Birds of a feather: Homophily in social networks. *Annual Review of Sociology, 27*, 415–444.

Maddock, G. M., & Vitn, R. L. (2008). Social media exposes the corporate psychopath. *Business Week Online*, August 26, p. 12.

Monge, P. R., & Contractor, N. S. (2003). *Theories of communication networks.* New York, NY: Oxford.

Ouellette, L., & Hay, J. (2008). *Better living through reality TV.* Malden, MA: Blackwell.

Palser, B. (2009). Hitting the tweet spot. *American Journalism Review, 31*(2), 54.

Papacharissi, Z. (2009). The virtual geographies of social networks: A comparative analysis of Facebook, LinkedIn and ASmallWorld. *New Media & Society, 11*(1/2), 199–220.

Polillo, S. (2004). *The network structure of the self: The effects of rituals on identity.* Paper presented at the annual meeting of the American Sociological Association. Online, available at: www.allacademic.com/meta/p108922_index.html (accessed May 26, 2009).

Ricoeur, P. (1985). *Time and narrative* (vol. 3). Chicago, IL: University of Chicago Press.

Rolling Stone. (2009). Follow the leader: The new gurus. *Rolling Stone*, June 11, p. 71.

Sohn, D. (2009). Disentangling the effects of social network density on electronic word-of-mouth (eWOM) intention. *Journal of Computer-Mediated Communication, 14*(2), 352–367.

Somers, M. R. (1994). The narrative constitution of identity: A relational and network approach. *Theory and Society, 23*(5), 605–649.

Tsetsura, K. (2007). *Discipline and control in negotiating female and professional identities in public relations.* Paper presented at the International Communication Association (ICA), San Francisco, CA.

Wenger, E. (1998). *Communities of practice: Learning, meaning, and identity.* Cambridge: Cambridge University Press.

Wenger, E., McDermott, R., & Snyder, W. M. (2002). *Cultivating communities of practice: A guide to managing knowledge.* Cambridge, MA: Harvard Business School Press.

Wiley, N. (1994). *The semiotic self.* Chicago, IL: University of Chicago Press.

Williams, S. L., & Moffitt, M. A. (1997). Corporate image as an impression formation process: Prioritizing personal, organizational, and environmental audience factors. *Journal of Public Relations Research, 9*(4), 237–258.

Chapter 12

Look At Us

Collective Narcissism in College Student Facebook Photo Galleries

Andrew L. Mendelson and Zizi Papacharissi

In recent years the popularity of social network sites (SNSs), such as Friendster, MySpace, and Facebook, has expanded, enabling a culture of remote connectivity for young adults maintaining a variety of social ties to primary and secondary groups of contact. This is especially true for college-age adults who use SNSs to stay connected with friends and family dispersed across remote or nearby locations. These networked platforms of socially oriented activity permit an introduction of the self via public displays of connection (boyd & Ellison, 2007; Donath & boyd, 2004; Papacharissi, 2002a, 2002b, 2009). A subsequent networked presentation of the self involves performative elements, using a variety of tools and strategies to present tastes, likes, dislikes, affiliations, and in general, personality. Such a performative palette on sites like Facebook might include listings of interests and favorite music, films, and books, linking to groups sharing points of view or interests, posting of comments and responses, and, relevant to this chapter, posting and labeling of photographs of one's self and one's friends. The purpose of this chapter is to examine the use of photo galleries as an instrument of self presentation and a means of visual autobiography online.

Photographs have long served a significant function of preserving biographical memories. Albums of photographs—from tintype and cabinet card albums in the mid- and late 1800s to digital galleries in the twenty-first century—are used to tell and retell experiences shared by members of one's family and by one's wider social circle. These photographs serve as mnemonic devices for the moments that bond us together, sparking larger conversations within families (Chalfen, 1987). Further, they allows us, as Barthes (1981) suggests, to search through the past and rediscover the truth of our loved ones. Similarly, the manner in which college students portray themselves and tag others through photographs on Facebook is a contemporary means of introducing the self and performing one's identity. How do the photos selected, presented, and tagged help reify this mediated performance? If photos are taken for the purpose of being displayed and tagged, does this render the experiences and the social relationships presented more real? College students consciously upload and tag displayed photographs, thus selecting certain subjects and events to emphasize. Inspired by Chalfen's (1987) examination of "how we construct, manipulate, interpret, live with, participate in, and generally use visual symbolic forms" (p. 5), we examine how visual imagery is employed to present the self and everyday college life via Facebook photo galleries. In this study, we interrogate the photographs college students present of themselves as important forms of symbolic creation of their worlds.

Self-Presentation and Social Network Sites (SNSs)

In everyday life, people consciously and unconsciously work to define the way they are perceived, hoping to engender positive impressions of themselves. This effort entails emphasizing certain characteristics, through dress, hairstyle, behavior, and/or speech, while hiding or diminishing other characteristics perceived as flawed, depending on context. Goffman (1959) uses the term "performance" to refer to "all the activity of a given participant on a given occasion which serves to influence in any way any of the other participants" (p. 15). Contemporary scholars from a variety of disciplines argue that identity is performed, in its many iterations, in contexts that are both virtual and real, mediated or not, offline or online (Buckingham, 2008; Butler, 1990; Turkle, 1996).

Research on self-presentation has moved from examining interpersonal interactions to displays through mass media (Mendelson, 2007; Meyrowitz, 1985) to more recent forms of new media in which elements of interpersonal and mass communications are merged, like personal homepages and blogs (Dominick, 1999; Papacharissi, 2002a, 2002b; Walker, 2000). New media, such as the World Wide Web, allow people the opportunity to present various forms of themselves to others at a distance. People are able to post only that information which presents a desired image. While people are purportedly presenting themselves, they are presenting a highly selective version of themselves. Social network sites (SNSs) present the latest networked platform enabling self-presentation to a variety of interconnected audiences.

boyd and Ellison argue (2007), "SNSs constitute an important research context for scholars investigating processes of impression management, self-presentation, and friendship performance" (p. 10). Indeed, SNSs afford a variety of tools that potentially extend and compromise impression management. In some cases, people create multiple versions of Facebook or MySpace pages for different audiences (not unlike how we present different versions of ourselves in face-to-face contexts); one for peers and one for parents.

Social network sites connect networks of individuals that may or may not share a place-based connection. SNSs support varying types of interaction on diverse and differing platforms. Some of the popular SNSs include MySpace, Facebook, Cyworld, LinkedIn, and Bebo, among others, in terms of millions of users attracted, but also in terms of public attention and scholarship focus. Even though most SNSs are structured around a profile and a display of connections or friends, they may vary to the extent that they support additional services, such as blogging (e.g., LiveJournal), audio/visual content sharing (Flickr, Last.FM, YouTube), professional orientation (LinkedIn), focus on status updates online and mobile connectivity (Twitter, Dodgeball), exclusive membership (ASmallWorld), or specific ethnic, religious, sexual orientation, and/or particular content genres (Orkut, CyWorld). Donath & boyd (2004) define SNSs as:

> on-line environments in which people create a self-descriptive profile and then make links to other people they know on the site, creating a network of personal connections. Participants in social network sites are usually identified by their real names and often include photographs; their network of connections is displayed as an integral piece of their self-presentation.
>
> (p. 72)

People use SNSs to present aspects of themselves to their network. These expressions can simultaneously express uniqueness and connection to others. These sites are about establishing, presenting, and negotiating identity, through the tastes and interests expressed (Liu, 2007), those who we friend and highlight (Donath and boyd, 2004), through the applications we add to our SNS pages, and through the pictures of us and our friends (boyd, 2004; Donath, 2007). In addition, these identity presentations are supported by comments from other users.

SNSs are most often used to connect with individuals people know from offline environments, rather than for meeting new people online, differentiating SNSs from online dating sites (Lampe, Ellison, & Steinfield, 2007; Lenhart & Madden, 2007). The number of people linked to SNSs is generally larger than those one would communicate with on a regular basis, and certainly beyond those who would see one's personal photo albums (boyd & Ellison, 2007; Donath, 2007). Little of the research into SNSs has examined the posted photographs beyond acknowledging them as elements of self-presentation. Still, photos play a large role in how identity is presented (Dominick, 1999). According to one study of teen use of SNSs, including Facebook, most users do post photos of themselves and their friends (Lenhart & Madden, 2007), with this activity being more popular with girls than boys. Facebook's published statistics, at present, report over 250 million active users and more than one billion photos uploaded every month (Facebook Press Room, Statistics, 2009). The photographs on Facebook pages present a series of performances strategically chosen by an individual.

The photographic life of young adults, including college students, is not much understood, and relevant research is presented in the following section. Thus, Facebook presents a useful case study into how college students construct their lives through photographs.

Personal Photography

Personal photographs are photographs made by ourselves, members of our family, or peer group for our own use, not by professional photographers and not for mass audiences (Chalfen, 1981; Slater, 1995). These images are part of a larger social practice which Chalfen (1987) refers to as the "Kodak culture," "whatever it is that one has to learn, know, or do in order to participate appropriately in what has been outlined as the home mode of pictorial communication" (p. 10).

While we think of personal photographs as rather haphazard, Chalfen (1987) and Musello (1980) argue that they are highly ritualized and conventionalized, with a rather limited range of subjects and events being recorded. While there is theoretically an unlimited range of subjects to document, cultural practice dictates a rather more limited set of subjects and moments. Personal photographs present ideals, emphasizing how we wish our lives to be remembered (Holland, 1997). The positive is always recorded over the negative, with moments of celebration emphasized (King, 1986; Slater, 1995), especially those associated with lifetime milestones: birthdays, holidays, weddings. As Holland (1991) argues, these private pictures are entangled within and influenced by larger cultural stories about community, family, and gender. Personal photographs reaffirm "culturally structured values" (Chalfen, 1987, p. 98) through what is shown (Orhn, 1975).

Relationships are also key aspects of personal photography, demonstrating important bonds between family and friends. There is an evidentiary purpose to personal photographs, providing proof of experiences and relationships for ourselves and for others (Barthes, 1981; Jacobs, 1981). These moments and the relationships become sanctified through their documentation. They are deemed worthy of recording and preserving. Digital photography has expanded the range of subjects deemed photoworthy, with more emphasis on the everyday and banal (Murray, 2008; Okabe & Ito, 2003). Holland (1997) suggests that "Pictures of leisure activities increasingly include the carnivalesque—cross-dressing for the last-night party, sidling up to the Greek waiter, the club outing when everyone was impossibly drunk, the risqué nude image" (p. 137).

There is normally a strong interaction between subject and photographer in personal photographs. The photographer is most often known intimately by the subject, and both share an interest in making photographs that emphasize how people would like to be seen. Further, personal photography is a social activity, where people actively pose for each other. Holland (1991) argues that: "Recording an event has become part of that event—and perhaps the most important part" (p. 2; see also Boerdam & Martinius, 1980). Most subjects pose directly before the lens, looking straight ahead, highly aware of being photographed. The photographer holds the camera at eye level, emphasizing the normalness of the viewpoint (Jacobs, 1981). While the technology of personal photography allows pictures to be made with the subject unaware, this seldom occurs (Holland, 1991).

We therefore consciously and unconsciously transform ourselves before the camera, portraying a version of ourselves we hope to be (Barthes, 1981; Jacobs, 1981; Slater, 1995). Boerdam & Martinius (1980) also draw on Goffman: "People give a 'performance' when they allow themselves to be photographed, in the sense that they make allowance for a public that will ultimately see the photograph" (p. 109).

The presentation of personal photos is also highly ritualized. The social process dictates not only how these photos are made, but also to whom they are shown. These are not meant for mass audiences. They are meant for people who were known "personally" to the subjects in the images (Chalfen, 1987; King, 1986). The photos are produced for and consumed by those subjects and photographers and slightly larger circle of friends and relatives. Chalfen states that: "Ordered collections of home mode imagery are repeatedly telling the same 'stories' according to some master scenario-stories based on the pictorial rendering and unfolding of an interpretation of experienced daily life and the 'punctuation' of special experiences" (p. 142). These collections "deliver culturally significant tales and myths about ourselves to ourselves" (p. 142).

Most people's photographs are edited depending on the viewing audience. Some images are displayed at work, some in frames in the home, some in albums, and still others are kept for personal viewing only or destroyed. Personal photo albums are generally organized chronologically from oldest to newest, as well as around specific events (Miller & Edwards, 2007). Albums are not structured around a narrative. As Chalfen (1987) suggests: "The narrative remains in the heads of the picturemakers and on-camera participants for verbal telling and re-telling during exhibition events" (p. 70; see also Holland, 1991).

The production and presentation of personal photographs connects with Carey's (1975) notion of the ritual view of communication: "In a ritual definition, communication is linked to terms such as sharing, participation, association, fellowship, and the possession of a common faith" (p. 6). These types of photos help build and sustain social groups by communicating shared values and stories. These images play an important role in perpetuating memories for a group, calling up moments for reflection and reminiscence. They are the visual myths, capturing the best moments to be told and retold, or as Sturken (1999) says, photos are "an artifact used to conjure memory, nostalgia, and contemplation" (p. 178; see also Hirsch, 1999).

Little research has examined the photographic worlds from the early adulthood time of life after high school graduation. This is certainly because the albums Chalfen examined were controlled by parents and not the young adults themselves. Tinkler's (2008) overview of research on young people's photographic practices echoes this. She suggests "Until recently, however, most children had little say over how they were represented in amateur, commercial or institutional photographs" (p. 258). She goes on to argue: "Today, young people from across the social-class spectrum have a wider range of opportunities for photographic self representation due to the availability of cheap . . . cameras" (p. 258). Digital technology has placed cameras and photographs in the hands of almost all. And Facebook, Flickr, Snapfish, and other sites allow for sharing of photographs easily with others.

In networked environments that blend private and public boundaries, like SNSs, personal photographs can traverse a multiplicity of audiences, to which these photographic narratives are of variable coherence and relevance. Yet, since they all emanate from the ego-centered basis of SNSs like Facebook, they inadvertently communicate content of a performative nature to a variety of audiences. In order to better understand the worlds and accompanying narratives college students visually construct for themselves, our analysis is guided by the following general thematic questions: What kinds of visual narratives do college students construct through the display of photo galleries on Facebook? What are the defining elements of the visual rhetoric presented by Facebook photo galleries? Finally, what sense of self is presented via the visual storytelling media of Facebook? By examining visual depictions of behaviors broadcast to a simultaneity of public and private audiences, we hope to better understand the nature of identities that are performed on online spaces on the basis of experiences lived offline.

Method

We chose to analyze college students' photos qualitatively using methods based in visual anthropology and semiotics in order to capture the richness of the images, in addition to the more subtle aspects of the presentations. This qualitative analysis was guided primarily by Chalfen's (1987) "event-component framework" for analyzing home mode forms of communication. This framework contains two axes—events and components—each made up of five elements. The events Chalfen details are: *Planning*—"any action(s) in which there is a formal or informal decision regarding the production of a photographic image(s)" (p. 20); *Shooting: on-camera*—"any action(s) that in some way structures the person(s) or thing(s) that 'happens' in front of the operating camera" (pp. 21–22); *Shooting: behind camera*—"any action(s) not in front of the camera but which in some way still structures the use and operation of it" (p. 22); *Editing*—"any action(s) which transforms, accumulates, eliminates, arranges or rearranges images" (p. 23); and *Exhibition*—"any action(s) which occurs after shooting, in which photographic . . . imagery is shown and viewed in a public context" (p. 25). We adopted Chalfen's accompanying definition of public as "any audience that consists of more than the picture-taker or editor" (p. 25). We focused on the last event, the exhibition, in our analysis of photo albums as presented through Facebook. We also employed his five components of home mode imagery, as a guide for our analysis: *Participants*—this concerns "identifying people who take pictures, appear in pictures, and look at pictures" (p. 27); *Topic* "describes image content in terms of the subject matter, activities, events, and themes that are presented in pictures" (p. 29); *Setting* "refers to when and where a particular communication event takes place" (p. 30); *Message form*—"the physical form, 'shape' or kind of picture" (p. 31); and *Code* "includes the characteristics that define a particular message form or 'style' of image construction and composition," focusing on the conventions that define the nature of the photographic images (p. 32). In addition, Chalfen suggests that the visual alone is not enough to understand how these forms of communication are used. Scholars must also examine verbal information included with the images, such as captions or titles. To this end, we examined visual identifications of photographed subjects or "tags," and commentary accompanying all photographs.

In addition to Chalfen's framework, this analysis was informed by semiotic analysis, which attempted to qualitatively place content in a larger cultural context of meaning, looking for recurring patterns of presences and absences (Hall, 1975; Rose, 2001). The choice of one subject over another frames our understanding of an event. Thus, it is also necessary to consider what was not chosen for inclusion in the photographs (Fiske, 1990; Szarkowski, 1966; Trachtenberg, 1989; van Leeuwen, 2001). Choices of what to include are only one aspect; we must also examine how the different choices are combined. Meaning is created by the relationships among the present signs (Fiske, 1990). The entire body of work must be examined to ascertain these patterns of representation. While people are theoretically free to record and post pictures of anything, there are limitations based on these norms or conventions of what is acceptable or reasonable. Based on Chalfen, we examined the Participants, Topics, Setting, Form, Code (aesthetics), as revealed through the photos exhibited when clicking on the profile link, "See Photos of."

Participants in an online survey on Facebook uses (Papacharissi & Mendelson, 2008) were contacted by a graduate assistant for the purpose of accessing their photos. The participants were informed that their photos would be kept confidential. All photos of those agreeing to participate in this portion of the study were collected by producing portable document files of their photo pages. For this study, we examined the "photos of" each person to get a sense of how college students are portrayed by themselves and their friends through the processes of posting and tagging photographs. This examination did not focus specifically on the albums each person posted, but on the overall collection of photos featuring the person whose pages we were examining. Currently, the architecture of Facebook groups all tagged photos of a person together, regardless of whether they are posted by the subject or by others. When a subject's Facebook page opens, there is a link under their profile photo which reads, "View Photos of me," containing all the images we analyzed. Based on the above method, the lead author examined every photograph found when clicking on the "Photos of" from the student's Facebook homepage and every comment posted about the photos, producing a total $n = 20{,}962$ photos examined, and $n = 13{,}543$ comments analyzed.

Analysis

Before going further into the qualitative analysis, we begin with some descriptive results from the close-ended survey of college students ($N = 333$) from which this sample was drawn in order to provide a descriptive sense of the popularity of photo posting and tagging. Women reported having more photos on their pages (4.36 vs. 3.48, on a 1–5 scale; $F(1) = 38.18$, $p = 0.000$), being more likely to post photos (3.22 vs. 2.51; $F(1) = 47.26$, $p = 0.000$), and more likely to tag photos than men (3.02 vs. 2.5; $F(1) = 20.6$, $p = 0.000$). Further, the size of one's social group, as defined by the number of friends participants reported having, was positively correlated with the number of photos a person reported having ($r = 0.39$, $p = 0.000$). Finally, the number of photos correlated most strongly with maintained ($r = 0.23$, $p = 0.000$) and bonding social capital ($r = 0.20$, $p = 0.000$) measures, reflecting the extent of past ties sustained and close ties strengthened respectively on Facebook. As we will see, the college students' photographs are focused most strongly on social relationships.

Qualitative Analysis

A total of 89 students who participated in the survey were willing to have their photos more closely examined. This sample comprised 37 males and 52 females. For this group, the number of photos ranged from 1 to 1,523 (mean $= 236$; $sd = 3.11$; median $= 124$), while the number of comments ranged from zero to 1,348 (mean $= 152$; $sd = 2.11$; median $= 83$). Not surprisingly, women had more photos of themselves (whether posted by themselves or others), averaging 337 to men's average number of photos of 93 ($t(58) = 4.6$; $p = 0.000$). Likewise women (mean $= 213$) had more comments about their photos than men (mean $= 66$; $t(69) = 3.9$; $p = 0.000$). The number of photos was highly correlated with the number of comments ($r = 0.716$; $p = 0.000$). Because these students were enrolled in an introductory mass communication class, most were freshmen or sophomores.

The results of this chapter are organized around Chalfen's categories of analysis: the subject matter present in the photographs (participants, topics, and settings) as well as what subject matter doesn't show up or shows up very little; the behavior of subjects; the photographic aesthetics of the images; the organization of the photographs; and, finally, an analysis of the comments.

Participants, Topics, Settings

Relationships are the dominant subject matter in all the photographs. The vast majority of the photos are of pairings or groups of friends, mostly of the same gender, posing for the camera at formal or planned events, such as parties or sporting events. This includes photos taken by a separate photographer and those shot by one of the subjects holding a camera out to photograph him or herself with a friend or friends, and was the norm for both men and women. Men were most often photographed with male friends, and women with women.

The dominance of the same-sex subjects in photos can most strongly be seen in high school prom photos encountered in the analysis. While there were photos of a person posing with his or her date, pinning on a boutonniere or corsage, or group shots of a series of couples posing in front of a house, the vast majority of photos presented either groups of female friends posing in their dresses together, or groups of male friends posing together in their tuxedos. The bonding of same-sex friends even at a couples' event was of the most importance. Similarly, high school graduation occasions often featured images of the subject posing with same-sex friends in their caps and gowns.

The prevalence of same-sex group photos does not imply the absence of photos of people of the opposite sex together. At party settings, both male and female participants were photographed with members of the opposite sex, posing in a platonic manner, or together, in large group photos featuring everyone present at the party. But overall, photographs revealed the importance of one's peer group, most often for these first- and second-year students, members of the same gender. Pictures with members of the opposite sex were posed in much of the same way as those with same-sex friends. They revealed mostly friendships rather than romantic connections or even significant flirtation.

Once a person has a significant other of the opposite sex, the content of the posted photographs do change. In those cases, the relationship became the main focus of the photographic narrative, through the frequent posting of pictures of the couple alone (taken by a third party or by themselves holding a camera out), or posing with a group of one of the partner's same-sex friends. The romantic relationships were also demonstrated and confirmed visually through the amount of physical contact, usually reflected through sitting on the other's lap, hugging each other, and heads together.

Certain events were repeated within and across most of the college student photo collections. These mostly included typical planned high school and college activities or rituals: parties, road trips with friends (to the beach, to New York City), dances and proms, school-year holidays (such as Halloween and St. Patrick's Day), college sporting events, and, to a lesser extent, professional sporting events, and high school graduation. The recording and posting of a subject's participation in the social rituals of college is central. For example, a series of a group of male friends painting their chest in team colors, each with a letter of the school on his chest, was photographed, both during the painting process and at the actual sporting event. Still, almost any moment shared by friends is worthy to be recorded. Several other photos depicted driving in a car, riding on the subway, walking someplace, or eating at a fast-food restaurant. Friendships were confirmed through the inclusion of road trip photos, showing friends posing on the beach in swimming suits, at sites in the location being visited, such as Times Square in New York City, or in restaurants around a table.

Parties presented by far the most common setting for photos. These were most often posed photographs of groups of friends, often with bottles of beer or plastic cups in hand. Occasionally there were bottles of hard liquor shown. Few photos showed cigarette smoking. Drug usage or paraphernalia were also not present. Because of the age group under study, bars were less often the setting for drinking. Still, there was little or no effort to hide or avoid photographing underage drinking. In fact, it was most often blatantly included in the frame, by holding the bottle or glass up high or out toward the camera.

The importance of parties is reflected in the prevalence of certain holidays, such as Halloween and St. Patrick's Day, both holidays associated with parties and drinking. The vast majority of students had photos of Halloween, most often posing before a party in one's apartment or residence hall in costume with one's same-sex friends. Outfits were important for St. Patrick's Day as well, as photos reveal the typical bright green shirt and green party hats. Apparel becomes important to the various rituals of college life. Costumes were naturally prominent in Halloween party photos, green outfits for St. Patrick's Day, while sporting events photos featured subjects donning team wear, displaying team or college affiliation. Photos would typically be taken in said outfits beforehand at one's apartment or dorm, on the subway, or in a car going to the event, tailgating beforehand in the parking lot, and sitting in the stands.

These rituals of college life seemed largely gender neutral, being equally common for male and female photographed subjects. In contrast, a visible gender divide became apparent in "hanging out" photos; that is, photos of relaxation or "down time" in one's apartment or dorm, in casual clothing, such as sweats and t-shirts (i.e., not dressed to go out), most often again with members of one's gender. Women were much more likely to have photos of these moments, and these included laughing together, eating pizza, dyeing someone's hair, and just talking. Another common photo for women was the reflection shot with another friend in a bathroom mirror. This could be in an apartment bathroom, but this was also seen in bar bathrooms. Most often these presented a series of at least three or four photos with the subjects playing with poses. Some women produced these mirror photographs of just themselves. Men were likely only to have pictures of actual formal events.

Portraits of the subjects alone were present, though they did not outnumber photos with friends. Portraits were taken by the subject holding out a camera, using a mirror, or by using a computer camera. Some men and women would play with poses of themselves, posting a series of photos made at the same time with different body positions or facial expressions.

Certain types of settings were not encountered often, although it bears repeating that the photos of each subject are not necessarily all the photos taken of this subject, but only the selection of photos that have been posted and tagged. With this in mind, most of the students displayed no images of themselves with family members, specifically with family members of older generations, including parents or grandparents. Similarly, few people had photographs with very young children. The few cases where parents appeared were at family functions such as holiday parties or weddings, or of parents socializing with the subject and his/her peer group. In one case, a mother and father were playing beer pong with their college-aged daughter and her friends at their house. Family members, when they did appear, were more often to show up in photos before college started, up through the summer before freshman year. A few (though very few) new baby pictures were present, in the form of children of siblings. Older people appeared in the form of a celebrity, an athlete, or service personnel at a resort or restaurant with whom the friends are posing.

Negative events, such as illnesses or serious accidents, were absent from these galleries. However, other, less somber yet embarrassing or "bad" photos remained, even when someone commented that this was awful or that they could not believe a photo was posted. The fact that the images and the comments were seen suggest that the commenter was not concerned enough to remove the image. One example is of a series of a girl dancing crazily with a drink in her hand, licking a girl's face, and licking the top of a girl friend's chest. The fact that the image remains posted suggests she did not feel this was embarrassing enough to take down, possibly containing some type of meaning for her and her peer group. To another embarrassing photo, the subject commented: "Bad hair!!!! DESTROY! DESTROY!" Similarly, another person commented on a different photo: "LMAO hey hey. i thought we had an understanding that this night never happened. shush, [name removed] babe. trying to find our buried secrets." Despite the private nature of the event described and the information revealed, these pictures remain on public display, suggesting that their publicity surpasses the stated discontent or embarrassment brought on by the displayed image.

Landscapes and cityscapes without people in them were seldom posted. Landscapes were seen in photos of the subject or the subject and friends posing in the foreground of a wider image while on a trip, thus documenting the shared experience of being someplace together. Most of the travel images were likewise images of the subject with his or her friends—for example, posing with characters at Disney World along with friends. Most of the subjects never appeared with animals, whether pets from their parents' house or pets they own in school. This latter example is not surprising since most of the subjects were still living in a dorm where pets are not allowed. Finally, images of students in classes or other academic campus buildings, or studying anywhere, were absent, thus visually removing the academic side of the college experience from the college-based presentation of the self.

Behaviors

Beyond subject matter, we looked at the types of activities and behaviors subjects were pursuing in the photos. What became immediately apparent was that subjects were almost always aware of and interacting with the camera/

photographer. There were few candid photos taken or photos where the subjects were caught completely unaware. Most of the behavior was intentionally photographic in what would be considered a formal pose, standing and smiling, facing the camera. Subjects were most often physically close to each other, with parts of their bodies touching and their heads leaning into each other. Whereas women were more likely to be hugging someone in the photo with them, men would merely stand physically close to each other or have their arms around each other. But even this difference diminished at parties (presumably through the presence of alcohol), as men can often be seen hugging as well.

Furthermore, there was much exaggerated behavior directed to the camera, reflecting a variety of poses and a playful attitude. This was apparent through broad gestures (e.g., arms up above the head), exaggerated poses and facial expressions, such as large grins or laughing, sticking out one's tongue at the camera. Other behavior directed at the camera was overt drinking, which included being photographed drinking with a friend, playing drinking games such as beer pong, or drinking from a liquor bottle. Most of these students are underage, and did not appear overly concerned with the illegality of underage drinking. The few candid photos were typically of play at a party, including drinking and drinking games, dancing and playing, often in a series with at least one image showing an awareness of the camera. People were also photographed outside of party situations, just goofing around with friends, playing outside, jumping on a friend's back, or laughing with friends.

Women were more likely to strike poses that were flirtatious or sexy. Women often posed in exaggerated sexy poses with each other, showing leg or exaggerating their cleavage. They also were more likely to cant their heads together for a pose. Their sexy poses were often recognized and complimented through comments from both male and female friends.

Many students generally have developed clear ways of posing for photographs by the end of their high school years. This is especially true for women. There are often series of images of women alone or with friends in a non-event setting, practicing posing. Mirror shots allow immediate feedback on how one is posing before the camera. In one example, a young women practices posing, a slight arch to her back, hand on hip, head slightly canted, even in self shots. This becomes her consistent poses throughout college images. Another guy is referred to in comments as always being in "picture mode," having a specific look for the camera even in casual situations.

There was seldom overt sexual behavior, including few photos of people kissing on the lips. Lip-to-lip kissing was an indicator of a more serious relationship, and limited to those with significant others. On the other hand, the kissing of another person's cheek was very common, both across and within the same gender. Kissing on the cheek was almost always highly exaggerated and comical, with laughter on the faces of both people. While this was very common for women, men could also be seen kissing the cheeks of women and, to a lesser extent, men (the latter was usually at a party and thus following the consumption of a certain amount of alcohol). The cheek kiss seemed to indicate a sign of close friendship.

Sexual behavior of any sort between non-serious couples was not photographed. There was only one photograph that showed a male subject at a distance kissing a girl. Comments revealed this was a one-time occurrence, with no other such "hook ups" documented and posted.

Aesthetics

The majority of the photos were centered and taken straight on with the subjects posed, looking at the camera/photographer. This is not surprising given that most of the photographers were not professionals and they were using point-and-shoot cameras. What would be considered more sophisticated composition (e.g., rule of thirds, selective use of focus, foreground framing, etc.) was seldom seen. Most were taken at a medium to close distance, thus limiting the amount of background in the photos. The context of the photos materialized largely in the minds of the participants and viewers. One party tends to look much like another to outsiders. Captions can reveal contextual information identifying a specific party, but, like family photo collections, captions weren't always included, beyond the tagged names of the subjects in the photos. The distance between the subjects and the photographer mainly depended upon the number of people to be included in the photographs. The majority of group shots were a single horizontal line facing the camera: the more subjects, the further back the photographer had to stand. Wider shots were used when proof of a shared experience was needed, such as a wider shot with a football stadium in the background or a wider shot of friends posing in Times Square.

Another common aesthetic format was the "self shot," holding the camera out to capture one's self and, at times, friends. The photographer/subject's arm was thus seen extending to the corner of the frame and this often led to a slightly tilted horizon line. The act of including others in a self-shot photo demonstrates both a certain spontaneity ("we must capture this moment now") and confirms the closeness of the friends ("I want to take a photo with you"). Whereas a photo taken by someone else could be set up, self-shot photos revealed a greater agency in determining the subject matter.

Webcam shots were often manipulated using the distortion controls of the image capture software. These allow for identity play by stretching or compressing one's image. Often, webcam photos appear in a series, revealing different facial expressions in each shot. Finally, photos that were badly composed, such as those where people were cut off or tilted, and those which were under- or over-lit, were still posted, assuming the content was of interest. People would still be tagged in a photo, even if only part of them could be seen.

Analysis—Organization

Similar to weblogs, the photographs of each subject were in a reverse chronological order, with the most recent images first. Further, like most family photo albums, there was no clear structured narrative, but pictures were just organized around time. Unlike most family albums, which are based around a single photographer, the "photos of" each person are collective, based on all the images posted by the subject and his or her friends through tags. The current architecture of Facebook collects all pictures tagged with a person's name under profile pictures, although individuals do have the option of "untagging," and thus removing their name, but not their image, from the photograph. In most family albums, the photographer is not often in the album or collection as often. With Facebook, the subject is often in most of the photos in a collection.

The collective nature of this photo collection can create a deviation from chronological orders, depending on when different people post pictures from the same event. Further, people often post intentionally "nostalgic" photos from childhood or even earlier in high school, before Facebook. As we will see in the next section examining comments, friends react to these images in a nostalgic way, remembering good times together in the past.

Finally, in all photos, the camera becomes part of the event. A number of people have and use cameras, as evidenced by the number of people posting images from the same event. Thus, there is a certain triangulation of the friendship circle, since the same groupings appear through the lens of multiple cameras. This is true for all events, even the most formal, such as proms. Moreover, the photographer is clearly known by and a member of the social cohort depicted. Poses that would be unlikely to an unknown photographer are quite common; including "hamminess" and "flipping off" the photographer in jest.

Comments

The comments posted by friends reinforce group cohesiveness and closeness. Comments are tied to the pictures, not to the individual, meaning that everyone tagged in the photos will have the same set of shared comments. The group nature of comments can be seen through the consistent use of nicknames, references to inside jokes or past events, statements of affection and compliments, and gentle ribbing of each other. All these examples are understood by those in the know. The context of friendship allows for statements that those outside the group cannot make or would possibly find offensive. Comments allow friends to relive the pictured events, emphasizing the shared good times. Examples of this include statements such as, "OMG THIS IS SO SWEET! i remember this! We were interviewedddddd!" (*sic*). There are also references to longing or missing members of one's friendship circle away at other schools, such as, "aww I miss this" or "I miss you guys." Comments reinforce the group's participation in college rituals, for example this series of comments about posing with alcohol:

PERSON A: water???
PERSON B: if that's what you like to call it . . .
PERSON C: and mommy and daddy think your sooo innocent. not fair
PERSON B: that's why i'm the favorite:) (*sic*)

People also relive embarrassing moments through comments, especially related to behavior while drunk, such as craziness and passing out. For example, " left that shirt at my crib when u passed out in a bush . . ." (*sic*). Or "Whats that mark on my sweatshirt?" in reference to a stain from vomiting.

Many statements reflect a desire to be included in the group, whether to be included in the event pictured or to be tagged if one is pictured: "can someone please explain why no one tagged me in this!!!!" or "it still means ur ass needs to get the hellzz down there woman." This last quote supports the group of friends through their absence, by expressing the desire for the left out individual to come visit.

Typically, the same recurring group of people will tend to comment on the photos, again demonstrating the tightness of the social group. Comments are not always about the content of the photos. The photos often bring up the opportunity for an extended conversation about individuals in the social group. The conversations sparked by a photo can encompass many posts extending over a period of time (even more than a year between the first and last comment on a photo). Comments continue a dialogue for those at a specific event and those who were not there but are part of the extended social network. Thus, these photo collections, like Facebook in general, allow vicarious participation in friends' lives even at a distance. People use comments and the photos to keep updated on their friends, such as "wtf bro when was this?" (*sic*). Photos can be used to link up with more distant friends: "adorable! how ya been chica?"

Discussion

Carey (1975) emphasized a ritual view of communication, which helps foster community integration through the sharing of common experiences and values. This is clearly central to what is revealed in the collections of Facebook photos of college students. The commonality of the images within each student's collection, and between all the students, demonstrates that, while the outfits and locations change, the types of events documented and the nature of the poses do not. The same stories are told and retold in these photographs. These images are highly conventional, both in terms of their subject matter and their aesthetics. These images record social rituals of college life, with little of the academic side.

These Facebook photos do not necessarily represent all photos taken by or of a person. These merely represent those images that a student or a friend has chosen to post and tag for others. Thus, these photos represent a strategic representation of a social group and social life in college. More than anything, these photos allow college students to speak to each other visually, playing out their college lives for each other. These photos establish proof of an authentic college experience, one filled with friends and the rituals of college life, drinking, sports, and the closeness of a peer group. They do more than merely document the rituals. This is readily apparent by noticing what is lacking, images of parents and images without friends. These photos help confirm one's independence from family and childhood.

These images demonstrate the primacy of relationships. The photos are all about the connection among college students; and, for these primarily first- and second-year students, among those of the same gender. This echoes other authors who have argued that friends are especially important for members of Generation Y (Huntley, 2006), especially same-sex friends. It is interesting to see the change in focus of the photos as a serious relationship with a member of the opposite sex occurs. Images of the couple begin to dominate. Chalfen (1987) had pointed out that college life was absent in the albums he examined. This study allows a glimpse at the transition from being part of a family to an independent photographic entity in one's own right. Further, the transition to a couple reflected the possible beginnings of a family collection of photos, focused around a dyad and not a larger peer group. For the larger peer group, images of embarrassment as well as joy draw friends together, helping support the authentic college experience and bond one's friends. Close friends are expected to share both positive and negative moments, and only close friends would appreciate and decode embarrassing images in the correct spirit of group-bonding. These images are the equivalent of the gentle ribbing seen in the comments. Further, opening up oneself to potential ridicule demonstrates the trust extended to one's peer group.

Proof of the closeness of one's peer group is confirmed by both the quantity and nature of pictures displayed. The closer the relationships shared among friends, the more frequently they appear in photos with a student. Likewise, the more they appear, the more their friendship is confirmed. The poses and moments also reveal the closeness of friends. For women, this included moments of informal hanging out in one's residence. For both genders, this included physical closeness (including hugging and cheek kissing) and exaggerated poses. Physical closeness was most strongly seen when a student entered a serious relationship. Physical closeness indexes emotional closeness.

As stated earlier and consistent with previous work on personal photographs, the meaning of these images is constructed largely in the minds of the viewers and is intended for members of one's social group. Contextual information about location and time was largely absent. These photos facilitate the recall of already existing memories, as evidenced by the posting of older photographs from childhood, which required no caption. Members of the peer group recognized and responded to these nostalgic photos. By understanding the meaning in the photos, the cohesiveness of the social group was enhanced. Contextual elements, through backgrounds, are de-emphasized, suggesting the primacy of the human relationships and the existing knowledge in the minds of viewers required for decoding the images. Facebook images were clearly appropriated by a closed group, used to reinforce membership and cohesiveness. Group membership affords a full understanding of the overt and latent meanings of photos and, subsequently, identifying these overt and latent meanings potentially enhanced one's sense of belonging.

The photos portray college students suspended in sociality, perpetually bonding with friends and toasting the best of times. Events are opportunities to connect with friends, and by representing those moments in posted Facebook photos reinforces the bonds of the relationships. While one game blurs into another and one party into another, the photographs of them tell a larger story of the importance of shared experiences of college life with one's closest friends. Once posted, these photographs create instant "good old days" upon which friends can reminisce and feel nostalgic, even if the event occurred just last night. For men, the sociality ends at formal events, emphasizing the importance of "drinking buddies," for women, sociality exists in both formal and informal moments. Women's friendships are built as much at parties as they are lounging in dorm rooms, reinforcing previous work on the importance of girls' bedroom culture in establishing identity and friendships (Nayak & Kehily, 2008).

Because pictures are posted by multiple people, the photo galleries are dynamic. These collections of photos are potentially always changing, thus presenting a confluent plane of activity upon which performances of the self are enacted, and "tagged." Just as people remove individuals from their home photo albums when divorce happens, Facebook collections can also change as individuals remove photos. This action removes the photos from the collections of all who are tagged on the photos, as well as the comments attached. Thus, the convergent nature of the platform allows these performances to constantly evolve and forever elude permanence, as they are subject to the multiple redactions of numerous audiences. This convergent context simultaneously references spaces and evolves beyond space, presenting what de Certeau (1984) has termed "a moving map," upon which visual depictions of memories are pieced into narratives through the practice of "tagging." The fluid context upon which performances of the self are enacted affords reflexively shaped personal narratives of the self, which are indicative of what sociologists have described as a constant state of flux or liquid modernity (Bauman, 2005; Giddens, 1990).

Interestingly enough, the aesthetics and the form of the displayed photos place the self or multiple subjects at the center, frequently through camera placement that may appear awkward or unprofessional. The emphasis on the self is highlighted by the absence of contextual information, medium to close distance, limited background, awareness of the camera, and behaviors produced specifically for the camera by a single or several subjects. The totality of these behaviors reflect a collectively performed narcissism, through which a single or multiple subjects exhibit self-referential behavior, that is then exponentially tagged, re-tagged, commented, and referenced in further introspective moments that culminate to group cohesion. These traces of narcissism are present in photographs that contain a single, two, or multiple subjects; the theme in common, reflective of narcissism, is the connoted enamorment with the subject, dyad, or group photographed.

. Given the general content of these visual galleries, which are structured around articulating individual autonomy and signaling independence from family and affiliation with peer groups, it would be more meaningful and accurate to interpret these narcissistic lapses as a step toward self-reflection and self-actualization, rather than instances of uncontrollable self-absorption. Lasch (1979) connected narcissistic behaviors to hedonistic tendencies reflective of a materialistic culture, but also clarified that, while narcissistic behavior may be structured around the self, it is not motivated by selfish desire, but by a desire to better connect the self to society. Alternatively, in Sennet's (1974) terms, narcissism "takes the idea of the involuntary disclosure of character to its logical extreme," thus affording identity play and the performative extremes that we identified in this study. Moreover, the aesthetics of these photographs reflect what Mitchell (1995) calls "meta-photography," that is, photographs that reveal the process of picture-making. These meta-photographs demonstrate the manner in which the camera becomes an extension of the body for these young people, most explicitly demonstrated in the self-shot photographs. In addition to the narcissistic overtones, the form of these pictures is aimed at further blurring the line between producer and subject, through group photos in which picture-takers and picture-posers dynamically rotate, and audiences viewing the photos participate in photographic meta-constructions through commenting and tagging.

This study suggests some interesting directions for future research. First, it builds on the literature of personal photography by examining the more public use of personal photographs on SNSs. Most of the literature on personal photography has focused on how and what people present in the more private settings of the home. The Internet, as other media have before, blurs the distinction between private and public, thus upsetting conventions of storytelling and mnemonic recollection via photography. Second, this piece expands on Internet studies of self-presentation by focusing more closely on the photographic representation people offer of themselves. Finally, this chapter attempts to place the photographic presentation college students offer in the context of a larger visual youth culture.

Of course, the sample studied is limited to Facebook photos and is not meant to be representative of all college students. Still, the consistency of the photo types allows us to draw conclusions about how college students use photos to speak to each other visually. Future research could attempt to track the changing nature and uses of these photographic repositories, following a smaller sample of college students as they photographically move through college years and beyond. In-depth interviews would help gain understanding of the roles that photographs play in these students' lives. These interviews also could help differentiate people who post many photos from those who do not.

Facebook tagged photographs present more than random moments in a person's life. They present a suspended take on college life sociality, through a collage of scenes celebrating the self, group culture, and membership that are played out over and over again. The same scenes are repeated in a variety of photographed occasions as we find them comforting and reassuring. They provide visual evidence of social networks. Pictures reveal the transition from high school to college, but they do more than document; they allow photographed subjects to prove or confirm these milestones for each other; they validate the sense of a *real* college experience. Facebook pictures are where college students visually play out their lives for each other, demonstrating their identity as college student. These practices serve as performative exercises of identity and belonging, simultaneously declaring and corroborating shared experiences.

References

Barthes, R. (1981). *Camera lucida: Reflections on photography*. New York, NY: Hill and Wang.

Bauman, Z. (2005). *Liquid life*. Cambridge: Polity.

Boerdam, J., & Martinius, W. O. (1980). Family photographs—A sociological approach. *The Netherlands Journal of Sociology, 16*, 95–119.

boyd, d. m. (2004). Friendster and publicly articulated social networking. *CHI 2004 Proceedings*, 1279–1282.

boyd, d. m., & Ellison, N. B. (2007). Social network sites: Definition, history, and scholarship. *Journal of Computer-Mediated Communication, 13*(1), 11. Online, available at: http://jcmc.indiana.edu/vol.13/issue1/boyd.ellison.html.

Buckingham, D. (2008). Introducing identity. In D. Buckingham (Ed.), *Youth, identity, and digital media* (pp. 1–24). Cambridge: MIT Press.

Butler, J. (1990). *Gender trouble: Feminism and the subversion of identity*. New York, NY: Routledge.

Carey, J. W. (1975). A cultural approach to communication. *Communication, 2*, 1–22.

Chalfen, R. (1981). Redundant imagery: Some observations on the use of snapshots in American culture. *Journal of American Culture, 4*(1), 106–113.

Chalfen, R. (1987). *Snapshot versions of life*. Bowling Green, OH: Bowling Green State University Popular Press.

de Certeau, M. (1984). *The practice of everyday life*. Berkeley, CA: University of California Press.

Dominick, J. R. (1999). Who do you think you are? Personal home pages and self-presentation on the World Wide Web. *Journalism and Mass Communication Quarterly, 76*(4), 646–658.

Donath, J. (2007). Signals in social supernets. *Journal of Computer-Mediated Communication, 13*(1), 12. Online, available at: http://jcmc.indiana.edu/vol.13/issue1/donath.html.

Donath, J., & boyd, d. m. (2004). Public displays of connection. *BT Technology Journal, 22*(4), 71–82.

Facebook Press Room. (2009). Statistics. Online, available at: www.facebook.com/press/info.php?statistics.

Fiske, J. (1990). *Introduction to communication studies*. London: Routledge.

Giddens, A. (1990). *The consequences of modernity*. Cambridge: Polity.

Goffman, E. (1959). *The presentation of self in everyday life*. New York, NY: Anchor Books.

Hall, S. (1975). Introduction. In A. C. H. Smith (Ed.), *Paper voices: The popular press and social change, 1935–1965* (pp. 11–24). Totowa, NJ: Rowan and Littlefield.

Hirsch, M. (1999). Introduction: Familial looking. In M. Hirsch (Ed.), *The familial gaze* (pp. xi–xxv). Hanover, NH: University Press of New England.

Holland, P. (1991). Introduction: History, memory and the family album. In J. Spence & P. Holland (Eds.), *Family snaps: The meanings of domestic photography* (pp. 1–14). London: Virago.

Holland, P. (1997). "Sweet it is to scan . . .": Personal photographs and popular photo-graphy. In L. Wells (Ed.), *Photography: A critical introduction* (pp. 103–150). London: Routledge.

Huntley, R. (2006). *The world according to Y: Inside the new adult generation*. Crows Nest, NSW: Allen & Unwin.

Jacobs, D. L. (1981). Domestic snapshots: Toward a grammar of motives. *Journal of American Culture, 7*(1), 93–105.

King, G. (1986). *Say "cheese!" The snapshot as art and social history*. London: William Collins Sons and Co.

Lampe, C., Ellison, N., & Steinfield, C. (2006). A familiar Face(book): Profile ele-ments as signals in an online social network. *CHI 2007 Proceedings*, 435–444.

Lasch, C. (1979). *The culture of narcissism*. New York, NY: Norton & Co.

Lenhart, A., & Madden, M. (2007). Teens, privacy & online social networks: How teens manage their online identities and personal information in the age of MySpace. *Pew Internet & American Life Project*. Online, available at: www.pewinternet.org/ PPF/r/211/report_display.asp.

Liu, H. (2007). Social network profiles as taste performances. *Journal of Computer-Mediated Communication, 13*(1), 13. Online, available at: http://jcmc.indiana.edu/ vol.13/issue1/liu.html.

Mendelson, A. L. (2007). On the function of the United States paparazzi: mosquito swarm or watchdogs of celebrity image control and power? *Visual Studies, 22*(2), 169–173.

Meyrowitz, J. (1985). *No sense of place: The impact of electronic media on social behavior*. New York, NY: Oxford University Press.

Miller, A. D., & Edwards, W. K. (2007). Give and take: A study of consumer photo-sharing culture and practice. *CHI 2007 Proceedings*, 347–356.

Mitchell, W. J. T. (1995). *Picture theory: Essays on verbal and visual representation*. Chicago, IL: University of Chicago Press.

Murray, S. (2008). Digital images, photo-sharing, and our shifting notions of everyday aesthetics. *Journal of Visual Culture, 7*(2), 147–163.

Musello, C. (1980). Studying the home mode: An exploration of family photographs & visual communication. *Studies in Visual Communication, 6*(1), 23–42.

Nayak, A., & Kehily, M. J. (2008). *Gender, youth and culture: Young masculinities and femininities*. New York, NY: Palgrave Macmillan.

Okabe, D., & Ito, M. (2003). Camera phones changing the definition of picture-worthy. *Japan Media Review*, August 29. Online, available at: www.japanmediare-view.com/japan/wireless/1062208524.php.

Orhn, K. B. (1975). The photo flow of family life: A family photograph collection. *Folklore Forum, 13*, 27–36.

Papacharissi, Z. (2002a). The self online: The utility of personal home pages. *Journal of Broadcasting & Electronic Media, 46*(3), 346–368.

Papacharissi, Z. (2002b). The presentation of self in virtual life: Characteristics of personal home pages. *Journalism and Mass Communication Quarterly, 79*(3), 643–660.

Papacharissi, Z. (2009). The virtual geographies of social networks: A comparative analysis of Facebook, LinkedIn and A Small World. *New Media & Society, 11*(1/2), 199–220.

Papacharissi, Z., & Mendelson, A. L. (2008). *Friends, networks and zombies: The social utility of Facebook.* Paper presented to the Association of Internet Researchers 9.0, Copenhagen, Denmark.

Rose, G. (1991). *Visual methodologies.* London: Sage Publications.

Sennett, R. (1974). *The fall of public man.* New York, NY: Random House.

Slater, D. (1995). Domestic photography and digital culture. In M. Lister (ed.), *The photographic image in digital culture* (pp. 129–146). London: Routledge.

Sturken, M. (1999). The image as memorial: Personal photographs in cultural memory. In M. Hirsch (ed.), *The familial gaze* (pp. 178–195). Hanover, NH: University Press of New England.

Szarkowski, J. (1966). *The photographer's eye.* New York, NY: The Museum of Modern Art.

Tinkler, P. (2008). A fragmented picture: Reflections on the photographic practices of young people. *Visual Studies, 23*(3), 255–266.

Trachtenberg, A. (1989). *Reading American photographs: Images as history: Mathew Brady to Walker Evans.* New York, NY: Hill and Wang.

Turkle, S. (1996). Parallel lives: Working on identity in virtual space. In D. Grodin & T. R. Lindlof (Eds.), *Constructing the self in a mediated world: Inquiries in social construction* (pp. 156–175). Thousand Oaks, CA: Sage.

van Leeuwen, T. (2001). Semiotics and iconography. In T. van Leeuwen & C. Jewitt (Eds.), *Handbook of visual analysis* (pp. 92–118). Thousand Oaks, CA: Sage Publications.

Walker, K. (2000). "It's difficult to hide it": The presentation of self on Internet home pages. *Qualitative Sociology, 23*(1), 99–120.

Chapter 13

Copyright, Fair Use, and Social Networks

Patricia Aufderheide

Online social networks have made visible what was always true: the self is endlessly constructed with a constant stream of bits of culture that people use both to shape experience and relationships. People communicate with each other traveling along lines of taste and affection for shared and shareable culture. Online social networks facilitate and reinforce the building of one's personal social networks, which locate you in the world and to yourself.

Take Kira's twenty-sixth birthday party. Kira and her twenty-something friends met at a bar in downtown Washington, D.C., to get a list of absurd tasks (jump in a fountain; hug 10 strangers; do a group dance to Michael Jackson's "Thriller;" take a picture of the number 26 somewhere). They then headed off in teams to accomplish those tasks, recorded them faithfully on their cameras and cell phones, and came back to the bar to recount their achievements and peer onto each other's screens. Then they went home to post their recordings on Facebook, where their friends are now commenting and forwarding to others. Their online selves were completely integrated with their face-to-face selves.

Meanwhile, Kira's friend Alison (who won Kira's scavenger hunt, as you can find out on her Facebook page) found out about Keyboard Cat—an online video meme—from friends on Facebook. Or maybe it was some IM chat, or an email—she doesn't remember, really. Alison was puzzled at first, but quickly got the idea. Video of a real cat playing (thanks to an unseen master) the piano gets inserted into some piece of bad or over-the-top television. For instance, in "Play Haley Off, Keyboard Cat," in a segment from the TV show, *Walker, Texas Ranger*, a young boy tells Walker's friends that he knows he has AIDS. Suddenly, the keyboarding cat video is interpolated. Similarly, a pretty announcer for some international TV program suddenly vomits on screen—and there's the keyboarding cat. So every time Alison sees a particularly good keyboard cat, she posts it on her Facebook page. Now that her friends know the keyboard cat is on her radar, they're scouting for her too. Keyboard cat is currency in her social network.

Lauren, a co-worker of Alison's, has created a kind of contest on her Facebook page, to see who can track down and post particularly silly examples of 1980s culture. It started as part of an 1980s-theme day that swept her social network. The contest makes Lauren's Facebook page a destination, and creates incentives for her friends to scour YouTube for the odd, weird, and out-of-fashion. One of their favorite finds—and sometimes their own creation—is the "literal video version." Finding an egregious music video, people then rewrite the lyrics, creating new subtitles that literally spell out what is going on in the video (which is usually narrative nonsense) to the tune of the original song. (See, for example, "Total Eclipse of the Heart: Literal Video Version.") When one of her friends finds a delicious example, Lauren will repost that discovery on her Facebook page by Hat Tipping, or HTing. The online nature of this scavenger hunt doesn't make it any less real than Kira's scavenger hunt was. Lauren's online exchanges reinforce and facilitate her face-to-face social life.

The friends share not only their own work but professional work that also comments on and reshapes popular culture. For instance, the Media Matters for America site depends on Facebook flow to carry its critique of conservative media forward. Its "Fox News is a 24/7 Political Operation: the Untouchables Edition" uses clips from Fox News showing grossly biased announcers attempting to besmirch the Obama Administration, with interpolated intertitle commentary. The segment is posted on the Media Matters Facebook page, which Lauren then reposts on her page. Her association of the Media Matters page with her own network is a way of expressing her own political opinion, and an invitation to others to repost as well.

It has never been clearer that people, in this way, make new culture with existing culture, creating new meanings for it that are appropriate to—indeed, contribute to defining—their own networks. In a study of online video work incorporating copyrighted material, we identified a wide range of ways that people are making new culture with existing culture (Aufderheide & Jaszi, 2008). Social networking makes it breathtakingly easy to share entire swaths of popular culture in that process. The 1980s videos, the Fox news excerpts, the "Thriller" music—it's all copyrighted work. That fact poses some new challenges both to existing copyright holders and to makers of new culture in a digital era. When is it legally permissible to quote from your culture, which social network participants do every day?

Such uses are not going unchallenged; indeed, sometimes they are punished, and punished unjustly. Copyright holders have been ferocious in their pursuit of people who reuse their copyrighted work digitally. Online video sites such as YouTube—the mother lode of the copyrighted material circulating madly on social networking sites—are patrolled by content holders' automated identification system (often known simply as "robots" or "bots") for what some content companies call "piracy." The copyright holders issue take-down notices to the services, which then remove the postings within 48 hours. The target of the content companies' bots is posting of entire programs or films, but they often hit work by people who, accidentally or on purpose, are not only reusing but repurposing their work, in an entirely legal way. Remix-ers actually have the right to quote existing copyrighted work without licens-ing it, under the U.S. copyright doctrine of fair use. The posters also have the right to issue a counter-takedown notice when their work disappears, but often, intimidated or ignorant of their rights, they do not. Indeed, the new makers are often clueless about whether their actions are legal. They do not know what constitutes fair use in their own practice. They may well not only be intimidated by actions such as takedowns, but by their own fears and confu-sions. In one of our studies, we found there was a high level of anxiety among college-age makers of online video about the risks of violating copyright (Aufderheide & Jaszi, 2007).

Fair use, which is explained in detail below (p. 279f.), is context-dependent, and users need to decide in each case whether it's appropriate to their situations. They do so on the basis of some general considerations, referred to in the legisla-tion itself. Those terms, however, are so vague that they can be unhelpful. The law suggests calculating fair use on the basis of the nature of the original material, the kind of use being made, how much is taken, and the effect on the market. Each of these categories is too baggy for comfort, especially in the high-stakes world of copyright infringement. Fortunately, judges take seriously the norms of specific communities and situations, and so best practice codes have been a prac-tical, effective way to deal with interpretation of fair use (Aufderheide, 2007).

In 2008, a precipitating event in the world of online video provoked the Center for Social Media and the Washington College of Law's Program on Information Justice and Intellectual Property to team up and create the Code of Best Practices in Fair Use for Online Video. Google had purchased YouTube, the overwhelmingly major site for online video, and Viacom, a major media company, had promptly sued Google for permitting copyright infringement. Google and other companies running online video websites have claimed they were Internet Service Providers (ISP)—not curators, creators, or programmers of content—and as such were protected from secondary lia-bility for copyright infringement under the Digital Millennium Copyright Act. But in this litigation, Viacom charged that YouTube was in fact contributing to the infringement of Viacom's material, because it had given people the tools to infringe and encouraged them to do so.

These legal positions may be tested in Vicacom's lawsuit; much more likely, however, the suit will lead to a private settlement rather than a public resolution. The lawsuit is in limbo, but it is well understood in the industry that the large media companies ultimately want an environment in which they do not have to patrol the online video sites and issue takedowns, but rather can depend on the online video sites to patrol themselves and their customers. Instead of waiting for ISPs to remove offending material, as they do today, they would like YouTube to filter the content at the outset. If Google's past history in negotiating with stakeholders is any guide, at some point Google (an industry trend-setter) will accommodate content holders' demands in some way. Others in the industry are likely to follow suit.

If online video sites filter with pre-emptive, automated, or semi-automated detection systems, then fair use is at risk. And, if people cannot exercise fair use, they cannot conduct the ordinary business of communication as evidenced in social networking practices today. The actual and proposed systems filtering do not discriminate between fair use and infringement, because they are automated, as the Electronic Frontier Foundation has frequently noted. Indeed, its own proposed guidelines (still languishing without industry adoption) recommend human intervention to eliminate "dolphins" caught in copyright infringement "tuna" trawling (www.eff.org/issues/ip-and-free-speech/fair-use-principles-usergen). Industry discussions to date have uniformly been pious about developing filtering techniques that honor fair use; consult, for example, the corporate-created "Principles for User Generated Content Services" (ugcprinciples.com/). But no one, in 2008, had done more than pay lip service to the idea; no one had addressed how to define fair use within the online video and social networking environment. And without some clear understanding of how fair use applies to online video, it is difficult to think about how to preserve it.

It was thus with a sense of urgency that the legal scholar Peter Jaszi, from the Washington College of Law, and I worked with a team of experts to craft the Code of Best Practices in Fair Use for Online Video (reproduced below, pp. 279–290, and also at www.centerforsocialmedia.org/resources/publications/fair_use_in_online_video/). We focused on online video rather than any other digital expression because it was such a vivid part of all social networking, as well as being a stand-alone practice. We had created earlier codes of best practices in fair use with documentary filmmakers' organizations and with teachers' organizations. In this case, the practices were so new that there were no representative organizations for the vidders, the remix and mashup artists, the political commentators, the social networkers, and the fashion-watchers. So instead of working with established organizations, we built a blue-ribbon panel composed in part of leading lawyers with fair use expertise, and in part of scholars with a strong knowledge of—and commitment to—the emerging remix culture of do-it-yourself makers. They worked over months to craft the document, which promptly went viral—thanks to enthusiastic bloggers such as Cory Doctorow—on its release.

One of the most interesting things about the terms of the Code was what was not in it. The Code did not rely on the distinction between noncommercial and commercial work—an obviously unreliable line in a field that is developing so quickly. Rather, it emphasized the primary indicator of fair use identified by judges over the last two decades: "transformativeness." Many bloggers, online video creators, vidders, and the scholars who studied them feel strongly that they should be permitted to do what they like with copyrighted material, because they are not making money from it. This approach, however, is not a particularly sturdy argument as business models adapt to create commercial environments (such as the ad-filled YouTube) for both commercial and noncommercial work.

There were no industry criticisms of the Code, other than a non-lawyer's disparagement of it on the website of the Copyright Alliance (funded by large copyright holders and chartered to promote their interests in Washington, D.C. (blog.copyrightalliance.org/2008/07/the-remix-culture)). Patrick Ross wrote:

> This is a dangerous effort. We at the Copyright Alliance support education on fair use and have information on our site. But our information is intentionally broad; we do not want to be in the position of giving legal advice to specific end-users of copyrighted works. . . . But that is precisely what the best practices guide writers run the risk of doing. . . . What is implied suggests a significant expansion of the current established thinking of fair use, going far beyond legal precedent.

William Patry, the copyright scholar who was senior copyright counsel at Google, responded sharply on his blog (williampatry.blogspot.com/2008/07/patrick-ross-and-fair-use.html):

> Let's see what this means: a guy who isn't a lawyer, much less a copyright lawyer, thinks it is a dangerous effort for copyright lawyers, educators, and those who deal with real world fair use problems on a daily basis to address some of the common problems presented, not as legal advice, but as "best practices." The safe sex approach, according to Mr. Ross is the type of education that Mr. Patrick's group—a front for large corporate copyright owners—gives, namely always ask permission. . . . I can say, based on my over 25 years of experience with fair use, over 25 years more than Mr. Ross has, that the site doesn't "imply" "a significant expansion of the current established thinking of fair use, going far beyond legal precedent," as he states. Mr. Ross's purpose is not to engage in a constructive debate about specific examples and

whether those examples are appropriately a fair use, something reasonable minds might disagree on. Rather, his purpose is to silence those who try to provide responsible, thoughtful guidance to those on the ground, and ultimately to silence those who dare to suggest there can be fair use at all.

Patrick Ross did not respond. But Google did. Google funded the Stanford Fair Use Project and the Center for Social Media to make a short film about the Code. That video, created by Claire Darby, is called "Remix Culture: Fair Use Is Your Friend," and is available on YouTube among other sites, including the Center for Social Media.

Today, the vast majority of sound and image material on Facebook and other social networking sites is third-party, copyrighted work. Much of that copyrighted work is being reused legally, even if the users do not know that. But the creative practices that enable the construction of social networks online as well as offline are threatened by industry conflicts that have nothing to do with Kira, Alison, and Lauren, and by a deformed understanding of fair use and copyright policy generally by users themselves.

The social networking habits that incorporate copyrighted material will only grow. When YouTube and other online video services pre-emptively filter work that contains copyrighted material, nearly every MySpace and Facebook member will immediately feel the effect. Such filtering would directly change and limit the circulation of material that informs ordinary social interaction online (and, inevitably, offline) today. It is imperative for users of this emerging environment for self-expression and self-formation, as well as their teachers, mentors, and allies, to understand the potential and the limits of fair use—the major copyright exemption from copyright ownership. It is imperative that they both exercise and defend their rights to employ fair use, as they reference, access, and transform their own culture.

Fair use enables the creation of new culture; it is remix culture's friend. For that reason, employing, teaching about, and sharing the Code of Best Practices in Fair Use for Online Video are acts in favor of creative culture production.

Appendix: Code of Best Practices in Fair Use for Online Video

centerforsocialmedia.org/remix
A Future of Public Media Project, funded by the Ford Foundation
June 2008

Code of Best Practices Committee

Co-chairs

Peter Jaszi, Professor of Law, Faculty Director of the Glushko-Samuelson Intellectual Property Clinic, Washington College of Law, American University
Patricia Aufderheide, Professor, Director of the Center for Social Media, School of Communication, American University

Members

Michael C. Donaldson, Esq., Los Angeles
Anthony Falzone, Lecturer, Executive Director, Fair Use Project, Stanford Law School
Lewis Hyde, Richard L. Thomas Professor of Creative Writing, Kenyon College; Fellow, Berkman Center for Internet and Society, Harvard University
Mizuko Ito, Research Scientist, School of Cinematic Arts, University of Southern California
Henry Jenkins, Professor, Program Head, Comparative Media Studies, Massachusetts Institute of Technology
Michael Madison, Associate Dean for Research, Associate Professor of Law, University of Pittsburgh School of Law
Pamela Samuelson, Richard M. Sherman Distinguished Professor of Law and Information, University of California, Berkeley
Rebecca Tushnet, Professor, Georgetown University Law Center, Georgetown University
Jennifer Urban, Clinical Associate Professor of Law, Director of the Intellectual Property and Technology Law Clinic, University of Southern California
centerforsocialmedia.org/fairuse

Introduction

What This Is

This document is a code of best practices that helps creators, online providers, copyright holders, and others interested in the making of online video interpret the copyright doctrine of fair use. Fair use is the right to use copyrighted material without permission or payment under some circumstances.

This is a guide to current acceptable practices, drawing on the actual activities of creators, as discussed among other places in the study *Recut, Reframe,*

Recycle: Quoting Copyrighted Material in User-Generated Video (centerforsocialmedia.org/recut) and backed by the judgment of a national panel of experts. It also draws, by way of analogy, upon the professional judgment and experience of documentary filmmakers, whose own code of best practices has been recognized throughout the film and television businesses (centerforsocialmedia.org/fairuse).

What This Isn't

This code of best practices does not tell you the limits of fair use rights.

It's not a guide to using material people give permission to use, such as works using Creative Commons licenses (creativecommons.org). Anyone can use those works the way the owners say that you can.

It's not a guide to material that is already free to use without considering copyright. For instance, all federal government works are in the public domain, as are many older works. In most cases, trademarks are not an issue. For more information on "free use," consult the document "Yes, You Can!" (centerforsocialmedia.org/files/pdf/free_use.pdf and www.copyright.cornell.edu/public_domain).

It's not a guide to using material that someone wants to license but cannot trace back to an owner—the so-called "orphan works" problem. However, orphan works are also eligible for fair use consideration, according to the principles detailed below.

How This Document Was Created

A distinguished panel of experts, drawn from cultural scholarship, legal scholarship, and legal practice, developed this code of best practices, informed by research into current personal and nonprofessional video practices ("user-generated video") and on fair use. Full identification of panelists is on the back cover of this document.

Background

Video is increasingly becoming a central part of our everyday landscape of communication, and it is becoming more visible as people share it on digital platforms. People make and share videos to tell stories about their personal lives, remixing home videos with popular music and images. Video remix has become a core component of political discourse, as the video "George Bush Don't Like Black People" and the "Yes We Can" parodies demonstrated. Both amateur and professional editors are creating new forms of viral popular culture, as the "Dramatic Chipmunk" meme and the

"Brokeback to the Future" mashup illustrate. The circulation of these videos is an emerging part of the business landscape, as the sale of YouTube to Google demonstrated.

More and more, video creation and sharing depend on the ability to use and circulate existing copyrighted work. Until now, that fact has been almost irrelevant in business and law, because broad distribution of nonprofessional video was relatively rare. Often, people circulated their work within a small group of family and friends. But digital platforms make work far more public than it has ever been, and cultural habits and business models are developing. As practices spread and financial stakes are raised, the legal status of inserting copyrighted work into new work will become important for everyone.

It is important for video makers, online service providers, and content providers to understand the legal rights of makers of new culture, as policies and practices evolve. Only then will efforts to fight copyright "piracy" in the online environment be able to make necessary space for lawful, value-added uses.

Mashups, remixes, subs, and online parodies are new and refreshing online phenomena, but they partake of an ancient tradition: the recycling of old culture to make new. In spite of our romantic clichés about the anguished lone creator, the entire history of cultural production from Aeschylus through Shakespeare to *Clueless* has shown that all creators stand, as Isaac Newton (and so many others) put it, "on the shoulders of giants."

In fact, the cultural value of copying is so well established that it is written into the social bargain at the heart of copyright law. The bargain is this: we as a society give limited property rights to creators, to reward them for producing culture; at the same time, we give other creators the chance to use that same copyrighted material without permission or payment, in some circumstances. Without the second half of the bargain, we could all lose important new cultural work just because one person is arbitrary or greedy.

Copyright law has several features that permit quotations from copyrighted works without permission or payment, under certain conditions. Fair use is the most important of these features. It has been an important part of copyright law for more than 150 years. Where it applies, fair use is a right, not a mere privilege. In fact, as the Supreme Court has pointed out, fair use keeps copyright from violating the First Amendment. As copyright protects more works for longer periods than ever before, it makes new creation harder. As a result, fair use is more important today than ever before.

Copyright law does not exactly specify how to apply fair use, and that is to creators' advantage. Creative needs and practices differ with the field, with technology, and with time. Rather than following a specific formula, lawyers and judges decide whether an unlicensed use of copyrighted material is "fair" according to a "rule of reason." This means taking all the facts and circumstances into account to decide if an unlicensed use of copyright material generates social or cultural benefits that are greater than the costs it imposes on the copyright owner.

Fair use is flexible; it is not uncertain or unreliable. In fact, for any particular field of critical or creative activity, lawyers and judges consider expectations and practice in assessing what is "fair" within the field. In weighing the balance at the heart of fair use analysis, judges refer to four types of considerations mentioned in the law: the nature of the use, the nature of the work used, the extent of the use, and its economic effect. This still leaves much room for interpretation, especially since the law is clear that these are not the only necessary considerations. In reviewing the history of fair use litigation, we find that judges return again and again to two key questions:

- Did the unlicensed use "transform" the material taken from the copyrighted work by using it for a different purpose than that of the original, or did it just repeat the work for the same intent and value as the original?
- Was the material taken appropriate in kind and amount, considering the nature of the copyrighted work and of the use?

Both questions touch on, among other things, the question of whether the use will cause excessive economic harm to the copyright owner.

If the answers to these two questions are "yes," a court is likely to find a use fair. Because that is true, such a use is unlikely to be challenged in the first place.

Another consideration underlies and influences the way in which these questions are analyzed: whether the user acted reasonably and in good faith, in light of general practice in his or her particular field. Online video makers' ability to rely on fair use will be enhanced by the Code of Best Practices in Fair Use that follows. This code of best practices serves as evidence of commonly held understandings—some drawn from the experience of other creative communities (including documentary filmmakers) and supported by legal precedents, and all grounded in current practice of online video. Thus, the code helps to demonstrate the reasonableness of uses that fall within its principles.

Video makers can take heart from other creator groups' reliance on fair use. For instance, historians regularly quote both other historians' writings and textual sources; filmmakers and visual artists reinterpret and critique existing work; scholars illustrate cultural commentary with textual, visual, and musical examples. Equally important is the example of commercial news media. Fair use is healthy and vigorous in daily broadcast television news, where references to popular films, classic TV programs, archival images, and popular songs are constant and routinely unlicensed.

Unlike many traditional creator groups, nonprofessional and personal video makers often create and circulate their videos outside the marketplace. Such works, especially if they are circulated within a delimited network, do enjoy certain copyright advantages. Not only are they less likely to attract the attention of rights holders, but if noticed they are more likely to receive special consideration under the fair use doctrine. That said, our goal here is to define the widely accepted contours of fair use that apply with equal force across a range of commercial and noncommercial activities, without regard to how video maker communities' markets may evolve. Thus, the principles articulated below are rooted squarely in the concept of "transformativeness."

In fact, a transformative purpose often underlies an individual creator's investment of substantial time and creative energy in producing a mashup, a personal video, or other new work. Images and sounds can be building blocks for new meaning, just as quotations of written texts can be. Emerging cultural expression deserves recognition for transformative value as much as more established expression.

Best Practices

This code of practices is organized, for ease of understanding, around common situations that come up for online video makers. These situations do not, of course, exhaust the possible applications of fair use to tomorrow's media-making techniques.

But first, one general comment: Inevitably, considerations of good faith come into play in fair use analysis. One way to show good faith is to provide credit or attribution, where possible, to the owners of the material being used.

One: Commenting On or Critiquing of Copyrighted Material

Description: Video makers often take as their raw material an example of popular culture, which they comment on in some way. They may add unlikely subtitles. They may create a fan tribute (positive commentary) or ridicule a cultural object (negative commentary). They may comment or criticize indirectly (by way of parody, for example), as well as directly. They may solicit critique by others, who provide the commentary or add to it.

Principle: Video makers have the right to use as much of the original work as they need to in order to put it under some kind of scrutiny. Comment and critique are at the very core of the fair use doctrine as a safeguard for freedom of expression. So long as the maker analyzes, comments on, or responds to the work itself, the means may vary. Commentary may be explicit (as might be achieved, for example, by the addition of narration) or implicit (accomplished by means of recasting or recontextualizing the original). In the case of negative commentary, the fact that the critique itself may do economic damage to the market for the quoted work (as a negative review or a scathing piece of ridicule might) is irrelevant.

Limitation: The use should not be so extensive or pervasive that it ceases to function as critique and becomes, instead, a way of satisfying the audience's taste for the thing (or the kind of thing) that is being quoted. In other words, the new use should not become a market substitute for the work (or other works like it).

Two: Using Copyrighted Material for Illustration or Example

Description: Sometimes video makers quote copyrighted material (for instance, music, video, photographs, animation, text) not in order to comment upon it, but because it aptly illustrates an argument or a point. For example, clips from Hollywood films might be used to demonstrate changing American attitudes toward race; a succession of photos of the same celebrity may represent the stages in the star's career; a news clip of a politician speaking may reinforce an assertion.

Principle: This sort of quotation generally should be considered fair use and is widely recognized as such in other creative communities. For instance, writers in print media do not hesitate to use illustrative quotations of both words and images. The possibility that the quotes might entertain and engage an audience as well as illustrate a video maker's argument takes nothing away from the fair use claim. Works of popular culture typically have illustrative power precisely because they are popular. This kind of use is fair when it is important to the larger purpose of the work but also subordinate to it. It is fair when video makers are not presenting the quoted material for its original purpose but to harness it for a new one. This kind of use is, thus, creating new value.

Limitations: To the extent possible and appropriate, illustrative quotations should be drawn from a range of different sources; and each quotation (however many may be employed to create an overall pattern of illustrations) should be no longer than is necessary to achieve the intended effect. Properly attributing material, whether in the body of the text, in credits, or in associated material, will often reduce the likelihood of complaints or legal action and may bolster a maker's fair use claim.

Three: Capturing Copyrighted Material Incidentally or Accidentally

Description: Video makers often record copyrighted sounds and images when they are recording sequences in everyday settings. For instance, they may be filming a wedding dance where copyrighted music is playing, capturing the sight of a child learning to walk with a favorite tune playing in the background, or recording their own thoughts in a bedroom with copyrighted posters on the walls. Such copyrighted material is an audio-visual found object. In order to eliminate this incidentally or accidentally captured material, makers would have to avoid, alter, or falsify reality.

Principle: Fair use protects the creative choices of video makers who seek their material in real life. Where a sound or image has been captured incidentally and without pre-arrangement, as part of an unstaged scene, it is permissible to use it, to a reasonable extent, as part of the final version of the video. Otherwise, one of the fundamental purposes of copyright—to encourage new creativity—would be betrayed.

Limitation: In order to take advantage of fair use in this context, the video maker should be sure that the particular media content played or displayed was not requested or directed; that the material is integral to the scene or its action; that the use is not so extensive that it calls attention to itself as the primary focus of interest; and that where possible, the material used is properly attributed.

Four: Reproducing, Reposting, or Quoting in Order to Memorialize, Preserve, or Rescue an Experience, an Event, or a Cultural Phenomenon

Description: Repurposed copyrighted material is central to this kind of video. For instance, someone may record their favorite performance or document their own presence at a rock concert. Someone may post a controversial or notorious moment from broadcast television or a public event (a Stephen Colbert speech, a presidential address, a celebrity blooper). Someone may reproduce portions of a work that has been taken out of circulation, unjustly in their opinion. Gamers may record their performances.

Principle: Video makers are using new technology to accomplish culturally positive functions that are widely accepted—or even celebrated—in the analog information environment. In other media and platforms, creators regularly recollect, describe, catalog, and preserve cultural expression for public memory. Written memoirs for instance are valued for the specificity and accuracy of their recollections; collectors of ephemeral material are valued for creating archives for future users. Such memorializing transforms the original in various ways—perhaps by putting the original work in a different context, perhaps by putting it in juxtaposition with other such works, perhaps by preserving it. This use also does not impair the legitimate market for the original work.

Limitation: Fair use reaches its limits when the entertainment content is reproduced in amounts that are disproportionate to purposes of documentation, or in the case of archiving, when the material is readily available from authorized sources.

Five: Copying, Reposting, and Recirculating a Work or Part of a Work for Purposes of Launching a Discussion

Description: Online video contributors often copy and post a work or part of it because they love or hate it, or find it exemplary of something they love or hate, or see it as the center of an existing debate. They want to share that work or portion of a work because they have a connection to it and want to spur a discussion about it based on that connection. These works can be, among other things, cultural (Worst Music Video Ever!, a controversial comedian's performance), political (a campaign appearance or ad), social or educational (a public service announcement, a presentation on a school's drug policy).

Principle: Such uses are at the heart of freedom of expression and demonstrate the importance of fair use to maintain this freedom. When content that originally was offered to entertain or inform or instruct is offered up with the distinct purpose of launching an online conversation, its use has been transformed. When protected works are selectively repurposed in this way, a fundamental goal of the copyright system—to promote the republican ideal of robust social discourse—is served.

Limitations: The purpose of the copying and posting needs to be clear; the viewer needs to know that the intent of the poster is to spur discussion. The mere fact that a site permits comments is not enough to indicate intent. The poster might title a work appropriately so that it encourages comment, or provide context or a spur to discussion with an initial comment on a site, or seek out a site that encourages commentary.

Six: Quoting in Order to Recombine Elements to Make a New Work that Depends for its Meaning on (Often Unlikely) Relationships Between the Elements

Description: Video makers often create new works entirely out of existing ones, just as in the past artists have made collages and pastiches. Sometimes there is a critical purpose, sometimes a celebratory one, sometimes a humorous or other motive, in which new makers may easily see their uses as fair under category one. Sometimes, however, juxtaposition creates new meaning in other ways. Mashups (the combining of different materials to compose a new work), remixes (the re-editing of an existing work), and music videos all use this technique of recombining existing material. Other makers achieve similar effects by adding their own new expression (subtitles, images, dialog, sound effects or animation, for example) to existing works.

Principle: This kind of activity is covered by fair use to the extent that the reuse of copyrighted works creates new meaning by juxtaposition. Combining the speeches by two politicians and a love song, for example, as in "Bush Blair Endless Love," changes the meaning of all three pieces of copyrighted material. Combining the image of an innocent prairie dog and three ominous chords from a movie soundtrack, as in "Dramatic Chipmunk," creates an ironic third meaning out of the original materials. The recombinant new work has a cultural identity of its own and addresses an audience different from those for which its components were intended.

Limitations: If a work is merely reused without significant change of context or meaning, then its reuse goes beyond the limits of fair use. Similarly, where the juxtaposition is a pretext to exploit the popularity or appeal of the copyrighted work employed, or where the amount of material used is excessive, fair use should not apply. For example, fair use will not apply when a copyrighted song is used in its entirety as a sound track for a newly created video simply because the music evokes a desired mood rather than to change its meaning; when someone sings or dances to recorded popular music without comment, thus using it for its original purpose; or when newlyweds decorate or embellish a wedding video with favorite songs simply because they like those songs or think they express the emotion of the moment.

Conclusion

These principles don't exhaust the possibilities of fair use for online video. They merely address the most common situations today. Inevitably, online video makers will find themselves in situations that are hybrids of those described above or will develop new practices. Then, they can be guided by the same basic values of fairness, proportionality, and reasonableness that inform this code of practices. As community practices develop and become more public, the norms that emerge from these practices will themselves provide additional information on what is fair use.

Common Fair Use Myths

If I'm not making any money off it, it's fair use. Noncommercial use is indeed one of the considerations for fair use, but it is hard to define. If people want to share their work only with a defined closed-circle group, they are in a favorable legal position. But beyond that, in the digital online environment, wholesale copying can be unfair even if no money changes hands. So if work is going public, it is good to be able to rely on the rationale of transformativeness, which applies fully even in "commercial" settings.

If I'm making any money off it (or trying to), it's not fair use. Although nonprofit, personal, or academic uses often have good claims to be considered "fair," they are not the only ones. A new work can be commercial—even highly commercial—in intent and effect and still invoke fair use. Most of the cases in which courts have found unlicensed uses of copyrighted works to be fair have involved projects designed to make money, including some that actually have.

Fair use can't be entertaining. A use is no less likely to qualify as a fair one because the film in which it occurs is effective in attracting and holding an audience. If a use otherwise satisfies the principles and limitations described in this code, the fact that it is entertaining or emotionally engaging should be irrelevant.

If I try to license material, I've given up my chance to use fair use. Everyone likes to avoid conflict and reduce uncertainty, and a maker may choose to seek permissions even in situations where they may not be required. Later, a maker still may decide to employ fair use. The fact that a license was requested—or even denied—doesn't undercut an otherwise valid fair use claim. If a rights holder denies a license unreasonably, this actually may strengthen the case for fair use.

I really need a lawyer to make the call on fair use. Fair use is a part of the law that belongs to everyone. A lawyer usually works for a client by reducing risk; in copyright law, that often means counseling purchase of rights for all uses of copyrighted material. If clients tell lawyers that they want to assert their rights (something that has a very low risk, if they understand what their rights are) then lawyers can recommend appropriate policies; but lawyers need to be told what their clients want.

And, finally, a special note from the lawyers among us: Be careful not to draw too much from specific past court cases. A good example of one decision that easily can be over-interpreted is the California District Court decision in *L.A. Times* v. *Free Republic*, 56 U.S.P.Q.2D (BNA) 1862 (C.D. Cal. 2000), which ruled that a right-wing electronic bulletin board that invited reader comments on mainstream media content was not fair use. This anomalous case predates a Supreme Court decision (*Eldred* v. *Ashcroft*, 537 U.S. 186, 2003) that clearly asserted the link between fair use and free speech. Furthermore, decisions like *Bridgeport Music, Inc.* v. *Dimension Films*, 410 F.3d 792 (6th Cir. 2005), dealing with infringement standards in music sampling, are widely cited for fair use principles when in fact they do not concern fair use at all. While case law is of essential importance in establishing legal norms, it is the *trend* in case law that determines such norms. The trend in case law about fair use has strongly been in the direction of supporting transformativeness as a core measure of fair use. This puts the judgment about fair use back squarely in the hands of the new creators and platform providers, who must look carefully at how videos repurpose copyrighted works.

The Program on Information Justice and Intellectual Property, led by Professor Peter Jaszi, promotes social justice in law governing information dissemination and intellectual property through research, scholarship, public events, advocacy, and provision of legal and consulting services. The program is a project of the Washington College of Law at American University in Washington, D.C., led by Dean Claudio Grossman.

The Center for Social Media, led by Professor Patricia Aufderheide, showcases and analyzes media for social justice, civil society, and democracy, and the public environment that nurtures them. The center is a project of the School of Communication, led by Dean Larry Kirkman, at American University in Washington, D.C.

Funded by the Ford Foundation, as part of the Center for Social Media's Future of Public Media Project

Feel free to reproduce this work in its entirety. For excerpts and quotations, depend upon fair use.

centerforsocialmedia.org/fairuse

Aufderheide, Patricia, and Peter Jaszi. 2007. The Good, the Bad, and the Confusing: User-generated Video Creators on Copyright. Washington, D.C.: Center for Social Media, School of Communication, American University.

——. 2008. Recut, Reframe, Recycle: Quoting Copyrighted Material in User-Generated Video. Washington, D.C.: Center for Social Media, School of Communication, American University.

References

Aufderheide, P. (2007). How documentary filmmakers overcame their fear of quoting and learned to employ fair use: A tale of scholarship in action. *International Journal of Communication*, Winter. Online, available at: http://ijoc.org/ojs/index.php/ijoc/article/view/10/26 (accessed October 29, 2009.

Aufderheide, P. & Jaszi, P. (2007). *The good, the bad and the confusing: User-generated video creators on copyright*, April, 20 pp.

Aufderheide, P. & Jaszi, P. (2008). *Recut, reframe, recycle: Quoting copyrighted material in user-generated video*. Center for Social Media, January 2008, 17 pp.

Chapter 14

Artificial Agents Entering Social Networks

Nikolaos Mavridis

Introduction

Social network sites (SNSs), which have recently become tremendously popular,[1] have so far been exclusively populated by human actors. On the other hand, at least part of the functionality of such networks relies on software agents implementing artificial intelligence techniques—for example, in order to implement recommendation systems for friends or other entities. However, such agents were not playing actor roles within the network. Recently, the monopoly of human actors within SNSs has been broken; disembodied or even physically embodied intelligent software agents are just starting to populate SNSs. A huge range of potentialities exists regarding useful roles for such artificial agents, which might furthermore have varying degrees of autonomy. In this chapter, I will start by introducing a concrete example of such an agent: Sarah the FaceBot, a robotically embodied intelligent artificial agent, which carries out natural language interactions with people, physically present or remote, and which utilizes and publishes social information on Facebook—even having her own automatically updated page. Then, five areas of open questions that have arisen will be presented, as well as an exposition of the potentialities for other artificial agents in SNSs, either in actor or in other roles, which are promising to unleash new possibilities and beneficially transform social networks.

Sarah the FaceBot

Sarah (Mavridis et al., 2009a; Mavridis, Kazmi, & Toulis, 2009c) is a physical mobile robot with Face Recognition, natural language dialogue, as well as navigation/mapping capabilities (Figure 14.1). Furthermore, it is a robot that is also equipped with an interaction database (keeping information about previous interaction episodes) as well as a social database (keeping personal info as well as friendship relations for the people the robot knows). Most importantly, the robot also has a live connection to the Facebook social network site—and utilizes online information toward crafting dialogues with humans, as well as publishing information on its own Facebook page. Sarah has three kinds of human friends: those that she has met physically, but which are not her friends on Facebook (P), those that she has met physically, and which are also friends with her on Facebook (PF), and those that she has not (yet) met physically, but which are friends with her on Facebook (F). Interaction with human friends can happen over a number of channels: real-time natural language dialogue with physically present friends, real-time dialogue over chat for friends which are currently online on Facebook, as well as offline Facebook messaging and posting.

A transcript of a typical interaction with Sarah follows:

// Greetings/Recognition:

R: Hello! My name is Sarah. Welcome to the interactive robots and media laboratory.

R: Hi! Are you Panos Toulis? (from Face Recognition).

H: Yes (Robot changes its online status to "interacting with Panos Toulis").

Figure 14.1 Our robot, Sarah the FaceBot, while interacting with a human.

// Query of overall state:
R: Hey, Panos Toulis, are you doing well today?
H: Yes, pretty well.
// General news-based discussion:
R: Let me tell you some interesting news that I've heard.
R: The latest windows release will be available to everyone after a surge in demand crashed the Microsoft website on the 9th of January (item taken from BBC news online).
R: Have you heard about this?
HR: Yes.
R: That's great!
// Robot discusses Facebook status of human:
R: I see you are chasing robots in the desert.
// Robot gives news about a mutual friend, acquired through Facebook:
R: Did you know that our friend Shervin Emami has posted a new photo on Facebook? (information acquired from Facebook minifeed).
H: No.
// Robot sends reminder to human:
R: I am sending you a message about this to check it out.
// Robot remembers past encounter with mutual friend:
R: I saw Shervin yesterday evening and he was doing well. (information acquired from interaction database).
// Robot gives news about a mutual friend, acquired through Facebook:
R: Did you know that our friend Chandan is "waiting for Sarah to have that little sweet conversation with me"? (information acquired through Chandan's Facebook status).
H: Yes, of course.
// Robot connects an online friend with the human:
R: One of our friends, Nikolaos Mavridis, is online—would you like me to send him a message?
H: Yes ("Nikolaos, Panos says hello" is sent).
// End of interaction:
R: Hey, Panos, it was nice talking to you! I have to go now. See you later!
(Robot continues wandering).
Thus, currently Sarah is capable of producing dialogue turns for:

D1. Recognition/Greeting.
D2. Querying the *state* of the human.
D3. Relaying customized *general news*.
D4. Relaying Facebook *minifeed-based news* about human or common friends.
D5. Relaying previous *interaction-based memories* about human or common friends.

D6. Performing a *real-time connection with a third* common friend which is online.

D7. Saying goodbye.

It is worth noting that all of these turns contribute toward real-time information diffusion within the social net; and, apart from these, Sarah's updated Facebook page contents as well as messages also diffuse information, but in a non-real-time manner.[2]

Sarah was originally created in order to test an interesting hypothesis in the field of HRI (Human–Computer Interaction), which was formulated in Mavridis et al. (2009a): "Can reference to *shared memories* and *shared friends* in human–robot dialogue create more meaningful and sustainable relationships?"

Motivation for positing this question was provided by disappointing early results on long-term human–robot interaction experiments, as exemplified by Mitsunaga et al. (2006)—although robots seem to be exciting and interesting to humans at first, upon multiple encounters quite quickly humans lose interest. Thus, the following chain of argument led to the postulated hypothesis:

> Let us examine random human encounters, without explicit purpose of interaction—say, short chat with a colleague or friend. What is their content? First, there seems to be continuity in these dialogic episodes, connecting the current with the previous encounters; a common, *shared past* is being created, and reference to it is often made in the dialogue. Second, this common past is not exclusive to the two partners conversing at the moment; it actually extends to their circle of mutual acquaintances—and thus news and memories regarding *shared friends* are often being mentioned. Thus, let us try to create a conversational robot that can refer to shared memories and shared friends in its dialogues; and examine whether this will lead to better long-term human–robot relationships.

Upon closer examination, and in AI terminology, in a sense Sarah is a form of a chatterbot; and there exists a long line of such systems in the literature, starting with the classic ELIZA (Weizenbaum, 1966). But there are a number of important differences between FaceBots and classic chatterbots; not only is Sarah physically embodied, but most importantly her dialogues are driven by a rich context of previous interactions as well as social information, acquired physically or online, and which is dynamic and conversational-partner specific.

Two further comments are worth making: first, regarding "shared" entities; and second, regarding implicit teleology. The primary hypothesis that Face-Bots were created for, is concerned with two postulated "shared" entities and their effect on human–robot relationships: shared past and shared friends.

Both of these belong to a wider set of shared entities that might prove to be important: shared interests, shared goals—actually often quite correlated with shared past and shared friends, at least in certain contexts/for certain subsets. All of these shared entities can be hypothetically unified under the "intersection" $I(A(t),B(t))$ of the two actors (human and robot in our case), at a given time instant t—a time-varying concept. It might well be that the creation, maintenance, and synergistic co-evolution[3] of such an intersection turns out to be a crucial factor toward long-term human–robot relationships.

Before proceeding to five areas of open questions that have arisen from this project, a short note on teleology: the casual conversations that Sarah is attempting to replicate seem not have an explicit purpose from the conversational partner's point of view. However, their teleology is probably better localized not at the personal or the dialogic-partners level—but at the social network level. The establishment of an adequate intersection enabling understanding and co-reference, the flow of local-context relevant information, and the resulting bonding might well be three main components—ultimately tied to collective social capital.[4]

Five Areas of Open Questions

Apart from the original motivation behind the creation of Sarah the FaceBot, this line of research opened up a number of interesting avenues as well as questions related to artificial agents and social networks:

Q1. *Interaction patterns of agent*: What will be the interaction patterns of such agents with physically present or remote humans? For example, what will be the frequency, duration, and content of such interactions?

In practice, for artificial agents within social networks, this would amount to logging and analyzing the different types of interaction events that will occur—synchronous or asynchronous, mutually visible or unidirectionally visible: viewing a profile or photo, sending a message, chatting, adding a friend, etc. For agents that also have a physical embodiment, such as Sarah the FaceBot, proxemics, gaze, and other such external measurements might also be utilized.

Q2. *Friendship graph of agent*: What will be the form and temporal dynamics of the friendship graph of such agents? (a snapshot of Sarah's graph can be found in Figure 14.2). What will the connectivity patterns, tie strengths, as well as the individual social capital (Coleman, 1988) be?[5]

One might expect significant differences with human actors in this respect;[6] for example, the sustainable social circle size of technologically unassisted humans is constrained by cognitive limitations—which seem to be somewhat relaxed in the case of artificial agents. On the other hand, one should also note that there also exist important limitations of the current state of agents as

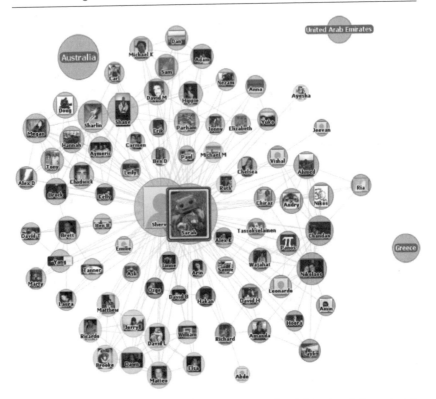

Figure 14.2 The "touchgraph" depiction of the first-level friends of the robot in March 2009, before public opening of friendships: 79 first-level friends, 13,989 second-level friends.

compared to humans (for example, in unconstrained natural language dialogic capabilities).

Q3. *Effect of introduction of agents in social network*: How will the interaction and structural patterns of the existing social network be affected by the introduction of such agents? Will connectivity patterns be disrupted? Will the evolutionary dynamics or node distributions change?[7] How will collective social capital (Putnam, 1993) be affected? How about diffusion patterns? Here, we move from the ego-centric viewpoint of the agent toward the collective viewpoint of the network, which is where human actors belong—and which is ultimately the locus of importance.

Q4. *Relation of agents with multimedia content of SNSs*: How will the image or video content of SNSs be altered through such agents? For example, what is their potential in posting photos and videos, and/or recognizing faces, objects, places, and events in posted photos and videos, on the basis of their own observations or other pre-tagged photos?

Given that human actors do not live in a symbolic/language-only world, and they populate SNSs with multimedia content, it is important for artificial agents to be able to handle and/or contribute such content. On the other hand, again given the different domains and activities on which the current state of agents is more capable as compared to humans, and vice versa, this also creates an opportunity for overall benefit.

Q5. *Social engineering potential of such agents for SNSs*: How will such agents be designed/positioned in order to affect connectivity patterns, diffusion patterns, social capital, and other such important parameters at will? How will one exploit the different capabilities of artificial agents for such a purpose?[8]

From a practical point of view, this is the most important question—and we will return to some aspects of this in the last section of this chapter.

Currently, some very early answers to aspects of Q1 and Q2 for the case of Sarah have been reported in Mavridis et al. (2009c), together with an extensive discussion of the synergies between SNSs, interactive robotics, and face recognition. Furthermore, the use of live photos in conjunction with online photos toward better face recognition, as well as algorithms utilizing social context toward better and/or faster recognition through such agents, is discussed and algorithms are given in Mavridis, Kazmi, Toulis, & Ben-AbdelKader (2009b). Also, simple algorithms for empirically estimating the social graph given only photos containing co-occurring faces are presented.

Of course, this is just a very early stage regarding the questions and avenues listed above—and much more work remains to be done in order to reach a more mature stage. Also, one can pose the above questions (Q1–Q5) not only in their predictive form ("What will be?"), but also in their potential form ("What could be?"), their normative form ("What should/would one want to be?"), and their engineering form ("How should we act in order to reach . . .?"). Thus, we can, for example, ask not only: how will social capital change with the introduction of artificial agents? But also: how could it change? As well as: how would one want it to change? And also: what action plan should be followed so that the introduction of artificial agents within social networks changes social capital toward the desired direction?

The Physical vs. Online and Symbolic vs. Sensory Realms

Expanding upon Q4, another interesting observation regarding embodied artificial agents in actor roles arises: such artificial actors, as human actors do, belong to an actual social network, a subset of which is re-represented within Facebook. Also, as mentioned before, they have three categories of friends: physical only (P), physical who are on Facebook (PF), and Facebook only (F).

Their perceived identity thus depends on different primary sources for each of the three categories of friends (physical presentation vs. online); and the effect of differences and misalignments across these can thus be studied.

Yet one more observation is concerned with the relationship of the linguistic/symbolic with the sensory realms for such agents. Both realms are accessible physically as well as online; although different projections/selections of the two realms exist in the two. For example, consider photos; these belong to the sensory realm—and the robot has access to snapshots from its own camera (physically), as well as to Facebook-posted photos (online). For example, consider the friendship relationship between two individuals; say, George and Jack. This linguistic/symbolic information might be available through the online friendship graph on Facebook, or might be acquired by direct/indirect questioning, through the robot's dialogue system. On the other hand, this linguistic/symbolic piece of information is not uncorrelated to the sensory realm; as a simple statistical analysis can show (see Mavridis et al., 2009b), we expect that "The face of X appears in photos together with the face of Y" (a sensory-realm relation) is a strong predictor for "X is a friend of Y" (a linguistic/symbolic-realm relation). In essence, this is yet one more instance of symbol grounding (Harnad, 1990)—which is normally performed by human actors, and which in this case could potentially be transferred over to the artificial actors (Mavridis, 2007). Thus, a quartet of vertices arises: sensory/physical (capturing a photo through the robot's camera), linguistic-symbolic/physical (hearing that X is a friend of Y), linguistic-symbolic/online (reading that X is a friend of Y from Facebook), sensory/online (seeing a photo on Facebook), and the bidirectional connections among these vertices are to be resolved by the actors involved.

Now, having seen a brief introduction to FaceBots as an example of a robotically embodied artificial agent in an actor role within the Facebook SNS, let us move on toward a wider perspective: a basic taxonomy and an exposition of the potentialities for other artificial agents in SNSs (either as an actor or in other roles) will be presented, followed by a discussion of their possible effects toward beneficially transforming human social networks.

The Space of Potentialities for Artificial Agents

The space of potentialities for artificial agents within social networks is quite vast, and a number of basic degrees of freedom/dimensions (D) will be introduced here.

D1. One first obvious choice is concerned with the *Appearance* of the Agent to the human actors of the network; one possibility for the agent is to have an active Actor role within the SNS, with a profile, a friendship network, and interactions—such as the case of Sarah—and either for it to be declared as an artificial entity or to posit itself as a human actor. Another is for it not to appear as a human actor, but as a distinct entity (for example, an installable Facebook application) or as part of the architecture of the SNS itself (as is the case of the friend recommendation system of Facebook). Yet another, quite interesting, possibility is for its existence to be unknown to the human actors; where the agent can be acting by effectively modulating what might appear as random events; for example, the order of presentation of items within a list, pushing forward and thus emphasizing some items in order to increase their availability in the human's mind.

D2. One other degree of freedom is concerned with the *Physicality* of the agent. One can have, for example, a physically embodied agent; a virtual character with a cartoon-like body; or a totally disembodied entity. Of course, this degree does not only cover form, but also movement and body dynamics of the agent.

D3. Yet one other interesting dimension is *Autonomy*; the artificial agent might be completely autonomous, or exhibiting adjustable autonomy through human assistance at specific times or in certain levels of abstraction. Such a configuration sometimes combines the best of both worlds (artificial and human), and enables successful application of agents to areas where their current state of the art would not allow them to be applied alone. Some recent examples of adjustable and sliding autonomy in the agents and robotics literature are Schurr, Marecki, Tambe, Lewis, and Kasinadhuni (2005) and Sellner, Heger, Hiatt, Simmons, and Singh (2006)—and analogous guiding principles can be followed in creating effective man–machine hybrid agents participating in SNSs.

D4. In the case of an agent in an actor role, another important dimension is that of the apparent perceived *Identity* of the agent; the profile information, linguistic style, dialogue system, posted pictures, friendship circles, as well as interaction behaviors of the agent, all contribute to this. As noted, the agent is performing his or her identity in two stages: the physical and the online stage. Simple software tools for crafting artificial actor identities have not yet appeared; although one would envision that with appropriate machine learning techniques, information mined from the profiles, dialogues, and the other traces of the actor's performed identity would enable the creation of congruent identities for artificial actors, parametrized by a set of simple user choices. For example, one could envision the possibility of learning simplistic mappings from regional-socio-economic background (part of profile information) to linguistic style (mined from dialogues), for a limited dialogic range, and vice versa, and thus using these mappings in order to minimize authoring time when crafting the identities of new artificial actors.

D5. Finally, and quite importantly, there is the question of the overall *Purpose* of the agent. This will be considered in more detail in the next section.

Possible Purposes for Artificial Agents

Let us start with an observation: moving on from actor-role to non-actor-role agents, one of the crucial differences is concerned with their scope of visibility; usually, an actor-role agent can only have direct access to the resources opened to him or her via the adjusted security settings of the other agents that have chosen to connect on the network. In contrast, an overt non-actor agent, for example a Facebook application, often gets wider access to all data of the actors that have installed it; and even more so, an overt- or covert-non-actor agent that is part of the SNS itself, for example the friend recommendation system of Facebook, can have omniscient access to all actors within the SNS as well as their interactions. After this comment regarding the difference in scope of visibility between actor- and non-actor-role agents, let us move back to some possible choices for the purpose of artificial agents within social networks.

The purpose of the example agent presented above, Sarah the FaceBot robot, is to create sustainable relationships with humans—which could be translated into a metric containing components related to frequency and duration of interaction over a longer period, human satisfaction, as well as number of friends, for example. Another possible purpose for actor-role agents is teaching/education, specialist assistance, as well as multiple forms of persuasion (Fogg, 2002).

Also, artificial agents in actor roles can be quite beneficial for setting up experiments in order to test scientific hypothesis related to social networks—for example, questions regarding diffusion—as they are, in a sense, limited but perfectly reliable puppets. As long as their divergence from human behavior is not detrimental for the purpose of the experiment, they can be used to create predictable responses and gather measurements within the social network: for example, when studying diffusion, agents can act as pre-programmed filters or targeted redistribution nodes; or when acquiring friendship request acceptance prediction models, agents can be set up with the desired apparent identities and initial messaging response patterns, and gather results regarding the acceptance of their requests by various actors. The interchange between human actor and artificial actor for social network research is quite parallel to human/robot interchange when bi-directionally informing Human–Robot Interaction (HRI) by Human–Human Interaction studies and vice versa, for example (Mutlu et al., 2009); and as long as the nature of the experiment can benefit from the "limited but perfectly reliable puppet" constraint.

Another possible purpose for actor-role agents is to intervene within the information flow of the network—toward a number of potential goals: re-spreading news, monitoring for possible mutations, even counter-spreading information, or creating parallel flows and adjusting existing two-step flow of communication nets and influencers (Katz & Lazarsfeld, 1955). Another possible goal is the active acquisition of information: actor-role agents could potentially activate their own connections on demand, in order to seek, ask for, and relay back missing information.

One further possible purpose is restructuring the connectivity of the network, through suitable overt or covert recommendations; this might take place towards a variety of goals, for example related to useful matchmaking of actors toward personal or professional goals, which could be beneficial to the network or a sub-network as a whole—perhaps in terms of social capital. For example, an agent might try to actively detect and manipulate structural holes. Due to the benefits of a possible wider scope of visibility and non-interactivity in this case, non-actor agents are more suitable for this purpose.

Another primary role for non-actor agents is supervising/policing the network in order to detect possible criminal or otherwise harmful/illegal activity. Currently, there exist, for example, automated- or human-assisted picture censorship services within SNSs; but there exist many more areas that could potentially benefit from the appropriate form of supervision, given of course appropriate privacy and freedom concerns.

Finally, let us close this brief exposition of some possible purposes for agents within social networks with a relevant comment: when arbitrating visibility/action scope across a number of agents, often hierarchical structures are quite beneficial, sometimes augmented with hierarchy-breaking patches. A recent example of a hierarchical multi-agent cognitive architecture is, for example, EM-1 (Singh, 2006), where the idea of higher-order agents having access to the internals of lower-order agents and acting as "mental critics" is central.[9] One could thus envision similar hierarchies of visibility and action scope within hybrid multi-human/artificial agent systems operating on SNSs.

Conclusion

In this chapter we have discussed the entry of Artificial Agents, in embodied or disembodied forms, within human social networks. We started by introducing a concrete example of such an agent: Sarah the FaceBot, a robotically embodied intelligent artificial agent, which carries out natural language interactions with people, physically present or remote, and which utilizes and publishes social information on Facebook—and which publishes on her own automatically updated page. Then, there was a brief presentation of five areas of open questions that have arisen, a short discussion on relevant aspects of the quartet created by the physical/online and symbolic/sensory realms, and an exposition of the potentialities and purposes for such agents; either in actor or in other roles. In conclusion, artificial agents, which are currently increasingly populating social networks, are promising to significantly change these networked publics in a beneficial manner, and unleash numerous new possibilities.

Notes

1. Before the introduction and wider spread of SNSs, the primary means of online self-presentation were homepages, which while changeable, were not dynamic (Papacharissi, 2002).
2. Currently, and mainly due to speech recognition constraints, Sarah is mainly diffusing information acquired through online news, Facebook minifeed and status, and interactions; but there is not much direct acquisition of information from the human, except from a basic state query and "did you know x" queries. This is an active direction for extensions.
3. This co-evolution often indirectly relies on input from personal evolution and interaction with other entities inside or outside the shared circle of friends; such interactions might lead to the growth of the personal non-shared component of each actor, which in turn leads to novel input for co-shaping the intersection.
4. For an interesting and somewhat complementary evolutionary view, including a theory postulating the transformation of primate grooming into gossip, see Dunbar (1996).
5. For a concise introduction to the basic social network analysis (SNA) terms used here, one could look at the opening chapters of Marlow (2005).
6. Ultimately, after a number of layers, reducing to some of the differences between atoms and bits, in sense of Negreponte (1995), or at least to the differences between biological atoms and the current state of agents comprised by bits.
7. For example, the well-established power law distributions arising from the model of Barabasi (2002), depend on preferential attachment processes—which, for the sake of experimentation at least, artificial agents might not chose to follow—and linear growth of the net.
8. For example, the much larger interaction memory as well as social info storage of such agents, or the possibility of having distributed embodiments spanning large geographical distances, are two basic differences.
9. Such models are arguably quite reminiscent to implementations of the structures of a platonic republic, at least in some respects.

References

Barabasi, A. L. (2002). *Linked: The new science of networks*. Cambridge, MA: Perseus Publishing.

Coleman, J. (1988). Social capital in the creation of human capital. *American Journal of Sociology, 94* (Issue supplement: Organizations and institutions: Sociological and economic approaches to the analysis of social structure), S95–S120.

Dunbar, R. I. M. (1996). *Grooming, gossip, and the evolution of language.* Cambridge, MA: Harvard University Press.

Fogg, B. J. (2002). *Persuasive technology: Using computers to change what we think and do.* San Francisco, CA: Morgan Kaufmann.

Harnad, S. (1990). The symbol grounding problem. *Physica D, 42*: 335–346.

Katz, E. & Lazarsfeld, P. F. (1955). *Personal influence: The part played by people in the flow of mass communications.* Glencoe, IL: Free Press.

Marlow, C. A. (2005). *The structural determinants of media contagion.* PhD Thesis, Media Arts and Sciences, Massachusetts Institute of Technology, Cambridge, MA.

Mavridis, N. (2007). *Grounded situation models for situated conversational assistants.* PhD Thesis, Media Arts and Sciences, Massachusetts Institute of Technology, Cambridge, MA.

Mavridis, N., Datta, C., Emami, S., Tanoto, A., Ben-AbdelKader, C. & Rabie, T. F. (2009a). Facebots: Social robots utilizing and publishing social information in Face-book. *Proceedings of the IEEE Human–Robot Interaction Conference (HRI 2009).*

Mavridis, N., Kazmi, W., Toulis, P., & Ben-AbdelKader, C. (2009b). On the synergies between online social networking, face recognition, and interactive robotics. *Proceedings of the Computational Aspects of Social Networking Conference (CaSoN 2009).*

Mavridis, N., Kazmi, W., & Toulis, P. (2009c). Friends with faces: How social networks can enhance face recognition and vice versa. In A. Abraham, A. Hassanien, & V. Snasel (Eds.), *Computational social networks analysis: Trends, tools and research advances.* Berlin: Springer Verlag.

Mitsunaga, N., Miyashita, T., Ishiguro, H., Kogure, K., & Hagita, N. (2006). Robovie-IV: A communication robot interacting with people daily in an office. *Proceedings of IEEE IROS 2006*, 5066–5072.

Mutlu, B., Yamaoka, F., Kanda, T., Ishiguro, H., & Hagita, N. (2009). Nonverbal leakage in robots: Communication of intentions through seemingly unintentional behavior. *Proceedings of the 4th ACM/IEEE Conference on Human–Robot Interaction (HRI 2009).*

Negroponte, N. (1995). *Being digital.* New York, NY: Vintage Books.

Papacharissi, Z. (2002). The self online: The utility of personal home pages. *Journal of Broadcasting & Electronic Media, 46*, 346–368.

Putnam, R. D. (1993). The prosperous community: Social capital and public life. *American Prospect, 13*, 35–42.

Schurr, N., Marecki, J., Tambe, M., Lewis, J. P., & Kasinadhuni, N. (2005). The future of disaster response: Humans working with multiagent teams using DEFACTO. *American Association Artificial Intelligence (AAAI) Spring Symposium on AI Technologies for Homeland Security 2005.*

Sellner, B., Heger, F. W., Hiatt, L. M., Simmons, R., & Singh, S. (2006). Coordinated multiagent teams and sliding autonomy for large-scale assembly. *Proceedings of the IEEE, 94*, 7, 1425–1444.

Singh, P. (2006). *EM-ONE: An architecture for reflective commonsense thinking.* PhD Thesis, Media Arts and Sciences, Massachusetts Institute of Technology, Cambridge, MA.

Weizenbaum, J. (1966). ELIZA—A computer program for the study of natural language communication between man and machine. *Communications of the ACM, 9*, 1, 36–45.

Conclusion
A Networked Self

Zizi Papacharissi

Attention shapes the self, and is in turn shaped by it.
(Csikszentmihalyi, *Flow*, p. 13)

The Self in Convergent Architectures

The self, in late modern societies, is expressed as fluid abstraction, reified through the individual's association with a reality that may be equally flexible. The process of self-presentation becomes an ever-evolving cycle through which individual identity is presented, compared, adjusted, or defended against a constellation of social, cultural, economic, or political realities. Goffman (1959) described this as an information game: "a potentially infinite cycle of concealment, discovery, false revelation, and rediscovery" (p. 13). This somewhat ego-centered approach has been related by other sociologists to contemporary historical developments, which render the self more liquid (Baumann, 2000; 2005), reflexive (Giddens, 1991), or self-identity a process (Jenkins, 2004). Self-identity in public and private life thus traverses distinct yet connected planes of interaction or networks. Technology may provide the stage for this interaction, linking the individual, separately or simultaneously, with multiple audiences. Online social networks constitute such sites of self presentation and identity negotiation. *A Networked Self* introduced an anthology of discussions on what it means to present the self in online networked environments.

Social network sites enable individuals to construct a member profile, connect to known and potential friends, and view other members' connections. Their appeal derives from providing a stage for self-presentation and social connection. SNSs provide props that facilitate self-presentation, including text, photographs, and other multimedia capabilities, but the performance is centered around public displays of social connections or *friends*, which are used to authenticate identity and introduce the self through the reflexive process of fluid association with social circles. Thus, individual and collective identities are simultaneously presented and promoted. Online social networks like MySpace, Facebook, Cyworld, Orkut, LinkedIn, and Bebo reinforce the social affordances of online environments, by fostering interaction that is primarily interpersonal, and founded upon norms of everyday interaction adapted to the online setting. Enabling both identity expression and community building, SNSs are initially structured around a niche audience, although they frequently expand beyond that target market. SNSs cater to a variety of cultural and social interests, and vary to the extent that they support additional services such as blogging (e.g., LiveJournal), audio/visual content sharing (Flickr, Last. FM, YouTube), professional orientation (LinkedIn), focus on status updates online and mobile connectivity (Twitter, Dodgeball), exclusive membership (ASmallWorld), or specific ethnic, religious, sexual orientation, and/or particular content genres (Orkut, CyWorld).

The architecture of the technology that belies these networked platforms of interaction rests upon principles of convergence, which enable multiple and overlapping connections between varieties of distinct social spheres. The social platforms or spaces sustained by convergent technologies accentuate confluence, flexibility, and reflexivity of media content. Jenkins (2006) has broadly defined convergence as "a word that describes technological, industrial, cultural and social changes in the ways media circulates within our culture ... a situation in which multiple media systems coexist and where media content flows fluidly across them" (p. 282). Jenkins emphasizes that convergence references several common ideas, including the flow of content across media platforms, overlap between media industries, financing that serves the interest of combined processes of media production, migratory behavior on the part of audiences that virally follow content, and of course, the ability for audiences to interact with content as both consumers and producers. The convergent properties of media render them both *remixed* and *remixable*; the product of institutions and independent socio-cultural agents. It is helpful to understand social network platforms as hosting social resources that are both remixed and remixable, in the sense that they actively combine all aspects of our social identity into a singular sphere, which then further evolves as these distinct parts converge and evolve.

Needless to say, convergence as a property is neither exclusive to nor defining of all communication technology. While characterized by a confluence of information communication services and platforms, convergence of technologies brings forth and is sustained by a convergence of practices within and beyond technology, thus also proposing a convergence of spaces and practices. To this point, Deuze (2007) suggests that convergence "is not just a technological process," and must therefore also be recognized as "having a cultural logic of its own, blurring the lines between production and consumption, between making media and using media, and between active or passive spectatorship of mediated culture" (p. 74). The confluent properties of information technologies suggest particular possibilities for interaction, which tend to be structured around the potential for interaction to converge social spheres, remix social resources, and reorganize the time and space contours of sociability. It would be sensible to characterize these properties as the affordances of convergent technological architecture, that is, intrinsic potentialities of technologies that make them "easier to use them for some purposes than for others" (Buckingham, 2008, p. 12). Open to re-appropriation by individuals, affordances are negotiated and re-deployed, characterizing technology that is both "socially shaped and socially shaping" (Buckingham, 2008, p. 12; Williams, 1974).

The individual combines the affordances of both older and newer media to construct a social sphere that lends autonomy and fluidity to the way in which sociality is managed. A model of networked sociality emerges on online spaces, the architectural affordances of which inform human activity, by suggesting possibilities for interaction. Working in ways similar to the architecture of physical spaces, these affordances "organize an ensemble of possibilities and interdictions," which are then left to the individual to actualize or reappropriate (de Certeau, 1984, p. 98). The architectural environment presented through these affordances places the individual as the center and source of all interactions, which typically emanate from a locus that permits an online connection. Frequently this locus is domestic, although workplace and mobile connections introduce elements of flexibility and ubiquity to the sociability sustained via social network sites. The common element, however, among all these access points is that they command a private sphere of interaction, meaning that the individual engages socially through a private media environment located within the individual's personal and private space. This private sphere of social interaction is rhetorically established by the individual by utilizing existing and imagined geographies of place. Social activities may be pursued, then, through private domestic environments or via temporary moments of privacy attained at the workplace, via mobile access, or in other public environments. These privée spaces are socially enabled via networked technologies, and social network sites afford this form of networked, mobile, and flexible sociality.

Private Spheres of Sociality and Multiplied Audiences

Private spheres of sociality are sustained through SNS member profiles, networks of friends, and communicative capabilities different SNSs offer. It is within this architectural plateau that the networked self is actualized, taking advantage of the expressive and connective affordances of SNSs. Online social networks allow the individual to connect to local and remote spheres of family members, friends and acquaintances, and strong and weaker social ties. They further expand the communicative channels individuals may dedicate toward the cultivation of social networks. The flexibility of online digital technologies permits interaction and relations among individuals within the same networks or across networks, a variety of exchanges and ties, variable frequency of contact and intimacy, affiliation with smaller or larger, and global or local, networks formed around variable common matter. The individual gains access to a variety of multimedia tools that enable the possibility for more controlled and more imaginative performances of identity online. Users create a "face" for each interaction and develop "faces" for a variety of situational contexts (Goffman, 1959). These performances are enabled by a performative palette that combines multimedia elements with cultural references, elements of play, denotative and connotative expression, and a variety of tools. Goffman (1959) describes this performative palette as the "setting," for the presentation of the self; that is, the "furniture, décor, physical layout and other background items which supply the scenery and stage props," with which the individuals articulate the "front," or a general introductory performance of the self, as opposed to the "backstage," where a more authentic self resides (p. 97). SNSs expand the *expressive equipment* at hand, possibly allowing greater control of the distance between the *front* and *backstage* areas of the self; what is presented and that which is reserved.

The process of self-presentation is complicated in the context of SNSs that combine a variety of audiences, of variable privacy or publicity, into a single crowd of spectators observing the same performance, but from a variety of vantage points, depending on their relationship to the performing self. The individual must then engage in multiple mini performances that combine a variety of semiological references so as to produce a presentation of the self that makes sense to multiple audiences, without sacrificing coherence and continuity. The process of modifying behavior so as to be palatable to a variety of audiences is not new for individuals. In everyday cycles of self-presentation and impression formation, individuals perform on multiple stages, and in doing so, they blend social spheres online that may have been separate offline, thus confusing private and public boundaries. Meyrowitz (1986) describes these circumstances as subtle changes in the "situational geography of social life," and argues that electronic media frequently reorganize private and public boundaries in ways that expose individuals to a variety of potential audiences, some intentional and several accidental (p. 6). The architectural equivalent of lifting all walls physically separating rooms, houses, offices, buildings, and all concrete structures, this rearrangement of boundaries results in a loss of the unique connection of interaction to place, or in Meyrowitz's terms, the loss of *a sense of place*. Social interactions taking place on SNSs could be interpreted as suffering from a similar lack of private/public boundary delineation, and consequently, a sense of place.

While it is possible for this convergence to displace the situational character of some communication, non-verbal and verbal cues afforded by technology enable the mediation of situational information. Following the initial, and rather dramatic, collapse of place described by Meyrowitz, individuals become familiar with a multiplication of place, which emphasizes the propagation over the consolidation of audiences. Scannell (1996) has referred to the same process as a "doubling of place," explaining that in late modern life, "public events ... occur simultaneously in two different places: the place of the event itself and that in which it is watched and heard. Broadcasting mediates *between* these two sites" (p. 76). With converged technologies, the effect is further multiplied, creating a plurality of overlapping or mutually exclusive social audiences, which suggests that the "doubling" or "multiplying" metaphor may be a more accurate reflection of the role played by technology (e.g., Couldry, 2000; Couldry and McCarthy, 2004; Moores, 2004; Ross, 2004; Scannell, 1996). Consequently, social relationships are multiplied, creating the potential for multiple performances of the self occurring on a variety of different stages (Moores, 2004). This multiplication of social audiences does not *imply* a lost sense of place, but it does necessitate performances that are more aware, so as to make sense to a variety of audiences. These performances are crafted in fragments of polysemic pertinence, which are interconnected by the SNS member profile. The resulting space is a converged continuum of sociality that is "homogeneous, yet at the same time broken into fragments" (Lefebvre, 1991, p. 342).

Knowns and Unknowns

Given that identity is performed to multiplied audiences, via multiple tools and on multiple stages, what are the consequences of these polysemous performances for sociality? The growing popularity of social network sites frequently leads scholars, the media, and the public to ask what sorts of individuals these networks produce: More or less social? Research typically reveals that, following an initial phase during which avid use of a new medium displaces other habits, individuals return to their everyday routines, which now include a healthier integration of the new medium. Therefore, for most people, new media contribute to, rather than permanently dislodge, social and other routines. As a result, individual spheres of sociality are not necessarily enhanced or restricted, but they are reformed. Important as it may be to con-sider the impact of the technology on social behaviors, a binary focus on effects invites metric tendencies that are inherently misguiding. More meaningful questions lie in determining not sheer amount or presence of sociality but, rather, the patterns of sociality that emerge.

Similarly, the growing relevance of social network sites invites questions regarding the social character of these platforms, leading us to ask: Are these tendencies reflective of more or less social media? By definition, communica-tion media connect (and disconnect), thus inherently possessing social attributes. Decades of social science research on communication technologies have shown that media do not render people more or less social; they connect and, in doing so, afford all situations they mediate social properties. All media are social. Without question, media will foster some form of social connec-tion; more interesting questions lie in investigating who they connect, who they disconnect, and how.

Finally, popular interest in social network sites revolves around the extent to which these present more or less social spaces. Given the ability of people to populate space with activity that is social, via media that intrinsically permit connection, more interesting questions involve what makes a space social; why some activities are present in certain social spaces and absent from others; and how properties of space inform the ways in which we perform our sociality.

These are the questions on the minds of the researchers contributing to this anthology, as they approach social network sites as spaces where sociality is exercised, reformed, or borne out of. The focus of this volume rested on the construct of the self, and what happens to self-identity when it is presented through networks of social connections in converged mediated environments. The volume was structured around the core themes of identity, community, and culture, as these are iterated on social network sites. Identity, community, and culture present primary organizing points for most researchers interested in new media. Rather than organize the volume around these core themes, I chose to let these themes inform and rematerialize in the text of the chapters. Each contribution to this volume evokes these three themes in various ways, and in doing so, permits this collection to both address and move beyond these abstractions.

Albert-László Barabási keynoted the volume, and the day-long conference that accompanied this volume, hosted by the Department of Communication at the University of Illinois at Chicago, in May of 2009. Using the logic of net-works, Barabási examined laws and mechanisms that underlie communication in all types of networks, whether those are sustained by the Internet, biologi-cal systems, or social actors and their communities. Expressing attributes inherent of human behavior and human organisms, networks communicate relationships between a variety of intertwined nodes of variable strength and weight. The unique characteristics of these nodes and their shared connections afford each network its fundamental set of laws and systemic organization, that is, its underlying architecture. It is the sociality emerging via this networked architecture that the contributors to this volume pursued with their research.

The organizational logic of networks was integrated with the context of communication theory in the first three chapters of the volume, so as to assess the communicative potential of social network sites. Walther, Carr, Choi, DeAndrea, Kim, Tong, and Van Der Heide connected the study of social network sites to the theoretical legacy of decades of mass and interpersonal communication research. The question they asked involved the extent to which converged platforms of social interaction, like social networks, necessitate new analytical concepts or can be appreciated via the application of existing theoretical approaches. While technologies of convergence build upon the personal, interpersonal, and mass communicative potential of past media, they also reorganize social conventions, leading to subsequent convergence of social spaces and practices. Walther et al. proposed a new perspective, founded on the merger of various communication theories applied to the liquid social landscapes proposed by newer media technologies. To this end, Walther et al. suggested an analytical emphasis that recognizes, first, the proximity and simultaneity converged interfaces advance via a multiplicity of sources, and second, the wide range of interpersonal imperatives pursued through purposive, and frequently combined, use of a variety of communication channels.

Such a remediation of media theory would help interpret the utility of newer technologies that have refashioned previous media as much as they have themselves been fashioned by the trajectories of media past. This reorganization of media theory would require a contemporary operationalization of terms that have defined empirically driven research on traditional media, including the audience, the public, and audience activity and involvement. It would also require a theoretical apparatus that allows us to examine what concepts like identity, community, and culture, which have inspired a majority of new media studies, mean on networked places that prioritize personal connections.

Converged platforms of social interaction reorganize our conventional understandings of time and space in ways that afford opportunities to fulfill personal needs for communication. Walther et al. recommended that we focus our analytical efforts on these needs, by re-adjusting our theoretical canons and enriching them with contemporary language. danah boyd took this cue and interpreted social network sites as a genre of networked publics. Within this framework, the affordances provided by the architectures of networked publics shape and are shaped by the dynamics of networked interactions, in the same way that the physicality of offline spaces informs and responds to the social predispositions of individuals. boyd perceives the affordances of networked publics as being shaped by an architecture of bits, and identifies profiles, friend lists, and tools for public communication as central structural components of networked platforms that may shape the interactions of publics that act socially within them. These architectural components, along with the structural affordances of persistence, replicability, scalability, and searchability, create singular multimedia networked stages, upon which identities and relationships are performed.

The architectural affordances of SNSs present a compelling theoretical backdrop, upon which the utility, consequences, and everyday ecology of media habits, including online social networking, may be explored. It is the formation of the everyday ecology of media routines that LaRose, Kim, and Peng were interested in, as they explored the normalcy with which newer media habits are integrated with standing everyday routines. Examining the pathology of this integration, LaRose et al. asked whether social network use may become compulsive, problematic, or addictive. Resting on recent theoretical developments and employing empirical data, they suggested that most cases of intensive social networking present instances where users willingly yield an amount of self-regulation so as to indulge a favorite media pastime. Despite popular press accounts of "Facebook addiction," use of SNSs appears to be no more problematic than other media habits. Moreover, not all types of Internet use are associated with the same types of consequences, suggesting that the effects of certain types of Internet use may offset the effects of more dysphoric uses. This would imply that, rather than isolating the effects of SNS use, it is essential that we examine and contextualize them within the greater spectrum of an individual's media and interpersonal habits and routines.

And yet it is important to consider the affordances of SNSs for interpersonal interaction without neglecting how the economies of SNSs engage the individual as commodity and networked laborer. Andrejevic suggested that the networked sociabilities facilitated by SNSs are structured upon a separation of the user from the means of socializing, thus permitting "storable and sortable" collections of social data. These data, produced and shared by the networked users, breathe life into the network, which accumulates social and economic capital as data become richer and more complex. Not only may these data be used to design marketing campaigns, customize applications, and lend further value to third-party-run groups and applications, but they also form the content backbone of the network, without which the value of the network would diminish. Thus, the social resources of individual members present the basis of the content production process, in which uncompensated individuals contribute personal information and additional social labor toward the accumulation of collectively generated networks of sociability. These social resources are further reconfigured and returned to the users in the form of customized marketing efforts, which colonize these domains of personal self-presentation and sociality of personalized commercial narratives. Andrejevic suggested that SNSs need not follow the commercial model of social labor exploitation, and that the specific peer-to-peer affordances of the network, in fact, steer away from these avaricious scenarios. The structural affordances of a capitalist economy, however, do tend to limit non-commercially sensitive deployments of socially networked platforms.

Andrejevic concluded that these commercially guided interpretations of interactivity and sociability further limit our understanding of community. It is this possibly compromised sense of identity that Parks became interested in, in the next group of chapters considering textures and patterns of sociability emerging on SNSs. Recognizing that community presents an influential meta-phor for understanding the social textures of the Internet, Parks questioned whether SNSs could be perceived as virtual communities. In doing so, he examined MySpace and the social affordances the network provides in terms of membership, personal expression, and connection. While virtual com-munities were relatively rare on MySpace, personal and social connections were abundant, frequently between individuals living in close proximity.

This would suggest a more personalized expression of sociability, that develops *sans* community aspirations to satisfy individualistically determined social needs. Parks suggested that users approach a network like MySpace looking not for community, but for "theater," or an experience of the mass communication variety, or what others have termed "micro-celebrity" (Senft, 2008). Motivated by what Parks termed an "inflated sense of agency," these users approach the medium hoping to expand their networks and ties. Fre-quently, however, they must rely on mostly local networks to sustain online connections, thus reflecting a confluence, rather than separation of social behaviors.

For researchers, social behaviors that traverse and frequently converge a variety of behavioral and performative platforms suggest that we become equally convergent in our application of theory, combining approaches to understand users that are equally multi-purposive in their social orientations. Ellison, Lampe, Steinfield, and Vitak, through a growing body of work, found evidence of a variety of connection strategies employed by college-age Face-book users to sustain social ties of varying breadth and depth. Utilizing schol-arship on social capital and interaction patterns, Ellison et al. found that the technical and social affordances of Facebook permitted users to manage broader and more diverse networks and interactions. Moving further away from the traditional approach of measuring the social value of online interaction against the metaphor of community, Ellison et al. proposed a more flexible model of relationship management enabled by SNSs, fostering larger sets of weaker ties, the ability to render ephemeral connections persistent, and more convenient means of cultivating social relations with strong and weak ties.

Hargittai and Hsieh further investigated differences between individual uses of SNSs, by employing data to construct a typology of social network site usage. Non-random differences in the intensity and diversity of engagement with SNSs reflected the presence of particular types of use, which could be associated with user attributes and possibly consequences of SNS use. Interpreted together, these differences indicated that those with more Internet experiences and abilities were more likely to be more engaged with SNSs. While the data did not reflect causal patterns, the implications here are important in terms of access and literacy privileges that influence the intensity and texture of online behaviors, and the reverse, that is, heightened Internet savvy that possibly develops out of more intense use. Media involvement has always been an important, yet elusive, antecedent and consequence of media use. Understanding the levels of involvement with a variety of SNSs is an important step in describing and analyzing their place in the greater spectrum of an individual's media and interpersonal habits.

Within an organizational setting, SNSs may facilitate enhanced presentation of professional and personal identities, as well as support communication within and across organizations. Watson-Manheim advanced the concept of "communication repertoire" as a way of organizing and analyzing the variety of opportunities different communication channels afford to workplace communication. Communication repertoires are developed in response to organizational priorities as well as external social factors, but customized by employees to support individual social and professional routines. The extent to which communication media repertoires, including SNSs, may be retrofitted by individuals depends on the degree of flexibility both the institution and the medium afford. Watson-Manheim saw the adoption of SNSs in the workplace as primarily a grass-roots effort, facilitated in most organizations via the communicative routines of employees, rather than formally espoused. The blurring of private and public boundaries that SNSs thrive on present a complicated social landscape for companies and their employees, who must reconcile and navigate personal and professional aspects of their identity in order to sustain communication that does not compromise either their professional or their personal project (and performed) profile.

And yet, intuitive appropriations drive the uses and capital generated by SNSs, as users frequently converge and customize attributes to construct personalized social spheres. Johnson, Zhang, Bichard, and Seltzer examined specific genres of SNS interaction to understand the relevance of online social networks for political communication. Examining a national online panel of over 500 Internet users, Johnson et al. compared SNSs and YouTube as sources of political information to find that reliance on SNSs proved to be a more accurate predictor of political attitudes and behavior. Even though the demographic and political profiles of the two platforms of services were similar, individuals utilized YouTube to obtain political information, but tested out their political attitudes and behaviors on the interactive spaces of SNSs. The connective and interactive affordances of SNSs allowed individuals to pursue civic behaviors both offline and online. While neither YouTube nor SNS use predicted the likelihood of voting, study results indicated that the more users watched YouTube, the less likely they were to vote, thus reflecting possible frustration or growing cynicism with the number of divergent messages present on YouTube.

In a similar vein, Kaye compared communication sustained by SNSs and blogging networks. Following an initial cluster analysis that identified four groups of users, Dabblers (those who do not heavily use SNSs or blogs for political information), Social Networkers (those who heavily use only SNSs), Ambi-textrous (those who heavily use SNSs and blogs), and Blogophiles (those who heavily use only blogs), Kaye compared social networkers and blogophiles, to isolate differences between the two platforms. She found that Social Networkers tended to be young, female Democrats, while Blogophiles tended to be older, male Republicans. Social Networkers were also higher in trust, lower in self-efficacy, less interested and knowledgeable about politics and less knowledgeable about the 2008 election than Blogophiles. Social Networkers enjoyed comparing political ideas and attitudes with those of like-minded individuals within their networks, whereas Blogophiles were motivated to use blogs for non-mainstream political information for depth and analysis. These results indicated that SNSs could support the affirmation of political attitudes and behaviors, where more information-driven platforms, like blogs and YouTube, provide the fodder for the development of these attitudes. Future research could investigate these relationships further, as they certainly reflect connections between user orientation, type of use, and consequences, also underlined by Ellison et al. and Hargittai and Hsieh earlier in this volume.

Gilpin further explored the variety of uses individuals put specific genres of SNS to, by focusing on the affordances of Twitter for public relations professionals. Examining how twitter feeds influence the information and attitudinal scope of public relations practitioners, Gilpin analyzed some of the most prominent feeds to find that this form of micro-blogging primarily fulfilled needs of information sharing, networking, and professional affirmation.

Beyond this initial plane of converged information, social, and professional needs, Twitter permitted the more fluid management of offline and online spheres of interaction for professionals, thus forwarding a newer model for self-organized PR, structured around the self and the greater professional interests of the individual. Thus, Twitter emerged as both an impression management and network management tool, which could be manipulated and readjusted to fit the personal and professional imperatives of individual users.

Impression management and network management were of interest to Mendelson and Papacharissi, who examined this from the different scope of college student photo galleries displayed on Facebook. Looking at the photograph as both a mnemonic and symbolic device, they were interested in the role of photographs in visual performances of the self enacted on SNSs. They found that photographs tagged on Facebook tended to reinforce group membership and cohesion. In-group language, references, and inside jokes surrounding photographs symbolically connected a private sphere of friends within the publicly private realm of Facebook. Most photographs exhibited narcissistic tendencies, overt displays of affection, and playful behaviors produced exclusively for the camera. These collective exhibitions of friendship emanated from the ego-centered member profile and advertised collectively shared experiences to the world, inviting both intentional and accidental onlookers to a "look-at-us" taste of what college life might be like. Directly performative, these visual presentations supported the theater of personal and collective identity, as played out through the rituals of the college experience.

As identities are increasingly performed and managed online, via an architecture that combines bits and cultural references, ownership of the rights to the privacy and publicity of these performances becomes important. For Aufderheide, the pressing issue is that of copyright, as these self-performances frequently remix cultural content in order to effectively communicate mediated identities. It is on the basis of these shared and remixed cultural performances that individual SNS users express themselves and connect with others. Fair use and copyright are central issues, given the opportunities to reappropriate cultural content and create new, privately public, and publicly private meaning that SNSs afford.

What is interesting for us, as researchers, is copyright protection and fair use of remixed and performed identities, as these become visible to a variety of audiences that individuals feel more or less comfortable with. If indeed identity presented online becomes a performance, to what extent can that performance be protected, or exploited, in the manner that other cultural performances are repurposed and traded within the greater cultural marketplace? Can an individual protect an identity performance by copyright, thus preventing a current or potential employer, or other undesirable viewers, from accessing it, or using it as a measure of the individual's entire identity?

This question attains greater complexity as SNSs are increasingly populated by more actors, of both human and software origin. Beyond the embedded presence of software agents responsible for the functionality and appeal of these networks, SNSs also afford the integration of disembodied or physically embodied intelligent software agents, who may employ a variety of actor roles within online social networks. Mavridis presented one concrete example of such an agent: Sarah the FaceBot, a robotically embodied intelligent artificial agent, who recognizes, converses, and remembers Facebook friends, and employs this information to update her own member page and sustain long-term communication with other network actors. Thus, not only does identity performance contain remixed and remixable properties, but it becomes possible to construct identities entirely out of remixed and remixable interaction.

The common thread between all these chapters is woven around emerging patterns of networked sociality. These patterns combine old and newer social habits, reform and remediate several social routines of the past, and reflect social tendencies and tensions that take shape on networked planes of social activity. The first set of chapters situated these tendencies and tensions in theoretical context, and proposed re-worked theoretical frames through which we may interpret them. Within these frames, central themes revolve around (a) the ability of networked and converged social platforms to serve personal needs for social connection, (b) the possibility of networked publics coalescing around the networked architectures of SNSs, (c) the ways in which these newer habits are combined and integrated with older ones, and (d) the manner in which modes of economic and organizational hierarchy influence the autonomy of individuals employing these networks as social agents.

Sociality, Sociabilities, and A Networked Self

A reasonable next cognitive step develops as we consider the shape of this emerging and networked sociability, and how sociality is formed out of distinct sociabilities embedded and borne out of SNSs as social platforms. Even though the terms "sociality" and "sociability" are synonymous, sociality refers to the sum of social behaviors that permit the individual to traverse from the state of individuality to that of sociality and fellowship. Sociability, on the other hand, refers to the ability to perform the social behaviors that lead to sociality, and thus, reflects one's inherent potential to engage in such social behaviors. The second set of chapters, then, considers the ways in which we employ the affordances of SNSs to attain sociability, and the extent to which the emerging tendencies and tensions of networked sociability enable a shared sense of sociality. Recognizing that community is not the only means of practicing sociability and attaining sociality, these chapters examine how autonomous, yet connected, agents interact offline and online, from the domestic and work-related, public and private, spheres. The emerging sociability moves beyond community, recognizes identity as performance, and defines as culture a converged set of practices that are social, political, economic, personal, and work-related, as long as they contain a semiology that affords connection. What emerges, then, is a networked self, socially enabled by the affordances of SNSs.

A networked self, communicated across collapsed and multiplied audiences, seeks social opportunities for expression and connection. These opportunities take a variety of forms, organically generated by relatively autonomous social agents pursuing social goals reified via the affordances of SNSs. A broad range of examples of networked sociability are visited in the last set of chapters, ranging from behaviors that connect social actors as citizens, teenagers as collective narcissists, remixed content to remixed identity, and, finally, human social agents to networked non-human social actors. What is clear is that sociability no longer stands for what it used to be. Human actors have been conditioned to recognize physically active and extroverted behaviors as social; in the networked context of sociability, we observe varieties of behaviors that are unquestionably social, yet also practiced from variably passive states of engagement or via the more introspective exercise of narcissistic photography or self-expression.

So-called social media enhance a particular type of sociability—networked sociability. And they contain affordances that permit persons to maintain the individuality of their private sphere as they traverse to sociality. Networked and remixed sociabilities emerge and are practiced over *multiplied* place and audiences, that do not necessarily collapse one's sense of place, but afford sense of place reflexively. A sense of place is formed in response to the particular sense of self, or in response to the identity performance constructed upon that place. This presents the modus operandi for the networked self, and the context of newer patterns of sociability and routes to sociality that emerge. The ability for individuals to efficiently avail themselves of the potential of SNSs depends on the individual level of access, literacy, and general comfort with socially networked platforms of interaction. Adept navigation of the social landscapes of SNSs implies that identity is performed, but is also edited across multiplied and converged audiences. It requires some mastery of the expressive equipment at hand, or the ability to maneuver in what Castells (2001) termed, the "technical geography" of SNSs. The ability to edit, or *redact*, one's own, multiple self-performances may afford a sense of place, even if temporarily so, for the individual. And thus, redactional acumen becomes a survival skill, as individuals exercise, become comfortable with, and play with a networked sense of self.

References

Bauman, Z. (2000). *Liquid modernity*. Cambridge: Polity Press.

Bauman, Z. (2005). *Liquid life*. Cambridge: Polity Press.

Buckingham, D. (2008). Introducing identity. In D. Buckingham (Ed.), *Youth, identity, and digital media* (pp. 1–24). Cambridge: MIT Press.

Castells, M. (2001). *The Internet galaxy*. Oxford: Oxford University Press.

Couldry, N. (2000). *The place of media power: Pilgrims and witnesses of the media age*. London: Routledge.

Couldry, N. & McCarthy, A. (Eds.) (2004). *MediaSpace: Place, scale and culture in a media age*. London: Routledge.

de Certeau, M. (1984). *The practice of everyday life*. Berkeley: University of California Press.

Deuze, M. (2007). *Media work*. Cambridge: Polity.

Giddens, A. (1991). *The consequences of modernity*. Cambridge: Polity.

Goffman, E. (1959). *The presentation of self in everyday life*. New York, NY: Doubleday.

Jenkins, H. (2006). *Fans, bloggers and gamers: Media consumers in a digital age*. New York, NY: New York University Press.

Lefebvre, H. (1991). *The production of space* (D. Nicholson-Smith trans.). Oxford: Blackwell. Originally published 1974.

Meyrowitz, J. (1986). *No sense of place*. New York, NY: Oxford.

Moores, S. (2004). The doubling of place: Electronic media, time–space arrangements and social relationships. In N. Couldry & A. McCarthy (eds.), *MediaSpace: Place, scale and culture in a media age* (pp. 21–36). London: Routledge.

Papacharissi, Z. (2010). *A private sphere: Democracy in a digital age*. Cambridge: Polity.

Ross, A. (2004). Dot.com urbanism. In N. Couldry & A. McCarthy (Eds.), *Media Space: Place, scale and culture in a media age* (pp. 145–163). New York, NY: Routledge.

Scannell, P. (1996). *Radio, television and modern life: A phenomenological approach*. Oxford: Blackwell.

Senft, T. M. (2008). *Camgirls: Celebrity and community in the age of social networks*. New York, NY: Peter Lang.

Williams, R. (1974). *Television, technology and cultural form*. London: Routledge.

About the Editor

Zizi Papacharissi (PhD, University of Texas at Austin, 2000), is Professor and Head of the Communication Department at the University of Illinois-Chicago. Her work focuses on the social and political consequences of online media. Her book *A Private Sphere: Democracy in a Digital Age* (Polity Press, 2010) discusses how online media redefine our understanding of public and private in late-modern democracies. She has published three books and over 40 journal articles, book chapters, or reviews.

Contributors

Mark Andrejevic is Associate Professor in the Department of Communication Studies at the University of Iowa. He is the author of *Reality TV: The Work of Being Watched* and *iSpy: Surveillance and Power in the Interactive Era*, as well as articles and book chapters on surveillance, digital media, and popular culture.

Patricia Aufderheide is a Professor in the School of Communication at American University in Washington, D.C., and director of the Center for Social Media there. Her books include *Documentary: A Very Short Introduction*, *The Daily Planet*, and *Communications Policy in the Public Interest*. She won career achievement awards in 2006 from the International Documentary Association and in 2008 from the International Digital Media and Arts Association.

Albert-László Barabási is Professor at Northeastern University and Lecturer of Medicine at Harvard Medical School. His research focuses on complex networks, and their applications to biological, social, and technological systems. Barabási is the author of *Linked: The New Science of Networks*, and the forthcoming *Bursts: The Hidden Pattern Behind Everything We Do*.

Shannon L. Bichard is an Associate Professor of Advertising in the College of Mass Communications at Texas Tech University. Her research interests focus on public opinion and consumer behavior, with an emphasis on online communication and engagement. Her research has appeared in journals such as *Journalism & Mass Communication Quarterly*, *Journal of Computer-Mediated Communication*, and *Health Communication*.

danah boyd is a researcher at Microsoft Research and a fellow at Harvard's Berkman Center for Internet and Society. Her research investigates everyday practices involving social media, with specific attention to youth. She recently co-authored *Hanging Out, Messing Around, and Geeking Out: Kids Living and Learning with New Media*. She also blogs at www.zephoria.org/thoughts/.

Caleb T. Carr is a PhD student in the Department of Telecommunication, Information Studies and Media at Michigan State University. His research addresses implications of new media in self-presentation perceptions, particularly in groups and organizations. He has most recently co-authored a chapter in *The Dynamics of Intergroup Communication*.

Scott Seung W. Choi holds a Master of Arts in Advertising from Michigan State University and a Bachelor of Arts in French Literature from the Hankuk University of Foreign Studies (South Korea). His research interests lie primarily in mediated communication and organizational communication, specifically in how newly emerging mediated communication technologies affect social relationships and organizations.

David C. DeAndrea is a doctoral candidate in the Department of Communication at Michigan State University. He is beginning a line of research that examines interpersonal processes and new media technology. His primary interest revolves around attributions of online behavior that are discrepant with offline impressions.

Nicole B. Ellison is an Assistant Professor in the Department of Telecommunication, Information Studies and Media at Michigan State University. Her research explores issues of self-presentation, relationship development, social capital, and identity in online environments such as online dating and social network sites.

Dawn R. Gilpin is an Assistant Professor at Arizona State University studying complexity, networks, and narrative in public relations and social media. Recent publications include the book *Crisis Management in a Complex World* with Priscilla Murphy (Oxford University Press, 2008), and articles in the *Journal of Public Relations Research* and the *Handbook of Crisis Communication*.

Eszter Hargittai is Associate Professor of Communication Studies at Northwestern University, where she heads the Web Use Project, and Fellow at Harvard's Berkman Center for Internet & Society. Her work focuses on the social and policy implications of information and communication technologies. She is editor of *Research Confidential: Solutions to Problems Most Social Scientists Pretend They Never Have*, recently published by the University of Michigan Press. Copies of her papers are available at www.webuse.org.

Yu-li Patrick Hsieh is a doctoral student in the Media, Technology & Society program at Northwestern University. His research interests include the influences of information technology uses on social engagement, as well as their effects on social, psychological, and economic well-being. He is currently working on a project that investigates whether there is a systematic relationship between social capital and Web-use skills. Yu-li received his MA in sociology from the University of Illinois at Chicago in the United States and another MA in social informatics from Yuan-Ze University in Taiwan.

Thomas J. Johnson is the Amon G. Carter, Jr. Centennial Professor in the School of Journalism at the University of Texas at Austin. He is the author of *The Rehabilitation of Richard Nixon: The Media's Effect on Collect Memory*. He has co-edited two books: *International Media Communication in the Global Age* and *Engaging the Public: How the Government and the Media Can Reinvigorate the American Democracy*.

Barbara K. Kaye (PhD, Florida State University, 1994) is Professor in the School of Journalism & Electronic Media, University of Tennessee-Knoxville. She researches how the Internet, blogs, and social media influence political attitudes and media use behavior. She has co-authored three textbooks, published more than 30 journal articles and has taught in Italy and Austria.

Jinsuk Kim is a PhD candidate in the Department of Communication at Michigan State University. Her research focuses on impression management and relationship development in online environments. Recently she has investigated the effects of culture and gender on self-disclosure in social networking sites. She is currently working on a book chapter on online self-disclosure.

Junghyun Kim (PhD, Michigan State University) is an Assistant Professor at the School of Communication Studies at Kent State University. Her research interests include the effects of new media on young people's psychological well-being, building and breaking of unhealthy media-use behaviors of children and young people, and virtual group identity and in-group bias. She has published articles in *Journal of Computer-Mediated Communication*, *Journal of Health Psychology*, *Computers in Human Behavior* among other journals.

Cliff Lampe is an Assistant Professor in the Department of Telecommunication, Information Studies and Media at Michigan State University. He received his PhD from the University of Michigan School of Information in 2006. He studies the intersection of social and technical systems, and the effects of those interactions.

Robert LaRose is a Full Professor in the Department of Telecommunication, Information Studies and Media at Michigan State University. His current interests include the impact of broadband in rural America, online privacy, and the formation of media habits. He is the co-author of *Media Now*, a popular introductory textbook.

Nikolaos Mavridis is the director of the Interactive Robots and Media Laboratory and an Assistant Professor of Intelligent Systems at the UAE University. He has a PhD from the Massachusetts Institute of Technology Media Laboratory, where his work was centered on building robots that can learn sensory, sensory motor, or teleological meaning models of words, and which can converse in natural language about current, imagined, or past situations. His current interests include interactive and social robotics, robots and the arts, as well as cognitive systems.

Andrew L. Mendelson is Associate Professor and Chair of the Department of Journalism in the School of Communications and Theater at Temple University in Philadelphia. His research focuses on the role(s) that photographic images play in society and how people understand the world because of the photograph.

Malcolm R. Parks is Professor of Communication at the University of Washington where he conducts research on social networks, online interaction, and relationship development in a variety of settings. His recent book, *Personal Relationships and Personal Networks*, received the Gerald R. Miller Book Award from the National Communication Association.

Wei Peng is an Assistant Professor in the Department of Telecommunication, Information Studies and Media, Michigan State University. Her primary research interest is to understand the persuasive impacts of interactive technologies, including digital games, social network sites, etc. Her recent publications appear in *Journal of Communication*, *Health Communication*, *Computers in Human Behavior* among other journals.

Kelly Quinn is a PhD candidate in the Department of Communication at the University of Illinois at Chicago. Her research focuses on how the technology practices of adults contribute to the creation and maintenance of their social relationships. She has co-authored a chapter on visual communication in the *Handbook of Political Communication* (forthcoming August, 2010).

Trent Seltzer is an Assistant Professor in the Department of Public Relations at Texas Tech University's College of Mass Communications. His research interests include agenda building, framing, and relationship maintenance in political and sport communication, as well as organization–public relationship management, measurement, and evaluation.

Charles Steinfield is a Professor and Chair of the Department of Telecommunication, Information Studies and Media at Michigan State University. His research examines the ways in which new media such as online social network sites are implicated in individual and organizational efforts to engage in collective action and build social capital.

Stephanie Tom Tong (MA, Michigan State University) is a PhD student in the Department of Communication at Michigan State University. Her research focuses primarily on interpersonal relationships in computer-mediated contexts. Specifically, she is interested in the areas of self-presentation, impression formation, message production, and relationship development and maintenance. Recent work has appeared in publications such as the *Journal of Computer-Mediated Communication* and *Human Communication Research*.

Brandon Van Der Heide (PhD, Michigan State University) is an Assistant Professor of Communication at the Ohio State University. Generally, his interests concern social influence and impression formation in a variety of online environments. His ongoing work explores how interpersonal impression formation and relational communication processes occur on social networking websites and in immersive virtual environments.

Jessica Vitak is a PhD student in the Telecommunication, Information Studies and Media department at Michigan State University, and a consultant for the Pew Internet Project. Her current research focuses on interaction and identity in online environments, specifically on social network sites and in online games. She has co-authored reports on online privacy and teens' gaming habits.

Joseph B. Walther is a Professor of Communication and of Telecommunication, Information Studies and Media at Michigan State University. The author of several theories and numerous empirical studies pertaining to computer-mediated communication in personal relationships, groups, and organizations, he has twice been recognized by the National Communication Association for specific articles that have changed conceptualizations of communication over time. He is currently directing studies on the juxtaposition of multiple sources of online influence, and examining the effects of virtual group work on the reduction of interethnic prejudice.

Mary Beth Watson-Manheim is Associate Professor of Information and Decision Sciences at the University of Illinois at Chicago. She is actively involved in research on the use of information and communication technologies (ICT) in the geographically distributed workplace, and the changing nature of work in this environment. She was a Fulbright-Nehru Senior Research Scholarship to India in 2009–2010.

Weiwu Zhang is an Assistant Professor of Public Relations in the College of Mass Communications at Texas Tech University. He is president of the Midwest Association for Public Opinion Research. He has published in diverse areas of public opinion, mass communication, and public relations. His current research interests include new media and politics, framing and public relations, media relations, and political public relations.

Index